ISSUES IN BIOMEDICAL ETHICS

Choosing Tomorrow's Children

ISSUES IN BIOMEDICAL ETHICS

General Editors
John Harris and Søren Holm

Consulting Editors
Raanan Gillon and Bonnie Steinbock

The late twentieth century witnessed dramatic technological developments in biomedical science and in the delivery of health care, and these developments have brought with them important social changes. All too often ethical analysis has lagged behind these changes. The purpose of this series is to provide lively, up-to-date, and authoritative studies for the increasingly large and diverse readership concerned with issues in biomedical ethics—not just health care trainees and professionals, but also philosophers, social scientists, lawyers, social workers, and legislators. The series features both single-author and multi-author books, short and accessible enough to be widely read, each of them focused on an issue of outstanding current importance and interest. Philosophers, doctors, and lawyers from a number of countries feature among the authors lined up for the series.

Choosing Tomorrow's Children

The Ethics of Selective Reproduction

Stephen Wilkinson

CLARENDON PRESS · OXFORD

OXFORD
UNIVERSITY PRESS

Great Clarendon Street, Oxford OX2 6DP

Oxford University Press is a department of the University of Oxford.
It furthers the University's objective of excellence in research, scholarship,
and education by publishing worldwide in

Oxford New York

Auckland Cape Town Dar es Salaam Hong Kong Karachi
Kuala Lumpur Madrid Melbourne Mexico City Nairobi
New Delhi Shanghai Taipei Toronto

With offices in

Argentina Austria Brazil Chile Czech Republic France Greece
Guatemala Hungary Italy Japan Poland Portugal Singapore
South Korea Switzerland Thailand Turkey Ukraine Vietnam

Oxford is a registered trade mark of Oxford University Press
in the UK and in certain other countries

Published in the United States
by Oxford University Press Inc., New York

British Library Cataloguing in Publication Data

Data available

Library of Congress Cataloging in Publication Data

Library of Congress Control Number 2009941590

Typeset by Laserwords Publisher Services, Chennai, India
Printed in Great Britain
on acid-free paper by
MPG Books Group, Bodmin and King's Lynn

ISBN 978–0–19–927396–6

10 9 8 7 6 5 4 3 2 1

PREFACE

Work on this book was supported by the Arts and Humanities Research Council, Keele University, and the Wellcome Trust's Biomedical Ethics Programme. I would like to record my thanks for these awards.

All of my close colleagues at Keele University deserve thanks for their help over the last few years, especially for their willingness to talk about ethics. Eve Garrard, however, must be singled out for special thanks. She has read and provided incisive comments upon the majority of the text and, as always, has made it a lot better than it otherwise would have been. Eve and I have also worked together on some of these issues and my thinking on these matters has been greatly improved by talking them over with her. Other Keele colleagues who deserve a specific mention are Ruth Fletcher and Marie Fox, both of whom provided helpful and detailed feedback on an early version of Chapter 8.

Turning to people outside Keele, this work has been gestated for quite a few years and so I have doubtless forgotten a lot of the numerous helpful contributions that people have made during that period. Those I have no trouble remembering though are: Bob Brecher and Søren Holm, both of whom provided valuable feedback on the first draft of the whole manuscript; Rosamund Scott, who read and commented on several chapters and with whom I spent many informative and pleasant hours discussing the issues; and Sally Sheldon, whose advice, help, and support have been invaluable.

Sections 3.2 and 3.3 draw on a paper written jointly with Eve Garrard, which appeared in *The Monist* in 2006.[1] An earlier version of Section 4.2 was written jointly with Sally Sheldon and appeared in the *Journal of Medical Ethics* in 2004. Similarly, part of Section 4.3 is based on joint work with Sally Sheldon; this was originally prepared for a joint conference presentation at the University of Western Ontario in November 2007 and subsequently published in a collection entitled *The 'Healthy' Embryo*.[2] I would like to thank Eve and Sally for their help with these topics and for allowing me to

---

[1] Eve Garrard and Stephen Wilkinson, 'Selecting Disability and Welfare of the Child', *The Monist*, 89 (2006), 482–504.

[2] Sally Sheldon and Stephen Wilkinson, 'Should Selecting Saviour Siblings Be Banned?' *Journal of Medical Ethics*, 30 (2004), 533–7; Sally Sheldon and Stephen Wilkinson, 'Saviour Siblings, Other Siblings, and Whole Organ Donation', in Jeff Nisker, Francoise Baylis, Isabel Karpin, Carolyn McLeod, and Roxanne Mykituk (eds.), *The 'Healthy' Embryo* (Cambridge: Cambridge University Press, 2009).

make use of our previous collaborative work. Section 6.5 is based upon my 'Eugenics, Embryo Selection, and the Equal Value Principle' which appeared in the inaugural issue of *Clinical Ethics*, while Sections 8.1 to 8.4 draw on my 'Sex Selection, Sexism, and "Family Balancing" ', which first appeared in the *Medical Law Review* in 2008.[3] For all of the above, I would like to thank the editors for permitting me to make use of this material.

Last but not least, I would like to thank my parents. Without their unwavering support over many years, this book would not exist.

[3] Stephen Wilkinson, 'Eugenics, Embryo Selection, and the Equal Value Principle', *Clinical Ethics*, 1 (2006), 26–51; Stephen Wilkinson, 'Sex Selection, Sexism, and "Family Balancing" ', *Medical Law Review*, 16 (2008), 369–89.

CONTENTS

1

Introduction: The Ethics of Selective Reproduction

This introductory chapter aims to do several different things. It starts (in 1.1) by briefly describing three real cases of selective reproduction before (in 1.2) going on to offer a general account of what selective reproduction is. This account is developed in 1.3, which explains in more detail the idea that selective reproduction involves choosing between different (possible, future) people. Next, 1.4 and 1.5 discuss some of the methodological and theoretical assumptions that underlie my research, while 1.6 contains some remarks on the moral status of the embryo and explains why this issue does not figure prominently in subsequent chapters. Finally, 1.7 outlines the structure of the rest of the book.

1.1 Some Cases

The Masterton Case (Scotland, 1999)

Nicole Masterton, a 3-year-old girl, died following a bonfire accident. Shortly after her death, Nicole's parents (Alan and Louise) approached the Human Fertilisation and Embryology Authority (HFEA, the UK regulatory body) to ask if they could use preimplantation genetic diagnosis (PGD) to 'sex select' another daughter.[1] This would involve creating several embryos *in vitro* and implanting only female ones into Louise Masterton. The Mastertons already had four sons (who, it was reported, would 'love another sister') and wanted another daughter (Nicole having been the only one) to 'rebuild the female dimension' of their family. The Mastertons were ultimately unsuccessful because HFEA rules allowed embryonic sex selection only in order to avoid sex-linked genetic disorders, not for 'family-balancing' purposes or merely to

---

[1] G. Harris, 'Grieving Couple Fight to Choose Sex of Next Baby', *The Times*, 13 Mar. 2000, 11; M. Mega, 'Couple Fight to Pick Sex of Baby', *Sunday Times*, 12 Mar. 2001, 32.

satisfy parental preference. *Would offering the Mastertons 'family-balancing' sex selection have been ethical and ought it to have been permitted by the HFEA?*

The Nash Case (USA, 2000)

Molly Nash (aged 6) had Fanconi anaemia, a hereditary condition that weakens the immune system and usually causes death by the age of 7. She could be cured by using cells from the umbilical cord of a newly created sibling (a 'saviour sibling').[2] In order to do this, it would be necessary to create several embryos *in vitro* and to subject them to genetic testing and tissue-typing, implanting only 'compatible' embryos into Lisa Nash (Molly's mother). The procedure was carried out and Adam Nash, reportedly the world's first saviour sibling, was born in September 2000. Molly Nash received umbilical cord material and was reported to be doing well as recently as June 2003.[3] *Was this procedure ethically acceptable and should it have been permitted?*

The McCullough and Duchesneau Case (USA, 1996)

Candace McCullough and Sharon Duchesneau were an American deaf lesbian couple who wanted to have deaf children. To achieve this, they deliberately selected a congenitally deaf sperm donor to inseminate Sharon Duchesneau, thus maximizing the chances of having a deaf child.[4] They were successful and Duchesneau gave birth to a deaf daughter in 1996. *Was what they did ethical? If a couple (lesbian or otherwise) asked doctors to help them achieve the same result using PGD (or some other biomedical technique), should the doctors refuse? And ought this kind of selection to be lawful?*

1.2 What Is Selective Reproduction?

By 'selective reproduction' I mean the attempt to create one possible future child rather than a different possible future child. The reason for wanting to practise selective reproduction is normally that one possible future child is, in some way, more desirable than the alternatives. As the cases just described indicate, the kinds of desirability that people have in mind are many and varied, and the question of what counts as 'desirable' is controversial. There is however one *relatively* (though by no means entirely) uncontentious example: selection to avoid disease. If one possible future

---

[2] Mary Dejevsky, 'Parents Have Baby to Produce Life-Saving Stem Cells for Sister', *The Independent*, 3 Oct. 2000, 13.

[3] Dani Garavelli, 'Live and Let Live', *Scotland on Sunday*, 22 June 2003, 15.

[4] David Teather, 'Lesbian Couple Have Deaf Baby by Choice', *The Guardian*, 8 Apr. 2002, 2.

child would have a disabling, excruciating, and life-shortening disease, while another would not, then (to many of us) ensuring that the disease-free child is created seems like the sensible thing to do (all other things being equal). Disease-avoidance is then perhaps the most prevalent and widely accepted rationale for selective reproduction, particularly within the context of Western reproductive medicine.

Recent biotechnological developments (notably, the advent of preimplantation genetic diagnosis, the possibility of determining sex by sperm sorting, and the ever increasing sophistication of prenatal tests) have made selective reproduction a pressing policy issue for regulators and lawmakers, and a 'hot topic' in academic bioethics and the media. However, selective reproduction *need not* be 'high tech' and has been around in technologically unsophisticated forms for a very long time. Perhaps the most obvious example of this is using contraception or sexual abstinence to delay conception. For instance, a (philosophically inclined) 16-year-old girl might think to herself:

> *If I have a child now, then it will have a much worse life than an alternative child conceived when I am 26. Therefore, I'll wait for a decade and create the better-off child instead. Furthermore this will be good for my own quality of life.*

This is an instance of selective reproduction: choosing a (supposedly) better off possible future child over one that would be less well off. Interestingly, there is very widespread agreement that this sort of selective reproduction (avoiding teenage pregnancy through abstinence or contraception) is not merely morally unproblematic, but good.

Another kind of 'low tech' selective reproduction is where a woman chooses a sperm donor with certain desirable characteristics (or indeed chooses to have sex with such a person) in the hope that some of his advantageous traits will be passed on to her children. A good example of this is the famous Repository for Germinal Choice. This was set up during the 1980s and dubbed the Nobel Prize Sperm Bank because it supposedly contained several Nobel Prize-winners' sperm: the idea being that at least some of their brilliance might have biological underpinnings that could be passed on.[5]

In its broadest sense, 'selective reproduction' can cover both choices like those just mentioned, ones *between different possible future children* and *decisions about how many children to have (if any)*. Choices of the latter kind have been termed *different number* (because we are choosing between one number of children and another) while those of the former kind are called *same number* (because we are choosing not *how many* but rather *which* possible future children to create).[6] The focus of this book is mostly on

---

[5] Chris Ayres, 'When IVF turns into an IQ test', *The Times*, 11 Dec. 2007, 14.
[6] This terminology originates in Parfit's seminal work *Reasons and Persons*. He writes: 'Different Number Choices affect both the number and the identities of future people. Same Number Choices affect the

same number choices, although occasionally it discusses the implications of various arguments and views for different number cases. The reasons for restricting the scope of the work in this way are threefold. First, for reasons explored later, it seems that there are important ethical differences between same and different number choices; thus, each deserves and requires a separate treatment, although ideally we would be able to come up with an overarching theory that dealt with both types of choice. Second, the ethics of selective reproduction is a complicated business and, as we will see, just dealing adequately with same number choices is a task that requires at least a book-length piece. There are only so many things that can be dealt with adequately in one book and a line has to be drawn somewhere. Finally, most (though by no means all) of the pressing ethical and policy issues generated by new selection technologies concern same number choices. For example, techniques like preimplantation genetic diagnosis, although they can be used to enable different number choice are usually oriented towards delivering same number choice: enabling us to choose between different 'candidates for existence' (in this case, embryos). I should, however, add that there are other vitally important political debates and policy questions, ones outside the remit of this work, which are concerned mainly with different number choices. For example, for centuries, there have been pressing and difficult environmental questions about whether the planet is overpopulated, about how population size might need to be weighed against the amount of resources and/or welfare per person, and about what measures to limit (or encourage) population growth are acceptable.

1.3 Different Possible Future People

In defining selective reproduction, I have talked about *creating one possible future child rather than another*. This is an awkward form of words (compared to talking about *choosing children's characteristics*, for example) but there is a reason for using it. For the cases in question are all (or nearly all) ones in which what we are considering is not *altering the characteristics* of a determinate future child (as we might do by, for example, subjecting him or her to prenatal surgery or genetic modification as an infant); rather we are choosing between different possible future persons. This may seem like a somewhat obscure distinction but it is important for reasons that will become clear later, particularly during the discussion of the welfare of the child. For now though (and without going into the many metaphysical complications surrounding this) I

identities of future people, but do not affect their number. Same People Choices affect neither.' Derek Parfit, *Reasons and Persons* (Oxford: Oxford University Press, 1984), 356.

just want to explain why a certain type of choice, embryo selection (for example, using preimplantation genetic diagnosis) is *identity-affecting*: that is, why it is a choice between different possible future persons. This is important because very often people overlook a crucial distinction between *altering the characteristics of a determinate future person* (making someone more or less healthy, for example) and *choosing between two distinct possible future persons* (choosing a healthier one over one with a genetic disorder, for example).

First, what is preimplantation genetic diagnosis? In general terms, this involves creating several embryos outside the body using IVF. Each of them is then genetically tested, usually to detect the presence of a genetic disorder. Having carried out the test, one or more healthy embryos can be implanted in the prospective mother thus minimizing the risk of her child being one with a genetic disorder. Once the genetic tests have been carried out, we are faced with a set of embryos and could in principle implant any number of them (in the egg provider or indeed in any other woman). Imagine then (and this is of course only hypothetical) that we have five tested embryos and decide to implant *all* of them (in five different women) and that all goes well and they are all born alive. In this scenario, the following would have happened.

Scenario 1
- *Embryo A becomes Baby Amelia*
- *Embryo B becomes Baby Benjamin*
- *Embryo C becomes Baby Chloe*
- *Embryo D becomes Baby Daniel*
- *Embryo E becomes Baby Emily*

Amelia, Benjamin, Chloe, Daniel, and Emily are of course five distinct people.

Now imagine a slightly different scenario. Only the first three embryos (A–C) are implanted and carried to term and the others (D and E) are destroyed. In this scenario:

Scenario 2
- *Embryo A becomes Baby Amelia*
- *Embryo B becomes Baby Benjamin*
- *Embryo C becomes Baby Chloe*
- *Embryo D is destroyed; Baby Daniel does not come into existence*
- *Embryo E is destroyed; Baby Emily does not come into existence*

In Scenario 2, three people are created (Amelia, Benjamin, and Chloe) but two *possible future people* (Daniel and Emily) are not. Of course, merely possible future people are not normally given names, but they have been here just to help keep track of which possible entity is which.

By now it should be clear that when we choose between different embryos we choose between different possible future persons, not between (so to speak) different versions of the same possible future person. In Scenario 1, the one in which all five embryos are implanted, Embryo A becomes Amelia and Embryo E becomes Emily. Amelia and Emily are distinct babies, distinct people. If Emily and her gestational mother had been killed in a car crash during pregnancy (before Emily was born) this would make no difference to the existence or identity of Amelia (who, in this scenario, has a different gestational mother). Amelia would still exist, just as she would have if Emily had survived; they are distinct entities, distinct (actual, or at least possible, future) persons.

In the car crash scenario, Emily is a possible future person (an embryo) who did not make it into existence. As far as the 'who comes to exist?' question is concerned, there is no difference between the car crash case and one in which Embryo E is not implanted in the first place. The outcome is the same in both: Emily does not come to exist while Amelia does. So when we choose between different embryos for implantation, we are choosing between different possible future persons. And it is useful to think of embryo *non*-implantation as (in some, but clearly not all, respects) analogous to the car crash case: insofar as, in both cases, a possible future person does not come into existence.

As I mentioned not long ago the main reason why all this matters is because of its implications for the way in which we can deploy the ideas of harm and of the welfare of the child, something that I shall discuss in much more detail in Chapter 3. I will, however, very briefly outline what the problem is here because it is something to be kept in mind throughout.

Imagine then a different scenario. Two of the embryos have serious genetic impairments; three do not.

Scenario 3

- *Embryo A, if implanted, will become Baby Amelia, a child with a painful and life-shortening illness*
- *Embryo B, if implanted, will become Baby Benjamin, a child with a painful and life-shortening illness*
- *Embryo C, if implanted, will become Baby Chloe, a healthy child*
- *Embryo D, if implanted, will become Baby Daniel, a healthy child*
- *Embryo E, if implanted, will become Baby Emily, a healthy child*

Imagine that, in Scenario 3, the doctors and parents decide to implant Embryo A, despite knowing about the genetic disorder, and that Baby Amelia is born with an excruciating disease. When Amelia reaches the age of 18, the preimplantation situation and the fact that Embryo A was chosen is revealed to her (rightly or wrongly) so that she can understand her origins and the reasons for her pain. Amelia is understandably distressed by this and cannot understand why her parents did not select a disease-free embryo. What is more, she blames them for harming her, for (what she sees as) deliberately, or at least knowingly, giving her a disease. Her parents, although generally very sympathetic to Amelia's reaction, do however try to set her right about one thing. It is true, they admit, that they could have chosen a different embryo and consequently have had a child without the disease. *But that child would not have been Amelia.* It would instead have been Chloe, Daniel, or Emily, depending on which alternative embryo was selected. Thus, they tell her, although Amelia's life would certainly have been better if she had been born without a genetic disorder, that was not one of the options available to her parents. Rather *their* choice (as far as Amelia is concerned) was either to create her with the disease (by implanting Embryo A) or to create a different child altogether (for example, implanting C and creating Chloe). So while the disease is of course a source of regret, Amelia cannot reasonably claim that she has been *harmed* (made worse off) by her parents' decision, or been *given the disease* by her parents; for the only available alternative, for Amelia, was not a disease-free life but rather non-existence. So provided that Amelia does not feel, all things considered, that she would be 'better off dead', she cannot reasonably claim to have been *harmed* (made worse off) by her parents' reproductive decision because, had they chosen any other way, then she would not be better off, but rather non-existent. Of course, she can legitimately claim to have been harmed *by her disease* (meaning – *she would have been better off existing without it*, if that were possible) and to have been harmed by various painful episodes during her lifetime (meaning – *she would have been better off existing without such experiences*, if that were possible). But it does not follow from this that her parents' *reproductive* decision (to create Amelia rather than, say, Daniel) has itself harmed her because (as we have seen) the only practical alternative to being born diseased was not being born at all.

Many people find this kind of argument distinctly 'fishy' and troubling and it does require, and will get, much more discussion in Chapter 3. Nonetheless, this sketch of the problem should at least have made it clear both (a) why choosing between different possible future persons (what we might term *existential* or *identify-affecting* choice) is importantly different from altering the characteristics of a single determinate future person, and (b) why the idea of harm may not be readily applicable to these existential or identify-affecting choices.

1.4 Philosophical Bioethics

Having outlined the book's subject matter, I want now to say something about its methodology and the research underlying it. This is a philosophical work (in the analytic tradition, broadly defined) and so its approach to the various ethical and regulatory issues raised by selective reproduction is, not surprisingly, philosophical. What does this mean, though? Giving a full account of the nature of philosophy is itself a complex topic within philosophy and I shall not attempt such a thing here. What I shall do, however, is to sketch out the key elements of a philosophical approach to bioethics. These are:

1. Analysis of the form and structure of moral arguments (including the arguments for and against particular forms of law and regulation). *Thus, subsequent chapters (for example) look at arguments against selective reproduction which appeal to parental virtues, to the welfare of the child, and to concerns about treating children as commodities.*

2. An assessment of the quality of those arguments (especially, but not exclusively, their logic).

3. An analysis of the meaning, or meanings, of the key terms in the debate, and similarly of the nature of key concepts. *In ensuing chapters, the meaning(s) of key terms, such as 'commodification', 'enhancement', 'eugenics', and 'harm', are analysed.*

4. An analysis of the meaning and content of key moral principles and an assessment of their plausibility (for example, by spelling out their implications and the extent to which they cohere with other beliefs, policies, and values). *For example, later sections will explain and critically assess principles like* Procreative Beneficence, *according to which (where the requisite knowledge and selection techniques exist) we are obliged to create the possible future person with the best chance of having the highest quality of life.*[7]

These jobs are (or should be) the 'core business' of philosophical academic bioethics, not least because these are the aims that the resources of analytic philosophy are best suited to achieve.

This account of philosophical bioethics does however raise some questions that both bioethics researchers and their readers may want answering. First, how (if at all) does philosophical bioethics help answer the big questions about what we ought and ought not to do, both in terms of personal or professional ethics, and in terms of law and policy? Second, what about non-philosophical approaches to bioethics, such as the contribution of the social sciences? Third and finally, is there a place for ethical theory in this enterprise (and, if so, where)?

Taking the first question first: to what extent can philosophical bioethics help us to answer pressing moral questions about what we ought and ought not to do? The answer to this is that its role in answering these practical questions is indirect but indispensable. A vitally important part of coming to a rational view about what we ought to do is knowing which moral arguments for and against the action under consideration do and do not work. Indeed, as far as the morality of any given action is concerned, there is not much more to knowing whether we ought to do it than knowing which moral arguments work. For if there are decisive arguments for doing x and the arguments for not doing x are fallacious, then obviously we ought to do x. Things are rarely this straightforward however and sometimes the arguments on both sides appear equally good, perhaps because there is a 'stand off' about some

[7] Julian Savulescu, 'Procreative Beneficence: Why We Should Select the Best Children', *Bioethics*, 15 (2001), 413–26.

fundamental issue (like 'when does personhood begin?' or 'how do we weigh quality of life against number of lives saved?'). Alternatively, both sides in a given debate may have perfectly logical and coherent sets of views but disagree about an (as yet unanswered) *empirical* question: about an issue that (if it can be settled at all) can only be settled by scientific investigation, not through philosophical analysis alone.

This takes us to the second question: what about *non*-philosophical approaches to bioethics, such as the contribution of the social sciences? There is virtually no such work in this book, which (as I have said) is almost wholly philosophical. However, that is not to say that there is no place for such work within the overall field of bioethics. As I suggested above, philosophy on its own can only get us so far, because the moral issues will depend on empirical questions that the philosopher (qua philosopher at least) is ill-equipped to answer. Consequence-based arguments (such as that 'selecting out' disease will lead down the proverbial slippery slope towards 'designer babies' and a 'genetic underclass') are perhaps the most obvious examples of this and, as Zussman notes,

A good deal of medical ethics is based on consequentialist claims that social scientists are well equipped to deal with.[8]

This is the main way in which social science can contribute to bioethics, since knowing the likely social consequences of doing x will often be a crucial part of the moral case for or against doing x. Social science may also have some other indirect contributions to make. One of these is trawling for arguments and concerns. For instance, qualitative social science research might reveal that many people have deep-rooted concerns about eugenics. And while this would not be sufficient to show that these concerns were rational or well founded, it could at least perform an agenda-setting role: showing that academic bioethics ought perhaps to engage with these fears and either address or allay them, depending on how the arguments go. There is much more to be said about the role of empirical methods in bioethics but, since this is not a book on methodology, I shall move on, pausing to note that Eve Garrard and I have explored these issues in more detail in an earlier paper.[9]

Turning now to moral theory, one way of approaching bioethics is to select (and perhaps also argue for, although this may be outside the scope of *bio*ethics) a

---

[8] R. Zussman, 'The Contributions of Sociology to Medical Ethics', *Hastings Center Report*, 30 (2000), 7–11: 9.

[9] Eve Garrard and Stephen Wilkinson, 'Mind the Gap: The Use of Empirical Evidence in Bioethics', in M. Hayry, T. Takala, and P. Herissone-Kelly (eds.), *Bioethics and Social Reality* (Amderstam: Rodopi, 2005), 73-87. See also Erica Haimes, 'What Can the Social Sciences Contribute to the Study of Ethics? Theoretical, Empirical and Substantive Considerations', *Bioethics*, 16 (2002), 89-113; Mairi Levitt, 'Better Together? Sociological and Philosophical Perspectives on Bioethics', in M. Hayry and T. Takala (eds.), *Scratching the Surface of Bioethics* (Amderstam: Rodopi, 2003), 19–27.

particular normative ethical theory: a theory that tells us, in general terms, what we ought to do. Then, having chosen the theory, it is simply *applied* to whatever bioethical issue comes along. One very straightforward example would be hedonistic utilitarianism, according to which we must always create as much net pleasure or happiness as possible (net pleasure being the balance of pleasure over pain). Thus, if we were committed hedonistic utilitarians we would approach each bioethical issue by applying the theory, by working out for each question of policy, law, or individual behaviour, what course of action would maximize net pleasure, and then recommending that as the right (obligatory) action.

This approach is flawed, however, and not because of any defects in utilitarianism. The problem is this. Bioethicists (not to mention the recipients of bioethics research, such as practitioners and policymakers) face pressing moral, legal, and policy issues *now*, issues that must be decided one way or another in a relatively short time frame. One way of dealing with these questions would be first to decide on the correct moral theory and then to apply it, a process which (perhaps in conjunction with empirical evidence gathering) might yield definite answers to the pressing bioethical issues of the day. The difficulty with this method, however, is that the first part of it, coming up with decisive arguments for the correct moral theory (whatever that is) is likely to take a very long time, if the history of moral philosophy is anything to go by. For while there may be consensus among moral philosophers that some theories are more promising than others, there is still a great deal of fundamental disagreement about which moral theory is best, with no end in sight. As far as the 'pure' discipline of philosophy is concerned, there is no need to be troubled by this; perhaps normative ethical theory is essentially contestable and there will never be a decisive settlement of the debate. That is fine for philosophy. But it is a problem if we want to *use* moral theory to settle questions in bioethics, because the question 'which theory?' will loom large. And (using the 'top-down' theory-driven method) we will not be able to get going until it is answered. Or, worse still, people may (as they all too often do) just choose a theory that they like the look of, or which happens to fit their already formed moral views. All of this suggests that the 'applying theory to practice' approach is doomed to failure, at least when it comes to answering concrete questions in bioethics. That is not to say of course that applying theory to practice has *no* value. For it may (among other things) be a good way of finding out more about the nature and plausibility of theories.

1.5 Some Assumptions

All of which takes us to the question of what *my* theoretical commitments are. As far as normative ethical theory is concerned, I shall generally remain as neutral as possible, and I would not claim to *have* a normative ethical theory. That said, a handful of fundamental assumptions do underlie this work.

The first is what I term *Schematic Political Liberalism*. This is the view that the State is obliged not to prohibit a given activity, *x*, unless it can provide compelling reasons for doing so. So, for example, it must not ban human reproductive cloning, fox hunting, or smoking, unless it has a good argument for doing so. Another way of putting this is to say that there should be a *presumption* in favour of allowing things, but this is only a defeasible presumption and anything at all *could* legitimately be banned, provided that there were morally adequate reasons for doing so. Now clearly this is a very basic or minimal form of liberalism and it really only provides a schema for thinking about questions of law and regulation. Indeed, Schematic Political Liberalism could, in certain circumstances, be consistent with a very restrictive set of government policies, provided of course that these were all accompanied by adequate ethical justifications. Furthermore, many liberals wish to place restrictions on the kind of reasons that can justify legal prohibition, notably Mill, who famously writes:

the sole end for which mankind are warranted, individually or collectively, in interfering with the liberty of action of any of their number, is self-protection. That the only purpose for which power can be rightfully exercised over any member of a civilized community, against his will, is to prevent harm to others.[10]

This Millian view can be seen in the writing of contemporary ethicists, such as John Robertson, who writes:

I propose that procreative liberty be given presumptive priority in all conflicts, with the burden on opponents of any particular technique to show that harmful effects from its use justify limiting procreative choice.[11]

While for Millian liberals *harm to others* is the only legitimate reason for State prohibition (or other intervention), my Schematic Political Liberalism allows other moral reasons to count too. For example, in my view, the avoidance of harmless, but nonetheless wrongful, exploitation or instrumentalization could be valid grounds for State intrusion. (I am not saying that these *are* valid grounds, merely that they *could be*, and should not be ruled out a priori). Millians, however, would reject these as grounds for prohibition or regulation unless there was harm.

It might be said that *Schematic Political Liberalism* lacks content. There is some truth in this for, as we have seen, it certainly does not have *much* content; it does not rule much out. However it does underpin the general approach of this book to legal and regulatory issues, an approach which is in many ways *negative*. As we have seen, my

---

[10] John Stuart Mill, *On Liberty* (London: Watts & Co., 1929), 11.
[11] John Robertson, *Children of Choice: Freedom and the New Reproductive Technologies* (Princeton: Princeton University Press, 1996), 16.

view of State involvement is that it would be wrong to prohibit or regulate unless there were sound reasons for doing so. Therefore, in what follows, relatively little time is spent on positive arguments for the value of reproductive choice. Rather, my main interest is in the arguments for prohibition or restriction, or (in the case of purely ethical, as opposed to legal–regulatory, issues) in the arguments for certain kinds of choice or selection being morally wrong.

None of this means that I reject the view that reproductive choice is valuable or do not recognize that there are arguments for such a view. It is simply that (for reasons of space and focus) I do not choose to rehearse such arguments here. One such an argument is provided by John Robertson:

> reproduction is an experience full of meaning and importance for the identity of an individual and her physical and social flourishing . . . If undesired, reproduction imposes great physical burdens on women, and social and psychological burdens on both women and men. If desired and frustrated, one loses the 'defence 'gainst Time's scythe' that 'increase' or replication of one's haploid genome provides, as well as the physical and social experiences of gestation, childrearing, and parenting of one's offspring. Those activities are highly valued because of their connection with reproduction and its role in human flourishing.[12]

On this view, the principle of procreative autonomy is grounded in the importance that most people assign to reproduction, in the practical implications that a decision to reproduce (or not) has for individuals, and in the close relationship between reproductive decision-making and human flourishing.[13] By and large, views like this are not inconsistent with this book's main conclusions, although I do not engage with them in this work and I am not committed to them myself. Rather, my concern (as far as law and regulation are concerned) is seeing whether the State has a good case for regulating and restricting selective reproduction (or particular practices within selective reproduction): whether any of the arguments offered *against* selective reproduction work. If the State does not have such a case (and I shall argue that, in many areas, it does not) then we do not even need to get into thinking about the positive value of procreative autonomy because, given

---

[12] John Robertson, 'Procreative Liberty in the Age of Genomics', *American Journal of Law and Medicine*, 29 (2003), 439–87: 450.

[13] Examples of this kind of view include the following. Emily Jackson tells us that 'when we disregard an individual's reproductive preferences, we undermine their ability to control one of the most intimate spheres of their life. Our reproductive capacity or incapacity indubitably has a profound impact upon the course of our lives, and decisions about whether or not to reproduce are among the most momentous choices that we will ever make': Emily Jackson, *Regulating Reproduction: Law Technology, and Autonomy* (Oxford: Hart Publishing, 2001), 7. Nicolette Priaulx says that the value of reproductive autonomy 'lies in its instrumentality in fostering basic human needs and one's sense of self': Nicolette Priaulx, 'Rethinking Progenitive Conflict: Why Reproductive Autonomy *Matters*', *Medical Law Review*, 6 (2008), 169–200: 173.

the presumption against State prohibition, there is no case to answer. In other words, reproductive liberty would prevail because there would be no reason for it not to.

Turning now from the legal and regulatory side of things to 'pure' ethics, the *morality* of selective reproduction, here I advocate a principle that is analogous to Schematic Political Liberalism: the *Presumption of Permissibility*. This says that we should presume that an action is merely permissible (neither wrong, nor obligatory, nor supererogatory) until an argument can be found that shows it to be otherwise. The Presumption of Permissibility again leads to a rather negative method. For I shall generally start with the assumption that selection is permissible and then search for an argument that might overturn this. In many cases, as we shall see, this search will be unsuccessful, in which case the presumption that it is permissible is retained (and bolstered by the knowledge that no argument against it has been found). I shall, however, concede that we have good reasons to be concerned about *some* selection practices and I am not wedded to a wholly libertarian or permissive view.

I should also add that, in some chapters, I do not get as far as explicitly discussing legal or regulatory implications. The examples I have in mind are those where the moral–philosophical analysis of the arguments (that is, arguments for the prohibition of, or for the moral wrongness of, certain selection practices) reveals them to be fundamentally flawed. In these cases, there is no question of the arguments having legal or regulatory implications (since they fail, as it were, before they even get to that stage) and so no need for a separate discussion of these.

1.6 The Moral Status of the Human Embryo

I now want to explain an omission: something that could have been in a book on the ethics of selective reproduction, but which has been left out, in order to pay more attention to other higher priority items. The omission is a detailed discussion of concerns about the destruction of embryos (and/or foetuses) and of the moral status of the human embryo. Given that embryo selection is referred to extensively throughout, this may strike some readers as odd. There are, however, several reasons for not saying much about this 'moral status' issue.

The first is that selective reproduction need not involve the selection and destruction of embryos. For, as we have seen, sexual abstinence, contraception, and gamete selection (such as sperm sorting for sex selection and the use of 'Nobel Prize' sperm banks) can all be selective reproduction techniques and these do not involve doing anything (directly) to embryos. There is then a distinction between objections to prospective parents *making certain types of choice* about the nature of their future offspring (determining sex, height, longevity, or whatever) and objections to the *means* that parents (or doctors) deploy in order to get what they want ('folk' medicine, gamete selection, preimplantation genetic diagnosis (PGD), abortion, infanticide, or whatever). This book's primary concern is the former: what *types of choice* about the nature of their future offspring can parents permissibly make (assuming, for the sake of argument, that morally unproblematic *means* of delivering these choices are available)? Because, as this book goes to press, PGD is one the most interesting and promising ways of delivering selective reproduction, many of the examples concern this. In addition, many of the recent legal and regulatory debates about selective reproduction have concerned the question of what types of embryo selection should be permitted. So in order to maximize the relevance of the discussion to contemporary bioethical and policy debates, my focus is often on PGD. However, most of the arguments considered apply with equal force to *all* other selective reproduction techniques. Thus, if it were discovered (as has been believed in some cultures) that a certain sexual position vastly increases the chances of having a boy, then using that sexual position intentionally to sex select would (as far as most of the arguments discussed here are concerned) be morally on a par with using sperm sorting or PGD to achieve the same end. Interestingly, new scientific evidence *has* recently come to light suggesting that some seemingly very innocuous forms of behaviour could be used for sex selection: for example, it is claimed that prospective mothers can increase their chances of giving birth to a son by eating breakfast cereals and by increasing their calorific intake.[14] If one objects to sex selection per se (rather than the means used) then presumably deliberately altering one's diet to have a boy would be just as objectionable as using sperm sorting or embryo selection to achieve the same end. However, when it comes to the legal and regulatory issues, there may be other relevant and important differences: not least the impracticability of policing people's eating habits or choice of sexual positions, and the immense invasion of privacy that that would involve (compared to, say, regulating fertility clinics).

The second reason for not discussing concerns about the destruction of embryos is that these are really *too general* to underpin arguments that count specifically against selective reproduction. So while it is not suggested that concerns about the status of the embryo are irrelevant here (they clearly are when embryos are destroyed) these objections do not count *specifically* against selection, but instead against a very wide range of practices including IVF, abortion, and some birth control techniques.

Third and finally, there are pragmatic reasons for not tackling 'head-on' questions about abortion and the status of the embryo in a book about the ethics of selective reproduction. One is that these questions have already been addressed, and in many cases addressed excellently and in considerable detail, by philosophers and others

[14] Jeremy Laurence, 'Mother's Diet Linked to Baby's Sex', *The Independent*, 23 Apr. 2008, 16.

and so it is best to avoid 'reinventing the wheel' by rehashing the abortion debate here.[15] Another is that many of the disagreements about abortion and related practices appear intractable. Hence, basing our arguments on a particular view of the status of the embryo would probably lead straight to argumentative deadlock. So it would be better for all sides if alternative arguments were explored, ones which *do not* rely on contentious assumptions (one way or the other) about the status of the embryo.

1.7 Outline and Structure

The view of philosophical bioethics advocated earlier was that its main job is to analyse and critically assess arguments and to explicate concepts. The structure of this work reflects that view of bioethics. Thus, rather than devoting chapters to particular types of selection, the material is distributed along argumentative and conceptual lines. So, for example, there are dedicated treatments of arguments based on parental virtue, of instrumentalization arguments, and of commodification arguments. All these arguments are supposed to apply to a wide range of selection practices. For instance, we can find them surfacing in debates about sex selection, about saviour siblings, and about cosmetic selection (selection based on appearance).

That said, I have also chosen to match up certain selection practices with particular arguments or concepts, on the grounds that some selection practices seem especially vulnerable to certain arguments or criticisms. So, for example, Chapter 3 is about both child welfare considerations generally and about attempts to deliberately create a child with a disability (as in the McCullough and Duchesneau case, mentioned above). The rationale for this is that child welfare arguments are particularly relevant to selecting for disability, because an influential argument against selecting for disability is that the children created will, so it is alleged, have objectionably low levels of welfare. Similarly, I have allied the discussions of commodification and instrumentalization in Chapters 4 and 5 with the treatment of selecting saviour siblings. Again, the rationale for this is that commodification and instrumentalization arguments are particularly relevant to selecting saviour siblings, since many people have objected to this practice on the

[15] E.g. R. Card, 'Infanticide and the Liberal View of Abortion', *Bioethics*, 14 (2000), 340–51; John Finnis, 'The Rights and Wrongs of Abortion', *Philosophy and Public Affairs*, 2 (1973), 117–45; Susanne Gibson, 'The Problem of Abortion: Essentially Contested Concepts and Moral Autonomy', *Bioethics*, 18 (2004), 221–33; Rosalind Hursthouse, 'Virtue Theory and Abortion', *Philosophy and Public Affairs*, 20 (1991), 223–46; Donald Marquis, 'Abortion and Human Nature', *Journal of Medical Ethics*, 34 (2008), 422–6; Warren Quinn, 'Abortion: Identity and Loss', *Philosophy and Public Affairs*, 13 (1984), 24–54; Judith Jarvis Thomson, 'A Defense of Abortion', *Philosophy and Public Affairs*, 1 (1971), 47–66; Michael Tooley, 'Abortion and Infanticide', *Philosophy and Public Affairs*, 2 (1972), 37–65; Roger Wertheimer, 'Understanding the Abortion Argument', *Philosophy and Public Affairs*, 1 (1971), 67–95.

grounds that the children created are treated as commodities or mere means. So the book consists of a set of chapters, each of which examines one or several *types of argument* against selective reproduction. Generally speaking, arguments that are applicable to a wide range of selection types have been prioritized. (By *selection types*, I mean grounds for selection, such as sex, appearance, health, and so on.) However, one exception to this is Chapter 8, which deals with arguments that might count specifically against sex selection.

Turning now to the book's content and structure, Chapter 2 looks at a set of arguments or positions, each of which criticizes selective reproduction by claiming it to be inconsistent with certain duties that parents have (such as the duty to love their children unconditionally), or certain virtues that they ought to have (such as the Virtue of Parental Acceptance). The most important conclusion of Chapter 2 is that these arguments fail. The main (though not the only) reason for this is a difficulty with applying arguments from parental duty or virtue to *reproductive* decision-making. The problem is that, in many important respects, the moral position of prospective parents is different from that of actual parents (parents of children that already exist). So even where it can be established that x is a parental duty or virtue, it does not follow from this that x is a duty or virtue that *prospective* parents have, or ought to have.

Chapter 3 addresses two questions. First, is there anything wrong with selecting for disability, with using selective reproduction deliberately to create a child with a disability (when a non-disabled alternative is available)? Second, under what circumstances (if any) do concerns about the welfare of (possible, future) children constitute good reasons not to practise selective reproduction, or indeed positive reasons to select in particular ways? These questions are related because much of the hostility towards selecting for disability is grounded in concern for the welfare of the child. The conclusions drawn in Chapter 3 are not straightforward and one thing that becomes obvious during the discussion is that appealing to child welfare considerations to justify reproductive decisions is a more complicated business than many people realize (except perhaps some specialist academic lawyers and philosophers who have been discussing these complexities for many years).

The main conclusion of Chapter 3 is that child welfare arguments do have a role, that they do provide us with reasons to practise or avoid certain forms of selective reproduction. However, this role is more limited and child welfare considerations less decisive than is commonly assumed. One reason for this is that (as mentioned above) the idea of harm only applies in very extreme cases, cases where the person created has a life that is so awful that she would be 'better off dead'. Another is that the relationship between disability and quality of life is more complicated and less direct than is sometimes thought.

When it comes to questions of policy, for these reasons (and others discussed in Chapter 3), I suggest that general bans on selecting in favour of disability, such as that enshrined in the UK's Human Fertilisation and Embryology Act 2008, are probably not warranted, or at least cannot be justified on child welfare grounds alone. This particular prohibition states that:

Persons or embryos that are known to have a gene, chromosome or mitochondrion abnormality involving a significant risk that a person with the abnormality will have or develop—

(a) a serious physical or mental disability,
(b) a serious illness, or
(c) any other serious medical condition,

must not be preferred to those that are not known to have such an abnormality.[16]

Having said that, the inclusion of the word 'serious' (depending on how this is interpreted in practice) may make this measure less objectionable than it would otherwise have been: especially if seriousness comes to be understood in terms of an 'all things considered' assessment of the (possible, future) child's quality of life, one that includes contextual and social factors as well as purely biomedical and functional ones.

Chapters 4 and 5 consider several quite different but linked matters. First, the Cost of Care Argument is evaluated. This is a further argument against selecting for disability, one that (unlike those considered in the preceding chapter) relies not on appeals to the welfare of the child created but on concerns about the costs that selecting for disability would (it is alleged) impose on the health service (and other people more generally). Second, there is a discussion of deliberately creating a 'saviour sibling'. Finally, there is an analysis of the concepts of instrumentalization and commodification, and a discussion of the claim that selecting saviour siblings involves the wrongful instrumentalization and/or commodification of children. What links these seemingly disparate topics is the idea that a (possible, future) child may be selected not for reasons connected to *her own* health or welfare but for reasons relating to *other people's* well-being. The saviour siblings case is the most obvious example (because selection is for the sake of an existing child) but the Cost of Care Argument is also about selecting (or not selecting) because of effects not on the person created, but on other people. Likewise, choosing to create a person for the sake of a third party invites the criticism that the person will be used as a mere means to an end, or treated as a commodity.

The two chapters' main conclusions are as follows. First, I offer several reasons for being sceptical or cautious about using Cost of Care Arguments to justify reproductive decisions. Second, I review the case against selecting saviour siblings and conclude

---

[16] Human Fertilisation and Embryology Act 2008 (c. 22), Section 14(4).

that it does not give us an adequate reason to prohibit the practice or to view it as unethical, although unsurprisingly there may be *extreme versions of* this practice that are objectionable (for instance, if the parents planned to discard the saviour sibling once it had 'served its purpose'). Third, as regards the alleged commodification of saviour siblings, it is argued that such claims are generally confused and unjustified. On the best available understandings of 'commodity' and 'commodification', embryo selection does not necessarily involve treating children as commodities, nor is there much reason to believe that there is a contingent connection between embryo selection and the commodification of children. Much the same goes for instrumentalization and the claim that embryo selection involves treating children as mere means. Embryo selection may well involve the instrumentalization *of embryos* (as opposed to children) and gamete selection may well involve the instrumentalization *of gametes*. But, it is argued, this should not be troubling for anyone who does not regard embryos or gametes as persons or 'ends-in-themselves'.

Chapter 6 looks at two arguments that have been used against selective reproduction generally, but especially against the widely accepted practice of screening out disability and disease: the Eugenics Argument and the Expressivist Argument. The Eugenics Argument says that selecting out disability and disease is a form of eugenics and that eugenics is wrong (or at least morally problematic). Therefore, it is argued, selecting out disability and disease is wrong (or problematic). The view defended in Chapter 6 is that the Eugenics Argument cannot overcome the following problem. Eugenics can be defined normatively, such that only wrongful forms of selection count as eugenic. But if this normative definition is adopted, then it is far from obvious that the types of selection we are considering (such as using PGD to avoid serious genetic disorders) really are eugenic. Alternatively, a broader and more descriptive definition of 'eugenics' can be adopted, in which case perhaps the practices under consideration *are* eugenic. But then (for reasons explored in the chapter) it may well be that this is an acceptable form of eugenics (although, having said that, it is not clear that *calling* it 'eugenics' is terribly helpful, because of the very negative connotations of that word, and because the word tends to cause confusion because of the various definitions of it that are in play).[17]

Turning now to the Expressivist Argument, this says that what is wrong with selecting out disease and disability is that it sends out a negative and damaging message: that the world would be a better place if people with diseases and disabilities did not exist. The analysis starts with a distinction between (a) communication problems, difficulties caused by the way in which 'selecting out' is presented and

---

[17] Stephen Wilkinson, 'Eugenics, Embryo Selection, and the Equal Value Principle', *Clinical Ethics*, 1 (2006), 26–51, and ' "Eugenics Talk" and the Language of Bioethics', *Journal of Medical Ethics*, 34 (2008), 467–71.

discussed, and (b) more fundamental concerns, specifically that the underlying rationale for 'selecting out' contains a negative message about people with disabilities, and so 'selecting out' inevitably sends out a negative message *regardless of how sensitively it is talked about*. Having sidelined the communication issues (which are, in theory at least, easy to deal with) I explore what the different rationales for 'selecting out' might be. I conclude that many of these are defensible and hence do not send out a morally problematic message. However, some are less defensible and, against these, the Expressivist Argument does work.

So the Eugenics Argument is entirely unsuccessful, while the Expressivist Argument is largely unsuccessful, but does work in a qualified way in a limited range of cases.

Chapter 7 examines the view that there is something especially bad about using selective reproduction to create *enhanced* children. The chapter does four things. First, it analyses and clarifies different accounts of enhancement (a concept which turns out to be more complicated and difficult than many people seem to think). Second, it identifies and explains some ethical views about enhancement: notably, the view that it is especially morally problematic (compared to, say, therapy or disease-avoidance). Third, it provides a critical assessment of these views. Finally, it asks what implications (if any) the most defensible of these positions have for the ethics of selective reproduction and also for questions of law and regulation.

The chapter's overall conclusion is that the most important arguments against enhancement selection fail, with one possible limited exception. The exception concerns positional goods (which are, as I explain in Chapter 7, only indirectly linked to the idea of enhancement). Some characteristics are *non-relationally* advantageous. These are properties (such as health perhaps) that it is beneficial to possess (or to have more rather than less of) regardless of the extent to which other people possess them. Such properties are contrasted with relationally advantageous ones, or positional goods. Purely positional goods are properties that it is good to possess (or to have more of) *only* because this gives the person a competitive advantage *over other people* (perhaps tallness and fashionableness are like this, in some cultures at least).

In Chapter 7, I discuss several arguments for restricting access to embryo selection for positional goods; the most important and most convincing one is as follows. If embryo selection for positional goods were left to the 'free market' then this would most likely result in greater inequality and injustice, and harm to the children of parents who could not afford it (and this would be harm proper since these 'unselected' children's existences are not at stake). But if public resources were used to fund embryo selection for positional goods then (assuming that everyone got the same level of enhancement) no one would be any better off (because the pursuit of purely positional goods is, by definition, a 'zero-sum game') but a great deal of public money would have been squandered. This then is the essence of the case against allowing embryo selection for positionally advantageous characteristics: either it would result in additional unfairness accompanied by harm, or in the wasting of public recourses (or possibly both).

Finally, Chapter 8 addresses the issue of 'social' sex selection (that is, sex selection for reasons other than the avoidance of sex-linked disorders). Many of the general anti-selection arguments discussed in earlier chapters apply to sex selection. However, selection for sex, nonetheless, also merits a chapter of its own because there is a set of special arguments (including notably ones to do with sexism and population sex imbalance) that apply uniquely to this practice.

After having outlined the legal and regulatory context in the UK, Chapter 8 proceeds to examine the view that so-called 'family-balancing' sex selection is morally preferably to other forms and should enjoy a privileged legal or regulatory status. Sex selection is 'family balancing' if the family in question has more children of one sex than the other (say, four girls and three boys) and then selects (in this case) a boy with the aim of evening things up, of reducing or eliminating the sex differential within the family. The main arguments for privileging 'family balancing' are that it is less likely to be sexist and less likely to cause population sex imbalance than other sorts of social sex selection. Sections 8.3 and 8.4 review these arguments, concluding that 'family balancing' is not (or need not be) any better than other forms of sex selection.

The remaining part of Chapter 8 considers the more fundamental question of whether *any* form of sex selection is permissible and reviews several further arguments against it. The conclusion ultimately arrived at is a complex one. It is argued that, while sex selection is not intrinsically or necessarily wrong, many actual instances of it are wrong, either because of their negative effects (for example, on population sex ratios) or because they are based on sexist beliefs and attitudes. Context then is crucial to the moral assessment of sex selection and, while it may be innocuous in some *relatively* non-sexist Western countries, it is less likely to be so in cultures where a strong preference for sons is the norm. So, as regards the ethics of sex selection, the view defended is that it is morally problematic insofar as it is sexist or harmful, and that often it is both (and hence problematic). However, I also argue (with some caveats) against the legal prohibition of social sex selection (using either PGD or sperm sorting) in the UK and in other relevantly similar Western countries. Two of the main reasons offered for this are, first, that it would be possible to regulate sex selection in ways that make it fairly harmless and, second, that any sexism enshrined in a British system of regulated sex selection would be no worse than that contained in many other permitted practices; and, while all sexism is morally to be condemned, making all of it *illegal* is neither practicable nor desirable.

2

Parental Duties and Virtues

The arguments considered in this chapter criticize selective reproduction by suggesting that it is incompatible with certain parental duties and virtues. I start by looking at the idea that parents ought unconditionally to love their children and by asking (a) whether this is true, and (b) whether, if it were true, it would apply to prospective as well as to actual parents. I then look at the Virtue of Parental Acceptance and again ask whether it applies to prospective parents and whether it is incompatible with selective reproduction. During this discussion, I also consider the claim that children should be regarded as gifts. I then examine and reject an argument offered by Hilary Putnam based on the supposed value of diversity. Finally, I look in some detail at the claim that children have a Right to an Open Future and the idea that this generates correlative duties for both actual and prospective parents; during this discussion I also address some wider questions about promoting and respecting autonomy.

The ultimate conclusion of Chapter 2 is that these arguments based on (supposed) parental duties and virtues are weak. One of the main reasons for this is the fact that prospective parents are, in important respects, in a morally different situation from actual ones.

2.1 Unconditional Love

> Designing in the sense of having a list of features and characteristics in a child and putting them together ... does seem to me to undermine the open and unconditional nature of parental love and to clearly attempt to set the life path of a child.[1]

Selective reproduction is often criticized on the grounds that it is incompatible with, or shows a lack of, unconditional love. Other reproductive practices have been on the receiving end of this criticism too; Elizabeth Anderson, for example, appeals to

---

[1] Anon., 'Choosing Designer Babies "Beyond Science and Law" ', *London Evening Standard*, 23 Apr. 2003.

unconditional parental love in her critique of commercial surrogacy.[2] This section critically assesses the Unconditional Love Argument against selective reproduction which, in its basic form, goes as follows:

1. Parents ought to love their children unconditionally (the Principle of Unconditional Parental Love).

2. *Therefore*: parents ought to love their children regardless of whether they have F (where F is some characteristic, such as being male, blonde, deaf, athletic, or tall).

3. *Therefore*: when choosing which possible children to create (for example, in embryo selection cases) prospective parents ought not to care whether their future children have F and ought not to choose between possible future children on the basis of their having (or not having) F.

There are two major problems with this argument. First, the Principle of Unconditional Parental Love is questionable. Second, even if parents were obliged to love their existing children unconditionally, it would not (I shall argue) follow that their attitudes to merely possible future children must be similarly unconditional. In other words, (2) (above) does not entail (3).

I shall examine each of these problems in turn. Taking the first one first: are parents really obliged to love their (existing) children unconditionally, in all circumstances and regardless of what characteristics they have? Before proceeding to answer this, some preliminary complications should be noted. First, there is a big philosophical question (not one I shall answer here) about what love is and thus about what counts as loving a child. Given that the philosophy of love is an immensely complicated and murky area, and that a detour into definitions of love would take us a long way from selective reproduction, I shall sidestep the definition of love and assume, for the time being, that we have a reasonably good grasp of what it is for parents to love their children.[3] Second, there is a similarly large question about what constitutes parenthood and thus about who (if anyone) is obliged unconditionally to love whom. For instance, there are debates about whether being a sperm provider is necessary and/or sufficient for being a father, and about whether gestation is necessary and/or sufficient for being a mother.[4] Again, I shall disregard these complications for the

[2] Elizabeth Anderson, 'Is Women's Labor a Commodity?' *Philosophy and Public Affairs*, 19 (1990), 71–92.

[3] Les Burwood, 'How Can We Assess Whether It Is Rational to Fall in Love?' *Journal of Social Philosophy*, 30 (1999), 223–35; Stan van Hooft, 'Commitment and the Bond of Love', *Australasian Journal of Philosophy*, 74 (1996), 454–66; Hugh LaFollette, *Personal Relationships: Love, Identity, and Morality* (Oxford: Blackwell, 1995).

[4] David Archard, 'What's Blood Got To Do With It? The Significance of Natural Parenthood', *Res Publica*, 1 (1995), 91–106; Tim Bayne and Avery Kolers, 'Parenthood and Procreation', in Edward Zolta (ed.), *The Stanford Encyclopedia of Philosophy* (Stanford: Centre for the Study of Language and Information), <http://plato.stanford.edu>; Giuliana Fuscaldo, 'Genetic Ties: Are They Morally Binding?' *Bioethics*,

present and leave to one side the question of what constitutes parenthood, for this does not have a direct bearing on the question in hand, which is whether parents (whoever they are) are obliged unconditionally to love their children. Third, some people cast doubt upon the whole idea of obligations to love, pointing out that we cannot be *obliged* to love people because love is involuntary; we cannot help whom we do and do not love. While this is an interesting line of argument, I am going also to disregard it for the present because, if this works at all, it works against love of *all* kinds, not just the unconditional variety. My concern however is specifically with objections to the view that parents should love their children *unconditionally*, not with problematizing the whole idea of morally required love. Furthermore, since I shall be arguing *against* the view that one reason not to practise selective reproduction is the moral requirement to love one's children, I could happily accept the claim that there is no such requirement without its adversely affecting my argument (except perhaps insofar as it renders my argument unnecessary).

Having dispensed with these preliminaries, we can now ask: are parents obliged to love their children unconditionally? One reason for thinking that they are not is the existence of counterexamples in which withholding parental love seems both reasonable and morally permissible. Perhaps the clearest cases are ones in which the child has carried out evil acts. Thus, the parents of rapists, serial killers, and torturers are arguably entitled to withdraw love from their children, although perhaps loving them would still be supererogatory (morally good but not morally required). As ever, much will depend on the context and the details of the case. For example, serial killers and torturers who have themselves been on the receiving end of abuse and whose evil behaviour was largely a result of this may be more deserving of continuing parental love; while parents who are themselves partly to blame for their children's bad behaviour may have stronger obligations to carry on loving than those who are blameless.

This counterexample works against an unqualified version of the Principle of Unconditional Parental Love. For surely we should not condemn a parent for withdrawing love from a child who (for reasons that are not the parent's fault) has become an evil 'monster'. We can expect parents to be extremely tolerant of their children's bad acts (compared to the tolerance required of strangers) but there surely must come a point at which the withdrawal of parental love is an appropriate response. This intuition seems to be a good reason to reject the view that parents should love their children unconditionally. However, it is not a *decisive* reason because, as is always the case with argument by counterexample, proponents of unconditional love may

20 (2006), 64–76; Avery Kolers, 'Cloning and Genetic Parenthood', *Cambridge Quarterly of Healthcare Ethics*, 12 (2003), 401–10; Liezl van Zyl, 'Intentional Parenthood and the Nuclear Family', *Journal of Medical Humanities*, 23 (2002), 107–18.

simply bite the bullet and say that parents must not withdraw love regardless of how evil and monstrous their children become.

Defenders of the Principle of Unconditional Parental Love may respond to the 'evil child' case by saying that it only shows that there are special circumstances in which children *forfeit* their rights to parental love, on account of their morally bad behaviour. Thus, it may be argued, the requirement to give parental love is unconditional *in all circumstances except forfeiture*. Furthermore, as far as selective reproduction is concerned, forfeiture is hardly likely to be relevant, since we are usually talking about selecting between different embryos or gametes, beings which have not yet had an opportunity to forfeit their putative rights to parental love. Hence, a slightly qualified version of the Principle of Unconditional Parental Love (one that allows for forfeiture) will be as good as (have the same ethical implications as) an unqualified version, so long as we focus just on selective reproduction.

So are there any other counterexamples other than the 'evil child'? Another candidate would be a case in which a child was either born with a mental impairment that was so severe that it lacked the kinds of personal characteristics (and the capacity to develop them) in virtue of which people are generally loved. An extreme example of this is anencephaly, which results in babies being born lacking a large part of the brain. Babies with this condition are 'usually blind, deaf, unconscious, and unable to feel pain'.[5] Many of us will feel that parents are not obliged to love such a child although, in such an extreme case, perhaps the thought is that there is no child there to be loved, only a 'body' or 'shell'. More controversial then would be a range of less severe cases in which the child was conscious but very severely mentally impaired (for example, such that it could never communicate or form anything other than the most rudimentary thoughts). As I just mentioned, much will depend on the details of the case and ethical arguments based on counterexamples are generally contestable. But I think we can say that there will be some examples of this kind (ones appealing to mental impairment rather than forfeiture) that do lead us to at least have some doubts about the Principle of Unconditional Parental Love.

A further, more theoretical, argument against unconditional parental love is provided by Stephen Hales. According to Hales, unconditional love is:

love that is not conditioned upon (dependent on, in virtue of) *any* properties of the beloved. Anything short of this would be love that is conditional upon some properties of the object of love, and hardly an honest candidate for unconditionality.[6]

---

[5] National Institute of Neurological Disorders and Stokes (US), NINDS Anencephaly Information Page, <www.ninds.nih.gov/disorders/anencephaly/anencephaly.htm#What_is> (last accessed: Sunday, 12 Apr. 2009).

[6] Steven Hales, 'The Impossibility of Unconditional Love', *Philosophy and Public Affairs*, 9 (1995), 317–20: 317.

He then goes on to point out that so-called 'unconditional' *parental* love is, by its very nature, conditional. For even if Jessica and Jack love their boy, Johnny, regardless of his behaviour and beliefs, their love is still:

conditional upon at least one of Johnny's properties, namely the property of *being their child*. That he has this property explains why they would continue to love Johnny should he become an axe murderer even though they do not love other axe murderers. The others lack the property of being their child.[7]

So 'unconditional *parental* love' is an oxymoron because love of this kind depends on one of the beloved's properties: in this case, *being Jessica and Jack's child*. Thus, if they were to discover that Johnny was not biologically their child after all (for example, due to a mix-up at birth) or if Johnny stopped being socially their child following a parent–child 'divorce', love would (or could) be withdrawn. Hales however concedes that this perhaps does not quite capture what concerns unconditional love enthusiasts. What they care about rather is:

love that won't vanish no matter what happens, or no matter what the actions of—or changes in—the beloved.[8]

According to Hales, the best way of construing this modified commitment to unconditional parental love is as the view that parents' love should be conditional only upon the *essential* characteristics of their children. This view forms part of a larger picture in which the best forms of love are those which depend only (or mainly) on the beloved's essential features, while the worst depend on features that are not only contingent but also transient and easily lost:

Johnny's parents love him because he is their child. *Being their child* is not a property that Johnny can ever lose. So no matter what Johnny does, or how he changes, his parents' love for him will abide. Weaker sorts of love will be those that are conditional upon contingent properties. Juanita does not love José because of his essential properties, but because of his contingent ones. This is why his drunken philandering could cause her to stop loving him. The weakest kinds of love are those conditional on properties that might easily be lost, such as physical beauty. Stronger sorts will be conditional upon properties or clusters of properties that will be hard to lose. The strongest possible love will be love based upon essential properties.[9]

But even this modified principle seems to me (and to Hales, though for different reasons) to be flawed.

First, there is a distinction to be drawn between the *strength* of a love and (one aspect of) its *moral status*. Saying what exactly it is for a love to be 'strong' is tricky and, as I said earlier, I would rather avoid a protracted detour into the philosophy of love. That

[7] Hales, 'The Impossibility of Unconditional Love', 318.
[8] Hales, 'The Impossibility of Unconditional Love'.
[9] Hales, 'The Impossibility of Unconditional Love', 319.

said, it does seem that one important aspect of a love's strength is the likelihood of its persisting. (Another is the extent to which the lover is willing to sacrifice her own interests for the sake of the beloved's.) Hence, it is no surprise that love grounded in a thing's essential properties will be strong, because a thing cannot lose its essential properties (or, at least, not while continuing to be the same thing). Conversely, it is no surprise that love based on transient features will be weak. However, a strong love is not necessarily a good or appropriate love. What if (for example) Jessica and Jack love Karen because she is Kenneth's daughter, or because she is a featherless biped, or because she was conceived in 1999? Arguably, all of these properties are *just as essential as* Johnny's being the son of Jessica and Jack, but they are hardly good grounds for love. So it is difficult to see why essentiality per se makes a property a good basis for love.

Second, however, even the claim that loves based on essential properties are stronger than other loves requires qualification. This is because the fact that a property is essential does not mean that it is obvious or perceptible. For example, let us grant (as is widely held) that having a particular biological father is an essential attribute. Thus, if Jack is Johnny's (biological) father then part of Johnny's essence is having Jack as a (biological) father. However, at least until the recent advent of genetic paternity tests, attributions of biological fatherhood were notoriously unreliable and hence this essential characteristic may not have been readily accessible to the putative father, or indeed to anyone. So what if Jack, who until now has loved Johnny based largely on the belief that he is Johnny's (biological) father, discovers that (owing to a mix-up at a clinic) he is not Johnny's father? At this point a love based (and conditional) upon a *supposed* essential feature may well fade. Hence, we must qualify the claim that loves based on essential properties are stronger because, although actual essential properties cannot change, we have to take into account people's epistemic frailties: the fact that they can easily make mistakes about those properties on which they base their love. Thus, the strength of a love may depend (inter alia) both upon the modality of the property on which it is based (i.e. it is essential?) *and* on the reliability (or otherwise) of the lover's belief in that property.

A third problem with the 'essential properties view' is that the issue of what features of a person are essential is complicated and contested. Many people do believe that A's biological origins (in particular, coming from particular gametes) are essential to being A. But not everyone thinks this and any theory of parental love that depends on essentiality is a hostage to metaphysical fortune—vulnerable to new arguments and findings in metaphysics about which things are and are not essential to a person's identity. And furthermore some theorists ('anti-essentialists') argue that there is no legitimate distinction to be drawn between essential and accidental properties, and/or that there are no essential properties.[10]

---

[10] See e.g. David Lewis, *On the Plurality of Worlds* (Oxford: Blackwell, 1986), Ch. 4; Nathan Salmon, *Reference and Essence* (Oxford: Blackwell, 1982); Anthony Wrigley, 'Genetic Selection and Modal Harms',

In the light of these considerations (both the theoretical ones and my earlier counterexample) I contend that the Principle of Unconditional Parental Love (including the 'modified' version) is at best questionable.

Nonetheless, this is not all that important, because there is a less extreme and more plausible alternative which, to a limited extent, can take its place. This is simply the view that *parental love ought not to be withheld or withdrawn on trivial or morally irrelevant grounds*. The intuitive plausibility of this is clear when we think about various cases in which parents disown their children. These include rejecting the child for having the 'wrong' religious beliefs, for marrying the 'wrong' person, for being gay, or even for supporting the 'wrong' sports team. I suggest that to withdraw parental love on these grounds is wrong (except perhaps in the most extreme cases—for example, if the selected religious beliefs, spouses, or sports teams were themselves thoroughly evil). Of course, controversy about what counts as a morally relevant and significant consideration is ubiquitous; for example, there are (unfortunately) many people in the world who would regard homosexuality as a significant moral wrong and who would regard it as a sufficient reason for disowning one's children. Thus, the view that parental love ought not to be withheld on trivial or morally irrelevant grounds, while providing a schema, does not in and of itself offer substantive moral guidance because a lot depends on the controversial question of which things are morally relevant and significant. Thus, there are difficult and interesting debates to be had about whether a child's being a burglar, a recreational drug user, a sex worker, or whatever, would be sufficient to justify the withdrawal of parental love.

2.2 Actual and Prospective Parents

I said earlier that the Unconditional Love Argument against selective reproduction has two major weaknesses: doubts about the Principle of Unconditional Parental Love itself and the fact that *even if* parents were obliged to love their existing children unconditionally, it would not follow from this that prospective parents are required *now* unconditionally to love their (presently non-existent) *future* children. The second of these weaknesses is the stronger objection and is subject of this section. In addition, the section looks at some wider issues about the extent to which actual and prospective parents are in the same moral position.

Before moving on to consider this, however, I should reiterate one of the key points made in Chapter 1: that this book is about the ethics of pre-existential selective

The Monist, 89 (2006), 505–25; Stephen Yablo, 'Essentialism', in Edward Craig (ed.), *Routledge Encyclopaedia of Philosophy*, <www.rep.routledge.com>.

reproduction, specifically of choosing the characteristics of *possible future children*, of ones that presently do not exist (or at least not as children or persons). It is important to mention this again because some people will say that the reason why obligations of parental love apply to (for example) embryos is that embryos *are* children. And, of course, the logic of that position is right: that is, *if* embryos are children and *if* parents ought unconditionally to love their children, then parents ought to love their embryos unconditionally too.

I am, however, (for reasons discussed in more detail in Chapter 1) ruling such arguments out of court. This is not because I substantively disagree with them (although, as it happens, I do) but rather because my interest here is in selecting *future* children. If someone believes that conception is the point at which embryos (or pre-embryos) become persons (or children, or human beings, or whatever the relevant category is) then I can still have a debate with them about pre-existential selective reproduction (in my sense of the term) but it would have to be a debate about selection decisions taken *prior to conception*. Thus, the debate with these people may well end up being rather more (although not entirely) 'science fiction' than a similar debate with someone who believes that preimplantation genetic diagnosis, and the like, are forms of pre-existential selective reproduction. Conversely, and at the other extreme, I could have essentially the same debate with someone who believed that very young children are not persons and that infanticide is, in principle, a permissible form of pre-existential selection—without questioning her views on killing infants per se, but rather focusing just on the selection issue. As with the 'pro-lifer', the rationale here is not that I agree with the proponent of selective infanticide, but just that the issue under consideration is neither 'when does life (personhood, etc. . . .) begin?' nor 'which beings have rights to life?' but rather 'which forms of *pre-existential* selective reproduction are (in principle) permissible?' Anyhow, for our present purposes, the thing to keep in mind is that the 'embryos are children' argument is being sidelined because, if they were, I would simply shift my attention to pre-conception selection, in order to keep the debate focused purely on the issue of selection. So I shall not, in this work, be arguing for a particular view about which reproductive practices are cases of pre-existential selective reproduction (as opposed to things done to children); but I shall sometimes assume (for the sake of argument and for stylistic economy) that the 'early' selection cases (gamete and embryo selection) are pre-existential.

We can now ask the substantive question: is unconditional love obligatory in the case of merely possible future children? One obvious reason for answering 'no' is that it is pretty hard to make sense of what loving a merely possible future child, or indeed a merely possible future anything, would be like. It looks as if it may be logically, or at the very least psychologically, impossible to love such merely possible things—not least because there are so many of them.

Perhaps though this misunderstands the relevant obligation; perhaps it is more like this. Parents are not, at the point at which they make reproductive decisions, obliged to love all of their merely possible future children. As I have said, this would be, at best, excessively demanding and, at worst, impossible. However, they *are* required to have the following attitude to their future children: 'whatever child comes along, we will love it unconditionally'. In terms of the logic of parental obligation this seems about right. Consider this analogy. Parents have an obligation to clothe and feed their children. Now they do not, in any straightforward way, have obligations prenatally to clothe and feed their merely possible future children, if indeed we can make any sense of such obligations. But perhaps they *are* required to have the following attitude at the point of reproductive decision-making: 'when a child comes along, we will do our best to clothe and feed it'. Indeed, this suggests the following universalizable schema:

> *If parents are under an obligation to do x for their (existing) children then, when deciding whether to have children, or which children to create, prospective parents ought to have the following attitude, or make the following commitment: 'when our child arrives, we will (do our best to) do x for it'.*

One difficult and interesting question that this schema raises is: what about cases in which parents know in advance that they will not be able to do x (say, clothe and feed their children)? Does this generate an obligation not to create the child in the first place? This question (and, more generally, the idea of 'wrongful life') is the subject of Chapter 3 and will not be discussed further here. With the schema in place, the position as regards unconditional love seems to be this. Assuming (for the sake of argument) that parents ought to love their existing children unconditionally, then prospective parents ought to *expect and/or plan* to love their future children unconditionally, once they arrive.

There is a further question, however, that needs answering before we can read off anything about selective reproduction: what kinds of selection (if any) are incompatible with planning to love one's future children unconditionally? One thing that *would* be incompatible with this is not selective reproduction per se but rather *intending to reject one's future children after birth* if it turns out not to have all the desired characteristics. Thus, one might, for example, use selective reproduction techniques in an attempt to create a blue-eyed child while having the following attitude: 'if the selection process fails and the child is brown-eyed, then we will give it up for adoption'. This appears morally reprehensible and starting the reproductive enterprise with such an attitude would fall foul of the Principle of Unconditional Parental Love. However, it is important to note that it is not the *desire to select* that violates the principle in this case, but rather the *plan to reject* the child if it does not live up to expectations. This is important because it is entirely possible to want to select characteristics while not having this problematic attitude of rejection. For instance, prospective parents might prefer a boy and try to sex select, but nonetheless be committed to loving the child regardless of sex and just as much if it is a girl, as if it is a boy.

There is a distinction to be made then between, on the one hand, preferring and attempting to create a child with characteristic F and, on the other, being disposed to reject a future child if it fails to have F. Table 2.1 illustrates this point, using the example of sex selection.

Table 2.1.

(A) The prospective parents prefer a boy and attempt sex selection. However, they'll love whoever comes along, regardless of sex.	(B) The prospective parents prefer a boy but do not attempt sex selection. They'll love whoever comes along, regardless of sex.
(C) The prospective parents prefer a boy and attempt sex selection. If they get a girl, they'll abandon her and try for a boy later.	(D) The prospective parents prefer a boy but do not attempt sex selection. If they get a girl, they'll abandon her and try for a boy later.

Table 2.1 makes it clear that there are four kinds of case and that concerns about parents abandoning their children if they do not have the desired characteristics are logically distinct from the question of whether or not the parents attempt to select. Thus, it is possible for parents who *do not* sex select to fall foul of the Principle of Unconditional Parental Love (by being disposed to reject a child of the 'wrong' sex) and conversely possible for parents who *do* sex select to act in accordance with the principle, provided that they are disposed to accept whoever comes along.

This is a decisive objection to the view that selective reproduction is wrong on account of its (supposed) incompatibility with the Principle of Unconditional Parental Love. For not only is the principle itself questionable but selective reproduction per se is not incompatible with it. For, as we have just seen, what matters is not people's attempts to select characteristics but rather their attitude of acceptance. Thus, I would suggest that scenarios (A) and (B) (the unshaded cells in Table 2.1) are morally unproblematic (at least as far as unconditional love is concerned) while (C) and (D) (the shaded cells) raise serious concerns (not least about the welfare of the child). And this is despite the fact that (C) does, and (D) does not, involve sex selection.

At this point, defenders of the Unconditional Love Argument may fall back to an empirical version of the argument and say that while *logically* selective reproduction need not violate the Principle of Unconditional Parental Love, *in fact* parents who select are more likely than others to reject (or otherwise mistreat) their children on the grounds that they have the 'wrong' characteristics. Rosamund Scott, for example, says that:

it must be stressed that this is necessarily speculative [but] to care one way or the other about your child's hair, eye colour or height so that you test and choose an embryo on this basis, could indicate a somewhat problematic attitude toward parenthood.[11]

As Scott herself notes, though, this is mere speculation and hence, insofar as the unconditional love objection relies on it, it is weak. In defence of the empirical claim, it might be argued that the desire to (for example) sex select is symptomatic of being overly concerned with the child's sex. This is especially so if selection entails a lot of cost, discomfort, and inconvenience, as in reality it seems to at the moment. Flinter, for example, reports that:

A preimplantation diagnosis cycle is a major undertaking for any couple, and the psychological, medical, and financial costs are considerable. A single cycle costs £4,000–7,000 . . . (including drugs).[12]

Thus, the proportion of the set of people who sex select that is unduly concerned with having (for example) a male child will probably be higher than the equivalent proportion in the general population. This may well be true just as, for example, people who have elective cosmetic surgery are perhaps more likely to be vain (or ugly) than the general population. But it does not follow from this that there is anything wrong with the act of sex selection. All that follows from it is that it is a practice that will appeal to people with a certain kind of bad attitude. But crucially it is not *only* attractive to these people, just as cosmetic surgery is not attractive *only* to the vain. Furthermore, nothing here suggests that there is a *causal* link between sex selection and insufficiently accepting parental attitudes. So sex selection cannot be condemned for *making* parents less accepting; it is just that under-accepting parents will be attracted to it, along with other forms of selective reproduction. Of course, it is open to someone to *claim* that the availability of techniques, such as sex selection, does make parents less accepting but this is just more empirical speculation which, as far as I am aware, is not well evidenced.

Finally, an additional practical consideration, one that counts in favour of sex selection, should be mentioned at this point. It is claimed (against sex selection) that

[11] Rosamund Scott, 'Choosing between Possible Lives: Legal and Ethical Issues in Preimplanation Genetic Diagnosis', *Oxford Journal of Legal Studies*, 26 (2006), 153–78: 167.

[12] Frances Flinter, 'Preimplantation Genetic Diagnosis Needs to be Tightly Regulated', *BMJ* 322 (28 Apr. 2001), 1008–9. In a 2006 paper, Donna Gitter reports US prices of around $15,000 for one cycle of IVF with PGD: Donna M. Gitter, 'Am I My Brother's Keeper? The Use of Preimplantation Genetic Diagnosis to Create a Donor or Transplantable Stem Cells for an Older Sibling Suffering from a Genetic Disorder', *George Mason Law Review*, 13 (2006), 975–1035: 982. According to the Bridge Centre's website (in April 2009) PGD costs £2,100 for 'test development (including HFEA application if necessary)' and then £1,050 per cycle for embryo biopsy and testing: see <www.thebridgecentre.co.uk> (last accessed: Sunday, 12 Apr. 2009).

parents who sex select are more likely than other parents to reject their children but, if sex selection were done effectively, then there would not be many such rejections because most parents would end up with what they wanted (at least with respect to the sex of their child).

So the Unconditional Love Argument fails. The Principle of Unconditional Parental Love on which it is based is implausible. And, even if parents *were* obliged unconditionally to love their children, it would not (as we have just seen) follow from this that *prospective* parents were obliged unconditionally to love their merely possible future children.

2.3 The Virtue of Parental Acceptance

In this section, I consider some views that, in some respects, resemble the Unconditional Love Argument. I start off by looking at McDougall's idea that there is a distinct Virtue of Parental Acceptance and then proceed to consider the Symmetry Principle, which says that if it would be wrong to withhold or withdraw parental love from an existing child for having characteristic F, it would be similarly wrong to deselect a possible future child on the grounds that it would have F. Finally, I examine the frequently made claim that children are, or should be treated as if they were, gifts.

The Virtue of Parental Acceptance

Rosalind McDougall is one proponent of this approach. She claims that:

Because a child's characteristics are unpredictable, acceptance is a parental virtue. The flourishing of the child is facilitated by the parent's embracing of the child regardless of his or her specific characteristics. Unless the parents act acceptingly toward the child's characteristics, the child's contentment and self esteem, and the parents' ability to enjoy that child, are all in jeopardy.[13]

McDougall thinks that the Virtue of Parental Acceptance can ground an objection to sex selection (and presumably other forms of selection too):

By sex selecting, the agent puts himself or herself into the parenting role yet fails to act in accordance with that role. The sex selecting agent acts wrongly not because acting on a preference for a child of a particular sex is necessarily inconsistent with being a good parent to the child so produced. That the sex selected child happens to be loved and adequately parented does not preclude condemnation of the sex selection act that brought that child into existence. The wrong is the sex selecting agent's failure to act in accordance with a

---

[13] Rosalind McDougall, 'Acting Parentally: An Argument Against Sex Selection', *Journal of Medical Ethics*, 31 (2005), 601–5: 603.

parental character trait, acceptance, which is intrinsically linked on a general conceptual level to the flourishing of children. Sex selection is wrong because it is not in accordance with the parental virtue of acceptance, regardless of the outcome for a specific child.[14]

For the time being, let us allow (as we did for unconditional love) that there is such a virtue and that actual parents (i.e. the parents of existing children) ought to have it. We can then focus our attention solely on the question of whether this virtue is applicable to *prospective* parents, to people who are planning to create a child and who are deciding whether or not to practice some form of selective reproduction. McDougall says that prospective parents who select put themselves 'into the parenting role' but how plausible this is depends on what exactly putting oneself into the parenting role amounts to. On her view, and in order for her argument to work, it must involve being in the same moral position as actual parents, with the same duties and virtue requirements. But, as we saw in the previous section, it is far from obvious that parents and prospective parents are in the same moral position. Hence, we need some kind of *argument* for McDougall's suggestion.

McDougall does offer an argument of sorts, although it is unconvincing. She says:

It is a necessary feature of the desire to sex select that it is part of a broader desire to become a parent; you could not want to have a son specifically without wanting, more generally, to be a parent. The sex selecting agent is thus necessarily in the situation of deliberately seeking to have a child; the sex selection decision is part of an overall project of parenthood. As Vehmas has suggested, the decision to procreate itself 'puts the potential parents morally in the position of parenthood'. Because the sex selecting agent has deliberately adopted the project of parenthood, he or she has created a situation in which the criterion of right parental action is relevant, despite the fact that no child yet exists.[15]

So are prospective parents morally in the same position as actual parents and, if so, why? Unfortunately McDougall does not properly address this. She makes two claims: that wanting to sex select entails wanting to become a parent; and that sex selecting entails deliberately adopting 'the project of parenthood'. Both assertions are believable but unremarkable, since neither requires us to think that actual and prospective parents should have their actions judged by reference to the very same virtues. When it comes to the crucial issue, McDougall does not provide an argument but simply quotes Simo Vehmas who says that prospective parents are 'morally in the position of parenthood', which is not of course an argument but an assertion of the hypothesis under consideration.

Perhaps then we should turn to Vehmas's original work to see what, if anything, justifies this assertion. Vehmas tells us:

[14] McDougall, 'Acting Parentally', 604.   [15] McDougall, 'Acting Parentally', 603.

conscious assent to parenthood means committing oneself to acting and evaluating one's actions and decisions in the light of the project of parenthood. One dimension of parenthood is committing oneself to caring for any kind of child. Parents who rejected their child who became seriously disabled due, for example, to a car accident would probably be considered as acting morally wrong [sic] *as parents*.[16]

How is this argument supposed to work? First, we have the innocuous suggestion that 'conscious assent to parenthood means committing oneself to acting and evaluating one's actions and decisions in the light of the project of parenthood'. This seems fair enough: prospective parents should certainly *take into account* their impending parenthood project and are (prima facie) obliged not to do things now that would jeopardize it or harm their future child. Vehmas then goes on to say that an aspect 'of parenthood is committing oneself to caring for any kind of child'. Since, in reality, not all actual parents will commit to this, I assume that this is a *moral* claim: parents *ought to* be ready to care for any kind of child. As noted in the discussion of unconditional love above, this may well be too strong but let us allow it to pass for the time being and grant that parents ought to care for any kind of child. Vehmas then goes on to say:

In the same way, prospective parents who have decided to procreate are *morally* parents and they should take a similar, unconditional attitude toward their prospective children as parents should take toward their actual children.[17]

This is problematic. First, Vehmas seems to have overlooked the distinction I made earlier between (a) a prenatal commitment to accepting and loving your child, *once it arrives*, and (b) refraining from selective reproduction. As I suggested earlier, (a) does not logically require (b); or at least we are still waiting for an *argument* that links (a) and (b). Thus, there are two ways of understanding Vehmas's claim. On the first interpretation, he is saying that prospective parents should have (a), the commitment to love whoever comes along, once s/he comes along. This is reasonably plausible (leaving aside my reservations about unconditional love) but tells us little or nothing about the permissibility or otherwise of selective reproduction because (a) does not entail (b). Alternatively, perhaps what he means is (b): that prospective parents' unconditional attitudes should involve not preferring (for example) a boy to a girl, or at the very least refraining from acting on such preferences. But if that is what he means then (b) has just been asserted and we are still waiting for the *argument* for it, for the argument that links (a) and (b) (or for some other supporting argument).

The McDougall–Vehmas view then is unjustified. Even if we grant that parents should have the Virtue of Parental Acceptance, this does not entail that *prospective*

---

[16] Simo Vehmas, 'Response to "Abortion and Assent" by Rosamund Rhodes and "Abortion, Disability, Assent, and Consent" by Matti Hayry', *Cambridge Quarterly of Healthcare Ethics*, 10 (2001), 433–40: 439.

[17] Vehmas, 'Response to "Abortion and Assent" by Rosamund Rhodes and "Abortion, Disability, Assent, and Consent" by Matti Hayry'.

parents should have this virtue. Furthermore, it is possible for prospective parents to have an attitude akin to the Virtue of Parental Acceptance (committing themselves to loving, within very broad parameters, whoever comes along) without eschewing selective reproduction, because (as we saw in 2.2) striving to get the child you want does not entail being disposed to reject the child if it does not fit with your preferences.

The Symmetry Principle

Vehmas's article suggests another general principle: the Symmetry Principle, which says that:

> *If it would be wrong to withdraw parental love from an existing child for having F, it would be wrong to deselect a possible future child on the grounds that it will have F.*

So, according to this principle, if it would be wrong to reject one's child for having red hair, it would be wrong to deselect a possible future child on the grounds that, if created, it would have red hair. Or (to use Vehmas's example) if it is wrong for parents to abandon a child who becomes disabled in a road accident then it must be wrong to deselect a possible future child on the grounds that it would be similarly disabled. The Symmetry Principle is narrower in scope, and rather less extreme, than the view that prospective parents have *all* of the duties of actual parents. Rather, the principle posits a specific relationship between the wrongness of abandoning a child on certain grounds and the wrongness of deselecting possible future children on those same grounds. The Symmetry Principle however, if accepted, would have very restrictive implications, because if there are very rarely circumstances in which parents are justified in abandoning their children then (according to the Symmetry Principle) there must be similarly few circumstances in which prospective parents are justified in deselecting a possible future child.

So why am I sceptical about the Symmetry Principle? The fundamental reason is just that it seems to be unmotivated, i.e. there is no reason to believe it, given some of the distinctions that I have been drawing in this chapter. In particular, the fact that parents can commit to love a (future) child regardless of whether it has F but at the same time attempt to select against F seems pretty decisive in severing the link between the obligation of actual parents not to abandon and the (putative) obligation of prospective parents not to deselect.

This is bolstered by a number of supplementary arguments. One is that abandonment of existing children will normally be painful for those children. Indeed, to be abandoned by one's parents on trivial grounds (such as appearance) would in many cases be devastating; whereas there is no pain of this sort when embryo selection is used to accommodate prospective parents' cosmetic preferences. Also relevant are the moral bonds and obligations generated by social parenting. This is complicated territory but I would suggest that the existence of an ongoing personal and emotional relationship between a parent and a child creates additional moral obligations over and above any that exist in virtue of the bare fact of biological parenthood. Thus, a parent who raises and lives with a child will (other things being equal) have more and/or stronger moral obligations to the child than a *merely* biological parent who was (for whatever reason) separated from her child at birth. If this is right then we have another reason to view actual 'social' parents and prospective biological parents differently since only the former have ongoing relationships of a kind that could generate these additional obligations.

Finally, perhaps a useful analogy here is spousal love of the sort that may exist within successful monogamous (and other) relationships. It seems that some of the differences between the moral position of actual and merely prospective spouses mirror (some of) the differences between the moral position of actual and merely prospective parents. Consider, for example, the position of Olivia, a woman who is seeking a husband on the internet using an online agency. Generally speaking, we would think that at this stage of a relationship (or 'pre-relationship' perhaps) it is okay for Olivia to select and deselect prospective husbands on relatively frivolous grounds, especially if there are lots of candidates to choose from and Olivia does not have time to meet them all. Thus, she might decide to 'screen out' men who are shorter than her, earn less than her, support Leeds United Football Club, enjoy the music of Leonard Cohen, and prefer white wine to red. Now we may or may not think that these are good aesthetic or lifestyle choices, and we may or may not think that these are good criteria for husband selection, but most of us would (I imagine) think that her screening-out process is *at least morally permissible*, especially in a context where detailed engagement with all the candidate husbands is impracticable. That is not to say that 'anything goes' at this stage and there may be concerns about deselection criteria that were based on morally reprehensible attitudes (racism perhaps). Nonetheless, it seems sensible to take quite a permissive line about what Olivia may select at the pre-relationship stage. Things, however, would be quite different, say, three years into a marriage, or even several months (or perhaps even weeks) into a 'dating' relationship. For at these later stages we will probably think that 'dumping' the man on the grounds listed above would be wrong, or at least morally problematic in ways that deselecting him 'pre-relationship' would not be. Thus, deselection (pre-relationship) on the basis of a man's wine preferences would be okay but 'dumping' (ending an ongoing relationship) on the same grounds would not. Why? One reason is that, as I suggested in the earlier discussion of social parenting, the existence of an ongoing personal relationship often generates additional moral obligations, obligations that one does not have to strangers, or to merely prospective children. A second is that 'dumping' is more likely to be painful than non-selection (although that is not to say that the latter is necessarily painless). So my suggestion (and this is, I admit, more of an explication of a view then an argument for it) is that the difference between actual and prospective parents resembles the difference between Olivia's position 'pre-relationship' and her position within a marriage. In other words, it would be *much* worse for parents to *abandon* a child with whom they have an ongoing relationship on trivial grounds (appearance, eating habits, or whatever) than it would be for them to deselect an embryo on similar grounds. For even if (as some might argue) they have a relationship of sorts with the embryo, it is very different from the sort of developed relationship that they would usually have with an existent child.

Children as Gifts

Finally in this section, I consider the idea that children are gifts. To provide a flavour of the claims that interest me, here are some quotations from four different English newspapers. The pieces from which they are drawn concern (respectively) sex selection, lesbian parenting, and (two on) using ART (assisted reproductive technology) to help older women to have children.

[E]very baby is a gift to be cherished unconditionally, regardless of its sex.[18]

A LESBIAN is hoping to make history by giving birth to her girlfriend's test tube baby . . . Martin Foley, of pro-life charity Life, said: 'Children are a gift—they should not be used as guinea pigs.'[19]

Having a baby is a gift—not a right that medical science can achieve at a cost.[20]

[A] 67-year-old [woman] is now seven months pregnant with twin girls. She looks in her 90s and said she was too busy in her earlier life to give birth. 'I have a choice and a right to have children,' says this misguided old woman. Oh no, she does not. Children are a gift, not a right. And no child will be happy to have a crone as a mother.[21]

As these quotations illustrate, 'child-as-a-gift' claims often go hand-in-hand with ones about unconditional parental love. And they are often used to rebut the (supposedly wrong headed) view that people have a right to a child (i.e. to any child at all, as in the lesbian and older mother cases) or that they have a right to a particular sort of child (as in the sex selection case). The question that I am going to address here is this: can the claim that children are gifts underpin a distinct ethical argument against selective reproduction and, if so, is that argument sound? I shall break this down into two questions. What does it mean to say that a child is a gift? And, if children were gifts, what ethical prescriptions (if any) would flow from this? What would their

---

[18] Anjana Abuja, 'The Ethics of Sex Selection Should Not Be Down to the Public', *The Times*, 12 Nov. 2003, 22.

[19] Jacqui Thornton, 'Lesbian Bid to Have Girlfriend's IVF Baby', *The Sun*, 19 Apr. 2005, 22.

[20] Karol Sikora, 'How Old is Too Old to Be a Mother?' *The Observer*, 7 May 2006, 12.

[21] Maureen Messant, 'Mum's Too Old', *Birmingham Evening Mail*, 7 Jan. 2005, 24.

being gifts entail for issues such as sex selection, lesbian parenting, or postmenopausal motherhood?

One important preliminary question is whether talk of children being gifts is inherently religious. For often when people say that children are gifts, what they mean is that they are gifts *from God*. For our purposes, it is necessary to sideline religious construals since, if the proposed argument depends on the existence of a particular God, it must necessarily be weak. This is not because I am assuming that God does not exist; (s)he may or may not. Rather, the point is that people's views about the existence and nature of God are many and varied and this is a very contested (and perhaps essentially contestable) issue. Hence, particular beliefs about God will fail to provide a generally acceptable starting point for, or premiss in, an ethical argument. Similarly, since demonstrating the existence of God through rational argument and/or scientific evidence is notoriously difficult, any ethical argument which relies upon the existence of a particular God will inevitably be weak and speculative, containing what is essentially an article of faith. In this particular respect, religious ethical arguments are rather like those that rely on speculation about social consequences. Both types of argument are weak insofar as they contain an un(der)-evidenced premiss (although social consequence arguments are in a slightly better position because their 'known unknowns' are generally more straightforward and more epistemically accessible than those relied upon by religion). Religion is then by no means the only body of belief to suffer from this problem and elsewhere Eve Garrard and I have argued that some secular ethical theories may well have similar difficulties.[22]

For moral arguments that rely on an ethical theory (secular or religious) can be no more convincing than the underlying argument for the theory itself and this can cause problems for theory-driven arguments within bioethics given that (like religion) moral theory is a hotly contested area. For our purposes then, we must leave to one side religious construals of gift talk and confine ourselves to secular understandings. None of this of course implies that people with strongly held religious beliefs cannot come up with convincing ethical arguments. Clearly they can, provided that they confine themselves to valid inferences and well-evidenced premisses. Finally on the subject of religion, it is worth noting in passing that, for people who believe that God created the whole universe, there is surely a sense in which *all* things are gifts from God. Therefore, even if we were to accept the theists' view that children are gifts from God, there would remain a question about why this makes having children special, or imposes special ethical obligations on parents.

So what secular sense, if any, can be made of the claim that children are gifts? The first, and perhaps rather obvious, point to make is that (having sidelined the religious

[22] Eve Garrard and Stephen Wilkinson, 'Does Bioethics Need Moral Theory', in Matti Hayry and Tuija Takala (eds.), *Scratching the Surface of Bioethics* (Amsterdam: Rodopi, 2005), 35–45.

view) children are not literally gifts. This perhaps requires qualification since a child could be given to one set of (social) parents by another as a gift. But at least in the cases that we are looking at, cases in which prospective parents use ART to create their own biological children, there does not seem to be any giving involved. Someone could pay for IVF or PGD as a gift but even this would not be the giving of a child, any more than charging for ART services is the selling of a child. So the secular interpretation of the gift claim must be that children are *like* gifts in certain respects and/or should be *treated or regarded* as gifts in some ways.

There are two main construals of this. According to the first, to say that children are gifts means simply that prospective parents do not have a right to them, the idea being that gifts are not deserved or entitlements. (Actually, it is not obvious to me that gifts cannot be deserved, or even that there cannot be a right to a gift, but I will not pursue that worry any further here.) So what does it mean to say that prospective parents do not have a right to reproduce? One possible meaning is that parents are not entitled to publicly funded ART services, or that there are limits to any such entitlement. Another is that society, perhaps through law and regulation, is morally permitted to interfere with people's attempts to reproduce, or to reproduce selectively. Now both of these claims may well be true, but neither of them adds a great deal to the existing set of arguments against selective reproduction. The fundamental reason for this is that to invoke such rights-claims is *question-begging*, assuming and importing an *answer* to the question we are considering, rather than giving us an independent *reason to believe* in that answer. Let us say, for example, that some prospective parents want to use selective reproduction to create a fair-haired child. Now there may or may not be sound moral arguments against this, but to assert that they *have no right* to choose a blonde child is not one of them. Why? Because this simply assumes and asserts the view that they ought not to do this, or the view that we are entitled to stop them from doing it (depending on the precise nature of the rights-claim). So invoking rights in this way is not much better than simply saying that it is 'just wrong' and expecting that to be taken as a *reason* not to do it. Furthermore, almost everyone in the selective reproduction debate would agree that there is no *unfettered* right to reproduce: that there are *some* circumstances in which selection would be wrong and/or in which society should intervene. What they disagree about is a range of more specific questions about rights and duties—under which particular circumstances are reproduction and/or selection permissible? So, for this reason too, merely denying that there is an absolute right is unhelpful.

On the second understanding, the view that children are gifts is a conjunction of two other claims. First, there is the idea that parents should respond to their children (especially perhaps their new ones) with an attitude of good fortune and gratitude, regardless of the child's particular characteristics. They should, in short, be glad to have their child, no matter what it is like. Second, there is the view that parents ought not to predetermine their children's characteristics. Both of these claims are meant to follow from the child-gift analogy. In the case of the first, the idea is that it would be wrong to receive a gift and then to bemoan the fact that it lacks certain specific features. Rather, the virtuous attitude towards gifts is one of acceptance and gratitude. In the case of the second, the feature of gifts that is appealed to is the fact that the recipient does not choose the precise nature of the gift.

Both of these claims are problematic. The first difficulty is that each relies on an overly narrow and selective understanding of the nature of gifts. Thus, we might ask whether recipients are obliged always to respond to gifts with attitudes of good fortune and gratitude, and I think we will find that the plausible answer is 'no'. For instance, I might receive a hideous gift, or one with excessively high running costs (a 'white elephant'). Whether appreciation is appropriate in such cases will depend on many different contextual features but it seems certain that there will be *some* cases where it is permissible not to react with feelings of gratitude. And if this is true of gifts then (if we accept the child-gift analogy) the same can be said of children. Hence, the child-gift analogy fails to support the claim that parents are required to feel appreciative of their children no matter what they are like. Similar considerations apply to the claim that recipients do not choose the precise nature of their gifts. This is simply false. There are many cases in which people choose what they would like for a gift. In response to this, it might be said that people *ought not* to choose their gifts, but to condemn all those people who construct their own birthday or wedding lists is surely going too far. Perhaps, I concede, having people not select their own gifts is often advantageous in various ways (for example, it enables the giver to express herself and provides the recipient with a nice surprise) but surely it would be a step too far to say that allowing people to choose their own gifts was morally wrong. And so, *if* we were to accept the child-gift analogy, then we would surely be compelled to say: if it is okay for people to choose the features of their gifts (which it is) then it is similarly okay for them to choose the characteristics of their children.

Another difficulty is that even if the above-mentioned claims (that parents should be grateful and that they ought not to predetermine their children's characteristics) did follow from the child-gift analogy they still would not add much to the argumentative state of play. Taking the second one first, the claim that parents ought not to predetermine their children's characteristics seems to beg the question, to assume the very thing that is at issue, and is tantamount to a bare assertion that selective reproduction is wrong. Hence, it fails to provide an independent *argument* against selective reproduction. Someone could of course try to avoid this question-beggingness problem by saying that there is an independent reason to believe that parents ought not to predetermine their children's characteristics, namely the fact that children are (or are like) gifts. But, as we have seen, this is a weak argument, for there are reasons to doubt both whether children are (like) gifts in any significant sense and whether, even if they are, it follows from this that their characteristics ought not to be chosen.

The reason why the first claim (about parental gratitude) does not add much to the argumentative state of play is that it is very similar to something already discussed, and taken account of, the Virtue of Parental Acceptance. Indeed, the claim about gratitude seems just to be a more extreme version of a principle of parental acceptance: the idea that parents must not only accept but must be pleased with their children.

I conclude then that the claim that children are gifts is incapable of underpinning an additional argument against selective reproduction. Some talk of children being gifts is misguided and based on a false idea of what gifts are; other talk of their being gifts is more justifiable but is reducible to other (generally clearer) ways of making essentially the same point, such as the Virtue of Parental Acceptance.

2.4 Diversity

I turn now to look at an argument suggested by Hilary Putnam in his 1998 Oxford Amnesty Lecture, 'Cloning People'; while the lecture is specifically about human reproductive cloning, his remarks are intended to apply to selective reproduction generally. According to Putnam, a distinctive and important feature of the parent–child relationship is the absence of choice. He writes:

In any other relationship, one can choose to some extent the traits of one's associates, but with one's children (and one's parents) one can only accept what God gives one to accept. And, paradoxically, that is one of the most valuable things about the love between parent and child: that, at its best, it involves the capacity to love what is very different from one's self.[23]

This, Putnam thinks, grounds an argument against selective reproduction. For the use of selective reproduction (particularly cloning) would, in all probability, mean that we would end up with children 'just like us' and therefore miss out on the experience of loving 'what is very different from one's self'.

Before moving on to look at some other things that Putnam says, it is worth flagging an initial difficulty with his position: the fact that the absence of choice and the presence of difference are only contingently connected (if connected at all). So if what is supposed to be bad about pre-conception choice is that it reduces difference and/or diversity, then this is something that will have to be established empirically: for while some prospective parents would use selective reproduction to create children

---

[23] Hilary Putnam, 'Cloning People', in Justine Burley (ed.), *The Genetic Revolution and Human Rights: The Oxford Amnesty Lectures* (Oxford: Oxford University Press, 1999), 1–13: 10.

'just like them', others may not. For instance, parents who regard themselves as aesthetically mediocre might seek to have an extremely beautiful child, parents with hereditary diseases might select children free from these conditions, or (more generally) parents who value diversity and difference (as Putnam does) may seek to use selective reproduction to generate variety within their households. Even cloning could be used to create internal family diversity, for a family could choose to clone someone quite different from any of its existing members. So Putnam's pro-difference and pro-diversity stance will only count against selective reproduction (including even cloning) if it can be established empirically that most people, if offered choice, would use it to create children 'just like them' (whatever that means).

Moving on, Putnam's main concern about cloning, and the like, is that there is a close link between people's personal moral and familial values and broader societal values. Thus, he argues, 'the moral image of the family' should:

reflect our tolerant and pluralistic values, not our narcissistic and xenophobic ones. And that means that we should welcome rather than deplore the fact that our children are not us and not designed by us, but radically Other.[24]

He continues:

the unpredictability and diversity of our progeny is an intrinsic value and . . . a moral image of the family that reflects it coheres with the moral images of society that underlay our democratic aspirations.[25]

So the argument is that if we are politically committed to tolerance and pluralism (as Putnam thinks we should be) then we should (a) positively welcome, rather than resist, the prospect of our children being radically different from us and (b) not seek to 'design' our children.

This argument, however, is unsatisfactory and has several flaws in addition to the one already mentioned (i.e. the fact that choice does not entail lack of difference or diversity).

First, Putnam talks about welcoming (looking forward to and preferring) difference and diversity, but this seems too strong in the context of familial relationships, since it suggests that parents should be disappointed if their child is a 'chip off the old block', or indeed if they have identical twins. Surely a more appropriate and virtuous attitude would be acceptance of difference and diversity coupled with a similar acceptance of sameness and uniformity. In other words, how much you love and value your child should not depend on its being *either* the same as *or* different from you (and/or other family members). Neither sameness nor difference per se are good grounds for rejection or acceptance.

---

[24] Putnam, 'Cloning People', 12.   [25] Putnam, 'Cloning People', 13.

Second, there are good reasons for thinking that diversity per se is not intrinsically valuable. One such reason is the existence of cases in which adding diversity makes things worse. Say, for example, that the evil inventor creates and inflicts upon the world a brand new range of pains, diseases, and disabilities. This world has more diversity in it than before the evil inventor's action but it seems to be a worse place. Furthermore (and crucially) not only is it a worse place but on the 'balance sheet', so to speak, diversity does not seem to figure as a positive at all. Thus, it would be weird (and false) to say—'well, all that extra pain and suffering is regrettable but, looking on the bright side, at least there is some extra diversity'. Similarly, we can imagine a situation where a society in which everyone is moderately happy is turned into one in which only 80 per cent are moderately happy, 10 per cent are miserable, and a further 10 per cent are in excruciating pain. Again, that the second society is more diverse does not seem to count in its favour at all. So diversity is not always or necessarily good.

One reply is to say that what matters is not diversity generally but rather *certain specific kinds of* diversity. For example, some people think that biodiversity is intrinsically (as well as instrumentally) valuable, while others believe that cultural and religious diversity are goods. But even in these fairly favourable cases diversity looks to be in some difficulty. For we can imagine cases in which increased biodiversity or increased cultural or religious diversity were thoroughly bad things. Imagine, for example, a case where a very happy community comprising six different cultural groups (whatever that amounts to) is joined by a seventh group of committed Nazis, and an eighth group of misanthropic fanatical terrorists. Imagine also that these new groups do not exactly get along with the first six (or each other) and that much strife and violence ensues. Again, in a scenario where extra diversity causes so much harm, it would be odd (and wrong) to say—'well, all that social strife is regrettable but, on the positive side, at least there is some extra diversity'. Or, in the case of biodiversity, if we could (without any adverse effects) eliminate malaria or HIV-AIDS then it would be strange to mourn the loss of biodiversity that this would entail.

In case anyone thinks that I am arguing *against* diversity, I should add that the very same objections can be levelled at the view that homogeneity is a good thing. For instance, there will be counterexamples where a highly valued cultural group or species is destroyed, or an individual dies, about which it would be strange to say—'well, it is sad, but at least it cuts down on the diversity'.

Another general difficulty with the idea that diversity should be valued is that, if we leave to one side 'instrumental' considerations (such as biodiversity's being useful to humans, or cultural diversity's making us more educated and tolerant) the claim that diversity per se is a good seems obscure and arbitrary. For it is hard to see what would lead one rationally to prefer more diversity to less; such a preference seems a mere whim. Similar considerations apply to complexity. As with diversity, it would be hard to justify (non-instrumentally) a preference for more rather than less. Why not prefer simplicity?[26]

Finally, it is important to raise, once more, the distinction between trying to shape your future child's characteristics before it exists and accepting what comes along, once the child arrives, regardless of whether or not it meets your preferences. I said earlier that it is the latter that matters and that this is consistent with attempts at selective reproduction. This applies equally to Putnam's claims. If what matters is tolerance and pluralism then this may well entail a commitment to accepting one's existing children (up to a point) regardless of their characteristics. But it does not follow from this that attempting, before they exist, to shape their characteristics is impermissible, because this is consistent with a virtuous attitude of parental acceptance, once they come along.

Putnam's diversity-based argument is therefore unconvincing.

2.5 The Child's Right to an Open Future

Finally in this chapter, I want to look at the idea that some kinds of selection are inconsistent with what, following Feinberg, has become known as the Child's Right to an Open Future. Like the other arguments considered in Chapter 2, this Open Future Argument starts by positing certain parental obligations (in this case, those relating to the Child's Right to an Open Future) and then attempts to deduce from these the wrongness of selective reproduction. The Open Future Argument therefore faces two challenges (again, like other arguments discussed). First, do the supposed parental obligations really exist? Is there a Child's Right to an Open Future? And second, if there were such a right, would it extend to merely possible future children, and would it impose obligations on merely prospective parents? Before tackling these questions though we must first ask what the Child's Right to an Open Future is supposed to be.

What is the Child's Right to an Open Future?

According to Feinberg, the 'child's right to an open future' is a convenient shorthand for a set of rights with a certain form, a 'vague formula' that 'simply describes the form of the particular rights in question ... not their specific content'.[27] These are 'rights-in-trust', which:

[26] Stephen Wilkinson, *Bodies for Sale: Ethics and Exploitation in the Human Body Trade* (London: Routledge, 2003), 214.

[27] Joel Feinberg, 'The Child's Right to an Open Future', in Joel Feinberg (ed.), *Freedom and Fulfilment: Philosophical Essays* (Princeton: Princeton University Press, 1980), 76–97: 77.

look like adult autonomy rights . . . except that the child cannot very well exercise his free choice until later when he is more fully formed and capable. When sophisticated autonomy rights are attributed to children who are clearly not yet capable of exercising them, their names refer to rights that are to be *saved* for the child until he is an adult, but which can be violated 'in advance', so to speak, before the child is even in a position to exercise them. The violating conduct guarantees *now* that when the child is an autonomous adult, certain key options will already be closed to him. His right while he is still a child is to have these future options kept open until he is a fully formed, self-determining adult capable of deciding among them.[28]

The idea of *rights-in-trust* is a useful way of conceptualizing certain moral issues. Take, for example, a case in which a mother decides that her young daughter would be better off not having children and so asks a doctor to sterilize her. Most of us, I imagine, would think that this sterilization ought not to happen (except perhaps in very exceptional circumstances). This is partly for welfare reasons; the child will be distressed and may miss out on the opportunity of having positive parenting experiences. But even leaving welfare aside (or even if we think the daughter really would be better off without children) moral objections to the sterilization remain. One of these is the Child's Right to an Open Future with respect to procreation. When she becomes an adult woman she will have a right to procreative autonomy. She does not presently have this right; rather, she has a right-in-trust. But if we sterilize her now then we will (as Feinberg puts it) be 'violating in advance' her right to procreative autonomy before she has a chance to exercise it.[29]

This is a relatively, though not entirely, uncontentious application of the Child's Right to an Open Future. More controversial are cases in which parents (and others) seek to determine children's beliefs and values.[30] For example, Feinberg discusses some American cases in which Amish communities have tried to keep their children out of State accredited schools. State schooling is thought to be incompatible with the goal of Amish education which is:

to prepare the young for a life of industry and piety by transmitting to them the unchanged farming and household methods of their ancestors and a thorough distrust of modern techniques and styles that can only make life more complicated, soften character, and corrupt with 'worldliness'.[31]

For several reasons, cases like this are more perplexing. One is that, if we take seriously the Amish claim that State education is polluting of young minds, it looks

---

[28] Feinberg, 'The Child's Right to an Open Future', 76–7.

[29] Dena Davies, *Genetic Dilemmas: Reproductive Technology, Parental Choices, and Children's Futures* (London: Routledge, 2001).

[30] J. Morgan, 'Religious Upbringing, Religious Diversity, and the Child's Right to an Open Future', *Studies in Philosophy and Education*, 24 (2005), 367–87.

[31] Feinberg, 'The Child's Right to an Open Future', 81.

as if future options will be foreclosed whatever educational choice is made. For if corrupted (by State schooling) as a child one cannot, as an adult, simply *choose* to become uncorrupted; it may be irreversible. A second is that the extent to which options are foreclosed by education is uncertain, since the effect of exposing children to different kinds of schooling is relatively unpredictable. Third, it should be noted that many widely accepted parenting and schooling practices are themselves designed to foreclose options. For example, they attempt to stop people from deciding to become criminals.[32] So one might ask whether 'mainstream' education is so fundamentally different from Amish education in this respect. For both are, as it were, biased in favour of generating adults who will make certain choices, the difference being over which choices are favoured.

For our present purposes, the (putative) Child's Right to an Open Future is of interest principally because of the correlative parental duties that it is supposed to underpin. In general terms, these will be duties not to close down certain future options for one's children although, as we have seen, spelling out exactly which options ought to be left open is tricky.

Is there a Right to an Open Future?

The idea of a Child's Right to an Open Future is problematic in a number of respects. First, it is hard to say what counts as a more or less open future because it is hard to come up with a non-arbitrary way of individuating and counting options. For instance, someone who sends her son to a disciplinarian music academy may say that his number of options is increased. She may claim that, although he is now only qualified to be a musician and ill-equipped to do anything else, he can play seventy-two instruments in 476 styles, whereas he has only lost out on a few other options: for example, being a health care professional, being an academic, or being a construction worker. Similarly, someone else who sends his daughter to a disciplinarian sports academy may say that her options are increased. For although she is now ill-equipped to be anything but a sportswoman, she can play seventy-two sports in 476 styles etc. So given the difficulty of non-arbitrarily individuating and counting options, it is going to be almost impossible to say which futures are the most open.

Second, *just how* open should children's futures be? Or to how much openness do children have a right? One answer is that parents should maximize openness, keep as many options open as possible, but this is implausible on at least two counts. First (like other maximizations) it is likely to impose excessive or impossible demands on parents. Second, it is likely to harm children because having one's options kept open

[32] Claudia Mills, 'The Child's Right to an Open Future?' *Journal of Social Philosophy*, 34 (2003), 499–509: 500.

is not cost-free and may compete with other goods; children who are made to do 'a bit of everything' may end up being good at nothing. Another (non-maximizing) approach would be to posit some *threshold* of openness, to say that children have a right to a certain number of options, at least in some areas of life. However, this is also going to be dogged by worries about arbitrariness and by the above-mentioned problems with counting and individuating options.

These considerations, combined with others discussed in more detail elsewhere, lead me to believe that talking about the Child's Right to an Open Future is not terribly helpful, both in general and a fortiori when discussing selective reproduction scenarios in which the putative rights bearers do not even exist yet.[33] That said, the concept of Child's Right to an Open Future is an attempt (albeit a flawed one) to articulate some more plausible underlying ethical principles, particularly those relating to autonomy.

Autonomy

One such principle (although this too faces difficulties) is that parents should not foreclose their children's options without good reason: that there should be a presumption in favour of keeping children's options open. Of course, this is *only* a presumption and there will be very many cases in which there *is* a good reason for shutting down options (for example, to prevent harm). Nonetheless a parent's *default* position should be that she will not shut down options unless there is a compelling reason to do so. Now while this is quite a plausible principle (after all, why close down an option without good reason?) it faces one of the same problems as the Child's Right to an Open Future: namely, is there a non-arbitrary way of counting and individuating options? For, as we saw in the earlier cases of the disciplinarian music and sports academies, there may be lots of cases in which it is not clear which policy would count as a closing, rather than an opening, of options. And this limits the usefulness of the principle when it comes to addressing substantive ethical issues.

Perhaps a better principle or view, then, is that there is a set of 'privileged' options that should be kept open in all but the most exceptional circumstances. What particular options (if any) fall into this category will be contested but one relevant candidate for our purposes is reproductive choice; others may include moral and religious beliefs and practices, choice of marital and/or sexual partners, or choice of career. What justifies a choice making it on to this list of 'privileged' options will also be a complex and contested issue and is not something I can get into here. It is however

[33] Stephen Wilkinson, ' "Designer Babies", Instrumentalisation and the Child's Right to an Open Future', in Nafsika Athanassoulis (ed.), *Philosophical Reflections on Medical Ethics* (London: Palgrave-Macmillan, 2005), 44–69.

worth noting, because it has particular relevance to our present concerns, that some writers have sought to justify privileging reproductive (procreative) autonomy on the grounds that reproduction generally has special significance for people.[34]

On this view, the value of procreative autonomy is grounded primarily in the importance that most people assign to reproduction, in the practical implications that a decision to reproduce (or not) has for individuals, and in the close relationship between reproduction and flourishing.

Finally, and most plausibly, there is the view that parents ought to do what they can to ensure that their children develop into autonomous adults who are capable of making independent rational choices, based on autonomously held beliefs and desires. Here, it is important to distinguish two different senses in which the word 'autonomy' is used. In one of its senses, autonomy is used to mean roughly 'being allowed to do what you want' and respecting autonomy is taken just to mean 'letting people do (or have) what they want'. In the second sense of 'autonomy', which is more useful and relevant for our purposes, autonomy is a psychological property of persons and 'respect for autonomy' is a term for the moral constraints that a person's having this psychological property places on the way in which we should treat her. For example, it is commonly claimed that to interfere with an autonomous person's body without her valid consent is, among other things, a failure to respect her autonomy, a failure to act in accordance with the moral constraints that her possessing autonomy places on other agents.

I will not attempt to say much here about what exactly the psychological property of autonomy is since this is an immensely complicated issue in its own right and philosophers have provided a wide range of complex and differing accounts.[35] One common understanding of autonomy (which I broadly support) is in terms of our capacity rationally and reflectively to endorse, reject, and rank (in terms of their relative importance to us) our desires (wants, preferences, etc.). For example, suppose that you have two conflicting desires: to stick to your diet (since you want to lose weight) and to eat the delicious chocolate cake in front of you. In such a case, you might exercise your autonomy by thinking carefully about the relative importance to you of (a) weight loss and (b) pleasurable cake eating, and by subsequently acting

---

[34] John Robertson, 'Procreative Liberty in the Age of Genomics', *American Journal of Law and Medicine*, 29 (2003), 439–87: 450.

[35] Gerald Dworkin, *The Theory and Practice of Autonomy* (Cambridge: Cambridge University Press, 1998); Harry Frankfurt, 'Freedom of the Will and the Concept of a Person', *Journal of Philosophy*, 102 (1971), 129–39; Lawrence Haworth, *Autonomy: An Essay in Philosophical Psychology and Ethics* (New Haven: Yale University Press, 1986); Richard Lindley, *Autonomy* (Basingstoke: Palgrave MacMillan, 1986); Catriona Mackenzie and Natalie Stoljar (eds.), *Relational Autonomy: Feminist Perspectives on Autonomy, Agency, & the Social Self* (New York: Oxford University Press, 2000).

on whichever desire you judge, all things considered, to be most important. So a central case of autonomous action would be a person acting on those desires which on reflection she has decided to endorse. In addition, in order for an action (or a belief, or any other mental state) to count as autonomous it must not result from 'controlling' or 'distorting' forces, such as brainwashing or other sorts of 'mind control'—although drawing the distinction between those influences that are 'controlling' or 'distorting' and those that are not is far from easy.

One interesting question is how the above mentioned views—(A) that there are some special options which must be kept open in all but the most exceptional circumstances and (B) that parents should develop their children's (future) autonomy—are related. Both are underpinned by the thought that personal autonomy is something of value and/or worthy of respect. In the case of (A), the idea is that there are certain options which are so important that to take them away from an autonomous person (or at least to do so without special justification) would be a *failure to respect* her autonomy. In the case of (B), the thought is simply that, given the value of autonomy, it should be *promoted* in one's children. (A) and (B), however, are different (though not necessarily incompatible) views and it is important to keep in mind that while (A) is about *respecting* autonomy (about the moral constraints that someone's autonomy places on our actions towards her), (B) is about *promoting* autonomy (about helping people to develop more autonomy). Thus, (A) and (B) relate to the issue of foreclosing options in rather different ways. In the case of (A) (the *respect for* autonomy view) the reason not to foreclose options is that this constitutes a failure to respect the person's (present or future) autonomy, not that it will *make the person less* autonomous. In the case of (B), however, (the *promotion of* autonomy view) the question of whether certain options ought or ought not to be foreclosed will boil down to one about consequences: in particular, to which methods of child-rearing (or which decisions in selective reproduction) are most likely to generate autonomous adults. Given this, the question of which options ought to be foreclosed will generally depend on quite practical considerations. Crucially, because the aim is *causing* children, as they develop, to acquire the psychological property of autonomy, it is not obvious that leaving options open is the best (the most autonomy promoting) course of action, since this may not be the most effective *means of fostering* autonomy. Perhaps it is, but whether it is an essentially empirical matter and it is entirely possible that a disciplinarian approach to parenting, one in which relatively few choices are given to children, is the best means of developing autonomy in the long term. Indeed, this point is not unique to children and it is at least in theory possible that an authoritarian state is the best way to promote and protect adults' autonomy, by keeping them safe from autonomy-corrosive influences, such as addictive drugs, gambling, and religious cults.

Two Worries about Future People's Autonomy

So corresponding to (A) and (B) (above), there are two distinct autonomy concerns raised by selective reproduction. I will call them the Failure to Respect Autonomy Worry and the Failure to Promote Autonomy Worry.

The Failure to Respect Autonomy Worry is about the following sort of scenario. Prospective parents choose to create Thomas. Thomas will, if all goes to plan, grow into an autonomous adult; he will have the psychological property of being autonomous. However, Thomas is also chosen on the grounds that he has some physical limitation. (It need not be physical but will be in the more straightforward cases.) Thomas's physical limitation, in adulthood, will prevent him from doing things that he autonomously chooses to do; his autonomous desires and plans will be frustrated. This will not make him less autonomous; he will retain the psychological property of being autonomous. Nonetheless, it could be argued that to subject him to this limitation (in the absence of a special justification) is a failure to respect his (likely, future) autonomy. This is probably what Dena Davies has in mind when, in a discussion of prospective parents who wish to 'select for deafness', she says:

A decision made before a child is born that confines her forever to a narrow group of people and a limited choice of careers so violates the child's right to an open future that no genetic counsellor should acquiesce to it. The very value of autonomy that grounds the ethics of genetic counselling should preclude assisting parents in such a decision.[36]

It is also worth noting that the sterilization case mentioned above would fall into this category (that is, it raises a Failure to Respect Autonomy Worry) because the objection to sterilizing a child is not that it *stops her from being* autonomous but that it is likely to lead, later on, to the frustration of her autonomously chosen desires and projects.

Turning now to the Failure to Promote Autonomy Worry, this is about the following sort of scenario. Prospective parents choose to create Katie. Unlike Thomas, Katie has been selected because she will develop only limited autonomy. For example, she might (to use a rather far-fetched example) be genetically predisposed to accept uncritically the prospective parents' view of morality and religion, or be disposed to be malleable and susceptible to brainwashing and indoctrination. The prospective parents choose Katie with a view to ensuring that their particular culture, language, and religion are preserved. They could in principle achieve similar results without resorting to selective reproduction: by, for example, deploying special parenting techniques and sending their child to a special school. However, by choosing Katie

---

[36] Dena Davies, *Genetic Dilemmas: Reproductive Technology Parental Choices and Children's Futures* (London: Routledge, 2001), 65.

they increase their chances of success and, if they leave things to chance, may instead end up with a strong-willed and independently minded young woman who questions and rejects their values—not a prospect that they would welcome.

Applying the Autonomy Worries to Selective Reproduction

Let us start with the Failure to Promote Autonomy Worry, as this is in some respects more straightforward. Since our concern is with pre-existential selective reproduction, the scenario we are looking at is one in which the prospective parents are choosing between different possible future children. Let us assume (so as to screen out epistemic complications) that they know, with a high degree of certainty, that they have a choice between Andrew who will be fully or highly autonomous, Bobby who will only be borderline autonomous/non-autonomous, and Cheryl who (perhaps owing to a genetically based mental impairment) will never become autonomous.

Anyone who values autonomy, who thinks that (*ceteris paribus*) the world would be a better place if people were more autonomous (or if more people were autonomous), must also hold that there are autonomy-based reasons for choosing Andrew. For if all other things are equal (if there is otherwise nothing to choose between Andrew, Bobby, and Cheryl) and if Andrew will have more of a valuable property than the other candidates for existence, then why would anyone (or at least anyone who values autonomy) not choose Andrew, not choose the possible future world which has more of a thing of value rather than less. All that this commits us to is that there is *some* reason to prefer (people like) Andrew in situations where *all* other things are equal. Hence, the possibility of countervailing reasons remains, as does the possibility of those reasons being strong enough either to justify not choosing (randomizing) or choosing another candidate. It does, however, seem that, insofar as we focus exclusively on the Failure to Promote Autonomy Worry, the best way to meet it is to ensure that (in cases where all other things are equal) the possible future person selected is the one who is most likely to be autonomous. The Failure to Promote Autonomy Worry then is not a consideration that tells against selective reproduction. Rather, it counts only against *certain kinds* of choice: notably against choosing to create future people whose autonomy will be limited (in cases where a more autonomous alternative exists). Indeed, very often, the Failure to Promote Autonomy Worry may be best dealt with by having *more* selective reproduction, not less: by selecting super-autonomous future persons instead of those who will be merely averagely autonomous.

This is an interesting conclusion because we started off with what is ostensibly a way of *objecting to* selective reproduction, the claim that it is incompatible with the Child's Right to an Open Future. But it turns out that part of the underlying rationale for this (putative) right, the commitment to the value of autonomy, gives us a reason *to favour* certain kinds of selection, those that will increase autonomy.

Turning now to the Failure to Respect Autonomy Worry, this can be best illustrated by a variation on the sterilization case discussed above. Prospective parents are deciding whether to select (possible, future) Child A or Child B. Child A would, if created, have normal reproductive capabilities. Child B would, if created, be incurably infertile. To keep our attention focused solely on the autonomy issues, we need to make a number of assumptions, many of which would in reality be improbable or unknowable. In particular, we need to assume that all other things are equal including (notably) welfare levels. Thus, we are assuming that A and B are equally likely to have happy lives, perhaps because being unable to bear children either would have no net effect on B's welfare (having children does, after all, have disadvantages as well as advantages, and closes options as well as opening them) or because B has some other compensating advantages over A. Our question then is, would selecting B constitute a failure to respect her (likely, future) autonomy?

Crucial to this question is the fact that the choice facing us is an *existential* one; it is about (among other things) whether B will come into existence. We are not choosing between a future world in which B exists and is incurably infertile and another in which she exists with normal reproductive capacities. If we were, then the choice would be fairly easy and there would be a clear autonomy-based case for preferring the latter. Our choice though is between a future world in which B is incurably infertile and one in which she does not exist at all, one in which A exists instead. So the respect for autonomy question boils down to this: are we morally required to respect the (presently merely possible) autonomy that B would have were she to be created and, if so, does this respect require us to prevent B from coming into existence, to choose A over B?

These questions raise many of the same issues that are dealt with during the discussion of wrongful life in Chapter 3 and so what I say here will be relatively brief.

The fundamental question is: could allowing someone to come into existence, selecting someone for existence, itself constitute a failure to respect the autonomy that that person would (if created) come to have? One apparent reason for thinking that the answer to this is 'yes' is the existence of hypothetical cases like the following. Imagine that some reproductive technologists set themselves up as 'slave breeders' and sell specially selected children (children who will later become autonomous) into slavery. Surely, it will be argued, this is a failure to respect the autonomy that these poor children will come to have. I think that this is correct (with some qualifications). However (as I shall go on to discuss in Chapter 3) there is a distinction to be drawn between the act of creating or selecting and the act of selling the child into slavery. These are separable, at least as far as moral evaluation is concerned. And while it is clear that the selling into slavery is a failure to respect (future) autonomy (or, at the very least, an act of collusion with others who will not respect autonomy), it is not so clear that the decision to create the child, considered in and of itself, is a failure to respect (future) autonomy. So I would suggest that the Slavery Case is somewhat misleading because the primary failure to respect autonomy is not the *existential* decision but rather something done to a young child after birth, after the question of its existence is settled.

The purer and less confusing case (and what we need to focus on) is the one where there are no wrongful acts after birth and where the wrong, if there is a wrong, is *causing someone to be created* who will (for example) have serious physical limitations: limitations that will, in adulthood, lead to the frustration of her autonomous desires and the failure of her autonomously formulated aims and projects. As I have said, this is complicated and many of the difficult underlying issues are dealt with during the discussion of 'wrongful life' in Chapter 3. However, even without taking on these fundamental issues, it is evident that the Failure to Respect Autonomy Worry is not capable of underpinning a general objection to selective reproduction (although, as with the Failure to Promote Autonomy Worry, it may constitute an objection to particular types of selection). The main reason for this is that there is an important sense in which we are *all*, to some extent, in the position of Child B. That is to say, everyone has physical limitations and everyone (or at least all but the most fortunate, or the least ambitious of us) will suffer the frustration of autonomous desires and the failure of autonomously formulated aims and projects. For instance: *Charlotte* autonomously wants to be a world-class athlete but this cannot happen because she has the wrong physique; *Harry* autonomously wants to be a ballet dancer but cannot because he too has the wrong physique; *Joseph* autonomously wants Grace to love him but she will not because she finds him physically repulsive; *Ella* (aged 95) autonomously wants to walk up the stairs in her house but cannot owing to the debilitating effects of ageing. These situations are ubiquitous. We are *all* susceptible to the frustration of autonomous plans owing to physical limitation.

So *if* the fact that a (possible, future) person would (if created) have her (likely, future) autonomously formed desires frustrated owing to physical limitation is a reason to deselect that person, to prevent her from coming into existence, *then* it looks like we have a reason to deselect *all* candidates for existence—to stop all births! What follows from this? One conclusion is that since the Respect for Autonomy Worry applies to all (possible, future) persons then it fails to provide us with a reason to think that selective reproduction is *especially* problematic. Rather, if there is a legitimate Respect for Autonomy Worry at all (and maybe there is not) then it is an entirely general issue when we create people and will apply as much to 'natural' as to selective reproduction. A second conclusion is that, precisely because it is so general, the Respect for Autonomy Worry is not one we can sensibly have about merely possible future people: in other words, the fact that the worry is so generalizable serves as a *reductio ad absurdum*. Perhaps a useful analogy here is boredom.

We might worry about using selective reproduction to create people who will later on experience boredom. But then when we realize that this worry is entirely general (i.e. everyone will experience boredom at some point in their lives) it evaporates because the only alternative to creating people who will later be bored is to create no one. A third conclusion is that Respect for Autonomy Worry, if it counts for anything, counts *in favour of* some sorts of selective reproduction. For if the problem is that creating people with physical limitations is a failure to respect autonomy then one rather good way of alleviating this would be to use selective reproduction to create people with relatively few limitations. So the Respect for Autonomy Worry counts in favour of selecting (possible, future) people with relatively few physical limitations and conversely against using selective reproduction to 'select in' people with comparatively high levels of physical limitation.

The Failure to Respect Autonomy Worry then is not capable of supporting general opposition to selective reproduction. For *either* the worry itself is incoherent or irrational *or*, if it is not, then it seems actually to support certain sorts of selection.

Conclusion

The overall aim of Section 2.5 was to assess the view that some kinds of selection are inconsistent with the Child's Right to an Open Future. I argued that the idea that children have this right, or at least that 'Child's Right to an Open Future' *talk*, is confusing and problematic. One reason for this is that such talk encourages us to think in terms of more or less open futures with more or fewer options, but individuating and quantifying options is problematic and furthermore does not fully capture the morally relevant features that we want to capture: in particular, those relating to autonomy, which is the fundamental value underlying thoughts about the Child's Right to an Open Future.

I have suggested that whatever sound content the idea of a Child's Right to an Open Future has, is reducible to two more fundamental worries about autonomy, which I termed the Failure to Promote Autonomy Worry and the Failure to Respect Autonomy Worry. As we have just seen though, neither of these is capable of justifying general opposition to selective reproduction. Indeed, both 'worries' seem ultimately to count *in favour of* some forms of selection. The former gives us a reason to select in favour of future people who will be more autonomous and/or more likely to be autonomous; the latter gives us a reason to select future people with fewer limitations so that their autonomous plans and desires will not be frustrated.

Overall then it seems that both the Child's Right to an Open Future and the underlying worries about the autonomy of (possible, future) people fail to provide a general objection to selective reproduction.

2.6 Summary and Conclusions

In Chapter 2, I have looked at several arguments against selective reproduction, each of which seeks to show that it is incompatible with attitudes, duties, or virtues that parents, and crucially *prospective* parents, ought to possess. I have argued that all of these arguments are inadequate. In some cases, this is because the argument relies on an implausible premiss, such as the Principle of Unconditional Parental Love, or the idea that diversity is intrinsically good. In other cases, the problem is that the parental virtue posited does not apply to *prospective* parents, even if it applies to actual ones. Indeed, as I have suggested from time to time during Chapter 2, a general problem with arguments from parental duty or virtue is that, in many important respects, the moral position of prospective parents is different from that of actual parents (i.e. parents of children that already exist). So even where it can be established that X is a parental duty or virtue, it does not follow from this that X is a duty or virtue that *prospective* parents have, or ought to have.

That said, there may be some links between the duties of actual and prospective parents and earlier I suggested the following schema for linking the obligations of actual and prospective parents, one which is supposed to follow from the fact that prospective parents ought to aim and plan to act in accordance with their future obligations:

> *If parents are under an obligation to do x for their (existing) children then, when deciding whether to have children, or which children to create, prospective parents ought to have the following attitude, or make the following commitment: 'when our child arrives, we will (do our best to) do x for it'.*

Essentially, this is just an application of a much more general thought: the idea that people ought to aim to act in accordance with their future obligations (once the future arrives, as it were)—or at least they ought *not to intend not to* act in accordance with them. This thought is especially plausible when the future obligations are ones that are being voluntarily assumed as will be the case with many prospective parents. Thus (in our cases at least) it can plausibly be argued that those who are unwilling to accept or to act in accordance with parental duties and virtues ought not to undertake the project of parenting (just as, for example, people who are unwilling to act in accordance with spousal duties and virtues, whatever they might be, ought not to get married).

Finally, as the discussion of Table 2.1 makes clear, we need to keep in mind a crucial distinction between, on the one hand, preferring one's future children to have F (some characteristic, such as blue eyes) and trying to cause them to have F and, on the other, being disposed to abandon children who do not have F. Once this distinction is recognized, it becomes clear that such ideas as the Virtue of Parental Acceptance do not entail that selective reproduction is wrong, because it is possible to practise selective reproduction and to prefer children with F, *while at the same time being disposed to accept and love whatever child comes along.* This point is perhaps the most important of the chapter since it raises a problem that afflicts *all* arguments from parental duty and virtue.

3

Selecting for Disability and the
Welfare of the Child

In the long argument over designer babies, did anyone imagine that parents might prefer a designer disability? While we were all worrying about the bionic offspring of the super-rich, two deaf lesbians in America were going round the sperm-banks, trying to make a deaf baby. It sounds like the start of a bad joke, except that they have now managed it twice.[1]

These women are taking the idea of creating so-called designer babies to a horrible new level.[2]

A lesbian couple were branded 'barbarians' this week after revealing they deliberately set out to have a DEAF baby.[3]

In April 2002, an American lesbian couple, Sharon Duchesneau and Candy McCullough, 'attracted fierce criticism by deliberately having a deaf baby', using a friend with five generations of deafness in his family as a sperm donor.[4] As it happens, Duchesneau and McCullough did not need to resort to the use of novel biotechnology to achieve their aim and were able to get what they wanted just by carefully selecting a sperm provider. However, using embryo selection techniques, such as PGD to deliver similar results, is a possibility that prospective parents may wish to explore. Indeed, it has been contemplated by the UK's Department of Health

---

[1] Jeanette Winterson, 'How Would We Feel If Blind Women Claimed the Right to a Blind Baby?' *The Guardian*, 9 Apr. 2002, <www.guardian.co.uk/Archive/Article/0,4273,4390038,00.html> (last accessed: Sunday, 12 Apr. 2009).

[2] James Langton, 'Lesbians: We Made Our Baby Deaf on Purpose', *London Evening Standard*, 8 Apr. 2002, 9.

[3] Tim Spanton, 'A Designer Baby Would End Our Heartache', *The Sun*, 11 Apr. 2002, 51.

[4] John Kilner, *The Ends Don't Justify the Genes*, Center for Bioethics and Human Dignity, <http://www.cbhd.org/resources/genetics/kilner_2002-07-19.htm> 19 July 2002 (last accessed: Sunday, 12 Apr. 2009); Sheila McClean, *Modern Dilemmas: Choosing Children* (Edinburgh: Capercaillie Books, 2006), 67–9; David Teather, 'Lesbian Couple Have Deaf Baby by Choice', *The Guardian*, 8 Apr. 2002, <www.guardian.co.uk/international/story/0,3604,680616,00.html> (last accessed: Sunday, 12 Apr.2009).

which, in a 2005 consultation paper, cites the Duchesneau and McCullough case and 'commonly expressed concerns' about 'the possibility that techniques used to *screen out* disabilities or impairments could also be used for *screening in*', asking:

Do you think that there should be a prohibition on deliberately screening *in*, or selecting *for* impairments and disabilities—as opposed to screening *out*, or selecting against?[5]

More recently, in its 2006 *Making Babies* report, the Human Genetics Commission discusses (albeit briefly) the issues raised by Duchesneau and McCullough and concludes that selecting for disability (through gamete donation) should not be permitted:

Under current UK guidelines, someone who is deaf as the result of an inherited condition which could be passed on to offspring should not be accepted as a [gamete] donor. **While the exclusion of people with genetic disorders such as inherited deafness as gamete donors is controversial, we feel that current restrictions are reasonable and should be maintained.**[6]

More recently still, in December 2006, the UK Government announced that its reforms of the Human Fertilisation and Embryology Act would include a statutory prohibition on 'deliberately screening in a disease or disorder'.[7] And (as I mentioned in Chapter 1) a version of this provision is indeed contained in the Human Fertilisation and Embryology Act 2008:

Persons or embryos that are known to have a gene, chromosome or mitochondrion abnormality involving a significant risk that a person with the abnormality will have or develop—

    (a) a serious physical or mental disability,
    (b) a serious illness, or
    (c) any other serious medical condition,

must not be preferred to those that are not known to have such an abnormality.[8]

Thus what has been dubbed 'designer disability' is both a real possibility and a form of selective reproduction that has provoked vigorous ethical and legal debate (not to mention legislative action).[9] Furthermore, as Julian Savulescu points out:

---

[5] Department of Health, *Review of the Human Fertilisation and Embryology Act 1990—A Public Consultation* (2005), 42. The Human Fertilisation and Embryology Authority (HFEA) and the Advisory Committee on Genetic Testing (ACGT) asked similar questions five years earlier in their consultation document. See HFEA and ACGT, *Consultation Document on Preimplantation Genetic Diagnosis* (1999), 11–12, <http://www.hfea.gov.uk/cps/rde/xbcr/hfea/PGD_document.pdf> (last accessed: Sunday, 6 Sept. 2009).

[6] Human Genetics Commission, *Making Babies: Reproductive Decisions and Genetic Technologies* (Jan. 2006), <www.hgc.gov.uk>, 63 (last accessed: Sunday, 12 Apr. 2009). Emphasis in the original.

[7] Department of Health, *Review of the Human Fertilisation and Embryology Act: Proposals for Revised Legislation (including Establishment of the Regulatory Authority for Tissue and Embryos)* (Dec. 2006).

[8] Human Fertilisation and Embryology Act 2008, Section 14(4).

[9] The expression 'designer disability' comes is taken from Julian Savulescu, 'Deaf Lesbians, "Designer Disability" and the Future of Medicine', *BMJ* 325 (10 May 2002), 771.

These choices are not unique to deafness. Dwarves may wish to have a dwarf child. People with intellectual disability may wish to have a child like them.[10]

One of the main aims of Chapter 3 then is to ask whether deliberately creating a child with a disability, when a non-disabled alternative is available, is morally acceptable. And if (as many people seem to think) it is not, then what exactly is wrong with this form of selection?

This chapter's other main aim is more general and theoretical: I want to ask how child welfare considerations should impact on the ethics and regulation of selective reproduction. In particular, under what circumstances are concerns about the welfare of (possible, future) children capable of underpinning arguments either against selective reproduction in general, or against selecting particular kinds of (possible, future) children? The rationale for including this theoretical discussion is that the main reason advanced for not permitting selecting for disability is the allegedly low welfare levels of any children thus selected. Furthermore, the 'welfare principle' has been part of UK law since the passing of the Human Fertilisation and Embryology Act 1990. This stated that:

(5) A woman shall not be provided with treatment services unless account has been taken of the welfare of any child who may be born as a result of the treatment (including the need of that child for a father), and of any other child who may be affected by the birth.[11]

In its 2008 reforms, the UK Government decided to retain this provision, except that 'the need of the child for a father' was replaced by 'the need for supportive parenting'.[12] Thus, there are important and policy-relevant questions to be asked about whether such legal requirements are justified and about their conceptual and theoretical underpinnings.

3.1 Disability and Quality of Life

Our negative attitudes to disability lead to false assumptions about the quality of life of a disabled child: in other words, that such a life is not worth living; that the person would be better off dead.[13]

The scenario that concerns me is the following.

---

[10] Savulescu, 'Deaf Lesbians.'   [11] Human Fertilisation and Embryology Act 1990, Section 13(5).
[12] Human Fertilisation and Embryology Act 2008 (c. 22), Section 14(2).
[13] Anon., 'Striving for Perfection Is Fine, But Not at Any Cost', *The Press and Journal* (Aberdeen), 7 June 2006, 14.

The Selecting for Disability Scenario

Prospective parents, with the help of doctors, create several embryos using IVF. Each embryo could be implanted and carried to term. The parents and doctors are however committed to implanting only one and to donating the others for research. Given this commitment, the question that faces them is which to implant. To help them decide, they perform various genetic tests. These show that two of the embryos would go on to develop with major physical disabilities—disabilities which, while compatible with a worthwhile life, usually cause significant pain and loss of opportunity. The other embryos are, as far as anyone can tell, completely healthy. The parents decide that one of the first two embryos, those that will develop with physical disabilities, should be implanted. The doctors act in accordance with their wishes.

Have either the doctors or the prospective parents acted wrongly in this case?

As ever, before addressing the substantive ethical question, it is necessary to make some preliminary and clarificatory points.

First, it should be noted that the Selecting for Disability Scenario raises fundamental general issues about the permissibility of IVF and the destruction of embryos. As I explained in Chapter 1, however, I am not going to tackle these matters in this book.

Second, as I also explained in Chapter 1, I hold that cases like the Selecting for Disability Scenario, those in which we are in effect choosing between candidates for life, are importantly different from those in which we are simply choosing whether or not to create a single possible person and so, in this discussion of selecting for disability, I shall say relatively little about the latter ('different number' choices).[14] This is partly for reasons of space and focus, and partly because the majority of actual cases in which disability may be selected will, like the scenario sketched above, be 'same number' choices.

Third, for the purposes of this chapter, I am going to focus exclusively on those arguments against selecting for disability that are child welfare focused.

Fourth (and this is the main concern of this section) the prospect of selecting for disability raises questions about the relationship between disability and expected quality of life and, while this is not an issue that I am going to engage with in great detail, there are some aspects of it that need to be addressed here. Perhaps the best way into this is to look at an initial sketch of (one version of) the Child Welfare Argument against selecting for disability, which goes as follows.

Premiss 1: *Selecting for disability (at least usually, or on average) involves selecting (possible, future) people who will have less good (less happy, lower quality) lives than the (possible, future) non-disabled alternatives. In other words, selecting for disability involves choosing between lower and higher quality of life, and choosing lower over higher.*

---

[14] Derek Parfit, *Reasons and Persons* (Oxford: Oxford University Press, 1984), 356.

Premiss 2: *When given a choice between lower and higher quality (possible, future) lives, we are morally obliged to choose higher over lower (all other things being equal).*

Therefore, *selecting for disability is wrong, because it is incompatible with the principle expressed in Premiss 2.*

This is a formally valid argument; the conclusion follows logically from the two premisses. Any dispute then must be about the truth or otherwise of the two premisses. The moral principle encapsulated in Premiss 2 will be the subject of later discussion. Premiss 1 is my present concern: is it true that selecting for disability involves selecting lower over higher quality lives?

In fact, there are a number of different questions here and it is important that these are clearly distinguished. Foremost among them are:

1. Does selecting a (possible, future) person with a disability *inevitably* mean selecting someone with a lower quality of life?
2. In general, or on average, do people with disabilities have worse lives than those without?
3. If people with disabilities do have worse lives than those without, is this the result of social discrimination, or is it in the *nature* of disability?

The answer to (1) is clearly 'no'. It is possible for people with disabilities to have high-quality lives and for those without disabilities to have awful lives; the happiest people with disabilities are undoubtedly happier than the most miserable non-disabled people. One important implication of this is that if (as the Child Welfare Argument suggests) what matters is that we choose higher over lower quality lives, then there may be some cases in which selecting for disability is not merely permissible but obligatory, cases in which the (possible, future) person with a disability is the available candidate for existence who would (if created) have the happiest life, all things considered. Imagine, for example, the following scenario.

Given limited resources, we are able to offer fertility treatment to only one of the following couples.

Joshua and Kayleigh *are congenitally deaf and their (possible, future) child would be similarly deaf. They are nonetheless caring, loving, and skilled parents. They are also wealthy and could provide a child with many material advantages.*

Luke and Megan *are non-disabled and would probably have a non-disabled baby. However, they have a long track record of child abuse and would abuse any subsequent children. Furthermore, owing to a lack of social service resources where Luke and Megan live, removing a child from them later in order to prevent abuse is impracticable. Hence, if created, their child would almost certainly suffer terrible cruelty.*

This is a very thinly sketched case but we can nonetheless envisage a scenario in which Joshua and Kayleigh's child would have a much higher quality of life than Luke and Megan's. And that is all we need to show that selecting a (possible, future) person with a disability does not *inevitably* mean selecting someone with a lower quality of life. In cases like this, believers in the Child Welfare Argument seem compelled to say that we should select the (possible, future) person *with* the disability. Thus, not surprisingly, the real target of the Child Welfare Argument is (or should be) selecting (possible, future) children with *low welfare*, not selecting against disability per se.

Quality of life issues are not confined to disability and most of the arguments discussed in this chapter apply to *any* case in which a child with a lower level of welfare is selected. Thus, choosing to have a child in adverse social circumstances, when more favourable alternatives are available, is not fundamentally different from selecting for disability. This application of the Child Welfare Argument to 'social' issues, as well as to disability and health ones, is quite common in public debates about (for example) women who have children at either a very young age (teenage pregnancy) or a relatively old age (postmenopausal pregnancy). In both of these cases, the standard objection to early/late motherhood is that having your child in the 'normal' maternity age-range would produce a child with a better chance of a high-quality life.[15] In other words, if you are going to have a child, you ought to have it at the optimal age (whatever that might be) for delivering high quality of life. However, one additional complication in these cases is that probably a lot of early/late motherhood choices are not 'same number'. For often, and perhaps inevitably in the case of 'late' motherhood, the choice is not between different children, born at different times, with different welfare levels—but between this ('extra') child and no ('extra') child.

Because disability does not inevitably or necessarily lead to lower welfare, the Child Welfare Argument against selecting for disability must rely on auxiliary claims about the relationship between disability and welfare, which takes us to Question (2). Do people with disabilities, in general or on average, have worse lives than those without?

This question often leads to considerable conflict and confusion. One reason for this is that there is a sense in which it is an empirical matter but another sense in which it is not. It is an empirical matter (in one way) because, in order to find out

[15] In 2006, for example, reports suggested that 'women who delay having children until later in life risk damaging the fertility of their daughters'. Ian Sample, 'Older Mothers Risk Fertility of Daughters', *The Guardian*, 25 Oct. 2006, <http://www.guardian.co.uk/medicine/story/0,,1930727,00.html> (last accessed: Sunday, 12 Apr. 2009). See also Mark Henderson, 'Older Mothers "Put Their Daughters at Risk of infertility"', *The Times*, 25 Oct. 2006, <http://www.timesonline.co.uk/article/0,,11069-2419970,00.html> (last accessed: Sunday, 12 Apr. 2009).

whether disabled people's lives are happier or unhappier than other lives we could (in principle) conduct a huge quality of life study, count up the results, and then come to a view about whether people with disabilities are generally unhappier than others. Indeed, more nuanced versions of the survey could be carried out, distinguishing between different kinds of disability, and between other groups. Thus, we might (for instance) discover that actuaries with hearing impairments are happier (on average) than window cleaners without disabilities, or that that non-disabled taxi drivers are less happy (on average) than wheelchair users. Taking this survey approach, there is essentially no difference between comparing disabled and non-disabled people's welfare levels and comparing quality of life in Epsom with that in Hull. In both cases (and this is, of course, only an illustrative simplification) we simply collect survey data and use social science techniques to analyse it.

There is, however, a difference between comparing people with and without disability, and comparing the residents of Epsom with those of Hull. Let us say, for the sake of argument, that people in Epsom have lower quality lives than the people of Hull. If this is so, then the relationship between being less happy and living in Epsom is entirely contingent. There is, as it were, nothing in the *concept* of Epsom that connects it a priori with lower welfare. Rather, that is just the way the world happens to be and, for all we know, it could change over time and Epsom might overtake Hull in the quality of life league table. Things are different though when we compare disability with non-disability. This is because there is an a priori connection between disability and welfare or (as Glover puts it) flourishing:

Disability requires failure or limitation of functioning. But a limitation of functioning creates disability only if (on its own or *via* social discrimination) it impairs capacities for human flourishing. It would not be a disability if there were a failure of a system whose only function was to keep toenails growing. With arrested toenail growth, we flourish no less.[16]

As Glover rightly points out, characteristics only get to *count* as disabilities, as opposed to mere differences, if they impair the capacity to flourish. We might similarly say that features of a person only get to count as disabilities if they impair people's capacities to have happy or 'high-quality' lives. The relationship between people's actual levels of welfare and disability is indirect because (as Glover suggests) the a priori connection is not between being disabled and *not flourishing* but rather between being disabled and having a reduced *capacity to flourish*. Thus, actual people with disabilities can (and often do) flourish regardless of their disabilities and indeed whole communities of people with disabilities could flourish in this way, and may even flourish more than their non-disabled counterparts. In particular, disability's effects on a person's quality

---

[16] Jonathan Glover, *Choosing Children: Genes, Disability, and Design* (Oxford: Clarendon Press, 2006), 9.

of life depend both on her environment and her personal preferences. Glover offers the example of colour blindness:

suppose someone colour-blind does not want to become a pilot or do any of the other things that depend on normal colour vision. The incapacity does not reduce the person's flourishing. The choice is between saying that for him or her it is a harmless disability or saying it is not a disability at all. There is a verbal choice here, and in this case it does not greatly matter which way we go.[17]

So not wanting to do the thing that a disability makes you unable to do is one way in which its potential to reduce quality of life can remain unrealized; indeed, as Glover notes, we sometimes may not even want to count such inabilities as disabilities. Another, as suggested earlier, is environment, both social and physical (and, within the physical, both built and natural). So (for example) mobility disabilities can be made much less disabling through the provision of wheelchairs, ramps, and suitably designed vehicles, while deafness can be made much less disabling if most people use sign language and through technologies that convert auditory into visual information. As Asch puts it:

During the last twenty-five years . . . people with disabilities have argued that only some of their limitations and problems could be attributed to their physiology; others stemmed from rejecting attitudes, discriminatory practices, and physical and institutional obstacles that could be remedied. Using a sturdy wheelchair in an area without curbs, steps, and narrow doors, a girl could attend her neighborhood school. When she grew older, she could go to work if she could board the public bus; and she could live where and with whom she wished if she could obtain assistance with toileting, dressing, and cooking from people she hired and trained.[18]

This leads us on to Question (3): is the disadvantage associated with disability the result of social discrimination or is it something to do with the nature of disability? By now, it should be clear that the answer is, as Richard Hull puts it, 'generally a bit of both'.[19] As ever, Glover makes the point well:

There has been a debate over whether we should replace the 'medical' or 'functional' model of disability with the 'social-construction' model. It is time to give up this debate, as it is now unfruitful for the same reason that makes the 'nature–nurture' debate unfruitful. To many disabilities, there is a contribution from a variety of sources, including functional limitation *and* social context.[20]

---

[17] Jonathan Glover, *Choosing Children: Genes, Disability, and Design* (Oxford: Clarendon Press, 2006), 9.

[18] Adrienne Asch, 'Distracted by Disability', *Cambridge Quarterly of Health Care Ethics*, 7, (1998), 77–87: 78. See also Richard Hull, 'Defining Disability—A Philosophical Approach', *Res Publica*, 4 (1998), 199–210.

[19] Richard Hull, 'Cheap Listening? Reflections on the Concept of Wrongful Disability', *Bioethics*, 20 (2006), 55–63: 56.

[20] Glover, *Choosing Children*, 7–8.

As we have seen, in order to count as a disability (rather than a mere difference) a characteristic must impair people's capacities to flourish and hence the nature of disability does indeed contribute to disadvantage (although, as we have also seen, this potential can remain unrealized). At the same time, it is obvious that social discrimination can (and often does) worsen the lives of people with disabilities either actively (for example, when they are mocked or assaulted) or passively (for example, when needed and deserved facilities are not provided). Consider, for example, this description of social disadvantage by Ed Smith:

It's no fun being quadriplegic. We have to battle attitudes that believe us to be incapable of speaking for ourselves, unworthy of any accommodation of our physical needs, and something less than 'normal'. We wait in the snow or the rain outside hotel and restaurant doors that don't have automatic openers, hoping some kindly soul will see us and come running before we perish. We endure while waitresses and store clerks talk over our heads to our spouses or caregivers about what kind of pie or size shirt we want. We get stuck in cubby-holes in the back of theatres and movie houses. I have almost been physically attacked while asking an able-bodied motorist to remove his vehicle from a handicap parking space so we could get close to an entrance.[21]

The view of the relationship between disability and disadvantage that I am suggesting will undoubtedly be disputed by people on several different fronts. Some, for instance, would say that disability *is* (what I termed) mere difference and that there is no fundamental difference between the disadvantage suffered by (for example) black people in a racist society and that suffered by people with disabilities in a disablist society. I find this view implausible and hold that there is a relevant distinction between characteristics that are disadvantageous in and of themselves (even in the absence of social discrimination, but often *exacerbated* by social discrimination) and those which are neutral in themselves, but serve as a basis for harmful social discrimination. As Glover puts it:

We do not say someone's ethnicity is a disability, precisely because all its disadvantages are entirely socially imposed. In theory, social input is not in the same way essential for something to be a disability. Robinson Crusoe, alone on his island and unable to walk properly after a stroke, would still be disabled.[22]

Whereas having a particular skin colour, alone on a desert island, would not be disadvantageous (leaving aside varying propensities to sunburn and the like) because there is no possibility of social discrimination.

---

[21] Ed Smith, 'Death, Not Disability, is the End of the World', *CBC News Online*, 3 Feb. 2005, <http://www.cbc.ca/news/viewpoint/vp_disabilitymatters/smith_20050203.html>, (last accessed: Sunday, 12 Apr. 2009).

[22] Glover, *Choosing Children*, 9.

Of course, saying whether a condition is intrinsically disadvantageous, detrimental even in the absence of social discrimination, is not always easy and there are countless tricky borderline cases. What about, for instance, facial scarring? Is this a disability even when functionality (eating, talking, etc.) is unimpaired? Perhaps not, if *the entire* disadvantage is due to people's negative attitudes and reactions. And what about extreme shortness? In our developed technological world, most of the disadvantages related to shortness seem not to be intrinsic, but rather are caused either directly by people's hostility, or by the unsuitability of the built environment. So perhaps extreme shortness is not a disability either but rather (like race, sex, and sexuality) a possible ground of discrimination. Shortness is, however, more complicated than disfigurement because we can imagine desert island scenarios where shortness *is* detrimental; it may, for example, stop people from being able to reach tall branches, or from fending off attacks by animals. On the other hand, we can equally imagine desert island situations in which shortness is useful: for example, a person might have more shelter available because of her ability to get under small bushes. So this reveals another complication which is, when deciding whether something is disadvantageous, we need to specify a background environment. And, as we have seen, a characteristic may be advantageous in one environment but disadvantageous in another. Hence, the question of whether a given characteristic is 'intrinsically' disadvantageous and thus a possible disability may well be environment-relative, in which case we should not say *categorically* that F is a disability but rather that F is a disability *in environments a, b, and c*, etc.

These complications arise in the case of deafness, the example with which I opened the chapter and prospective parents who actively seek a deaf child, have argued that deafness is not intrinsically disadvantageous. As BBC News puts it, they see 'deafness as a cultural identity, not as a disability'.[23] Thinking along these lines, Candy McCullough reportedly said:

Some people look at it like 'Oh my gosh, you shouldn't have a child who has a disability!' but, you know, black people have harder lives. Why shouldn't parents be able to go ahead and pick a black donor if that's what they want? They should have that option. They can feel related to that culture, bonded with that culture.[24]

Similarly, Neil Levy quotes Roslyn Rosen's remarks:

I'm happy with who I am [. . .] and don't want to be 'fixed'. Would an Italian-American rather be a WASP? In our society, everyone agrees that whites have an easier time

---

[23] BBC News, *Couple 'Choose' to Have Deaf Baby*, 8 Apr. 2002, <http://news.bbc.co.uk/1/hi/health/1916462.stm> (last accessed: Sunday, 12 Apr. 2009).
[24] Teather, 'Lesbian Couple Have Deaf Baby', See also Merle Spiggs, 'Lesbian Couple Create a Child Who Is Deaf Like Them', *Journal of Medical Ethics*, 28 (2002), 283.

than blacks. But do you think a black person would undergo operations to become white?[25]

So there is a view that being deaf is, in relevant respects, like being black: not intrinsically disadvantageous and hence not a disability.

There is no clear-cut answer to the question of whether deafness is 'intrinsically' disadvantageous. There are certainly many imaginable desert island scenarios in which deafness would be disadvantageous (for example, not being able to hear oncoming predators could be dangerous) and there appear also to be many disadvantages in our society, even leaving aside social discrimination. For example, people with severe hearing impairment are unable (at least unaided) to appreciate music, or the auditory aspects of drama and conversation. However, as Lillehammer notes:

Human deafness is an unusual disability in several respects. First, it is a moderate disability compatible with living a very good life of its kind. Second, the existence of special forms of communication like sign language and lip reading enables deaf people to participate in a valuable form of social life without removing their particular disability. These facts have enabled a strong deaf culture to develop in many countries.[26]

Similarly, Draper and Chadwick raise the case of Philip and Linda, a deaf couple, who:

want the [embryo] with congenital deafness to be implanted first . . . [and] justify their decision by arguing that their quality of life is better than that of the hearing. As far as they are concerned, giving preference to the affected embryo is giving preference to the one which will have the best quality of life. They are very concerned that any hearing child they have will be an 'outsider'—part neither of the deaf nor of the hearing community at least for the first five or so years of his/her life.[27]

So what conclusions should we draw about deafness? Well, obviously it involves functional limitation, but is this a limitation that will impair the person's capacity to flourish? The answer to this has to be a (somewhat unsatisfying) 'it depends'. There are certainly possible scenarios in which the advantages of being deaf, such as the sociocultural ones cited by Lillehammer, Draper and Chadwick, are so great that they outweigh any disadvantages caused by the functional limitation (and associated social discrimination). Similarly, we can imagine natural environments in which deafness is advantageous: for example, ones containing agonizing loud noises. Furthermore,

[25] Neil Levy, 'Reconsidering Cochlear Implants: The Lessons of Martha's Vineyard', *Bioethics*, 16 (2002), 134–53: 137.

[26] Hallvard Lillehammer, 'Benefit, Disability, and the Non-Identity Problem', in Nafsika Athanassoulis (ed.), *Philosophical Reflections on Medical Ethics* (London: Palgrave-Macmillan, 2005), 43.

[27] Heather Draper and Ruth Chadwick, 'Beware! Preimplantation Genetic Diagnosis May Solve Some Old Problems But It Also Raises New Ones', *Journal of Medical Ethics*, 25 (1999), 114–120, 116.

the effects of functional limitation can be limited by practical measures, such as supplementing auditory information with visual. But, on the other hand, there are also possible situations in which the sociocultural advantages of being deaf are negligible and in which being unable to hear impacts negatively on quality of life. Moreover, as Julian Savulescu notes, it may not be necessary to be deaf in order to access some of the goods that membership of the deaf community provides:

Hearing children of deaf parents can learn to sign, just as children of English parents can learn to speak Chinese as well as English. It is better to speak two languages rather than one, to understand two cultures rather and one. (It would be disabling for children of English parents living in China if their children spoke only English, even though it might be easier for their parents to communicate with them.)[28]

So everything depends on the detail of the case and it is inadvisable to generalize about the relationship between disability (or even deafness) and quality of life.

Where does this leave the Child Welfare Argument against selecting for disability? Faced with these complicated and murky questions about which disabilities confer net advantage and which are disadvantageous (and in which environments, etc.), the best strategy for proponents of the Child Welfare Argument is to change their conclusion from 'selecting for disability is wrong' to a more qualified 'selecting for disability is wrong *when this will lead to the creation of a person with a less happy life (a lower quality of life, diminished capacity to flourish, etc.) than that of the alternative (possible, future) persons*'. They can then focus on establishing the general principles of the argument without becoming bogged down in discussions of individual disabilities. However, if the Child Welfare Argument was ever going to be applied to practice or policy then of course these discussions about individual characteristics and people would need to take place. What I am suggesting here is that these issues can be saved for another day so that a discussion of the Child Welfare Argument's underlying principles can take place. For the rest of this chapter then I am going to allow the proponents of the Child Welfare Argument, just for the purposes of discussion, the assumption that selecting for disability means selecting a lower quality of life—even though, as I have noted, this is certainly not true of all cases.

3.2 Harm and Wrongful Life

A couple of deaf lesbians went to extraordinary lengths to produce two deaf kids. They wanted their children to be just like them, they explained. Right. So does

---

[28] Savulescu, 'Deaf Lesbians', 771.

that mean a one-legged father or mother should be allowed to chop off their babies' legs? Or that a blind parent would think it okay to put out their children's eyes. The logic is exactly the same.[29]

But is the logic exactly the same? Is there anything wrong with selecting for disability and, if so, what? Given the assumption that disability leads to reduced quality of life, an obvious answer is that the child created is *harmed* by its disability. However, for reasons that have been well rehearsed elsewhere, this view is problematic.[30] In particular, it is problematic in the light of two distinctions: that between identity-affecting and other choices and that between lives which are and are not 'worth living'.

Identity-affecting decisions are those which affect not what life will be like for a fixed future population or person, but instead affect which persons (out of a set of possible future persons) come to exist in the future. So where we have a choice between implanting Embryo A and implanting Embryo B, this choice is an identity-affecting one, a decision to create one rather than another (possible, future) person. These choices are contrasted with non-identity-affecting decisions, such as whether or not to subject a foetus or a child to surgery.[31]

So (for the reasons outlined in Chapter 1) when we choose between embryos, we choose between different (possible, future) persons. For this reason, the welfare arguments discussed here concern themselves solely with Selecting for Disability Scenarios that are identity-affecting (which includes all embryo selection cases), not with actions which modify or mutilate foetuses or children. In such cases, different principles apply, and it is a lot easier to account for the wrongness of intentionally maiming existing children than it is to account for the (putative) wrongness of selecting for disability. The opening quotation of this section therefore contains a fundamental, if understandable, error. If a father were to blind his child then he would have harmed her in a very straightforward manner. However, if he were to select

---

[29] Joan Burnie, 'A Poor States to Be In; Let's Just Ban the USA', *Daily Record* (Glasgow), 12 Apr. 2003, 25.

[30] Derek Parfit's *Reasons and Persons* (Oxford: Oxford University Press, 1984) is widely regarded as seminal treatment of the non-identity problem. See also Dan Brock, 'The Non-Identity Problem and Genetic Harms—the Case of Wrongful Handicaps', *Bioethics*, 9 (1995), 269–75; John Harris, *On Cloning* (London: Routledge, 2004), 68–9, and 'The Welfare of the Child', *Health Care Analysis*, 8 (2000), 27–34; Jeff McMahan, 'Wrongful Life: Paradoxes in the Morality of Causing People to Exist', in J. Coleman and C. Morris (eds.), *Rational Commitment and Social Justice* (Cambridge: Cambridge University Press, 1998); James Woodward, 'The Non-Identity Problem', *Ethics*, 96 (1986), 804–31.

[31] I do not go as far as to claim here that identity-affecting modifications are completely impossible, although the modification would have to be of a rather extreme kind: it might, for instance, be one that brought about the death of one person and the 'occupation' of the organism by another new person. However, for the present, it will suffice to say that: (a) selective reproduction is by definition identity-affecting; and (b) that embryo selection is a case of selective reproduction, not a case of (non-identity-affecting) modification.

an embryo for implantation on the grounds that it would, if implanted, grow into a blind child, it is not so clear that this can be called harmful because the alternative for that embryo was not a life with sight, but rather no life at all. For either it is selected (and will become a blind child) or it is not, in which case it will not become a child at all.

The second distinction is between lives that are and are not 'worth living', although I regard this terminology as problematic. Buchanan et al. draw the distinction as follows, and this is very much the contemporary bioethics orthodoxy:

A life not worth living is not just worse than most peoples' [sic] lives or a life with substantial burdens; it is a life that, from the perspective of the person whose life it is, is so burdensome and/or without compensating benefits as to make death preferable.[32]

In standard bioethics parlance then, a 'life not worth living' is one which, on balance, contains more negative than positive content (for instance, more pain than pleasure) 'from that individual's perspective'. The simplest way of thinking of this is in terms of net utility. If a person's future positive experiences are *less* valuable than her future negative experiences are disvaluable (if there is net negative disvalue) then she would be 'better off dead' and her life is not 'worth living'. Conversely, a 'life worth living' is one in which the person's future positive experiences are *more* valuable than her future negative experiences are disvaluable.

The 'life not worth living' terminology is rather unsatisfactory, however, as it excludes the possibility of reasons to carry on living, for a life's being 'worthwhile', which go beyond quality of life. For example, it is not difficult to imagine a case in which a person's future will be truly awful experientially, containing a great deal of pain and little else besides, but in which she keeps herself alive for moral reasons, perhaps to benefit third parties. In such cases, assuming that her reasons are good ones, her life would be 'worth living' despite its experiential quality being negative. I think it better therefore to distinguish negative quality of life from positive quality of life and (when thinking about whole lifetimes) between lives that contain negative net utility and those with positive net utility (for the person whose life it is). In this way, we can separate out experiential factors from other ideas about worthwhileness.

The reason for introducing this distinction between positive and negative quality of life is that I wish to concede from the outset that negative net utility cases are special. When selecting for disability creates a child with negative quality of life, then that child *does* have a valid complaint and *can* legitimately claim that it has been harmed by being created. For if the child could compare the state of affairs in which it exists (one with

---

[32] Allen Buchanan, Dan Brock, Norman Daniels, and Daniel Wikler, *From Chance to Choice* (Cambridge: Cambridge University Press, 2000), 224.

sub-zero quality of life) with another in which it does not (one with no life, and hence no quality of life) it would (and rationally should), other things being equal, prefer the latter.[33] I would suggest, however, that these 'wrongful life' cases are extremely rare and that most disabilities are nothing like as extreme as this. Most people with disabilities have a positive quality of life, even if their disabilities, or society's responses to them, cause them to have a lower quality of life than that of the average non-disabled person. In what follows I shall focus on cases in which the lives created are *not* ones with negative net utility then, not ones in which the child would be genuinely 'better off dead'.

I should, however, mention at least two possible challenges to my contention that sub-zero quality of life is very rare. First, someone might dispute it empirically and seek to show that disability's (or some disabilities') effects on quality of life are, as a matter of fact, worse than I have claimed—so bad perhaps that a majority of disabled lives are not 'worth living'. Of course, this *could* be true and, as a mere philosopher, I am not in a position decisively to refute (or confirm) it. To claim that most disabled lives are not 'worth living', however, would be a highly contentious, and hard to establish, premiss on which to base the Child Welfare Argument and thus the argument would be rather weak insofar as it relied on it. But, as I have said, this does not mean that it is not true; it may be. The claim that most disabled lives are not 'worth living' also seems rather at odds with the things that many people with disabilities tell us about their lives. Consider, for example, these positive remarks from Ed Smith who was earlier quoted saying 'it's no fun being quadriplegic':

Despite all this, the vast majority of spinal cord injured persons have a good quality of life. We have family and friends, hobbies and pursuits, occupations and pleasures. Life has changed irrevocably, but it has not become a hell so tormenting that we'd be better off dead. On good days it's downright bearable! I know several people with quadriplegia who swear up and down that they are really happy. Some of them have even said they're glad they had the accident because it changed their lives for the better. A friend who is also quadriplegic assured me not long ago that he didn't have a complaint in the world.[34]

Indeed, the surprisingly positive quality of life self-evaluations given by many people with disabilities have led some researchers to posit the existence of a so-called 'disability paradox'—the idea that:

many people with serious and persistent disabilities report that they experience a good or excellent quality of life when to most external observers these individuals seem to live an undesirable daily existence.[35]

---

[33] Jonathan Glover, *Fertility and the Family: The Glover Report on Reproductive Technologies to the European Commission* (London, Fourth Estate, 1989): 129.

[34] Ed Smith, 'Death'.

[35] G. Albrecht and P. Devlieger, 'The Disability Paradox: High Quality of Life Against All Odds', *Social Science & Medicine*, 48 (1999), 977–88.

That said, these positive accounts may not be representative and perhaps those with positive things to say are more likely to speak out, and more likely to be heard, than those whose experiences are negative. At any rate, we should certainly be cautious about accepting first person testimony; for even if it is accurate, it may be unrepresentative. So all we can say, it seems to me, about this particular issue is that no one knows for sure how many, if any, people with disabilities have lives that are 'below zero' and indeed, if they have such bad lives, whether this is an inevitable result of their disabilities or whether socio-environmental amelioration is possible. So on this issue we have, at least pending further empirical research, reached an impasse.

The second challenge to my view that people with disabilities very rarely have sub-zero quality of life comes from certain philosophers, notably David Benatar, who argue that there are a priori grounds for thinking that there are numerous cases in which people are harmed by their creation. Indeed, Benatar goes as far as to claim that 'being brought into existence is not a benefit but *always* a harm'; so there is (in his view) a sense in which *all* lives are 'wrongful'.[36] I will not go into Benatar's arguments for this here because, for my purposes, it will suffice to say that *if* Benatar were right then this would not help those who argue against selecting for disability on harm-avoidance grounds. This is because the creation (or selection) of *any* life, not just the lives of (possible, future) people with disabilities can (in Benatar's view) be argued against on harm-avoidance grounds. So those who are keen to avoid harm would have no reason to single out selecting for disability but should (absurdly) be against *all* births, although they may admittedly hold that disabled lives are generally *even worse* than other lives.

Finally in relation to the 'wrongful life' issue, some people deny the possibility of negative quality of life. One rationale for this is that:

it is not possible to compare existence and non-existence . . . non-existence is not any state in which somebody can be and so it is not possible for it to be better or worse than existence.[37]

I disagree with this for the reasons advanced by Feinberg:

When a miserable adult claims that he would be 'better off dead' . . . he is not making some subtle metaphysical claim implying that there is a realm of being in which even the nonexistent have a place. What he is saying is that he *prefers* to be dead, that is, not

---

[36] David Benatar, 'Why It Is Better Never to Come into Existence', *American Philosophical Quarterly*, 34 (1997), 345–55: 345. My italics.

[37] Benatar, 'Why It Is Better Never to Come into Existence', 350. In the passage quoted, Benatar is merely reporting this view, not endorsing it. See also David Benatar: 'The Wrong of Wrongful Life' *American Philosophical Quarterly*, 37, (2000), 175–83; 'To Be or Not to Have Been?: Defective Counterfactual Reasoning about One's Own Existence', *International Journal of Applied Philosophy*, 15 (2001), 255–66; *Better Never to Have Been: The Harm of Coming into Existence* (Oxford: Oxford University Press, 2006).

to *be* at all. Similarly, when we claim that some grossly deformed infant would have been better off unborn, we are expressing, belatedly, our belief that that state of affairs is preferable ... When one party says that another would have been better off had he never been born, he is claiming that the preference for one state of affairs over the other is a rational preference. Whether this is true or not, this is an intelligible claim without contradiction or paradox.[38]

That said, I could (for the present purposes) happily concede that there are no 'better off unborn' or 'sub-zero quality of life' cases. For this would strengthen my sceptical position regarding the appeal to harm, entailing that the appeal to harm is doomed to failure in *every* case, not (as I have claimed) just in the vast majority of cases.

Having noted that we are dealing with identity-affecting choices and sidelined those few cases in which there is sub-zero quality of life, I can now ask (again) whether selecting for disability harms the child created.

First of all, I note that it is possible to use the word 'harmed' very generally to mean 'wronged'. As Feinberg puts it,

to say that A has harmed B in this sense is to say much the same thing as that A has wronged B, or treated him unjustly. One person *wrongs* another when his indefensible ... conduct violates the other's rights.[39]

This is primarily a terminological rather than a substantive point, but I reject this wide usage (at least in this context) because using 'harm' in this extended way is confusing, obfuscating an important distinction between wronging people by harming them and wronging them in other ways. For example, it is analytically useful to be able to say that some cases of exploitation (such as paying someone desperately poor an excessively low wage for a day's hard work) wrong the exploited person *but without harming her* (because she is better off exploited than starving) whereas some other cases of exploitation are both wrongful *and harmful* (because they do make people worse off).[40] Similarly, some instances of wrongful failure to respect autonomy can be beneficial (paternalistic deception by doctors being a classic case); whereas others are generally harmful (non-consensual sex acts, for example). It is useful to be able to make such distinctions and the wide use of 'harm' to cover all wronging makes doing this difficult.

We must also leave to one side the extended sense of 'harm' which is used in relation to things without interests, such as plants and machines. In this sense, 'harm' means 'damage'. It is tempting to view this use of 'harm' as merely metaphorical, but even

---

[38] Joel Feinberg, *Freedom and Fulfillment* (Princeton: Princeton University Press, 1992), 17.

[39] Joel Feinberg, *Harm to Others: The Moral Limits of the Criminal Law*, i (New York: Oxford University Press, 1984), 34.

[40] The exploitation case is rather more complicated than I suggest here. See Stephen Wilkinson, *Bodies for Sale: Ethics and Exploitation in the Human Body Trade* (London: Routledge, 2003), 9–26.

if it is not, we can disregard it for the present since we are dealing with actual and possible persons.[41]

We should then leave open the possibility of harmless wrongdoing and reserve the word 'harm' for 'harm-to-interests'.[42] Feinberg defines this as 'the thwarting, setting back, or defeating of an interest'.[43] Interests can be set back by a wide variety of things, including accidents, and 'acts of God'. Hence, to say that someone has been subjected to harm-to-interests is not necessarily to make a moral judgement, because people can be harmed in this sense without being in any way wronged (by a disease or an earthquake, for example).

Harm-to-interests is a comparative concept: judgements about harm of this kind compare someone's relative levels of welfare in two actual or possible situations. Where these two comparators are actual, we are looking at a welfare differential over time. For example, we might say that someone has been harmed by an event, meaning that she is worse off after the event (and because of it) than she was before it. However, more often than not, statements about harm involve comparing the actual world with a merely possible world: the idea being that someone is harmed by X if *she would have been better off if X had not happened*. As I have argued elsewhere, harm claims can make reference to three different baselines and often disputes about whether a thing is harmful centre on the question of which baseline should be used. These baselines are as follows.[44]

> **The Pre-Interaction Baseline:** *an event harms a person relative to this baseline if it causes her to be worse off after it than she was before it;*
>
> **The Relevant Possible World Baseline:** *a person is harmed relative to this baseline if something causes her to be worse off than she is in the relevant alternative possible world;*
>
> **The Normative Baseline:** *a person is harmed relative to this baseline if something makes her worse off than she ought to be.*

With this apparatus in place, a good way of seeing whether harm is caused in the Selecting for Disability Scenario is to go through each of the baselines in turn. This means asking:

1. Is the child worse off *than before implantation?*
2. Is the child worse off *than in the relevant possible world?*
3. Is the child worse off *than it ought to be?*

The answer to (1) is 'no'. Preimplantation, either it had no welfare level or its welfare level was zero. Postimplantation, its welfare eventually rises to a positive level

[41] Feinberg, *Harm to Others*, 32.
[42] Wilkinson, *Bodies for Sale*, 69.
[43] Feinberg, *Harm to Others*, 33.
[44] Wilkinson, *Bodies for Sale*, 59–71.

(because the lives in question are not sub-zero). So either welfare has increased, or there is no legitimate preimplantation comparator and, either way, there are no grounds for saying that the child is worse off than before implantation.

The answer to (2) depends on what the relevant possible world is like. For the purposes of assessing the parents' decision, the relevant world will almost certainly be one in which they decide to implant a different embryo, one in which the child under consideration does not exist (because a different embryo would have resulted in a different child). Thus, the comparison again is with non-existence and the answer to (2) is also 'no'. For either non-existence does not provide us with a valid comparator or it gives us a zero welfare value. And, either way, there are no grounds for saying that the child is worse off, created than not.

Finally, is the child worse off than it ought to be? The chances of this being a 'yes' seem higher than for the first two questions because, at this point, one may try to import a super-zero (higher than zero) threshold for how well-off children ought to be. One candidate for this is what Steinbock calls 'minimally decent existence':

a child who does not have even a minimally decent existence is 'better off unborn'—that is, worse off for having been brought into existence. And if the child can be said to be 'worse off' for having been born, then the child can be said to have been harmed by being brought to birth.[45]

The basic idea here seems to be this. There are two relevant thresholds to consider. The first is zero lifetime utility. The bioethics orthodoxy is that this is the dividing line between 'lives worth living' and 'wrongful lives'. On this view, to create a child below the zero lifetime utility line would be both to harm and to wrong it because it would be better off dead, but children above the line are not harmed by being created (even if they have very low positive levels of welfare). Steinbock, however, suggests a second, higher, threshold for both harming and wronging 'minimal decency'. It may be an oversimplification to cash out Steinbock's view solely in terms of utility. Nonetheless, in effect, her proposal is that the threshold is not zero lifetime utility, but some higher positive value.

This super-zero threshold view meshes nicely with the normative baseline understanding of harm. For one could say: children ought to be at welfare level x (some super-zero level such as 'minimal decency') or above and, if their lives are below this, they have been harmed (by having been created) relative to this normative baseline. However, I have some doubts about such attempts to make use of a super-zero threshold.

One problem is non-arbitrarily specifying where the super-zero threshold is. Ought children to be at welfare level $+3$ or at $+19$ and what reason could there be for

[45] Bonnie Steinbock, *Life Before Birth: The Moral and Legal Status of Embryos and Foetuses* (New York: Oxford University Press, 1992), 122–3.

preferring one threshold to another? This then is one ground for preferring the bioethics orthodoxy. For the dividing line between lives containing net *positive* welfare and those containing net *negative* welfare (the 'zero line') seems not to be arbitrary in the way that some higher (or indeed lower) line would be.

A second challenge for the super-zero threshold view is how (or if) it can be distinguished from a pessimistic view of where the 'zero line' is (and/or of how many cases fall below it). Say, for example, that Professor Steinbock and Professor Pessimist both believe that 20 per cent of existing children should not have been born on account of their low levels of welfare. Steinbock believes that most of these unfortunate characters do have a 'positive' quality of life but not one that is 'minimally decent'; while Pessimist believes that they have a 'negative' quality of life. Both agree (to use Steinbock's words) that these children are worse off for having been born and have been harmed by being brought to birth. What then is the difference between Steinbock's view and Pessimist's? It seems to me that their positions are substantively the same and that any difference is merely terminological. Steinbock chooses to couch her pessimism (that is, pessimism about how many wrongful lives there are) in terms of a threshold (minimal decency) which is higher than the normal zero line. Whereas Pessimist sets the threshold for wrongful life at zero, but combines this with the (pessimistic) view that quite a lot of lives have sub-zero quality.

Consider this analogy. A thinks that the numerical grades given to students are, on the whole correct, but that the pass mark for degrees should be 50 per cent rather than 40 per cent, because people getting marks of 40–49 per cent are not really up to degree standard. B thinks that the pass mark should remain at 40 per cent but that people presently getting 40–49 per cent are being over-marked and should really be getting grades in the thirties. Like Steinbock and Pessimist, there seems to be no substantive difference between these views. They merely choose to express or operationalize their position in different ways: one by raising the threshold, the other by giving lower grades. We can see Steinbock and Pessimist as doing just this. The former, as it were, raises the pass mark for a life worth living; the latter keeps the pass mark where it is but assigns lower grades to people's lives.

The super-zero threshold view then does little or nothing to undermine my position that selecting for disability does not harm the child created, except in rather rare sub-zero quality of life cases. I would, however, concede that this sidelining of harm is dependent on my somewhat optimistic beliefs about how many 'lives not worth living' there are. And so if a more pessimistic view of this were correct (such as Steinbock's or even Benatar's) then I could no longer claim that wrongful life was 'very rare'. Having said that, if a *generally* pessimistic view of human welfare levels were to prevail then this would not count exclusively or specifically against selecting for disability and it may still be the case that selecting for disability is *no more harmful* than many other reproductive practices, including notably many cases of unassisted sexual reproduction. To continue with the exam marks analogy, if the pass mark is raised (or all the marks lowered) then there will inevitably be more fails across the board.

3.3 Slavery, Abuse, and Birthrights

In 3.3, I consider two challenges to the conclusion of 3.2: the Slavery Case and the Birthright Argument.[46] I also briefly discuss whether people with track records of child abuse should be permitted to access infertility treatment. This additional question is perhaps rather tangential, but nonetheless merits discussion here (a) because of the similarities between it and the Slavery Case, (b) because it is an important policy issue, and (c) because the spectre of child abusers using infertility treatment services is sometimes used (at least in the public policy arena) to bolster the Child Welfare Argument.

The Slavery Case

The first challenge to the conclusion of 3.2 is that (according to Archard) it commits me (and others) to saying the wrong thing about cases like the following:

For Robertson, Roberts and Harris, the parents who create a child—so long as it enjoys at least a barely endurable existence—do no harm and do no wrong. This seems to me to be deeply and obviously mistaken. Consider Gregory Kavka's example of the couple who produce a child they intend to sell at birth into slavery. Assuming that life as a slave is better than never existing, then—on the reasoning I have considered—they do not harm the child. Crucially in the absence of the offer from the slave owner they would not have a child. They were not planning to have one and do so only as a result of his offer. Thus their conception of the about-to-be-enslaved child is, in the requisite sense, unavoidable. I concur with Kavka in viewing their actions as morally 'outrageous'.[47]

I agree with Archard that the 'no harming, no wronging' view is implausible in the Slavery Case. However, since (I shall argue) it is different from the Selecting for Disability Scenario in important and relevant ways, his Slavery Case does not constitute an objection to my position. One of the main differences is that whereas the Selecting for Disability Scenario only involves one action or choice, the Slavery Case involves at least two. In the Selecting for Disability Scenario, the parents make a single choice: to have or not a child with a disability. (Of course, this single choice occurs

---

[46] David Archard, 'Wrongful Life', *Philosophy*, 79/3 (2004), 403–20.
[47] Archard, 'Wrongful Life', 412.

within a wider context that contains other options, including not having a child at all or adopting, but the choice facing them in the Selecting for Disability Scenario is a simple one—which embryo to implant.) The Slavery Case however involves at least two independently morally assessable components. One is to create or not to create the child. A second is to sell or not to sell the child. On my view, creating the child is neither harmful nor wrong; but clearly it would be both harmful and wrong to sell it into slavery. The Slavery Case then is less like the Selecting for Disability Scenario than it is like one in which parents have a healthy child with a view to mutilating it after birth. What we should say about this post-natal mutilation case is that there is nothing wrong with their *having* the child but that there clearly is a lot wrong with *mutilating* it after birth (and perhaps also with planning to do so).

One response to this is to point out that action individuation is a tricky business. As Harris reminds us:

It is a feature of any action that its description is almost infinitely expandable or contractable. My crooking my finger, is my pulling the trigger, is my shooting at Samson, is my hitting Delilah, is my killing the president, is my orphaning her children, etc., etc.[48]

Furthermore, it may be argued, even if creating a child per se is not wrong, creating a child with the intention to sell it into slavery is wrong, and that is what we are talking about; thus, my attempt to separate creation from selling into slavery is a distorted description which artificially and misleadingly attempts to cut off the underlying intentions and motivations from 'the act itself'.

An illuminating comparison here is buying a rail ticket with a view to carrying out a terrorist bombing of a train. Clearly this is (at least prima facie) wrong. However, I would maintain that there is nothing wrong with buying the ticket per se. Rather, it is planning a terrorist act that is wrong. When we talk about 'buying a rail ticket with a view to carrying out a terrorist bombing' this is a compound description referring to two things: the ticket buying and the terrorist planning. Since the latter is impermissible (and the former neutral) the conjunction of the two is impermissible, but this is *only because of the wrongness of conspiring to commit terrorist acts*. We can apply the same analysis to the Slavery Case. If asked, 'Is there anything wrong with creating a child in order to sell it into slavery?' we should answer, 'yes'. However, this too is a compound description referring to two things: creating a child and planning to sell the child into slavery. Creating the child per se is, on my view, permissible and, as in the train ticket case, the wrongness of the conjunction ('creating-a-child-in-order-to-sell-it-into-slavery') can be accounted for *solely by reference to the evil plan that accompanies it*. The Selecting for Disability Scenario, however, cannot be analysed in this way since it does not contain separable elements that can be independently morally assessed. The

---

[48] John Harris, *The Value of Life* (London: Routledge, 1985), 44.

parents must either select the disabled child, or select another child (or no child), for there is no accessible possible world in which the former can be born but without its disability. Hence, the two cases (Selecting for Disability and the Slavery Case) are not analogous.

A second response to my view is to claim that, although the conception and the enslaving are logically distinct, they are causally or practically conjoined because the child still would not have existed were it not for the slave owner's offer and the parents' willingness to accept it. This (which is an example of what I shall term the *Existential Manoeuvre*) amounts to saying to the child—'you can't complain about being a slave because if it weren't for the slavery deal you wouldn't exist'—and is supposed to be like the thought that children with disabilities cannot (or should not) complain about having been created with a disability if the parents' only alternative was not to have a child, or to have a different child. But again the two cases are different. One difference is that a world in which the child is not a slave is a genuine possibility, one that is not actualized only because of the parents' actions. Whereas in the Selecting for Disability Scenario, life without disability for that child is impossible. Another, perhaps more important, difference is that the conditional—'if it weren't for the slavery deal the child wouldn't exist'—is dependent on attitudes and choices that are themselves morally assessable and reprehensible. The relation between slavery and existence is only 'necessary' and 'inevitable' on account of the parents' voluntary and blameworthy attitudes and choices. Employing another analogy, it is one thing to say, 'You're cured but I'm afraid that removing your arms was a surgically necessary part of the treatment', but quite another to say, 'You're cured but I'm afraid our sadistic surgeon was only willing to save you if he was also, for his own amusement, allowed to cut off your arms.' In both cases, arm removal is causally necessary for survival, but in the latter case this 'necessity' exists only because of a morally reprehensible attitude on the part of the surgeon. Thus, there is a prima facie harm complaint against the surgeon in the latter case but not in the former. Thinking back to the earlier discussion of baselines, this harm complaint against the surgeon makes use of a normative baseline. For while the sadistic surgeon may well have made you better off than you were before she intervened, *and* better off than you would have been were it not for her intervention, she has made you *worse off than you ought to be*—because (arguably at least) you ought to have been saved *and* been left with your arms.[49] Applying this line of reasoning to the Slavery Case, we can say that the parents have harmed their slave-child, relative to a normative baseline, because they have failed to act in accordance with their duty not to sell her into slavery, and this breach of duty has caused the child to be worse off than she ought to be.

[49] Feinberg discusses a similar case. See Joel Feinberg, *Freedom and Fulfillment* (Princeton: Princeton University Press, 1992), 7.

A further reason for doubting that the parents in the Slavery Case can defend their actions by deploying the Existential Manoeuvre (by saying 'you can't complain about being a slave because if it weren't for the slavery deal you wouldn't exist') comes from considering another pair of cases.

> **Noah and Olivia** decide to have a child with the best of intentions. They plan to give it a happy life and a loving home. Later on however things go badly wrong for the family and Noah and Olivia end up selling the child to a gang of child abusers who torture her (such that the child has, all things considered, a barely worthwhile life).

> **Phoebe and Reece** decide to have a child for entirely evil reasons. They plan all along to sell her to a gang of child abusers who will who torture the child (such that she will, all things considered, have a barely worthwhile life).

Both Noah and Olivia's child and Phoebe and Reece's child may well claim to have been on the receiving end of *harm*. In their defence, Phoebe and Reece may use the Existential Manoeuvre and say that, were it not for their child-selling plans, their child would not exist. Thus, she cannot, all things considered, have been harmed because (*ex hypothesi*) her quality of life is not sub-zero and this is by definition better than, or at least not worse than, non-existence. This defence, however, is not available to Noah and Olivia because thoughts of selling the child had not entered their minds at the time of conception. Hence, Noah and Olivia's child's existence is not dependent in any way on its being sold and so they cannot legitimately use the Existential Manoeuvre.

What can we learn from comparing these cases? Well, if the Existential Manoeuvre were a legitimate defence of Phoebe and Reece's behaviour (indeed, even if it were just a consideration that counted in Phoebe and Reece's favour) then (other things being equal) their actions would be less bad than those of Noah and Olivia. But it will seem to many of us that Noah and Olivia's actions are *at least no worse than* those of Phoebe and Reece; indeed, many of us will feel that the actions of Phoebe and Reece, because they are *premeditated* child-sellers, are *even worse* than those of Noah and Olivia. Therefore, the Existential Manoeuvre seems not to be an acceptable defence of Phoebe and Reece's behaviour. For conceding that it was a legitimate defence would entail the unpalatable conclusion that Phoebe and Reece's behaviour is better than Noah and Olivia's. So either there is something wrong generally with the Existential Manoeuvre or there is some reason why it cannot be used by the likes of Phoebe and Reece.

There are, as I suggested earlier, cases in which the Existential Manoeuvre, explaining to a child that the only alternative to her allegedly harmed state was non-existence, can be a legitimate defence against an accusation of harm. There is, however, a reason why the Existential Manoeuvre cannot be used in cases like Phoebe and Reece, one already mentioned during the earlier discussion of the Slavery Case. It is that the primary source of harm, in cases of this kind, is not the creation of the child per se, even if that is done for morally reprehensible reasons. Rather, the harmful act is one that takes place after birth, during the child's lifetime: the act of selling it, abusing it, or whatever. So I would argue that Phoebe and Reece's actions are certainly no better than those of Noah and Olivia, and are not made better by the fact that they planned, pre-conception, to sell their child to abusers. Indeed, as I have suggested, the premeditation dimension may make it even worse. This is perhaps one source of confusion. We abhor the premeditated evil of someone who could, even pre-conception, be thinking about selling their child into a life of abuse or slavery. And this inclines us to think that *the act of bringing about conception* must itself be wrong because it is underpinned by such horrible motives. However, the correct picture, I suggest, is that the act of bringing about conception is, in and of itself, permissible—although clearly the motives that lie behind it are repugnant because they involve planning to act very badly towards a child.

So the Phoebe and Reece case and the Slavery Case then *do* resemble (and may even be worse than) the Noah and Olivia case; these cases also resemble ones in which parents intentionally mutilate their children. But they *do not* resemble the Selecting for Disability Scenario. In the Selecting for Disability Scenario, the Existential Manoeuvre can be validly deployed. For, assuming otherwise satisfactory parenting, there are no seriously harmful acts after birth. Parents who select for disability do not create a child with a view to harming it after birth; rather (in the case we are considering) they create a child which, owing to its genetic make-up, will *be born with* a disability. But in the Phoebe and Reece case and the Slavery Case, the Existential Manoeuvre *cannot* be legitimately used, because the ultimate decision to cause harm after birth is not itself an existential decision; it is a decision to harm an existent child, albeit in ways that may have been *planned* before the child existed.

I should add that selecting for disability and *then depriving the resultant child of a beneficial cure for its impairment* may well fall into the same category as the Slavery Case and this is different from, as it were, the *pure* Selecting for Disability Scenario because in 'deprivation of cure' cases the child is, during its lifetime, subjected to avoidable harm (namely, the withholding of medical treatment by the parents) although this only applies, of course, when the cure really would be beneficial to the child. This does not impact directly on the ethics of selecting for disability, but it does have an indirect effect in those cases where a beneficial cure is known to be available at the time of conception. Prospective 'selectors for disability' in these situations are faced with a dilemma. *Either* they can select for disability while planning to deprive their future child of medical treatment, in which case they are (to some extent) in the same morally problematic position as the parents in the Slavery Case; for they are planning to harm their child once it is born, albeit by omission and in a less extreme and malicious way than in the Slavery Case. *Or* they can select for disability while planning to provide their future child with a cure that will (in the most clear-cut cases at least) remove the very impairment that is selected for—in which case, if non-impairment is the eventual planned outcome, then selecting for disability, only to have it later removed, seems futile. Indeed, it will generally be worse than futile because it will be a waste of resources, and in some cases very unpleasant for the child (because of the side effects of the treatment).

The conclusion of this subsection then is that the Slavery Case does not provide a convincing argument against my view that (except in negative net disutility cases) the child created by selecting for disability is neither harmed nor wronged. In many cases where there *appears* to be harm, this is attributable to harmful actions (or omissions) after the child's birth, rather than to the creating of the child per se.

Should Abusive Parents be Allowed to Access IVF Services?

Before moving on to consider Archard's Birthright Argument, I want to look at the question of whether prospective parents with track records of child abuse (and who are likely to reoffend) should be prevented from accessing assisted reproduction services. For not only does this have a lot in common with the preceding discussion of the Slavery Case but it is also a real policy issue, with the HFEA's *Tomorrow's Children* consultation (2005), for example, asking about the possibility of parents who have 'a history of child abuse or neglect' and/or have 'been convicted of a child-related offence'—the worry being that such parents may abuse or neglect future children created using IVF.[50]

Given the overarching theme of this chapter, I will focus for the time being solely on the welfare of the child considerations and leave to one side other reasons for denying child abusers access to IVF. So, for example, I shall leave to one side cost arguments (for example, the costs of additional child protection measures) and also punitive considerations (for example, some might say that child abusers should be denied access to IVF as a punishment for their previous transgressions). I will also assume that the child abusers in question are not reformed characters, but are unrepentant and almost certain to abuse their future children; in other words, I will assume (for the sake of argument) that any child welfare concerns are well founded.

As regards the moral position of the prospective parents (prospective abusers) themselves this is just like that of the parents in the Slavery Case. Thus, I would say of these prospective parents that while creating the child per se may not be wrong (if its life will be above the 'zero line'), abusing it after birth clearly is wrong, and planning to do so should be condemned too. The policy question that interested

[50] HFEA, *Tomorrow's Children: A Consultation on Guidance to Licensed Fertility Clinics on Taking in* [sic] *Account the Welfare of Children to Be Born of Assisted Conception Treatment* (Jan. 2005), 6.

HFEA, though, was not about the (undoubtedly questionable) personal morality of prospective parents/abusers, but rather about the appropriate *regulatory* response. Should such people be *allowed* to access IVF? Thus, HFEA's question (and mine, at the moment) is about the ethics of third party (especially State) prevention and assistance, not something that I have said a great deal about thus far.

I will start with some relatively straightforward aspects of these child abuse cases. First, it seems obvious that child protection interventions after birth (for instance, by social service professionals) would be justified on harm-prevention grounds; thus there is nothing ethically problematic about trying to prevent abuse once the children in question are born. Second, preventing access to IVF will normally be fully justified in 'wrongful life' versions of the child abuse cases, specifically those where: (a) the abuse is very likely to occur (for example, because the abusers know how to elude the social services); and (b) the abuse is sufficiently bad to cause the child's quality of life overall to be below the 'zero line'. Third, in many 'same number' choice situations—for example, where we have to 'ration' publicly funded IVF services by choosing between competing sets of prospective parents—there will often be *impersonal* welfare reasons not to offer IVF to likely child abusers: that is, to select other prospective parents *instead of* likely child abusers. The rationale for this is that, given limited resources, we should, other things being equal, create the happiest available (possible, future) people, and abused children are likely to be less happy than non-abused ones. Impersonal welfare reasons of this kind are discussed in the next section.

So there certainly are *some* situations in which denying IVF to child abusers, and doing so on child welfare grounds, is permissible or obligatory. Things are less straightforward though when we are faced with a 'different number' choice (a child or no child), and when the abused (possible, future) child's life would be above the 'zero line'. Should prospective parents in these situations be prevented from accessing IVF? If they should (and maybe they should) it seems to me that the reason for this can be neither harm, nor the welfare of the child more generally. This is not a very pleasing conclusion but I think it is hard to resist, for reasons that have already been rehearsed in other contexts, in particular the fact that creating a person with a quality of life which is low but not sub-zero does not constitute a harm to that person.

There are, it seems to me, two main reasons why this conclusion feels uncomfortable (and I certainly share this discomfort). The first is that it looks as if we are condoning child abuse. This, however, is not the case. Indeed, the whole point of much of the preceding discussion was to show that the wrongness of child abuse (in certain circumstances) entails neither the wrongness of creating the children in question, nor the wrongness of *allowing* prospective abusers to create these children.

Second, those who (very reasonably) believe in preventing parents from harming their children may think that a legitimate means of doing this is to stop abusers from creating their victims in the first place—cutting off the problem at its source, as it were. When people think along these lines normally what they do is ignore, or at least sideline, the fundamental existential question of whether creation itself does or does not harm the child created, all things considered. Instead, they focus on particular (actual or potential) abusive episodes that take place during the child's life. Clearly, these events will be harmful and so, the argument goes, if denying access to IVF is the only (or best) available means of preventing these harmful events from occurring, then denying access to IVF on harm-prevention grounds is surely justifiable, especially given that (as Alastair Campbell notes, during a discussion of surrogacy):

> there is no such thing as the harm of non-existence . . . no one is denied anything if there is no person who exists—there is no abandoned pre-existing soul. It follows that regulation which might prevent some surrogacy arrangements and . . . resulted in no birth from the gametes of one or both of these parents, has caused no harm to any child. (It has of course caused harm to the parents, but this is not denied.) Thus no child is harmed by such regulation.[51]

So, people argue, because (a) we cannot harm the (possible, future) child by *not* creating it, and (b) we know that, if created, it will be harmed by episodes of abuse, harm-prevention tells in favour of not allowing the child to be created.

This is a superficially attractive, but flawed, line of argument. The problem with it is that *all* people will suffer harmful experiences of some sort during their lives and so, for *any* child, we could reason as follows:

1. If we create *Child A*, then *A* will be harmed when she experiences *Event E* (something that occurs during *A*'s life).
2. We can prevent this harm to *A* by not creating *A*.
3. Not creating *A* (for the reasons given by Campbell) would not harm *A*.
4. Therefore, we should not allow the creation of *A*, because that is the option that minimizes harm to *A*.

And of course if we allowed this line of reasoning to go through, it would entail not merely the restrictive regulation of assisted conception, but the banning of *all* conceptions, because *all* children will suffer some harm at some point. Therefore, this style of argument must be rejected. When we are deciding whether or not to permit a conception, what matters is not the avoidance of specific harmful incidents, but rather the overall balance of positive and negative experience over a lifetime. Only

---

[51] Alistair Campbell, 'Surrogacy, Rights and Duties: A Partial Commentary', *Health Care Analysis*, 8 (2000), 38.

if the negative outweighs the positive (which it may, but only the most extreme and unfortunate cases) should we contemplate banning a conception on harm grounds.

So where we are faced with a 'different number' choice (a child or no child), and where the abused (possible, future) child's life will be above the 'zero line', it is impossible to justify intervening to prevent the birth on child welfare grounds. That is not, however, to say that there are *no* possible grounds for prohibitive intervention; I have already mentioned two such possible grounds (social service costs and punishment of the abusers) and there may well be others (such as the desire to avoid a moral climate in which abuse is accepted). Furthermore, as I have already said, preventing abusive prospective parents from accessing IVF may well be justifiable on child welfare grounds in some other kinds of case: specifically, where the (possible, future) child would have a sub-zero quality of life, or where it is possible (so to speak) to 'replace' a (possible, future) abused child with a (possible, future) non-abused one—for instance, when we are choosing between candidate parents for publicly funded IVF programmes. Finally, one further consideration relating to State intervention is that legal and regulatory institutions may in practice be incapable of working with some of the complicated and fine-grained distinctions that I have been relying on here: for example, it may in practice be extremely difficult to tell which cases are 'same number' or 'different number', or to distinguish between future lives with sub-zero quality and those with merely low (but above 'zero') quality. Therefore, I would be the first to admit that a lot of work would have to be done to turn these somewhat abstract remarks on the ethics of State intervention into a practicable regulatory framework.

The Birthright Argument

Archard's second challenge to my view of harm and wrongful life rests on what he terms the Birthright Claim, the view that:

If a child should be guaranteed a set of rights then no child should knowingly be brought into existence lacking the reasonable prospect of enjoying these same rights.[52]

He argues that:

Deliberately conceiving a child who will be born to desperate social and economic circumstances violates that child's birthright. So too does deliberately conceiving a child who will suffer a dreadful handicap.[53]

Thus, selecting for disability is wrong, at least when the selected-for disability is bad enough to constitute a 'dreadful handicap', because it violates the child's birthright.

---

[52] David Archard, 'Wrongful Life', 404.   [53] Archard, 'Wrongful Life', 406.

Importantly, the Birthright Argument does not depend on the child's having been harmed by being created:

Thus I am happy to say that the parents who bring into existence a child knowing that she will enjoy a less than minimally decent life wrong the child even if they do not harm the child—either because non-existence cannot sensibly be compared with her miserable existence or because, *ex hypothesi*, her miserable existence is better than non-existence. The parents violate the child's birthright to a minimally decent existence.[54]

So what matters for the Birthright Argument is not harm, but a rights violation: a violation of the child's 'birthrights'. The Birthright Argument's conclusion is quite extreme. It is not just that, other things being equal, we should prefer the creation of a (possible, future) person whose rights are *not* violated to the creation of a (possible, future) person whose rights *are* violated. Rather, the conclusion is that it is wrong to create a child whose birthrights will be violated even where the alternative is no child at all: for instance, even in 'different number' cases. Thus, its scope is *not* confined to the 'same number' selection decisions that are my main concern.

The critical assessment of this Birthright Argument involves looking at two questions. First, is the Birthright Claim true? Second, what rights do children have and, in particular, do they have any rights which (in conjunction with the Birthright Claim) mean that selecting for disability is wrong? These two questions are separable because the Birthright Claim is only a view about the implications that the rights of actual children have for the ethics of creating (possible, future) children. As such, it does not commit us to any particular view of the rights of the child and, indeed, it is logically consistent with the view that children have no rights. For one could think both (a) that *if* children had rights *then* they should not brought into existence without a reasonable prospect of enjoying them (the Birthright Claim) and (b) that children have no rights. So the Birthright Claim is only a schema linking the rights of the child to the permissibility (or otherwise) of selecting certain (possible, future) children and so, unless it is allied with a particular substantive view of what rights children have, the Birthright Claim on its own will have few, if any, practical implications.

How are we to tell if the Birthright Claim is true? One way of testing it is to try to come up with counterexamples. If we are successful then we will have reason to reject the Birthright Claim; if not, then this will tell in its favour (although not decisively). The counterexamples we are looking for are cases in which (a) persons (including adults, for there is no reason to limit the scope of the Birthright Claim to children's rights, as opposed to human rights generally) have a moral right to *x* but in which (b) it would not (other things being equal) be wrong deliberately to create a person whose right to *x* is very likely to be violated.

[54] David Archard, 'Wrongful Life', 416.

I will briefly consider three candidate cases: children's rights to education; adults' rights to vote (or to have their political views democratically represented, one way or another); and people's rights to basic health care. One weakness of arguing by counterexample, especially in practical ethics, is that it relies on intuitions about cases and these may be unreliable and may vary from person to person. That said, I would suggest that there is a strong and reasonable moral intuition that the aforementioned rights exist and ought to be recognized. Furthermore these rights would be signed up to by most people in Western cultures and by most bioethicists (except perhaps those who eschew all rights-talk on theoretical grounds—and these bioethicists will, in any case, reject the whole Birthright Argument on the very same theoretical grounds). So I am suggesting that children should be educated, that there should be universal suffrage (at least for competent adults), and that people should be provided with basic health care. Of course the precise nature of these rights and obligations (issues such as when adulthood begins and what counts as basic health care) needs much more fleshing out but, for simplicity's sake, I shall leave these claims vague for the time being. *If* these rights exist and *if* the Birthright Claim is true then the following propositions must also be true:

1. It is wrong deliberately to create a child with no chance of a decent basic education. Prospective parents whose (possible, future) children have no chance of a decent education ought not to reproduce.

2. It is wrong deliberately to create people who will not be permitted to vote. Prospective parents whose (possible, future) children will not be permitted to vote (when they become adults) ought not to reproduce.

3. It is wrong deliberately to create a child who will not be provided with basic health care. Prospective parents whose (possible, future) children will not be provided with basic health care ought not to reproduce.

So are (1)–(3) true? My own view is that all of these are too strong. Do we (for example) *really* want to say that prospective parents whose (possible, future) children will never enjoy the right to vote ought not to have children at all? I think not. And, if this were true, then an enormous proportion of the world's population would be obliged to refrain from having children since only a minority of people live in democracies (depending of course on how one defines 'democracy'). This seems to me to be implausible. If I am right and (2) is false then there are two ways we can go. Either we can reject the Birthright Claim and say that, although there is a right to vote, it is nonetheless permissible to create people who will never enjoy that right. Or we can insist on the truth of the Birthright Claim and deny that there is a right to vote. Which way should we go?

This choice makes explicit an important structural feature of the Birthright Claim, which is that it is essentially a putative constraint (and rather a tough one) on what moral rights people can possess. For another, equally accurate, way of describing the Birthright Claim is as the view that people do not have a right to x *unless* it would be wrong (deliberately) to create people without x. On this view, existing people have no right to education unless it would be wrong to create new people with little or no chance of an education; existing people have no moral right to vote unless it would be wrong to create new people with little or no chance of enjoying voting rights; and existing people have no right to basic health care unless it would be wrong to create new people with little or no chance of basic health care. So accepting the Birthright Claim may well entail taking a rather minimalist view of what rights existing people have; it may, for instance, mean giving up on rights to education, voting, and health care. Alternatively, we could accept the Birthright Claim, have a more expansive idea of the rights that existing people have, but have a highly prohibitive view of reproduction such that there are very many cases in which parents ought to not reproduce.

This is a serious objection to the Birthright Claim. Essentially the problem is that the three cases mentioned above are, it seems to me, counterexamples to it. They are cases in which the existence of a right seems *not* to entail the wrongness of creating (possible, future) people who will not enjoy that right. Thus, I would want to assert a positive right to vote, but I *also* believe that it is permissible (at least in some cases) to create a child with no realistic chance of enjoying the right to vote. This is to some extent just an intuition about a case. But it is backed up by reasons too. In particular, we can easily imagine lives in which the moral right to vote is not recognized or enjoyed but which are otherwise very good lives and it seems bizarre and wrong to me to claim that these lives are wrongful, that it was wrong to create them in the first place. Rather similar things can be said about the rights to education and health care and to several other putative rights. I do not want to give up on the existence of these rights and nor do I want to claim that lives in which they are not enjoyed are necessarily wrongful. For these reasons I would reject, with one qualification, the Birthright Claim.

The qualification is that there may be *some* rights of which the Birthright Claim is true. Perhaps most obviously, one might posit the existence of a *right not to have a sub-zero quality of life*. This right may entail, inter alia, other rights around suicide, euthanasia, and the withdrawal of life-prolonging medical treatment, but it also plausibly entails the wrongness of creating people who will go on to suffer such a low quality of life. Thus, the Birthright Claim may well be true of some particular basic rights, but it does not capture a general structural feature of rights.

So I think that there are grounds for rejecting the Birthright Claim but, before moving on, it is worth paying some attention to what Archard says is the main argument for it. This is as follows:

1. 'I violate a child's given right, let us say her right to Ø, if I act so as to deny her the enjoyment of Ø.' This includes 'knowingly and avoidably putting her into a situation where she cannot enjoy Ø (or cannot reasonably be expected to enjoy Ø)'.[55]

2. 'If I know that a [possible] future child will be incapable of enjoying Ø and I nevertheless act to bring her into existence then I knowingly put her in a situation where she cannot enjoy Ø.'[56]

3. Therefore: to knowingly and avoidably create a child who cannot reasonably be expected to enjoy Ø violates that future child's right to Ø.

My main worry about this argument concerns the idea of *putting a person into a situation where she cannot enjoy Ø* (the thing to which she has a right) and, in particular, whether existential decisions and actions, those which cause a person to be created, should be counted as *putting a person into a situation* (under the relevant interpretation of this expression). To put it another way, I have some doubts about whether the second premiss is true—about whether creating a child who will not be able to enjoy Ø counts as *putting her in a situation* where she cannot enjoy Ø. Or alternatively, *if* creating a child who will not be able to enjoy Ø *does* count as putting her in a situation where she cannot enjoy Ø, then perhaps putting someone into a situation where she cannot enjoy Ø is not *necessarily* a violation of her right to Ø. In other words, perhaps the first premiss is false instead. At any rate, I doubt that *both* the first *and* second premisses can be true, since the plausibility of the first relies on an interpretation of *putting a person in a situation* which renders the second implausible, and vice versa.

Take, for example, the right to basic health care. There is, it seems to me, a moral distinction between, on the one hand, doing something to an existing person that will deprive her of health care and, on the other, creating an additional person who will not have access to basic health care. The first action will be a clear violation of the person's right to basic health care (at least in the absence of some special justification); she would have had health care and you have deprived her of it. But this is not obviously true in the second case. This is because you have *not deprived anyone of health care* by creating them. Rather, the deprivation, if indeed it is a deprivation, is of non-existence (you have, so to speak, 'deprived her of non-existence') and it is not clear to me that this is a violation of the right to health care or, if it is, it is not the *same kind of* violation as taking away an existing person's health care. Additionally, something will depend on the reasons *why* the (possible, future) people in question

[55] Archard, 'Wrongful Life', 405.   [56] Archard, 'Wrongful Life.'

will not have health care. If this is the fault of the person who creates her (for example, if the parents refuse to pay when they can and ought to) then of course there will be a wrongful deprivation of health care but the wrong here is in the way the child is treated after birth, not in the decision to create it per se. Cases like this are essentially the same as the Slavery Case. Alternatively, perhaps someone else (for example, other members of the community) ought to provide the health care in which case, again, the primary wrong is something that is done after birth. Or, in situations where access to health care is simply physically impossible (because, for example, of resource constraints) it is not so clear that there is any rights-violation (and presumably the right to health care must in any case be qualified so as to engage only when the delivery of health care is a realistic possibility).

As regards diagnosing where Archard's argument for the Birthright Claim goes wrong, what happens is that he asserts a principle that seems to be (and, on one understanding, is) plausible: that *putting someone in a situation* where she will not have Ø means *violating her right to Ø* (where such a right exists). But, for the reason just discussed, this is nothing like as plausible as it at first appears *if* 'putting someone in a situation where she will not have Ø' is taken to include existential choices and actions—those in which the person is 'put into the situation' by being created. Thus, I would contend, Archard's argument is based upon equivocation on the expression *putting a person into a situation where she cannot enjoy Ø* and so fails to justify the Birthright Claim.

3.4 The Same Number Quality Claim

Consider the following case.

The Mars–Moon Case.

The World President must choose between two space colonization projects: Mars or the Moon. The Mars–Moon choice is identity-affecting; different people will go, meet, breed, etc. The Mars–Moon choice is also a 'same number' choice: i.e., the same number of extra future people will be created on each. There is, however, one major difference. While in the short term, say the next two hundred years, the two colonies would be roughly equally happy, in the long term, Mars will (owing to environmental degradation) become a much worse place to live than the Moon. Hence, the Martian Colony would eventually contain much less happiness and much more misery than the Moon Colony.

Which colonization project ought the World President to choose? Clearly (if all other things are equal) she should choose the Moon Colony even if, because the choice is thoroughly identity-affecting, no individual colonist will be harmed by the decision, whichever way it goes. Why should she choose the Moon Colony? Because of some sort of impersonal (non-person-affecting) welfare principle, such as what Parfit terms the *Same Number Quality Claim*:

If in either of two possible outcomes the same number of people would ever live, it would be worse if those who live are worse off, or have a lower quality of life, than those who would have lived.[57]

If we subscribe to this principle, and believe that (other things being equal) we ought to select better rather than worse states of affairs, then there is an obligation to choose the Moon Colony. Such impersonal principles seem plausible. For in the absence of strong countervailing reasons (an important qualification) it is patently irrational, one might even say perverse, knowingly to select the worse of two states of affairs. Indeed, part of what it means to say that a state of affairs is 'better' is that we have reason to prefer it.

The Mars–Moon Case is essentially the same as the Selecting for Disability Scenario. In the former, the choice is between a worse-off and a better-off colony. In the latter, the choice is between a worse-off and a better-off individual. So the same principles apply, the only difference being the number of people involved. So can the Same Number Quality Claim explain and justify the intuition that selecting for disability is wrong? It goes some way, but *only* some way, towards doing this. My main reason for thinking this is that the Same Number Quality Claim cannot distinguish between selecting for disability and not selecting enhancement (by which I mean deliberately selecting a child with *super-normal*, better than normal, characteristics). To see why, consider the Non-Enhancement Scenario:

The Non-Enhancement Scenario

Prospective parents, with the help of doctors, create several embryos using IVF. Each embryo could be implanted and carried to term. The parents and doctors are however committed to implanting only one and to donating the others for research. Given this commitment, the question that faces them is which to implant. To help them decide, they perform various genetic tests. These show that two of the embryos would go on to develop with exceptionally strong immune systems and be unlikely to suffer from major diseases, such as cancer and cardiovascular illness. The other three embryos are, as far as anyone can tell, 'normal': i.e., without major genetic disorders, but lacking the super-normal (better than normal) features of the first two. The parents decide that one of the three 'normal' embryos should be implanted. The doctors act in accordance with the prospective parents' wishes.

As far as the Same Number Quality Claim is concerned, the parents' decision in the Non-Enhancement Scenario is morally the same as the decision in the Selecting for Disability Scenario. In both cases, it is wrong (other things being equal) and for

[57] Derek Parfit, *Reasons and Persons*, 360.

the same reason: a worse-off future person is created when a better-off future person could have been created instead (given the plausible assumption that having an exceptionally strong immune system, etc. is conducive to higher lifetime welfare). This is hardly surprising since the Same Number Quality Claim entails what, in the bioethics literature, has been called the Principle of Procreative Beneficence (perhaps slightly misleadingly, given that no identifiable individual is *benefited* in identity-affecting selection decisions). This view is that:

couples (or single reproducers) should select the child, of the possible children they could have, who is expected to have the best life[58]

One possible response to this is to accept that selecting for disability is merely an example of failing to 'select the best', a breach of the Principle of Procreative Beneficence that is not fundamentally different from the Non-Enhancement Scenario. However, many people will find this unsatisfying because they believe that selecting for disability is much worse than not selecting enhancement. Indeed, many believe that there is nothing wrong with failing to select a super-normal embryo, that it is a permissible choice, while there is something very wrong with selecting for disability. Furthermore, as we have seen, some want to go further and prohibit selecting for disability. For them, accepting that there is no difference between the Selecting for Disability Scenario and the Non-Enhancement Scenario will be very uncomfortable indeed; for doing so entails accepting that the case for prohibiting selecting for disability is (other things being equal) similarly a case for compulsory enhancement selection—not an implication many would accept.

So the argumentative state of play is as follows. The Same Number Quality Claim goes some way towards justifying the view that selecting for disability is wrong. But it fails to show that selecting for disability is worse than any other case of failing to have the 'best possible' child (where 'best possible' means 'the one with the highest level of welfare'). One implication of this is that the Same Number Quality Claim cannot on its own justify banning selecting for disability, because this would entail (absurdly, or at least unpalatably) an 'in principle' commitment to forcing parents to have the 'best possible' child in all cases. So we are still looking for an argument or principle capable of justifying the view that selecting for disability is *especially* morally bad, so bad perhaps that it should be prohibited. In Chapter 7, I shall look at some arguments which, it is claimed, do just this by appealing to a purportedly significant distinction between enhancement and disease-avoidance (the thought being that the latter is more morally defensible).

Before concluding Chapter 3, however, I should mention some general theoretical problems which afflict the Same Number Quality Claim and which, if unresolved,

---

[58] Julian Savulescu, 'Procreative Beneficence: Why We Should Select the Best Children', *Bioethics*, 15 (2001), 413–26: 415.

further weaken the Child Welfare Argument against selecting for disability. I suggested earlier that the Same Number Quality Claim was intuitively plausible and that part of its appeal was the underlying thought that it is rational to prefer, and obligatory to select, better rather than worse states of affairs, where all other things are equal. Specifically, we ought (other things being equal) to select states of affairs with more welfare (happiness, quality of life, or whatever) over those with less. Now this does look very plausible in 'same number' cases which, as it happens, are my main concern at present. However, one objection to the Same Number Quality Claim's underlying rationale is that it has unacceptable implications elsewhere.

One of these is that it might entail an obligation to 'create happy people', to create additional children in situations where this will lead to a state of affairs with more overall welfare in it: for example, if the child created would be very happy and the welfare costs to others, such as the prospective parents, would be relatively low. Various strategies for resisting this conclusion have been discussed at great length in the moral philosophy literature and I shall not attempt to summarize them here.[59] It does seem to me, however, that the conclusion that there is *some* reason to 'create happy people' is perhaps not so awful once countervailing reasons and welfare side effects are taken into account. For instance, as regards side effects, the fact that a person has a strong *desire* not to have children will often weigh heavily against having children because of the harm that would be caused to that person if she had a child solely out of duty, and because of the likely effects that being unwanted would have on the child's welfare. So this is one way of warding off the problematic scenario where someone is obliged to have a child she does not want—for the not wanting itself reduces the chances of there being an obligation to create a child (all things considered).

A second and more serious problem is that accepting the 'more welfare rather than less' principle may lead ultimately to what Parfit terms the Repugnant Conclusion.[60] To illustrate this (and this is *only* an illustrative simplification) it is useful to imagine that quality of life (or lifetime net welfare) can be simply mapped on a welfare scale of -10 to $+10$; 0 (the 'zero line') is the border between positive

---

[59] Also relevant is the large literature on whether there is a defensible 'person-affecting' version if utilitarianism. See e.g. Jonathan Glover, *Causing Death and Saving Lives* (Harmondsworth: Penguin Books, 1977); Jan Narveson, 'Utilitarianism and New Generations', *Mind*, 76 (1967) 62–72; Melinda Roberts, 'Is the Person-Affecting Intuition Paradoxical?' *Theory and Decision: An International Journal for Methods and Models in the Social and Decision Sciences*, 55 (2003), 1–44, and 'A New Way of Doing the Best That We Can: Person-based Consequentialism and the Equality Problem', *Ethics*, 112 (2002), 315–50; Jesper Ryberg and Torbjörn Tännsjö (eds.), The *Repugnant Conclusion: Essays on Population Ethics* (Dordrecht: Kluwer Academic Publishers, 2004).

[60] Derek Parfit, *Reasons and Persons*, 381.

and negative quality of life and so positive values denote 'lives worth living'. In the Mars–Moon case we were looking at a scenario like the following. The choice was between (say):

1. One million (possible, future) people at +7 (Moon), *and*
2. One million (possible, future) people at +4 (Mars).

I suggested that we should prefer to create the Moon population because this involves more total welfare. To use a crude additive method, we might say that whereas the Moon has 7 million units of welfare (+7 × 1 million people), Mars has only 4 million (+4 × 1 million people). Thus, the underlying rationale for preferring Moon to Mars seems to be (a version of) what Parfit calls the Impersonal Total Principle:

If other things are equal, the best outcome is the one in which there would be the greatest quantity of whatever makes life worth living.[61]

Since welfare, along with the allied notions of happiness and the absence of pain, are the subject of this chapter, I shall assume for the time being that this is what makes 'life worth living', although I am not necessarily wedded to that view more generally. Anyway, the underlying rationale for the Same Number Quality Claim appears to be the Impersonal Total Principle. But, as Parfit points out, the problem with the Impersonal Total Principle is that it leads to the Repugnant Conclusion. To illustrate what this is, consider the variation on the Mars–Moon Case shown in Table 3.1:

Table 3.1.

Planet	Population	Welfare Per Person	Total Welfare
Moon	1 million	+7	7 million
Mars	1 million	+4	4 million
Saturn	2 million	+4	8 million
Jupiter	5 million	+2	10 million
Uranus	12 million	+1	12 million
Neptune	130 million	+0.1	13 million
Venus	1,400 million	+0.01	14 million

The choice that faces us is which (possible, future) population to create and this reveals a problem with the Impersonal Total Principle: namely, that it entails (other things being equal) that we should select Venus. For although Venus has a very low level of average welfare—its people are generally pretty miserable and have lives

---

[61] Derek Parfit, *Reasons and Persons*, 387.

'barely worth living'—its total welfare level is high because it is so populous. This is a version of Parfit's Repugnant Conclusion. As he puts it:

For any possible population of at least ten billion people, all with a very high quality of life, there must be some much larger imaginable population whose existence, if other things are equal, would be better even though its members have lives that are barely worth living[62]

And, as its name suggest, this is supposed to be (and seems to me to be) an unacceptable implication.

So why is this a problem for the Child Welfare Argument against selecting for disability? As we saw earlier (given that it cannot, in most cases, use the idea of harm) the best version of the Child Welfare Argument relies on an impersonal welfare principle, specifically the Same Number Quality Claim. This in turn seems to rely on the Impersonal Total Principle which, as we have just seen, entails the Repugnant Conclusion. So the Child Welfare Argument depends on a principle that entails the Repugnant Conclusion.

Proponents of the Child Welfare Argument then are forced either to give up on the Child Welfare Argument or to accept the Repugnant Conclusion. Denying that the Repugnant Conclusion is really repugnant, so to speak, is of course an option, although I doubt whether this can be done convincingly.

Perhaps a more promising strategy for defending the Child Welfare Argument is to try to show that the Same Number Quality Claim does not lead inevitably to the Repugnant Conclusion. An enormous amount has been written on this since Parfit published *Reasons and Persons* in 1984 and I cannot hope to do justice to this here. Indeed, the Repugnant Conclusion merits a dedicated entry in the *Stanford Encyclopaedia of Philosophy* (one well worth reading) and this looks at no fewer than eight possible ways of dealing with it.[63] So, for now, all I can say is that whether the Same Number Quality Claim can be 'saved from' the Repugnant Conclusion is an open question in moral theory—and thus at least a *potential* weakness of the Child Welfare Argument.

Finally, I will briefly mention one possible (but ultimately unsuccessful) way of 'saving' the Same Number Quality Claim from the Repugnant Conclusion, because this often springs to people's mind when they are confronted with 'population ethics' case studies. This is the appeal to average welfare: the view that what matters, what we should be maximizing is *average* welfare, not total welfare. In 'same number' cases, of course, maximizing (mean) average and total welfare amount to the same thing. But

---

[62] Parfit, *Reasons and Persons*, 388.

[63] Jesper Ryberg, Torbjörn Tännsjö, and Gustaf Arrhenius, 'The Repugnant Conclusion', in Edward Zalta (ed.), *The Stanford Encyclopedia of Philosophy* (Spring 2006 edn.), <http://plato.stanford.edu/archives/spr2006/entries/repugnant-conclusion> (last accessed: Sunday, 12 Apr. 2009).

the two come apart in 'different number' cases like the multi-option space case (Table 3.1). Here, the total welfare view leads us to prefer Venus (1,400 people @ 0.01), but the view that we should maximize average welfare would lead us to prefer the Moon (1 million people @ 7). And you can imagine (for example) people having such thoughts about their own families: for example, that it is better to create three happy children at an average of +8 (total welfare, 24) than thirteen relatively miserable ones at +2 (total welfare, 26). The appeal to average welfare, however, has its own problematic implications in other cases. One is shown in Table 3.2.

Table 3.2.

Planet	Population	Welfare Per Person	Total Welfare
Moon	1 million people	+7	7 million
Mercury	just 10 people	+7.1	just 71

The Average Welfare Principle tells us to prefer Mercury, with a massive reduction in overall welfare and population levels, which seems to many people to be as bad as the Repugnant Conclusion. Another problem is shown in Table 3.3.

Table 3.3.

Planet	Population	Welfare Per Person	Total Welfare
Torture World I	1 million people	−9	−7 million
Torture World II	just 10 people	−9.1	just −71

The (possible, future) people in Torture Worlds I and II all have a substantially negative quality of life. The Average Welfare Principle tells us to prefer Torture World I, with a massive increase in overall suffering and in the number of people with horrendous lives, lives well below the 'zero line'. This seems to be the wrong conclusion; it would be worth having a slightly lower average quality of life (−9.1 rather than −9) if this meant avoiding the creation of 999,990 additional lives at −9.

3.5 Summary and Conclusions

This chapter has sought to address two main questions. First, is there anything wrong with selecting for disability, with using selective reproduction techniques deliberately to create a child with a disability (when a non-disabled alternative is available)? Second, under what circumstances (if any) do concerns about the welfare of (possible, future) children provide good reasons either not to practise selective reproduction, or not to select in particular ways? These questions are linked because most (though not all) opposition to selecting for disability is grounded in concerns about the welfare of the child.

1. Wrongful Life

First, there are possible cases of what is standardly termed 'wrongful life' or 'life not worth living', situations in which the person's quality of life is so bad that they would be 'better off dead' or 'better off not existing'. Cases where life has nothing to offer but pain and indignity will normally fall into this category. I accept much of the bioethics orthodoxy about these cases, in particular that it is wrong (in the absence of a special justification) to create a child that will have a sub-zero quality of life. So, when selecting for disability means creating a child with a 'life not worth living', selecting for disability is wrong (other things being equal). I have also suggested, however, that most cases of selecting for disability will not be 'wrongful life' cases, because the resultant child will have an overall positive quality of life. Some people (notably Archard, Benatar, and Steinbock) have taken issue with this but I hope that, during the course of this chapter, I have managed to ward off their attacks. So the upshot of this is that while a handful of selecting for disability cases can be condemned because the resultant child would be 'better off not existing', the majority cannot be criticized on this ground. Furthermore, we should remember that not all 'wrongful life' cases are to do with disability; some will be the result of socio-economic factors or abusive parents. So selecting for disability is not, as it were, uniquely awful in this regard.

2. The Same Number Quality Claim

I have also suggested that the Same Number Quality Claim is an intuitively attractive moral principle. In brief, this principle says that, all other things being equal, when faced with a choice between creating a child with a higher quality of life and one with a lower (but nonetheless positive) quality of life, we ought to choose the one with the higher quality of life. The Same Number Quality Claim is an *impersonal* moral principle. It is not claimed that, if we were to create a person with a lower (but positive) quality of life, that we would be harming or wronging them. Rather, the wrong would be of a general impersonal kind. We would have wrongly created a world with less, rather than more, welfare in it. If we accept the Same Number Quality Claim, it follows from this that it is wrong (other things being equal) to select for disability when this means selecting a child with a lower (but positive) quality of life—assuming the presence, of course, of available alternatives that would have a higher quality of life. So, as in the case of 'wrongful life', I have given reasons for thinking that *some* cases of selecting for disability are wrong. But it does not follow from the Same Number Quality Claim that *all* cases of selecting for disability are wrong because there are some situations (such as the Joshua, Kayleigh, Luke, and Megan case mentioned above) in which choosing a disabled over a non-disabled (possible, future) child is *required by* the Same Number Quality Claim. So one big practical question is *how many* cases of selecting for disability fall foul of the Same Number Quality Claim. I do not know the answer to this and I suspect that no one does. However, there is some reason to believe that many disabilities will lead to lower quality of life since (as Glover suggests) there is an a priori connection between being disabled and having a reduced capacity to flourish. Thus, states do not get to count as a disabilities (as opposed to a mere differences) if they do not diminish people's capacities to flourish (at least in certain environments). We cannot, however, read off from this that x per cent of cases of selecting for disability are incompatible with the Same Number Quality Claim, for this depends on unknown (and perhaps practically unknowable) empirical data.

In addition, as we have just seen, there are some potentially serious theoretical problems with the Same Number Quality Claim: in particular, the worry that it (or the principles underpinning it) may entail the Repugnant Conclusion. Fully exploring these theoretical issues is outside the scope of this chapter (and indeed this book). Nonetheless, we need to keep in mind that this is a further area of vulnerability for the Child Welfare Argument.

These are the main conclusions of this chapter, although that is not quite the whole story as far as selecting for disability and the welfare of the child are concerned. For in Chapter 4, I shall look at some arguments against selecting for disability that focus not on the welfare of the child created, but rather on the costs for other people of creating a child with a disability.[64]

---

[64] Many of the ideas in this chapter were developed with my colleague Eve Garrard to whom I am very grateful. See Eve Garrard and Stephen Wilkinson, 'Selecting Disability and Welfare of the Child', *The Monist*, 89 (2006), 482–504.

4

Choosing One for the Sake of Another

Some people feel that children should be conceived only for their own sake, and never as the means of providing benefits for others.[1]

This chapter and the next consider several quite different but nonetheless linked matters. First, I critically assess the Cost of Care Argument. This is an additional argument against selecting for disability, one which (unlike those considered in the previous chapter) relies not on appeals to the welfare of the child created but on concerns about other people's welfare, especially the costs that selecting for disability would (it is alleged) impose on the health service. Second, I consider the ethics of deliberately creating a 'saviour sibling' (or so-called 'spare part baby'), an additional child whose tissue can be used to save the life of an existing child.[2] Third, arising out of this discussion of saviour siblings, I look at the idea of instrumentalization (treating children as a mere means to an end) and at closely related concerns about so-called 'designer babies' and commodification (treating children as commodities).

What binds together these seemingly disparate topics is the idea that a (possible, future) child may be selected not for reasons connected to *her own* health or welfare, but for reasons related to *other people's* well-being, or indeed the satisfaction of other people's desires. The saviour siblings case is the most obvious example of this, for a (possible, future) child is selected so that an existing one might live, but plenty of other examples have basically the same form. Thus, one might, for instance, select a (possible, future) child in order to benefit its parents by satisfying their cosmetic preferences (assuming that having a blue-eyed daughter, or whatever, will be a benefit to them). Similarly, with the Cost of Care Argument against selecting for disability, what we are looking at is the claim that we ought

[1] HGC (Human Genetics Commission), *Making Babies: Reproductive Technologies and Genetic Decisions* (Jan. 2006), 50.

[2] The term 'saviour sibling' is taken from M. Spriggs and J. Savulescu, 'Saviour Siblings', *Journal of Medical Ethics* (2002), 289.

not to select for disability because of its detrimental effects on other people's welfare.

4.1 The Cost of Care

much of the enthusiasm for pre-natal screening and eugenic abortion stems from an unconscious fear of, and prejudice against, people with disabilities. An associated and very strong factor is the idea that eliminating those with congenital disabilities 'saves money'.[3]

There's some horrifying research out there in the literature which is based on cost-effectiveness: how much it costs to screen, how much it costs to keep a person alive, etc. When you read those you say to yourself—spot the difference between that and the kind of costing the Nazis did when they were eliminating disabled children. It makes your hair stand on end.[4]

The Cost of Care Argument can be used either as an objection to selecting for disability or as an argument for screening out (selecting against) disability and disease. For the time being, following on from the concerns of Chapter 3, I shall focus on the former, although nearly everything I say here applies equally to both versions of the argument, which goes as follows:

1. People with disabilities (at least on average) require more health and social service resources than other people.
2. *Therefore*: in societies with needs-based public health and social service systems (and in many other situations as well) deliberately creating a child with a disability, when a non-disabled alternative is available, imposes additional costs on the system and thus on other people.
3. These additional costs harm innocent third parties, most of whom will have had nothing to do with the decision to select for disability. The extra costs may be either monetary (higher charges or taxes) or may consist of service reductions because the additional child with a disability uses up resources that would otherwise have been available. Either way, there is harm (or risk of harm).
4. It is presumptively wrong to harm innocent third parties (that is, wrong in the absence of some special justification).

---

[3] Alison Davies, *A Disabled Person's Perspective on Pre-Natal Screening* (1999), <http://www.leeds.ac.uk/disability-studies/archiveuk/Davis/davis.htm> (last accessed: Sunday, 12 Apr. 2009).

[4] Anonymous, Expert interview with the author (2005).

5. *Therefore*: (assuming no special justification) selecting for disability is wrong.
6. Furthermore: even liberals (notably Millians)[5] hold that the State is entitled to prevent one citizen from harming an innocent other.
7. *Therefore*: as well as being morally wrong, there is a prima facie case for banning selecting for disability.

Although attractive at first glance, this argument suffers from a number of problems and will not ultimately succeed in justifying the view that selecting for disability should be banned, or even the view that it is morally wrong. In the remainder of this section, I shall consider three such problems. First, questions can be raised about its empirical premiss, the claim that people with disabilities 'cost more'. Second, as with many of the arguments considered in Chapter 3, it is not clear that the Cost of Care Argument can differentiate selecting for disability from non-enhancement, or from merely failing to select the 'best possible' child. Finally, there are some general theoretical worries about arguments of this kind, ones which I have discussed in detail elsewhere in relation to the debate about smoking and health care resource allocation.[6]

Do People with Disabilities 'Cost More'?

I am not a health economist and it is not for me to say whether people with disabilities do or do not consume more health and social welfare resources than others. Nonetheless, I can raise some queries of a general nature which cast doubt upon the claim that people with disabilities 'cost more'; or, at the very least, these queries should make us abandon the view that people with disabilities *obviously* 'cost more'.

First, it is worth reiterating that disability is a very broad category and the extent to which a person with a disability needs additional health and welfare resources depends on the nature of the disability. Thus, for some disabilities (deafness perhaps) there are many people whose lifetime consumption of health and welfare resources is at or below the national average. Whereas with other disabilities, those that prevent the person from dealing with her own basic care and hygiene needs, for instance, people are going to need much more care resource than the average. This diversity within disability means that the Cost of Care Argument applies, if it applies at all, only to those disabilities that cause extra need and extra cost.

Second, in order to assess things correctly and fairly, it is important to take a genuinely 'all things considered' approach to the costs that an individual's existence

[5] Mill famously claims 'that the only purpose for which power can be rightfully exercised over any member of a civilized community, against his will, is to prevent harm to others': Mill, *On Liberty and Other Essays* (Oxford: Oxford University Press, 1998), 14.
[6] Stephen Wilkinson, 'Smokers' Rights to Healthcare: Why the "Restoration Argument" is a Moralising Wolf in a Liberal Sheep's Clothing', *Journal of Applied Philosophy*, 16 (1999), 275–89.

imposes on society, which means taking account of not only the costs of health and personal care but also the consumption of other resources, and not just monetary ones. So, for instance, perhaps people with disabilities, on average, do less damage to the environment because they travel less and consume fewer products (since they have below average incomes). This is just speculation of course (although it does seem rather plausible) but the point is a more general one: that these *kinds* of things must be taken into account before judgements are made about the 'costliness' or otherwise of an individual. Furthermore, some people claim (as in the quotation below) that the existence of people with disabilities provides intangible moral benefits:

Caring for those with special needs or the disabled or vulnerable has the effect of changing us as individuals into less selfish and better people and making society as a whole more virtuous...bearing one another's burdens, bearing the burdens of others, and mutual burdens if you like, is not a negative thing at all, but a very positive thing that helps us to grow as a society and community. So I do not buy the argument that eliminating the 'weak' or having less 'weak' people in society improves our lot. I think it has a reverse effect on us morally.[7]

Now these intangible advantages may or may not exist; I am not arguing that they do. Rather, my point is that we must take a genuinely 'all things considered' approach to the costs and benefits of people's existence (including these intangibles) and, when we do, we may well come to see that people with disabilities are no more 'expensive' than others.

Third and finally (in relation to the cost question) health economics sometimes throws up some surprising results and this gives us further reason not to rely on apparently 'common sense' judgements about cost. A fascinating example of this is some work on the health care costs of smoking published in the 1990s. According to a study by Barendregt, Bonneux, and van der Maas:

Healthcare costs for smokers [per year] at a given age are as much as 40% higher than those of non-smokers[8]

However, because smokers are less likely to live into old age, smokers' *lifetime* health care costs are normally *less* than those of non-smokers:

The . . . non-smoking population lives longer and therefore incurs more costs . . . particularly in old age, when the costs are highest. On balance, the total costs for male and female non-smokers are 7% and 4% higher, respectively, than for a mixed [smoking and non-smoking] population, whereas for smokers the total costs are 7% and 11% lower.[9]

---

[7] Anon., *Expert Interview* (2005).

[8] Jan J. Barendregt, Luc Bonneux, and Paul J. van der Maas, 'The Healthcare Costs of Smoking', *New England Journal of Medicine*, 337 (1997), 1052–7: 1052.

[9] Barendregt et al., 'The Healthcare Cost of Smoking', 1055.

[Overall costs] if all smokers stopped smoking . . . would initially be lower . . . (by up to 2.5%) . . . With time, however, the benefit reverses itself to become a cost. The reason is that . . . smoking-related mortality declines and the population starts to age. Growing numbers of people in the older age groups mean higher costs for healthcare. By year 5, the benefit derived from the presence of the new non-smokers starts to shrink, and by year 15 these former smokers are producing excess cost. Eventually a new steady stage is reached in which costs are about 7% higher[10]

Barendregt et al.'s work is interesting because smokers are often vilified for, among other things, wasting health service resources which other ('innocent' and hence more deserving) patients could otherwise make use of. And this is of course meant to be an argument against smoking. However, if Barendregt et al. are right then this anti-smoking argument fails since, regardless of any philosophical merits that it might have, it is based on a false empirical assumption. Smokers do not cost the health service more than non-smokers; on the contrary, they cost less. Furthermore, this is before tobacco taxes are taken into account. Once these are also factored in then the health care costs argument against smoking looks even more shaky. Even ASH (a British *anti*-smoking campaign group) admits on its website that smokers probably pay several times more in taxes than it costs to treat smoking on the NHS, with tobacco taxation raising £9.5 billion and the treatment of smoking-related diseases costing a mere £1.7 billion.[11] So if only a quarter of the revenue generated by tobacco taxation was spent on the health service, it would be 'in profit'.

Now my point here is not that Barendregt et al. are right about smoking. They may or may not be. Rather, the point is that health-economic data can sometimes run against our intuitions such that even things which *seem obviously* to be costly may be cheaper than the alternatives. And, for all I know, some disabilities are like smoking in this respect. Actually, in the case of disabilities which reduce life expectancy, this is rather plausible because the main reason why smokers are supposed to save the health service money is that they die earlier than they otherwise would. As Persaud puts it:

Smokers . . . save the state money by dying early. Smoking tends to cause few problems during a person's productive years, and then kills them before social security and pensions payments are made.[12]

Of course much depends on the exact nature of the disability. Those that generate extreme dependency without reducing life expectancy may well be very costly for the health and welfare systems, whereas those that lead to a shortened but

---

[10] Barendregt et al., 'The Healthcare Cost of Smoking', 1056.

[11] ASH (website), *Tax and Smuggling: Frequently Asked Questions*, <http://old.ash.org.uk/html/smuggling/html/taxfaq.html> (accessed on Wednesday, 25 Oct. 2006)

[12] R. Persaud, 'Smoker's Rights to Healthcare', *Journal of Medical Ethics*, 21 (1995), 281–7.

generally independent life may well save money. Anyhow, my main point here is that we should not be too ready to just *assume* that disability is costly. If Cost of Care Arguments are going to be used then they need to be underpinned by very good economic data about particular disabilities and the costs and benefits associated with each. And, as I have suggested, this must include not just health economic data but a holistic assessment of all lifetime benefits and costs.

Disability vs Non-Enhancement

The second problem for the Cost of Care Argument is that it cannot separate selecting for disability from non-enhancement, or from merely failing to select the 'best possible' child. The form of this point is already familiar from earlier discussions of other arguments. In general terms the problem is that *if* it is reasonable to run the Cost of Care Argument against selecting for disability then it seems equally reasonable to run a version of the argument in which *selecting for disability* is replaced by *failing to practise health-enhancement selection* (such as selecting embryos that will go on to develop with exceptionally strong immune systems and resistance to major diseases). Specifically, one could argue as follows:

1. People who are created without the use of health-enhancement selection (at least on average) require more health resources than others.
2. *Therefore*: in societies with needs-based public health systems, creating people through means other than health-enhancement selection, when selection is available, imposes additional costs on the system and thus on other people.
3. These additional costs harm innocent third parties, most of whom will have had nothing to do with the decision not to use health-enhancement selection, etc.

And this will take us right through to the conclusion that failing to utilize enhancement selection is morally wrong and to the conclusion that there is a prima facie case for making health-enhancement selection compulsory and prohibiting 'natural' reproduction.

What does this show? Some people will simply accept this conclusion and say that there is indeed a duty to practise enhancement selection, or at least that it would be obligatory under certain circumstances: if it were reliable, safe, convenient, and cheap. These people may argue (and I must admit to having some sympathy with this) that using selective reproduction to create a child with a very good immune system is, in most relevant respects, no different from immunization programmes for existing children. So if, as some have argued, there are moral duties to participate in immunization programmes then there could (under certain conditions) be parallel moral duties to practise health-enhancement selection.[13] On this view, while selecting

---

[13] See Angus Dawson, *Vaccination Ethics: Law, Public Goods & Public Health* (Cambridge: Cambridge University Press, in press).

for disability will normally be wrong (at least when substantial extra cost is caused) it is not a *sui generis* evil but rather just an extreme version of failing to produce the child with the best possible health and lowest possible health care costs.

Alternatively, those who find the idea of a moral obligation (and a fortiori a legal obligation) to use enhancement selection unacceptable may take the view that the enhancement version of the Cost of Care Argument is a *reductio* of the argument. They may claim that since the argument is capable of generating such absurd or unpalatable conclusions then there must be something wrong with the argument (although exactly what remains to be specified).

Whichever one of these interpretations we accept, the Cost of Care Argument is weakened. On the second interpretation, this form of argument should be rejected. On the first, the argument is accepted but at the price of blurring the distinction between the putative wrongness of selecting for disability and that of merely failing to select the 'best' (healthiest) possible child.

It should, however, be noted that there are various ways in which one may try to salvage the supposed moral distinction between enhancement selection and other kinds; some of these are the subject of Chapter 7.

Cost of Care Arguments and Unpalatable Conclusions

As we have seen, one moral objection to smoking is that, in addition to any direct harm caused by passive smoking, it harms innocent third parties *indirectly* by using up health care resources. Because smokers (it is claimed) consume more health care resources than non-smokers, this means that (assuming a limited 'pot') there are fewer health care resources available to non-smokers than would otherwise be the case. And so there will be a number (perhaps a large number) of individual non-smokers who suffer and/or die because of a diminution in health resources caused by smokers' 'excessive' demands for health care. The position of smokers then is supposed to be like that of someone who, during a drought, consumes more than his fair share of water by putting a sprinkler on his lawns. This selfish behaviour harms other water users by leaving them without enough supply. This is also supposed to be the position of those who select for disability, where the disability in question carries with it extra health needs that will not be met privately. Like the smokers and the lawn sprinklers, these 'selectors for disability' voluntarily, knowingly, and unnecessarily impose additional burdens on public services, leaving others with less than they would otherwise have.

I have already mentioned some of the problems with these arguments, such as the possibility that many smokers and people with disabilities cost the taxpayer *less* than other citizens because of their reduced life expectancies. I want now to raise one further problem, a problem which seems to reveal a more fundamental flaw in arguments of this kind. We can see the problem by imagining a possible world in which smokers are 'cheaper' than non-smokers (that is, their lifetime health care costs are lower) and in which people with disabilities are (on average) similarly 'cheaper' than those without disabilities. Let us also, for simplicity's sake, assume that this is a world in which a range of selective reproduction technologies is freely available to all those who wish to make use of them. Thus, selecting for or against disability is easily done.

In this world, prospective parents have a choice between selecting for disability, not selecting at all, or selecting against ('screening out') disability. Now there are of course various arguments for and against each of these but, given our present concerns, let us focus for the time being on cost considerations. If you believe in the Cost of Care Argument you ought, in this world, to reason as follows. Given the assumptions in play, *any option other than* selecting for disability will involve deliberately, or at least knowingly, inflicting additional health care costs on the public system, something that may harm innocent third parties by depriving them of what would otherwise have been 'their' resource. And so, in this world, there is a prima facie 'cost of care' case *in favour of* selecting for disability and perhaps also in favour of its being compulsory, in order to protect the health care resources of innocent third parties. Similarly, there is a 'cost of care' case *in favour of* smoking, because of the deleterious effects that non-smoking has on health care resources.

One way of taking this is as a *reductio* of the Cost of Care Argument. Given that it is capable of producing such absurd results in possible worlds where disability and smoking are the 'cheaper' options, there must be something wrong with this style of argument. I have considerable sympathy with this interpretation and while it is not perhaps strictly a *reductio*, it has at least been shown that those who sign up to Cost of Care Arguments have made themselves hostages to empirical fortune. And, given what I was saying earlier about health economics sometimes throwing up surprising and counter-intuitive results, this is a precarious position to be in. So people who want to be able to resist the very counter-intuitive conclusion that there is a duty, on cost grounds, to smoke or a duty to select for disability would be well advised not to support Cost of Care Arguments.

Another response to this thought experiment, one which seeks to defend the Cost of Care Argument, is to import auxiliary empirical assumptions that tell against the unpalatable conclusion that there is a duty to smoke, or to select for disability. Someone might, for example, claim that any extra health costs caused by the creation of non-disabled children are more than offset by either the extra productiveness (and taxpaying) of people without disabilities, or by the higher quality of life that people without disabilities have. Now of course there are possible worlds in which such auxiliary empirical assumptions are true and, in these worlds, perhaps the unpalatable conclusion can be resisted. However, it is not clear to me that this helps the Cost of Care Argument all that much. This is first because, in these worlds, the unpalatable conclusion is false in spite of, rather than because of, the Cost of Care Argument; the Cost of Care Argument still tells in favour of the duty to smoke and the duty to select for disability. It is just that, in these worlds, there are countervailing considerations that outweigh the prima facie case delivered by the Cost of Care Argument. Second, the general point about proponents of the Cost of Care Argument being hostages to empirical fortune still stands, regardless of the fact that its defenders can come up with some more palatable possible worlds for us to consider.

Conclusions

In this section, I have considered the Cost of Care Argument against selecting for disability (which can also be used as an argument in favour of selecting against disability) and found it to be vulnerable to three kinds of objection. First, there is reason to doubt, or at least to question, the assumption that people with disabilities 'cost more' than other people, and clearly if they do not 'cost more' then the Cost of Care Argument cannot get off the ground. Second (and even if people with disabilities really do 'cost more') it is not clear that the Cost of Care Argument can differentiate selecting for disability from failing to use health-enhancement selection. Thus, while cost of care considerations might tell against selecting for disability, selecting for disability is not fundamentally different from other widely accepted actions and omissions, and so is not a *sui generis* evil (or, if it is, it is not so because of cost of care considerations). Finally, there seems to be something fundamentally problematic about basing ethics and policy on Cost of Care and (what I have elsewhere termed) Restoration Arguments.[14] This is principally because these arguments can, in certain circumstances, lead to unpalatable conclusions.

4.2 Saviour Siblings: The Welfare of the Child

In recent years, high-profile cases in Australia,[15] the UK,[16] and the USA[17] have brought to the public's attention the idea of using embryo selection to select a saviour

---

[14] Wilkinson, 'Smokers' Rights'.

[15] Julie-Anne Davies, ' "Designer" Baby Goes Ahead', *The Age*, 12 Mar. 2003, <www.theage.com.au/articles/2003/03/11/1047144972401.html> (last accessed: Sunday, 12 April 2009); Merle Spriggs and Julian Savulescu, 'Saviour Siblings', 289.

[16] BBC News, *Hashmi Decision Sparks Ethics Row*, 22 Feb. 2002, <http://news.bbc.co.uk/1/hi/health/1836827.stm> (last accessed: Sunday, 12 Apr. 2009).

[17] BBC News, *Genetics Storm Girl 'Responding Well'*, 19 Oct. 2000, <http://news.bbc.co.uk/1/hi/health/979884.stm> (last accessed: Sunday, 12 Apr. 2009); Sheila McClean, *Modern Dilemmas: Choosing Children* (Edinburgh: Capercaillie Books, 2006), 81.

sibling. By using HLA (Human Leukocyte Antigen) typing, commonly known as 'tissue-typing', in conjunction with preimplantation genetic diagnosis (PGD), doctors are able to pick an embryo for implantation which, if all goes well, will become a saviour sibling, a brother or sister capable of donating life-saving tissue to an existing child.[18] The most well-known UK case is probably that of the Hashmis.[19] Their son, Zain, had beta-thalassaemia, a blood disorder which could be cured using tissue from the umbilical cord of a sibling, but only if the sibling was a tissue match. The Human Fertilisation and Embryology Authority gave permission for the Hashmis to select a saviour sibling for Zain. This decision was swiftly challenged in the courts, with the UK High Court finding that the selection of a saviour sibling was unlawful.[20] In May 2003, the Court of Appeal overturned this decision, declaring that tissue-typing can be authorized under current legislation.[21] Prior to the more recent Court of Appeal ruling then it looked as if this form of preimplantation selection might be prohibited in the UK and my aim in this section is to assess whether this and similar bans are defensible and, more generally, whether using selective reproduction to create saviour siblings is morally wrong.

As regards the present legal position, the Human Fertilisation and Embryology Act 2008 permits saviour sibling selection under licence from the HFEA. It lays down specific criteria for this including:

1. That the proposed recipient of tissue is a biological sibling or half-sibling of the created/selected donor;

2. That the proposed recipient of tissue suffers from a 'serious medical condition' which could be treated by umbilical cord blood stem cells, bone marrow, or other tissue; and

3. That embryo selection is not carried out *solely* with a view to facilitating whole organ donation after birth.[22]

It can be seen that a number of ethical assumptions, visible in the regulatory regime derived from the 1990 Act and HFEA Code of Practice, continue to underpin these new provisions. First, the requirements suggest that the deliberate creation of a

---

[18] Many of the arguments discussed here are based on the following earlier works by Sally Sheldon and Stephen Wilkinson: 'Should Selecting Saviour Siblings Be Banned?' *Journal of Medical Ethics*, 30 (2004), 533–7, and 'Hashmi and Whitaker: An Unjustifiable and Misguided Distinction?', *Medical Law Review*, 12 (2004), 137–63.

[19] Sally Sheldon, 'Saviour Siblings and the Discretionary Power of the HFEA', *Medical Law Review*, 13 (2005), 403–11; John A. Robertson, Jeffrey P. Kahn, and John E. Wagner, 'Conception to Obtain Hematopoietic Stem Cells', *Hastings Center Report*, 32 (2002), 34–40.

[20] R (Quintavalle) v Human Fertilisation and Embryology Authority [2003] EWHC 2785 (Admin).

[21] R (Quintavalle) v Human Fertilisation and Embryology Authority [2003] EWCA Civ 667.

[22] Human Fertilisation and Embryology Act 2008, Schedule 2 (Activities that may be Licensed under the 1990 Act), Section 3.

saviour sibling remains a morally serious matter, not to be undertaken lightly. Indeed, significant debate centred on the question of whether it was sufficient to restrict this practice to those cases where an existing sibling was suffering from a 'serious' condition, on which interpretation might vary considerably, or whether it should rather be available only in the presence of a 'life-threatening' condition, which some believed to be a clearer and more restrictive form of words.[23] Second, the provision restricts use of this technology to saving a sibling, implying that this is seen as morally preferable to using it to save another family member (or an unrelated person). Finally, concerns expressed in the House of Lords (and elsewhere) that children could be created in order to be 'harvested' for organs, led to the successful introduction of the provision that an embryo cannot be selected with the aim of creating a child from whom a whole organ can be taken.[24]

Turning now to the moral arguments, I start by noting that, compared to many other forms of selective reproduction, the creation of saviour siblings starts off in rather a strong moral position because failing to use (or banning) embryo selection to create saviour siblings would lead to the death of a number of children who could have been saved by sibling donation.

As McClean notes:

the parents in these cases . . . are asking that available technology be used for purposes that most of us would regard as good; saving the life or improving the health of a sick child. Unless any of the ethical arguments against this hold water, they are not randomly or unreasonably trying to abuse or misuse technology.[25]

So, given that the *non*-availability of this practice will be fatal for a section of the existing population, the onus of proof rests very clearly with its detractors and the prohibitionists who must demonstrate that these children's deaths are less terrible than allowing this particular form of embryo selection. Whereas, for many forms of selective reproduction, we are just weighing procreative autonomy and parental choice against the various anti-selection arguments, in the case of saviour siblings, selective reproduction also has life-savingness on its side. This is, I suspect, why saviour sibling selection enjoys a relatively high degree of public support compared to other

---

[23] The original text of the draft Bill had preferred the term 'life-threatening' but this was changed to 'serious' on the recommendation of the Joint Parliamentary Committee charged with scrutinizing the draft legislation. For discussion of whether the term 'life-threatening' was, in reality, any more restrictive or less ambiguous, see HL Debs vol. 698 cols. 12–33 (21 Jan 2008); HC Debs vol. 476, cols. 102–4 (19 May 2008).

[24] The provision that the reference to 'other tissue' should be not be interpreted to allow the taking of a whole organ was introduced by an amendment tabled in the House of Lords by Baroness Royall of Blaisdon, a Government Minister, in response to concerns expressed during the Bill's Committee Stage. See Amendment no. 31, accepted at HL Debs vol. 698 col. 23 (21 Jan 2008).

[25] McClean, *Modern Dilemmas*, 81.

kinds of selective reproduction. One survey has claimed that almost two out of three Americans support this practice, while a British one (conducted in 2005) suggests that 58 per cent of the population agree that doctors and parents should 'be allowed to carry out genetic tests on IVF embryos before they are implanted into the mother's womb in order to select suitable blood donors for a sick sibling', with only 22 per cent disagreeing.[26]

The main 'anti'-saviour sibling arguments can be divided into three categories. First, there is the idea that saviour siblings would be wrongfully instrumentalized, treated as mere means rather than 'ends-in-themselves', or treated as commodities. Second, there are arguments suggesting that saviour sibling selection would have negative effects on society and the moral climate, leading to the acceptance of (so-called) 'customized conception' and 'designer babies'. Also in this 'social effects' category are arguments claiming that saviour sibling selection (or selection more generally) will eventually make society less fair and equal, and lead to the development of a 'genetic underclass'. Some arguments like this are considered in Chapter 7. Finally, there are the arguments that are the main concern of this section, those which focus on the welfare of saviour siblings. In Chapter 3, I considered some fundamental issues of principle relating to the welfare of the child. Here, I concern myself not with such general questions, but rather with how welfare considerations play out specifically in relation to saviour siblings.

Child Welfare Arguments against the selection of saviour siblings usually appeal to two kinds of alleged harm: harm to physical health caused directly by the PGD process and psychological harm. Let us start with physical health. As far as I am aware, most of the real world saviour sibling cases discussed thus far have been ones in which only the use of umbilical cord material was proposed. In these cases, any physical health problems for the saviour sibling must be ones caused by the selection process itself since no post-natal interventions are envisaged. It is, however, possible to envisage, and later I shall return briefly to consider, more dramatic cases in which a child is selected to become (for example) a bone marrow or kidney donor.

It is also worth noting that the use of umbilical cord stem cells to treat an existing sibling can take place without embryo selection because saviour siblings occur naturally from time to time. For example, press reports from March 2005 reveal the case of Nathan Howard, a boy whose 'whose life hung by a thread' and who 'has been given new hope by his baby sister':

a transplant of stem cells taken from the umbilical cord of his sister Hannah has extended his life by as much as a decade, giving researchers time to find a cure or longer-lasting

---

[26] Donna M. Gitter, 'Am I My Brother's Keeper? The Use of Preimplantation Genetic Diagnosis to Create a Donor of Transplantable Stem Cells for an Older Sibling Suffering from a Genetic Disorder', *George Mason Law Review*, 13 (2006), 975–1035: 983. See also McClean, *Modern Dilemmas*, 87.

treatment . . . His parents had hoped to have a 'designer baby', selected as an embryo to be a perfect match with Nathan. But a shortage of specialists and high number of parents seeking the procedure, meant they could have faced a long wait. So they gambled on having a baby without the screening procedure, although they were told the chances of it being a match for Nathan were only one in 16. But Hannah, born in November, was a perfect match. Blood cells, taken from her umbilical cord at birth, were injected into Nathan's heart in a 15-minute procedure at the Royal Manchester Children's Hospital[27]

If cases like Nathan Howard's are, as they are generally assumed to be, acceptable then this suggests that the practice of using umbilical cord material to save a sibling's life is, as one might expect, fairly harmless. Thus, any physical harm worries about selecting a saviour sibling must relate to the embryo biopsy process.

So, confining the discussion for the time being to these umbilical cord material cases, is PGD with tissue-typing physically harmful to these saviour siblings? A 2001 editorial in *The Lancet* suggested that 'embryo biopsy for PGD does not seem to produce adverse physical effects in the short term, but it is too early to exclude the possibility of later effects'.[28] What we *can* say though is that, as far as direct effects on physical health are concerned, there is no reason to think that saviour siblings will be any worse off than other children created using PGD. This is because embryos in both cases are subjected to the same process, the removal of just a few cells for testing. The only physical difference is what happens to cells *after* they are removed for testing and so it would be remarkable if this made any difference to the physical state of the embryo. Given this, a child welfare argument based on physical health considerations will either simply fail (because the evidence of harm is inadequate) or will prove too much, counting not only against the creation of saviour siblings but against *all* uses of PGD. Either way, the argument does not successfully single out saviour sibling selection for especially restrictive treatment.

An obvious response to this is to claim that a future child should be exposed to the risks of PGD only if she will derive enough benefit to outweigh those risks: a view that I will call the *net benefit principle*. On this view, the embryo is rather like an existing patient and doctors should expose her to risk only if, on the balance of probabilities, she will be a net beneficiary. If this principle is accepted, then (so the argument goes) there is an important difference between using PGD to select a saviour sibling and

---

[27] Jaya Narain, 'My Sister, My Saviour: Cell Transplant from Baby Girl Gives Boy Hope', *Daily Mail*, 23 Mar. 2005, 37.

[28] Editorial, 'Preimplantation Donor Selection', *The Lancet*, 358 (13 Oct. 2001), 1195. In its discussion of saviour siblings and tissue-typing, a recent New Zealand report on preimplantation genetic diagnosis also talks in terms of 'minimal risk to the embryo'. Human Genome Research Project (Dunedin, New Zealand), *Choosing Genes for Future People* (Dunedin: Otago University Print, 2006), 11. For further information on the risks associated with PGD, see also e.g. Frances Flinter, 'Preimplantation Genetic Diagnosis Needs to Be Tightly Regulated', *BMJ* 322 (28 Apr. 2001), 1008–9.

using it to screen for a serious genetic disorder since only the latter procedure benefits the child created, and so only the latter can be ethically acceptable.

However, this net benefit argument relies on some confused thinking: specifically, on the following model. When we screen for a disorder, an embryo (A) is subjected to an intervention (T) with the following effects:

(a) T prevents A from having a serious genetic disorder,

(b) T involves as yet unknown long-term health risks for A.

So subjecting A to T can (on this model) be justified by reference to A's interests because the benefit of (a) outweighs the harm or risk involved in (b). In saviour sibling cases, however, things seem not to be like this. For an embryo (B) is subjected to an intervention (T*) with the following effects:

(a*) T* will make B (more likely to be) a donor for an existing child,

(b*) T* involves as yet unknown long-term health risks for B.

T* cannot be justified by reference to B's interests since there is no (direct) benefit for B and some risk and so, if we accept the net benefit principle, inflicting T* on B is wrong. This then provides the *supposed* ethical basis for allowing preimplantation screening for genetic disorders, while not allowing saviour sibling selection—namely, that only the former conforms to the net benefit principle.

What is wrong with this model? The main difficulty is that it is not the case that T (PGD) prevents A from having a serious genetic disorder. Rather, A is *selected because* it does not have the genetic disorder in question (and so had A been naturally implanted, rather than implanted as a result of T, A still would not have had the disorder). So we cannot think of T as benefiting A because T has not cured A or removed a disorder. Instead, T involved choosing A on the grounds that it was already a 'healthy embryo'.

Given this, what can it mean to say that A has been benefited by T? The only way to make sense of this claim is to say that A derives benefit because T causes A to be implanted, and being implanted is better for A than not being implanted (assuming that, if implanted, A will go on to have a 'life worth living' and that the alternative to implantation is destruction). So, if there is any benefit at all for A, it is not being healthy rather than having a genetic disorder. Rather, the benefit is existential: existing rather than not existing.[29]

This style of argument raises a number of thorny philosophical problems (some of which were discussed in Chapters 1 and 3) and it seems to be based partly on a failure to realize that the decision to select a saviour sibling rather than some other (possible, future) child is identity-affecting. Also, for our purposes, the argument just outlined

---

[29] See the following for a discussion of this and similar arguments: Sally Sheldon and Stephen Wilkinson, 'Should Selecting Saviour Siblings Be Banned?', 533–7, and 'Hashmi and Whitaker', 137–63.

applies equally to screening for genetic disorders and saviour sibling selection. For if the relevant benefit is being caused to exist (rather than being cured of a genetic disorder) then clearly both A and B stand to gain more or less equally in this respect—since both are caused to exist by the selection process and probably would not have existed without it. And, furthermore, this will apply (again, more or less equally) to *all* selected embryos, except in those few cases where the life in question is so bad that it is 'not worth living'. So the net benefit principle, even if true, would fail to justify drawing a moral distinction between screening for genetic disorders and saviour sibling selection.

I turn now to the idea that saviour siblings will be psychologically scarred. The British Medical Association, in its submission to the *Consultation on the Review of the Human Fertilisation Act 1990*, told us that:

A key concern about such cases has been the possibility of psychological harm resulting to the child who would be selected and born to be a donor. Although likely to be as loved as any other child, concerns have been expressed that the child might resent being 'selected', feel less wanted or less respected as an individual.[30]

There seem to be two linked but analytically separate concerns here: first, that a future child may suffer psychological harm if she finds out that she was wanted not for herself, but as a means to save the life of a sibling; and second, that a child conceived for this reason is likely to enjoy a less close and loving relationship with its parents. However, even if we concede, for the sake of argument, that it would be hurtful or upsetting for a specially selected sibling (A) to discover that she had been conceived for the primary purpose of saving the life of an existing child (B), it seems unlikely that A would be *less* happy than another, randomly chosen sibling (C) who was unable to act as a tissue donor. For it could surely be argued here that A would benefit from B's company and may well derive pleasure from knowing that she has saved B's life. Furthermore, as Robertson et al. point out,

the fact that the parents are willing to conceive another child to protect the first suggests that they are highly committed to the well-being of their children, and that they will value the second child for its own sake as well.[31]

In contrast, imagine the psychological impact on C, born into a bereaved family and later to discover that she was a huge disappointment to her parents because of her inability to save B's life. Of course, a full consideration of the issue of psychological harm would involve marshalling substantial bodies of empirical evidence (not something that I can do here). But while this discussion remains speculative, I can at least say that

---

[30] People, Science, & Policy Ltd. (for the Department of Health), *Report on Consultation on the Review of the Human Fertilisation Act 1990* (Mar. 2006), 36.

[31] Robertson, Kahn, and Wagner, 'Conception to Obtain Cells', 35. See also Gitter, 'My Brother's Keeper?' 1023.

it is far from obvious that child welfare considerations should count against, rather than for, the practice of saviour sibling selection.

4.3 Saviour Siblings: Challenging Some Common Assumptions

In this section, I want to subject the following common ethical assumptions about saviour siblings to critical scrutiny.

1. Selecting a (possible, future) child so that it can be an organ (or bone marrow) donor at some point during its life would be morally much worse than selecting a saviour sibling whose only role is to provide umbilical cord blood.
2. The fact (when it is a fact) that the prospective parents want another child anyway and are not having an additional child *just* in order to save their existing child is a morally positive feature of the situation.
3. Saviour sibling selection is morally better, or less problematic, than other forms of saviour selection: for example, better than selecting a (possible, future) child to save its parent, another relative, or an unrelated person.

Organ Donation after Birth

> The Committee . . . recommends that the demands to be made on the child should be restricted to cord blood or bone marrow and that the harvesting of 'hard' or non-regenerating organs would be unacceptable.[32]

> Some people are concerned that once conceived as a 'saviour', it is difficult to place limits on the extent to which it is reasonable for the child to be used to benefit another person. Taking blood from the umbilical cord after birth causes no ill effects, but the removal of bone marrow is more controversial as it causes discomfort, although the long-term risk of harm is slight. However, once it is accepted in principle that children can be created to save the life of siblings, perhaps more extensive (e.g. the donation of a kidney) or repeated tissue donations may be seen as equally permissible.[33]

I want in this subsection to consider a seemingly more extreme saviour sibling case in which a (possible, future) person is created so that she can be a solid organ

---

[32] Ethics Committee of the Human Fertilisation and Embryology Authority, *Opinion: Ethical Issues in the Creation and Selection of Preimplantation Embryos to Produce Tissue Donors*, 22 Nov. 2001, ELC (12/03) 04—Annex A.
[33] HGC, *Making Babies*, 14.

donor at some point during her life. Is this practice morally worse than the standard saviour sibling case in which only umbilical cord material is used? And is it wrong, all things considered? As was noted earlier, many people think that the answers to these questions are *yes* and the Human Fertilisation and Embryology Act 2008 prohibits saviour sibling selection where this would be carried out *solely* in order to enable whole organ donation after birth.[34] So why is this view so compelling to legislators and others? There seem to be two main ethical concerns underpinning it. The first is a welfare worry: that, because being an organ donor is harmful (painful, risky, etc.), there will be a much greater (probable) negative effect on these saviour siblings, than on those whose role is merely to provide cord blood. The second is to do with the (future) autonomy and rights of the saviour sibling: the concern being that such siblings may be wrongfully forced, either physically or in more subtle ways, to be donors.

The first of these worries has some validity although it must be understood in the light of the previous discussion of harm and the non-identity problem. Thus, because the decision to create a saviour sibling is an existential choice (with the alternative being non-existence) I doubt that what we are looking at here is the saviour sibling's being *harmed* (by being created/selected) all things considered. And, for the same reason, it is likely that the saviour sibling (even in the organ donation case) will not have much to complain about in relation to the existential decision; for the act of creation will not itself have harmed or wronged her. So while, of course, she may well be subjected to harmful *events* within her life, as we saw earlier, this is not the same as being harmed by the act of creation or selection.

The welfare worry then, if indeed there is one, must be an impersonal one. For instance (in same number cases), one might object to selecting a saviour sibling on the grounds that this is incompatible with the Same Number Quality Claim: specifically because we would be choosing a (possible, future) person with lower welfare (because of the trials and tribulations of organ donation) rather than one with higher welfare (one who would not be an organ donor). Whether this constitutes a sufficient reason not to select the saviour sibling remains a moot point given the complications considered in Chapter 3. Furthermore, once we move to look at *impersonal* welfare considerations, it must make sense to take into account not just the welfare of the saviour sibling but also that of the *saved* sibling. And quite possibly the saved sibling's increased welfare and longevity will be a sufficient impersonal reason to select a (possible, future) saviour sibling—even where the welfare level of the new child created is lower than that of an available alternative (possible, future) child.

---

[34] Human Fertilisation and Embryology Act 2008, Schedule 2 (Activities that may be Licensed under the 1990 Act), Section 3.

Turning now to concerns about autonomy and consent, we must first distinguish cases in which the prospective donor is a competent adult from those in which she is not, and I start by considering competent adults. One possibility of course is forced tissue removal: a competent adult sibling could be physically forced to give up an organ. I take it that this would be wrong and that treating saviour siblings in this way would be like the Slavery Case discussed in Chapter 3. In other words, as with the Slavery Case, while there is nothing wrong with *creating* the saviour sibling, there undoubtedly is something wrong with forcibly removing her organs. We can then leave to one side forced tissue removal because it is clearly wrong but (using the Slavery Case analysis) not necessarily in ways that make it wrong to have created the sibling in the first place.

A more realistic and so perhaps more worrying scenario is that in which an adult, having been selected for the purposes of tissue donation many years ago (as an embryo) is expected by her family to donate life-saving tissue to a sibling:

tissue-typing scenarios raise a new series of concerns around the potential instrumentalization of the 'sibling saviour,' and the pressure the children might face to donate tissue or organs on a continuous basis, should the initial transplant fail to correct for the disease.[35]

As Simoncelli suggests (above) while the donation may be formally optional in these circumstances, the weight of family expectation and thoughts like 'we brought you into existence to save your sibling, and you would not exist if it were not for her' may mean that the prospective donor feels she has little or no choice in the matter, particularly if the result of her refusing to donate would be the death of her sibling. Hence, it might be argued, there is a significant risk of her being subtly coerced or manipulated into donating.

This concern about people being pressured to donate is without doubt a very proper one but it is not clear that it can underpin an argument against selecting saviour siblings. It is worth noting initially that the position of the (prospective) saviour sibling is not fundamentally different from that of many other prospective living related donors, since they too may be vulnerable to family pressure (although admittedly not to the claim that 'we brought you into existence to save your sibling').[36] In both cases, the prospective donor has a choice, to donate or not, but the voluntariness of that choice and quality of any subsequent consent may be called into question by the family's pressurizing behaviour, intentional or otherwise. Robert Truog notes:

With directed [live] donation to loved ones or friends, worries arise about the intense pressure that can be put on people to donate, leading those who are reluctant to do so to feel

[35] Tania Simoncelli, 'Preimplantation Genetic Diagnosis and Selection: From Disease Prevention to Customized Conception', *Different Takes*, 24 (2003). See also Gitter, 'My Brother's Keeper?' 1019.

[36] J. Harvey, 'Paying Organ Donors', *Journal of Medical Ethics*, 16 (1990), 117–19: 119.

coerced . . . Equally important . . . are situations in which people feel compelled to donate regardless of the consequences to themselves. In one instance, both parents of a child who was dying of respiratory failure insisted on donating lobes of their lungs in a desperate but unsuccessful attempt to save her life. Such a sense of compulsion is not unusual.[37]

As Truog says, though, health care professionals involved in tissue transfers have a duty to ensure that the consent given by the donor is valid, and in particular that it is genuinely voluntary—and we should assume, for our present purposes, that they act on this duty. I am not suggesting that they always would act on this duty, but if we do not assume this then we are muddying the waters by adding an independent wrong to the situation, one which is not directly related to saviour sibling selection.

Also, this concern about subtle pressure being exerted on (potential) adult donors is in essentially the same position as the worry about (potential) adult donors being physically forced. Both of these scenarios are structurally like the Slavery Case in that what is morally problematic about them is not the creation of the person per se but that she is wronged by something done to her during her life: in this case, the taking of her tissue without valid consent. And so while we should condemn these wrongful acts, it does not follow from this that we should condemn the original decision to create or select her.

To illustrate this consider the following analogy. Prospective parents live in a society in which the raping of women is rife. They are, nonetheless, keen to have a girl and select a female embryo for implantation (from a mixed group of viable embryos) knowing that there is good chance that their daughter will, at some stage, be raped. Their daughter's position then is (in some ways) like that of the coerced saviour sibling, since both will be wrongfully forced to do something. What should we say about the prospective parents' decision to select a female embryo? First of all, we can separate out the wrongness of rape from the putative wrongness of creating the daughter in the first place; for reasons explained during my earlier discussion of the Slavery Case, the wrongness of creating the daughter does not logically follow from the wrongness of the rape. We can, however, ask whether the fact that rape is foreseen provides a sufficient reason for not selecting the female embryo? Perhaps *in certain circumstances* it does. But *if* and *when* it does, the reason is an impersonal one, because of the identity-affecting nature of embryo selection decisions. Thus, assuming that the daughter will overall have a super-zero quality of life, it is not that she is harmed or wronged by being created (although evidently she *is* harmed and wronged by being raped). Rather, it is that, if a boy had been created instead, *his* quality of life would (*ceteris paribus*) have been higher than hers is, because he would not have been a rape victim. So it seems that, in order to mount a successful attack on creating prospective

[37] Robert Truog, 'The Ethics of Organ Donation by Living Donors', *New England Journal of Medicine*, 353 (4 Aug. 2005), 444–6: 444.

rape victims, we have to fall back on the Same Number Quality Claim, the limitations of which were discussed in some detail in Chapter 3. In other words, the reason not to bring into being people who will become rape victims is that we could have substituted them with other candidates for existence who (if created) would be less likely to be raped and so likely to have a higher quality of life overall. Essentially the same applies when it comes to the possibility of creating saviour siblings who are likely to be the victims of coerced tissue removal. There is perhaps a reason not to bring them into existence, but it is an impersonal reason: the fact that, had another child been created instead, one incapable of donating tissue, this alternative child would not be at risk of coerced tissue removal. So the rape case and the coerced tissue removal are essentially the same, except for one significant difference: one that I mentioned earlier but which is worth restating. In the saviour sibling case, there is a strong prima facie case in favour of selecting the saviour sibling, based on the fact that a life may be saved; whereas no such justification exists in the rape case.

Thus far in the discussion of organ removal I have focused on competent adults who are capable of giving independent consent to organ donation. I want now to look briefly at whether any special issues arise in relation to children: that is, in cases where a saviour sibling child (one who is 'pre-competent' and thus unable to consent for herself) is called upon to donate a solid organ to her sibling. The first thing to note here is that justifying child-to-child organ donation in general is a controversial area, regardless of whether or not the child has been specifically selected for this purpose. And so of course, all of the potential difficulties that apply in the case of naturally occurring child tissue donors will impact on selected ones as well.

In general terms, what might justify taking an organ from one child to save another? There seem to be three main answers (each of which may be used in both selected saviour sibling and other cases). The first is the idea that the donation, all things considered, normally benefits the donor because she benefits from her sibling's survival (and there is of course no reason why this line of argument would have to be restricted to siblings, since a donor could benefit from the survival of a parent, child, or friend).[38] Second, there is an impersonal utility-gain argument: that there may be some danger and suffering, and harm overall, for the donor, but this is outweighed by gains for the recipient. Finally, it might be argued that parents have the moral authority to consent to the donation on behalf of their children.

For my purposes, the question is whether *selected* saviour siblings are in essentially the same position as naturally occurring sibling donors. For, if they are, and if in general child-to-child donation is permissible (under certain conditions) then it looks as if donation by selected saviour sibling must be permissible too. So we need to ask

---

[38] Aaron Spital, 'Donor Benefit is the Key to Justified Living Organ Donation', *Cambridge Quarterly of Healthcare Ethics*, 13 (2004), 105–9.

whether these types of justification (benefit to the donor, impersonal utility gains, and parental authority) apply equally to selected and naturally occurring donors. Note that I shall not here get into the question of whether these justifications actually work, all things considered. That would be outside my present remit. And in any case, provided that we assume that child-to-child donation is (sometimes) permissible that is all we need for the present.

So, taking the benefit issue first, there is no reason why a selected donor stands to gain any less than a naturally occurring one. In both cases, the idea is that it is better for one's siblings to survive than to die and surely this remains true (if and when it is true) regardless of whether one was selected for this purpose. So the two types of donor (selected and naturally occurring) seem to be in the same boat as far as benefit is concerned. I should perhaps add that there is room for considerable scepticism about this kind of benefit, at least in certain cases. Siblings do not always get on and there are some advantages to being an only child; all of these things would need to be factored in when making a decision about the interests of the donor. Indeed, I think we can say with some certainty that the donor-benefit justification will not apply in every case, since there are numerous examples of siblings hating and hurting one another. Still, insofar as this justification works, it works for selected siblings as much as for anyone else. The same goes for the impersonal utility argument. It is hard to see any reasons why the benefits to the recipient and harms to the donor are going to be different by virtue of the fact that the donor was selected.

Finally, there is the question of parental authority. I should say first that I am also rather sceptical about this style of justification, at least insofar as it is supposed to be anything other than an indirect welfare argument (the idea being that parents are the best judges of their children's own interests). One worry about giving parents the job of decision-making in these situations is that, where the donation is not in the best interests of the prospective donor, they have a kind of a conflict of interest and are unable to act in the best interests of both children. But then, for anyone with more than one child, such situations are ubiquitous and there always has to be some weighing of one child's interests against the other's. Anyway, for our purposes, the question is whether parental authority as a justification for organ donation is any *more* problematic for selected child donors than for naturally occurring ones.

I think there is perhaps *some* reason to be more distrustful of parental authority in the case of selected saviour siblings than in other cases, although this is somewhat speculative. The worry is that if the parents have gone to all the trouble of selecting a saviour sibling, they can be presumed to have a very strong commitment both to saving their existing child's life and to the whole saviour sibling strategy (essentially, they must think that using the 'new' child as a donor is a good idea). And so when it comes to making a decision about whether or not the donation should actually take place they will have often, in decisional terms, gone beyond the point of no return.

Their commitment to the saviour sibling strategy will by then be so great, they will have invested so much in it, that they will be incredibly reluctant not to authorize the donation. For this reason, they are likely to be biased in favour of the donation and hence not perhaps the best decision-makers. As I say, this is speculative and, even if I am right, I have only identified a general tendency among this group of parents; it will not apply in every case.

If I am right, what follows from this? Probably all that follows is that, in selected saviour sibling cases, parents' rights to decide what happens to their children in terms of organ donation should be limited and decisions about whether donation takes place should be taken (after consultation with the parents) by more disinterested people, such as health care professionals or judges, based principally on the two other justifications for donation (donor benefit and overall utility). This safeguard should be sufficient to allay the fears just raised. And, in any case, it seems clear that *no* parents should have *unfettered* rights to decide whether their children donate organs or not (and indeed parents are not generally given such rights) because it is possible for *any* parent to become fixated on the interests of one child at the expense of another and so, for something as major as organ donation, safeguards and limits on parental authority are merited.[39] The position of selected saviour siblings then is again not fundamentally different from that of naturally occurring donors.

On this point, it is worth noting that, under English law, children (whether selected for the purpose or not) can only donate organs if several legal requirements are met. These include:

1. Appropriate consent from a mature minor or, for a younger child, someone with the legal power to consent on his or her behalf;
2. The approval of a court;
3. Permission from the statutory body charged with overseeing organ donation.

First, then, for any live organ donation, common law requirements relating to consent must be met. An older 'Gillick competent' child (that is, one who possesses the appropriate level of maturity and understanding) would be able to give consent to the donation.[40] Where a child is not 'Gillick competent', then either someone with parental responsibility or the court has the power to consent to an operation on his or her behalf, with such consent only to be given where this treatment is considered in

---

[39] McClean, *Modern Dilemmas*, 93.

[40] *Gillick* v *West Norfolk and Wisbech AHA* [1985] 3 All ER 402: a child is capable of giving valid, legal consent to her own medical treatment when she displays the necessary maturity and understanding to comprehend the proposed procedure. A higher level of maturity and understanding is required to consent to more serious procedures, such as that under discussion here. Section 2 of the Human Tissue Act 2004 requires that where the child is capable of giving consent, then the decision to consent must be his or hers.

the 'best interests' of the child. While generally the consent of one person with parental responsibility is sufficient, in the case of organ donation, one parent with parental responsibility would surely not be able to proceed in the face of opposition from any other parental responsibility holder without first seeking the court's approval.[41]

Second, even in cases where parents are in agreement in requesting solid organ donation, doctors would be well advised to seek prior court approval,[42] and such approval will only be forthcoming when the donation is felt to be in a child's best interests (or, more controversially, not against his/her interests). Consideration of a child's best interests would involve a holistic assessment, not limited to considerations of physical health but including psychological and social issues. On this basis, a series of American cases have suggested that in some instances, organ donation may be in a child's 'best interests' because of the psychological and emotional benefits to be derived from saving a sibling's life.[43]

While I know of no reported court decisions concerning donation by living children in the UK,[44] the operation of the same legal principles on this side of the Atlantic is well illustrated by the case of Re Y.[45] Although this dealt with a different set of facts (bone marrow donation from an adult patient with learning disabilities), the broad interpretation given to the best interests test remains instructive. Here, the donation was held to be in the best interests of an adult patient who did not have the capacity to consent to a procedure to take bone marrow from her to treat a desperately ill sibling, despite the fact that the two siblings rarely saw each other. This was because the procedure was low risk, there was no evidence that Y objected to it, and the donation

[41] The courts have held that there are 'a small group of important decisions . . . which, in the absence of agreement of those with Parental Responsibility, ought not to be carried out or arranged by one parent carer although she has Parental Responsibility': *Re J (Child's Religious Upbringing and Circumcision)* [1999] 52 BMLR 82 (CA) per Butler-Sloss LJ. See also *Re C (Welfare of Child: Immunisation)* [2003] 2 FLR 1095, where Thorpe LJ added 'hotly contested issues of immunisation' to that 'small group of important decisions'.

[42] In *Re W (a minor) (medical treatment)* [1992] 4 All ER 627 at 639: the Master of the Rolls said that organ donations were different from other treatments and that 'It is inconceivable that [the doctor] should proceed in reliance solely upon the consent of an under-age patient, however "Gillick competent", in the absence of supporting parental consent. In any event he will need to seek the opinions of other doctors and may be well advised to apply to the court for guidance'. While this is *obiter dicta* and phrased in terms of advice, it is a very strong statement from a senior judge and it would be a brave doctor who would choose to ignore it. Further, the Human Tissue Authority has noted that obtaining court approval to be 'good practice' prior to allowing a child to act as a donor and, as such, it is extremely likely that body will be unwilling to authorise such donation without such approval. Human Tissue Authority, *Code 2: Donation of Organs, Tissue and Cells for Transplantation* (2006), para. 28.

[43] *Hart v Brown* [1972] 289 A 2d A; *Strunk v Strunk* [1969] 445 SW 2d 145.

[44] Mason and McCall Smith report that their enquiries in the 1990s found no practising British surgeon who would be prepared to accept a live child as an organ donor. They found evidence of only one case which had occurred in the UK in the previous fifteen years; this concerned 17-year-old identical twins. See J. K. Mason and A. McCall Smith, *Law and Medical Ethics* (Oxford: Oxford University Press, 5th edn., 1999), 346–7.

[45] *Re Y (Mental Incapacity: Bone Marrow Transplant)* [1997] 2 WLR 556.

would have 'emotional, psychological and social benefit' for her. Extrapolating from *Re Y*, it is possible that a court would permit a higher risk procedure which brought considerable emotional, psychological, and social benefits to a child (e.g. balancing the loss of a kidney against the preservation of the life of a much-loved sibling). Yet the benefits to be derived from donation would clearly need to be extremely great in order to outweigh the pain and risks involved in donating a solid organ.

Third, in addition to these common law constraints, live organ donation is also now subject to the provisions of the Human Tissue Act (2004). All proposed living organ donations will be independently assessed and, in cases where the proposed donor is a child and the donation is of a solid organ or part thereof, a panel of at least three members of the Human Tissue Authority must decide whether the donation can take place.[46] No requests to allow a child to act as a solid organ donor have been reported.

In conclusion then, before solid organ donation from *any* child donor could proceed, all of the following would be required: appropriate consent (from a 'Gillick competent' child or parental responsibility holder); court approval confirming that the donation is in the child donor's best interests; and authorization from a three-person panel of the Human Tissue Authority.

It is difficult to imagine what further protection prospective child organ donors could be offered short of such a donation being completely prohibited. So in practice (at least in England) concerns about defective parental consent and about 'organ harvesting' in the case of saviour siblings seem unfounded.

Wanting Another Child Anyway

In public and press debates about saviour siblings, one question often asked is: will the saviour sibling be a loved and wanted child, desired for its own sake, or will it be *merely a means* of saving the existing child's life? Lying behind this are concerns both about the welfare of the child and about instrumentalization. One quite common response to the question is say that the parents wanted an additional child anyway: that is, regardless of their need for a saviour sibling. So, it is implied, they are not having an *extra* child for this purpose but merely selecting from 'candidates for existence', one of whom would have been chosen anyway, either through the use of another selection criterion, or randomly. For example, according to a report in *The Sun* newspaper, the Whitakers (at the centre of a widely publicized saviour sibling case):

argued they had always wanted a bigger family and insisted the saviour sibling would be just as loved as their other children.[47]

---

[46] Human Tissue Act 2004 (Persons Who Lack Capacity to Consent and Transplants) Regulations 2006.

[47] S. Brook, 'How Our Designer Baby Saved his Brother's Life', *The Sun*, 3 Feb. 2005, 36.

Similarly, in a more recent and less well-known saviour sibling case, the *Daily Telegraph* quotes Catherine Mariethoz's remark that:

To me, it is the same basic principle as IVF. With IVF you're choosing a healthy embryo. All you're doing is making sure that the second child—*which we would have had anyway*—is going to be a match.[48]

The 'we wanted another child anyway' claim does seem to be an effective way of deflecting charges of instrumentalization. For if the new child is wanted for reasons other than saving the existing child, then it is not desired just as a means of saving its sibling. Interestingly, however, there is another way in which the 'we wanted another child anyway' claim might tell *against* selecting a saviour sibling. To see why we need to think back to the distinction between 'different number' and 'same number' cases, a distinction that applies within the category 'saviour siblings' as follows:

> **Different Number Saviour Sibling Cases**—*ones where the prospective parents would not have had an additional child were it not for their need for a saviour sibling. Thus, they are choosing between: (a) creating a saviour sibling; and (b) not creating an additional child at all.*

> **Same Number Saviour Sibling Cases**—*ones where the prospective parents would have had an additional child anyway, regardless of whether or not they needed a saviour sibling. Thus, they are choosing between: (a) creating a saviour sibling; and (b) creating a child who (probably) would not be a saviour sibling.*

Rather counter-intuitively, there is an argument to suggest that, when it comes to child welfare considerations, same number saviour sibling selection (like the Whitaker and Mariethoz cases cited above) is morally *worse* than the different number selection (than cases in which the parents' *only* reason for having the child is the need for a tissue donor). The argument goes like this. As we saw earlier, the Same Number Quality Claim (the view that, *ceteris paribus*, we should select future people with more rather than less welfare) gives us some reason *not* to select saviour siblings in cases where being a tissue donor will reduce their quality (or indeed length) of life—as it may do if the donation of organs is being planned. Of course, the Same Number Quality Claim does not necessarily give us an *overriding* reason not to select saviour siblings since it has to be weighed against (inter alia) the value of saving existing children's lives. But it does at least count against this form of selective reproduction in same number cases. However, the Same Number Quality Claim does not apply to *different* number cases, those in which we are choosing between not creating a new person at all and creating a saviour sibling. Here, selecting a saviour sibling, provided that

---

[48] Nick Britten, 'Couple to Create "Saviour Sibling" ', *Daily Telegraph*, 6 May 2006, 6. My italics.

it will have a super-zero quality of life, is the option that seems to maximize overall welfare, because the alternative is not creating any additional child, which would mean zero additional welfare. So the welfare considerations, in the different number cases, all seem to push in the same direction: creating an additional person means extra welfare and the saved sibling's welfare (and/or longevity) will also be increased. Now, as I mentioned in Chapter 3, some people are unhappy with the view that we can create extra welfare by creating extra people and/or with the view that existence is a benefit. But even if we accept these sceptical views, it *still* looks as if the different number version of saviour siblings is less problematic than the same number version. For even if we said (of the different number case) that creating the extra person is neutral in welfare terms or that existence and non-existence are incommensurable, this is still better than in the same number case. For in the same number case, there is arguably a *reduction* in welfare caused by selecting the saviour sibling rather than selecting a (possible, future) person incapable of donating.

So there is a quandary. If parents would have had an extra child anyway, then it is a 'same number' case and they are vulnerable to the charge that they have selected a less well-off child than they could, and should, have done. (This, however, only applies to cases in which the saviour sibling's quality of life is worse than an alternative non-donor child's would have been; if its quality of life is the same or better than the alternative then there is of course no welfare problem.) On the other hand, the parents avoid this welfare problem if they would not have had an extra child were it not for their need for a saviour sibling, since it will then be a 'different number' case. But, in these cases, they are vulnerable instead to accusations of instrumentalization, because it will be claimed that they are having the child *solely* as a means of saving the existing child's life.

Organs for Parents

> although the HFEA has currently only permitted preimplantation tissue typing to save a sibling, and not a parent or other family member, this distinction could be difficult to maintain. If all lives are equally valuable, and it is generally good to save a life, whichever life it may be, it is arguably wrong to place limits on which lives can be saved by embryo selection.[49]

I want in this subsection to consider the view that saviour *sibling* selection is morally better, or less problematic, than other forms of saviour selection: for example, better than selecting a (possible, future) child to save its parent, another relative, or even someone unrelated. I shall focus on selecting a (possible, future) child so that its

---

[49] HGC, *Making Babies*, 51.

parent's life can be saved through donation, since this possibility has attracted a fair bit of attention and is generally frowned upon. For example, HFEA's Ethics Committee recommended in 2001 that 'the technique should not be available where the intended tissue recipient is a parent'.[50] There seem to be three main arguments for this view.

The first, which I shall largely disregard because it concerns mainly clinical and technical (as opposed to ethical) issues, is that saviour sibling selection is especially beneficial and effective because of the possibility of coming up with an ideal tissue match; whereas this would not apply if the donor is someone other than a sibling. Thus, saviour *sibling* selection (it is argued) delivers more expected net benefit to recipients and is to be preferred on those grounds. Additionally, if non-sibling donation is less effective, then the conventional alternatives to this form of selection (such as getting existing people to donate) become relatively more attractive than the conventional alternatives to saviour *sibling* selection (which are generally worse than sibling donation). But, as I have said, these arguments are essentially clinical and technical and (although important for practice and policy) not particularly interesting from a bioethical or philosophical point of view.

The second argument for preferring saviour *sibling* selection to other forms of saviour selection is suggested by (among many others) the Church of England, in its submission to the *Consultation on the Review of the Human Fertilisation Act 1990*. We are told that:

[tissue-typing] should only be allowed for the treatment of siblings . . . Trying to use this process for the treatment of parents would . . . introduce self-interest as a factor . . . there would be no prior evidence that the parents love and accept their children for themselves.[51]

The point here, like one discussed earlier in relation to the general Child Welfare Argument against saviour siblings, is a combination of concern about instrumental- ization and concern about the welfare of the child. The background thought is that instrumentalization and inadequate child welfare are more likely to occur when the beneficiary of saviour selection is a parent than when she is a sibling. Whether this is in fact the case though is certainly questionable and is not more than empirical speculation. For there may be cases in which a mother (for example) selects a (possible, future) child so that she can be saved herself but nonetheless loves and respects that child—perhaps more so than her other children because of the enormous debt of gratitude that she feels towards the saviour child. So, as with many arguments in this area, we await empirical evidence that would confirm or deny some of the claims made.

Third, there is an altruism argument lurking behind some concerns about parents selecting their own 'saviours'. For example, the Church of England quotation above

[50] Ethics Committee of the Human Fertilisation and Embryology Authority, *Opinion: Ethical Issues in the Creation of Embryos.*

[51] People, Science, & Policy Ltd., *Review of the Human Fertilisation Act 1990,* 38.

mentions the introduction of self-interest and the HFEA Ethics Committee, in its 2001 opinion, told us that:

preimplantation selection [for the benefit of the parent] appears *prima facie* to be morally less acceptable than selecting an embryo to provide tissue to treat a sibling, as it seems to replace concern for another with concern for oneself.[52]

So the thought seems to be that altruism is a good thing, that altruistic motives are morally positive features of actions, and so saviour sibling looks better in this respect than selection to save the parent herself. I have written elsewhere at length about altruism and am somewhat sceptical about altruism arguments of this kind.[53] I will not go over all of the reasons for this here but will briefly say why this particular altruism argument may not be as attractive as it at first appears. One reason is that saviour sibling selection may not be wholly altruistic and one might characterize some aspects of parents' desires to save their own children as self-interested, if understandably so. Parents in these situations will almost always have perfectly legitimate interests, but interests nonetheless, in their children's survival, in being able to experience their children's development into adulthood, and in avoiding bereavement. So I suspect that the ascription of *pure* altruism to the parents of (selected) saviour siblings may well be misguided. Conversely, there may be altruistic or beneficent motivations even for the parent who selects her own 'saviour'. For instance, as well as her own personal interest in her own survival she may want to carry on living in order to raise her other existing children, or to continue caring for a partner or parent, or indeed to achieve world peace and discover a cure for cancer. So we must remember that there may be moral and non-self-interested reasons for wanting to save oneself, although usually these are mixed with more ordinary selfish concerns.

Finally, we should not assume that altruism is an unqualified good, or that it is always a good-making feature of actions.[54] Two sceptical points about the claim that altruism is a good thing should be noted. First, altruistic acts are not *always* morally good. Indeed, they're not even always *permissible*. As McLachlan puts it:

Actions can be altruistic and wrong and worthy of discouragement . . . Altruism can be good in some contexts and can be bad in others. It can have good effects as well as bad effects. It can be done for good motives as well as bad ones: altruistic motives are not always good; self-interested motives . . . are not always bad.[55]

---

[52] Ethics Committee of the Human Fertilisation and Embryology Authority, *Opinion: Ethical Issues in the Creation of Embryos*.

[53] Stephen Wilkinson, *Bodies for Sale: Ethics and Exploitation in the Human Body Trade* (London: Routledge, 2003), 109–16.

[54] Wilkinson, *Bodies for Sale*.

[55] Hugh McLachlan, 'The Unpaid Donation of Blood and Altruism: A Comment on Keown', *Journal of Medical Ethics*, 24 (1998), 252–6: 253.

How can an altruistic act be wrong? This is best answered by simply listing some types of case. Perhaps not all of these will be accepted as possibilities, but I think it is pretty hard to maintain that *all* of the following are impossible.

1. The altruist is culpably mistaken about what is really in the interests of the person she is trying to help and ends up harming rather than helping.
2. The altruist benefits the person she is trying to help, but her intervention is wrongfully paternalistic.
3. The altruist benefits the person she is trying to help, but in so doing wrongfully harms innocent third parties.

McLachlan provides what seems to be a compelling example of (3) (or perhaps of something even worse than (3) if we think that these 'altruists' did not even manage to benefit anyone):

Often, altruism results in extremely wicked actions because people can, wrongly, be prepared to do for other people things which they would, rightly, be too ashamed to do solely for themselves. The recent suicide bombers in Israel, who killed over a dozen bystanders in a crowded marketplace and injured many more were not—or possibly were not—lacking in altruism.[56]

Generalizing, it is easy to think of more everyday cases in which A loves B so much that A is prepared to do bad things to a third party, C, in order to benefit B. Such cases range from minor wrongdoing to serious evil. So, as McLachlan points out, while many acts of altruism are paradigm cases of moral goodness, it is clear that others can be 'extremely wicked'.

It seems then that the ethical arguments against selecting a 'saviour' for a parent are not very convincing and that this form of saviour selection is no worse than the more widely discussed practice of saviour sibling selection.

Conclusions

In this section, I have looked at three ancillary issues relating to saviour siblings (or, more generally, saviour selection).

First, is selecting a (possible, future) child who can become an organ donor at some point during its life morally worse than selecting one whose only role is to donate umbilical cord blood? As far as the welfare of the child is concerned, the organ donation case may well be *slightly* worse than the umbilical cord blood case, just because (rather obviously) the latter has fewer (if any) detrimental effects on the saviour sibling. However, selecting a saviour sibling for the purposes of organ donation may still be justifiable, all things considered, because the legitimate welfare

---

[56] McLachlan, 'The Unpaid Donation of Blood and Altruism.'

worries here are impersonal ones; in particular, the saviour sibling will not normally have a valid harm complaint (with respect to the decision to create her) provided that her quality of life is greater than zero. And so once the value of saving another life is factored in, there is a good chance that selecting a prospective organ donor will be permissible. Another worry about the organ donation case relates to the (future) autonomy and rights of the saviour sibling: the concern being that such siblings may be wrongfully forced, either physically or in more subtle ways, to be organ donors. This concern about people being pressured to donate is without doubt a very proper one, but it is not clear that it can underpin an argument against selecting saviour siblings. This is partly because the coercion issue is really a question of how we treat these people during their lives rather than one about whether we should create them in the first place. Thus, while it may not be wrong to create a (possible, future) person who is a potential donor, it would be wrong to then force that person to donate against her will. It is also partly because the *selected* saviour sibling is, in most important respects, in the same moral and emotional position as the *naturally occurring* saviour sibling (those prospective sibling donors who were not selected but just happen to be potential donors). And most of the consent worries about selected saviour siblings are essentially just general ones about inter-sibling organ donations of all sorts.

The second ancillary question is: is it morally better if the prospective parents of saviour siblings want another child anyway and are not having an additional child just in order to save their existing child? The answer to this is that it is better in one way and worse in another. It is better because (arguably at least) the fact that they want another child anyway suggests that they are not regarding the saviour sibling as merely a means to an end, that they are not wrongfully instrumentalizing her. It may be worse, however, in terms of child welfare. In particular, same number cases (ones where they would have had the child anyway) will often fall foul of the Same Number Quality Claim whereas different number cases (those where they are *only* having the child because of the need for a saviour sibling) will not.

Finally, there is the question of whether saviour *sibling* selection is morally better, or less problematic, than other forms of saviour selection: for example, better than selecting a (possible, future) child to save its parent, another relative, or an unrelated person. As I have just suggested, contrary to popular option, it seems that this form of selection is not worse than saviour sibling selection.

4.4 Summary and Conclusions

In this chapter, I have done two main things. First, I looked at Cost of Care Arguments, which claim that certain (possible, future) people should (or should not) be created/selected in order to reduce health and social care costs. Such arguments can in principle provide reasons for practising or avoiding some forms of selective reproduction. However, when applied to disability avoidance (either as an argument against selecting for disability, or as an argument for 'screening out' disability) they are vulnerable to three objections and should therefore be approached with some scepticism. The objections are that: (a) the assumption that people with disabilities 'cost more' than other people is questionable; (b) cost arguments, if accepted, would count not just against selecting for disability (and for deselecting disability) but also in favour of enhancement; and (c) Cost of Care Arguments may lead to unpalatable conclusions.

Second, I looked at Child Welfare Arguments against selecting saviour siblings, finding these to be generally unconvincing. Not only is the empirical case for selected saviour siblings being worse off than relevant comparators speculative and weak, but the decision to select a saviour sibling is identity-affecting and so the child is unlikely to be harmed by the decision to create it.

In addition, I have challenged some common assumptions about the ethics of selecting saviour siblings, suggesting (among other things) that: (a) selection for the purposes of whole organ donation is defensible provided that there are adequate safeguards in place for *all* living organ donors; and (b) that forms of saviour selection other that saviour *sibling* selection (for example, selecting a donor to provide life-saving tissue for another relative, or for someone unrelated) may be acceptable (again, provided that there are adequate safeguards for living organ donors).

5

Treating Children as Commodities

Once we start to pick and choose our children's characteristics, we will be turning them into just another consumer commodity.[1]

As I suggested earlier, the main moral objections to selecting saviour siblings can be divided into three broad categories: child welfare arguments (discussed in the previous two chapters); social effects arguments (some of which will be looked at in Chapter 7); and the claim that (selected) saviour siblings would be wrongfully instrumentalized, treated as mere means rather than ends-in-themselves, or treated as commodities. Arguments in this last category are the concern of this chapter.

Selective reproduction of all kinds (not just of saviour siblings) is routinely objected to on the grounds that it involves treating or regarding children as commodities. It is this objection that, more often than not, underlies talk of 'designer babies'. Sometimes the claim is that selective reproduction is itself an instance of commodification; on other occasions, the claim is that selective reproduction will cause people to treat children as commodities. Consider, for instance, these recent quotations from British newspapers, which express (or report) commodification concerns about sex selection, the creation of 'saviour siblings', the 'IVF industry', and 'single mothers' (respectively):

The danger must be that [non-medical sex selection] would move society in the direction of creating children with certain characteristics. Increasingly, offspring might be seen as mere commodities. For designer handbag, read designer baby.[2]

The [HFEA] was accused yesterday of turning children into commodities after it relaxed the rules covering so-called designer babies. The decision means that dozens of parents will be allowed to have donor siblings[3]:

---

[1] David King, 'How Far is Too Far?', *Sunday Herald* (Glasgow), 25 June 2006, 12.

[2] 'An Affront to Human Dignity: Report's Backing of Gender Selection is Off the Mark', *The Herald*, 25 Mar. 2005.

[3] David Derbyshire and Jonathan Petre, 'Parents Win Right to Have Donor Babies', *Daily Telegraph*, 22 July 2004.

The ethos of the IVF industry—and this includes all other forms of assisted reproduction—remains questionable. Children are neither a right nor a commodity, and the IVF industry treats them as both.[4]

To set out from the outset with the intention of bringing a child into the world without a father is highly irresponsible and is treating children as commodities rather than the treasured people they should be.[5]

A 2006 report by the Human Genetics Commission also notes that some people:

are worried that the introduction of techniques enabling deliberate selection between embryos may lead to children being treated as commodities.   (HGC, 2006, para. 4.5)

This chapter's overarching aim is to interpret and critically assess the claim that some forms of selective reproduction are morally objectionable because they involve treating children as commodities. It starts by offering a general account of commodification. Commodification (in its moral sense) comprises two elements: instrumentalization (roughly, treating things that are ends-in-themselves as if they were mere means); and fungibilization (roughly, treating as interchangeable things that are not).

5.1 What Is Commodification?

A good starting point is, not surprisingly, is the idea of a commodity.[6] Kaveny, while introducing a special issue of the *Journal of Medicine and Philosophy* on commodification, identifies three essential characteristics:

First, every commodity has its price, which a seller will receive for surrendering it and a buyer will part with in order to acquire it.

Commodities are typically fungible, which means they are interchangeable with other goods of like type and quality. To use the language of contract law, one 'widget' is as good as any other.

A third basic feature of commodities is that their value is instrumental, not intrinsic.[7]

---

[4] Christina Odone, 'We All Lose in the Baby Business', *The Times*, 17 Jan. 2005.

[5] Norman Wells, quoted in Fiona Macrae, 'Fathers Surplus to Requirements', *Daily Mail*, 17 Aug. 2005.

[6] Some of the points made in this section are based on Stephen Wilkinson, 'Commodification', in Richard Ashcroft, Angus Dawson, Heather Draper, and John MacMillan (eds.), *Principles of Health Care Ethics* (2nd edn., Chichester: John Wiley & Sons, 2007), 285–92.

[7] Cathleen M. Kaveny, 'Commodifying the Polyvalent Good of Healthcare', *Journal of Medicine and Philosophy*, 24 (1999), 207–23.

So to treat a thing as a commodity is to treat it as if

1. It has a price; *and*
2. It is fungible; *and*
3. It has only instrumental value.

The next step is to distinguish descriptive from normative senses of 'commodification'. In the first of these, 'commodification' refers to a social practice and/or legal system under which rights over the thing in question are bought and sold.[8] To talk of commodification in this sense is not to make a moral judgement but merely to point out that, as a matter of fact, certain things are being treated as commodities.[9] In the second (normative or moral) sense to call something 'commodification' is to express moral disapproval and to refer to a distinctive kind of wrong: the wrong of commodification. Consider, as an illustration, the following criticism of organ sale from Brecher:

> the possibility of people's buying a kidney represents the further commoditisation [commodification] of human beings, [and] to that extent the practice resembles prostitution, certain forms of surrogacy, and . . . page three of *The Sun* in symbolising, partly constituting, and encouraging a moral climate within which the commoditisation [commodification] of human beings proceeds apace.[10]

Brecher's point here is not merely that permitting organ sale would constitute an extension of *the social practice of* commodification. That claim taken alone would be too obvious to be worth a mention and certainly would not constitute an argument for prohibition, but would be more like a description of what should be prohibited. Instead, his point seems to be that we ought not to permit these practices because doing so would be or cause a specific wrong: the commodification of human beings.[11]

It is this normative sense of 'commodification' which is most relevant to bioethics and which is my concern here. The key to understanding it is a distinction between proper and wrongful commodities. Proper commodities are those things that really are fungible and only instrumentally valuable; thus there is nothing wrong with treating them as fungible or as merely instrumental, because that is to treat them as what they are. Wrongful commodities, on the other hand, are things that are treated as if they are commodities despite their not being (really) fungible or merely

---

[8] Andrew Alexandra and Adrian Walsh, 'Exclusion, Commodification, and Plant Variety Rights Legislation', *Agriculture and Human Values*, 14 (1997), 313–23; David Resnik, 'The Commodification of Human Reproductive Materials', *Journal of Medical Ethics*, 24 (1998), 388–93; Stephen Wilkinson, 'Commodification Arguments for the Legal Prohibition of Organ Sale', *Health Care Analysis*, 8 (2000), 189–201.

[9] Mark Hanson, 'Biotechnology and Commodification within Health Care', *Journal of Medicine and Philosophy*, 24 (1999), 267–87: 269.

[10] Bob Brecher, 'The Kidney Trade: or, The Customer is Always Wrong', *Journal of Medical Ethics*, 16 (1990), 120–3: 122.

[11] Wilkinson, 'Commodification Arguments', 192.

instrumentally valuable. Thus, the distinctive wrong of commodification is treating something non-fungible and intrinsically valuable as if it were fungible and merely instrumentally valuable.

The idea of commodification is applicable not just to persons but to anything which is non-fungible and intrinsically valuable. Thus, commodification concerns may (for example) be raised about (non-human) animals, artworks, or the environment. For reasons of space and focus, however, my concern here is the commodification of people and people's bodies.

Before moving on to consider the idea of instrumentalization (treating embryos or children as mere means) in more detail, it is worth mentioning an interesting feature of the way in which commodification talk is used in debates about selective reproduction. This is that it is *not* restricted to contexts in which commercialization and payment are central moral issues. Indeed, sometimes prospective parents are accused of treating their (possible, future) children as commodities even though there is no question of the parents paying for them or selling them. I suspect that this is because although commodification's natural habitat, as it were, is debates about commercialization and payment, its essential *moral* content is a conjunction of concerns about instrumentalization and about treating things as fungible. And both of these can occur with or without money changing hands—although money and markets may well *encourage* them to occur, which is why money and markets are often deemed morally problematic. So when people cite commodification in non-monetary contexts, essentially what they are doing is appealing to concerns about instrumentalization and about treating things as fungible.

None of this is to say that there are not any monetary issues relating to selective (and, more generally, assisted) reproduction and the above quotation which accused the 'IVF industry' of treating children as commodities was a good example of this: the suggestion being that there is something additionally distasteful about *making money from* these so-called 'designer babies'. Furthermore, there are several practices in the assisted reproduction area in which the permissibility or otherwise of commerce is the main issue. These include the selling of human eggs (and, perhaps less controversially, sperm), 'egg sharing',[12] and paid surrogacy.[13]

---

[12] 'Paid egg sharing involves women or couples . . . who are undergoing fertility treatment, usually by in vitro fertilization (IVF), receiving free or reduced cost treatment in exchange for sharing some pre-agreed proportion (usually half) of their ovulated eggs with a woman or couple . . . who require egg donation for their own treatment.' Martin Johnson, 'The Medical Ethics of Paid Egg Sharing in the UK', *Human Reproduction*, 14 (1999), 1912–18: 1912.

[13] Elizabeth Anderson, for example, claims that the actions of surrogacy brokers (e.g. agencies) are 'morally on a par with baby selling': Elizabeth Anderson, 'Why Commercial Surrogate Motherhood Unethically Commodifies Women and Children: Reply to McLachlan and Swales', *Health Care Analysis*, 8 (2000), 19–26: 25. See also R. Kornegay, 'Is Commercial Surrogacy Baby-Selling?' *Journal of Applied*

5.2 Treating as a (Mere) Means

In their paper on saviour siblings, Boyle and Savulescu suggest that:

The commonest objection . . . is that it is wrong to bring children into existence 'condition-ally'. This objection finds its philosophical foundation in Immanuel Kant's famous dictum, 'Never use people as a means but always treat them as an end'.[14]

And this applies more generally to selective reproduction: that is, the commonest objection is that selection involves instrumentalizing the (future) child, wrongfully treating it 'as a means to an end' (a view which, as I suggested earlier, is sometimes expressed in talk of 'designer babies' or treating children 'as commodities').

In public debates about the ethics of selective reproduction, distinct objections and views often become entangled and an important part of the philosopher's task is to disentangle them so that each can be considered in isolation on its own merits. This is certainly true of many of the things that are said about instrumentalizing (possible, future) children and, in particular, worries about instrumentalization are very often allied with ones about the welfare of the child: the thought being that to instrumentalize a child is *both* wrong in itself *and* wrong because of its consequences for child welfare, since being regarded and treated as a 'mere means' by one's parents can hardly be conducive to well-being. But, while there probably is a causal connection between being instrumentalized and having reduced welfare I shall, for the purposes of this chapter, disregard the welfare dimension of instrumentalization, since welfare was discussed extensively in Chapter 3. And, as far as the welfare of the child is concerned, instrumentalization is just one of a number of causal routes through which selective reproduction (it is alleged) leads to reduced welfare. So, having sidelined welfare issues, we can turn now to evaluate the instrumentalization argument.

The first thing to say is that most straightforward versions of this argument are defective in one of two ways. First, many of them rely on a misunderstanding of 'Kant's famous dictum'. This does not prohibit treating people as means, but rather prohibits treating them *merely* or *solely* as means.[15] As Harris puts it:

We all . . . [treat people as means] perfectly innocuously much of the time. In medical contexts, anyone who receives a blood transfusion has used the blood donor as a means to their own ends[16]

Philosophy, 7 (1990), 45–50: 46; Stephen Wilkinson, *Bodies for Sale: Ethics and Exploitation in the Human Body Trade* (London: Routledge, 2003).

[14] Robert Boyle and Julian Savulescu, 'Ethics of Using Preimplantation Genetic Diagnosis to Select a Stem Cell Donor for an Existing Person', *BMJ* 32 (2001), 1240–3: 1241.

[15] Sheila McClean, *Modern Dilemmas: Choosing Children* (Edinburgh: Capercaillie Books, 2006), 88.

[16] John Harris, *The Value of Life* (London: Routledge, 1985), 143.

The Kantian anti-instrumentalization principle does not prohibit treating people as means. Rather, it asserts that we have a positive obligation always to treat them as ends. So treating people as means may be permissible (according to the principle) so long as we *also* treat them as ends. That this is the meaning of the Kantian principle should be unsurprising, because if it ruled out treating people as means altogether, it would be wildly implausible for the reasons suggested (above) by John Harris. On this Kantian view then there is nothing objectionable about creating a baby (more generally, treating a person) as a 'means to an end' provided that it is also viewed and treated as a human being. So even if it can be established that a particular practice involves treating a baby as a means, this will not prove anything unless it can also be established that it is being treated *merely* as a means.

The second common problem for instrumentalization arguments is that they must show why selective reproduction is *more* objectionable than having a child for other widely accepted reasons (or show that these widely accepted reasons should not themselves be accepted). Some people, for example, have children in order to 'complete a family', to provide a playmate for an existing child, to improve a marriage, to delight prospective grandparents, or to provide an heir. These reasons all, up to a point, involve parents viewing their (possible, future) children as means, which raises the question: are these behaviours are supposed to be condemned along with selective reproduction, since they all appear equally instrumental? If the answer is 'yes', this will make the instrumentalization arguments in general appear less plausible, for they will seem excessively restrictive and to 'prove too much'. This is true a fortiori if we are looking not just at ethics but also at legal prohibition, for surely having a child in order to provide a playmate for an existing child ought not to be banned, even if this is not a particularly good reason for conceiving—but if this is not restricted then why prohibit selective reproduction, if both are equally instrumentalizing?

So instrumentalization arguments against selective reproduction face these two challenges. Can they show that the reproductive practice under discussion involves not just treating children as means, but treating them *only* as means? And can they show that the degree and kind of instrumentalization is worse than that involved in many very normal and widely accepted scenarios?

Another fundamental question or challenge is: to what extent (if at all) are concerns about instrumentalization properly applicable to potential or possible, future persons? Or to put it another way: does the fact that it is wrong to treat existing people purely as means entail that it is wrong to have a purely instrumental attitude to *creating or selecting* possible, future people. This question is reminiscent of the earlier discussion of parental duties and virtues (in Chapter 2). At the end of that, I concluded that even where it can be established that x is a parental duty or virtue, it does not follow from this that x is a duty or virtue that *prospective* parents have, or ought to have. There is, it seems, no reason not to apply this general principle to instrumentalization: specifically, to parents' duties not to instrumentalize their (existing) children. Thus, it does *not* follow from the fact that parents ought not to instrumentalize their (existing) children that prospective parents ought not to instrumentalize their merely possible, future children. However, as I also noted in the earlier discussion of parental duties, prospective parents should be committed to not instrumentalizing their children *once they are born* (or whenever it is that they achieve sufficient moral status, which may be before or after birth depending on one's view of personhood).

As ever, it is helpful to think about these abstract and general points in relation to a particular (in this case, fictitious) example:

Victoria, William, Yasmin

Ten years ago, Victoria and William decided to have to have a fourth child, Yasmin. They used gametic sex selection technology to guarantee a girl. Their main reason for having Yasmin was that the Government, concerned about depopulation, was at that time rewarding people who had a fourth child by exempting them from Income Tax until the child reached the age of 21. In addition, because of independent concerns about a preponderance of males in the population, the Government was offering a cash bonus of £100,000 for parents who sex selected a girl. Victoria and William (who are, and were, quite well-off and therefore used to pay lots of Income Tax) are very clear that they would not have had an additional child at all were it not for the substantial tax incentive but, now that she exists, they love her and treat her very well, and she has had a high-quality life for these past ten years. Similarly, their only reason for sex selecting a girl was financial; they would otherwise have been equally happy with a boy.

Victoria and William's case suggests that it is possible to take an entirely instrumental attitude towards the creation of an additional person, and towards the selection of a (possible, future) person with particular features (in this case, femaleness) without this instrumentalizing attitude spilling over into the way that the created person is treated once she is born. In other words, it is possible entirely to separate one's attitude to the existential question (should a possible, future person be brought into existence?) from one's attitude to the person once she is created. The former can be wholly instrumentalistic while the latter is not. This seems a rather serious and fundamental objection to attempts to argue against selective reproduction on instrumentalization grounds—and to the view that an instrumentalistic attitude prior to conception or implantation must inevitably or necessarily lead to the instrumentalization of the child created.

There are two main ways of trying to save the instrumentalization argument from this objection.

First, it could be claimed that an empirical or indirect version of the argument still holds. In essence, this amounts to saying that, although it is *possible* for people like Victoria and William to have an instrumentalistic attitude to their future children pre-existentially without their having the very same attitude to the children after birth, this is *only a possibility* and, in reality, maintaining the distinction is both difficult and rare. Hence, the majority of parents will not be like Victoria and William, and will not be able to stop their instrumentalistic pre-existential attitudes from spilling over into the lives of their existent children. As suggested in Chapter 2, I am generally rather sceptical about arguments of this type. This is not because they are logically flawed but because, at least in debates about selective reproduction, they tend to be nothing more than speculation. So, while it would be nice to know whether instrumentalistic pre-existential attitudes would spill over, I suspect that no one yet knows whether they would. This is partly because the practices we are talking about are both new and practised only by a few, and partly because ascertaining through empirical social science the extent to which parents are 'instrumentalizing' their children would be a tremendously difficult undertaking. For example, identifying which particular behaviours count as instrumentalizing would be very hard.

The second, more radical response, is to claim that the Victoria and William Case is not as innocent as I suggested: that for them to have an extra child, in effect for money, is wrong *even if their attitude towards and treatment of Yasmin after birth are faultless.* This, however, seems rather implausible, principally because people have children for all sorts of different reasons, many of them self-interested ones. So, if we are going to condemn Victoria and William for having an additional child in order to achieve a selfish personal goal then we will have to condemn very many parents, perhaps even the majority of parents, too. As Katrien Devolder puts it in her article on saviour siblings:

parents have children for all kinds of instrumental reasons. Results of 'The Value of Children Project' (in 1973, before most assisted reproduction techniques were developed), coordinated by James Fawcett, indicated that one of the advantages of childbearing most frequently mentioned is the benefit for the husband–wife relationship. Other frequently mentioned reasons include 'immortality' of the individual, continuity of the family name, and the economic and psychological benefits children provide when their parents become old. This is not considered to be problematic, as long as the child is also valued in its own right.[17]

Conclusions

In general terms, instrumentalization is a valid *type* of moral complaint. We ought not to treat one another merely as means and ought to respect each other as persons and 'as ends'. However, specifying what exactly 'treating someone as an end' amounts to and saying what specific duties flow from this is notoriously controversial and

---

[17] Katrien Devolder, 'Preimplantation HLA Typing: Having Children to Save Our Loved Ones', *Journal of Medical Ethics*, 31 (2005), 582–6: 584.

problematic and this applies a fortiori to debates about selective reproduction, which in addition have their own complications and problems (not least the fact that we are dealing with possible or potential, as well as actual, people).

So how successful are instrumentalization arguments against selective reproduction? My answer is, in essence, *not very*. Instrumentalization arguments face three major challenges and it is not clear that they can meet any of them. First, in order to fall foul of the Kantian anti-instrumentalization principle, parents must treat their children *solely* or *merely* as means. So just pointing out that children (possible or actual) are treated as means, which is all that many instrumentalization claims do, is not enough. Second, the having of children for selfish reasons that are nothing to do with the interests of the (possible, future) child is ubiquitous. So proponents of the instrumentalization argument must establish that selective reproduction is somehow worse (as far as instrumentalization is concerned) than these other accepted practices. Otherwise the argument will be not so much against selective reproduction as against a very wide range of commonly accepted things. Third, I doubt whether there is really anything wrong with *prospective* parents having an entirely instrumentalist attitude to their *possible, future* offspring provided that this attitude does not spill over into the child's life. This is supported by a general principle established in Chapter 2: the fact that *actual* parents owe a particular duty to their child does not entail that *prospective* parents have the very same duty with respect to their (possible, future) child.

5.3 Fungibility

Treating People as Fungible

The second core element of commodification is 'fungiblization', which is to treat as fungible something that is not really fungible or which ought not to be treated as fungible. This section attempts to answer two questions. First, what is it to treat someone (or something) as fungible? Second, what if anything is wrong with treating people as fungible.

Straightforward examples of fungibles include bottles of beer, cans of baked beans, coins, and banknotes (excluding perhaps some 'collectables'), and sacks of sand or wheat. These are fungible because a rational agent would not care which particular object of the kind she possessed, since they are all the same in relevant respects (provided that the appropriate quality standards are met, since it is sensible of course to prefer a fresh beer to one past its sell-by date). 'Object of the kind' can be more or less narrowly specified. Thus, within beer, someone might care whether they get Cobra, Grolsch, or Peroni but then, such fussiness notwithstanding, fungibility will re-emerge at another level, *within* the brand instead, and the rational drinker again should not care (for example) which particular bottle of Cobra she is offered.

So to regard something as a fungible is not to care whether it is swapped for something else of the same kind. Thus, if someone raided my wallet and replaced my banknotes with others to the same value I would not care (leaving aside perhaps concerns about privacy). Or if someone siphoned the petrol from my car and replaced it with the same of amount of the same quality fuel, I would not care. There is then nothing wrong *in general* with treating things as fungible, but there is supposedly a subset of things, including notably persons, which are not fungible and should not be treated as such. In the subsequent discussion, I shall focus just on actual and future persons but note here in passing that other things could be the subject of (supposedly) wrongful fungibilization. Two examples of this are 'heritage' sites and pet animals. For instance, many people would think that there is something wrong with destroying the Ring of Brodgar or Stonehenge and replacing them with copies, even if the copies are excellent and only experts can tell them from the originals. Similarly, 'putting down' one's pet and replacing it with a 'cloned' version would be seen by many as importantly different, both emotionally and morally, from attempting to cure the original pet. These attitudes to pets and to historic sites may or may not ultimately be defensible. I merely note for the present that there is a widespread intuition that persons are not the only entities that should not be treated as fungible.

Turning now to the idea that there is something wrong with treating persons as fungible, let us start by considering some hypothetical cases:

Georgia

Georgia has been in a relationship with Katie for five years; they are sexual partners and have spent a lot of time together. Those who know them well describe their relationship as 'close, intimate, and loving'. For career reasons, Georgia has to move to Edinburgh; Katie has to stay behind in Brighton, 463 miles away. After only two days in Edinburgh, Georgia meets and (as she puts it) 'falls for' Keira and they very quickly embark upon an intimate sexual relationship. Keira is strikingly similar to Katie in many ways; they look alike and have the same sense of humour, same hobbies, same tastes in music, etc. When Georgia's friends ask her if she is missing Katie, she replies, 'Not much. I'm seeing Keira now and she's very much like Katie and gives me everything that Katie did. I'm really very happy.'

Scott and Evan

Scott is a regular user of Elliot's Barbershop. He insists on always having his haircut by a particular stylist called Sebastian. Evan, another Elliot's regular does not care which hairdresser does his hair so long as they do a decent job.

Hayden and Gabriel

Hayden is a regular user of commercial sexual services. He very much likes one woman, called Naomi, and insists on always seeing her. Gabriel uses the same sexual services agency but, unlike Hayden, insists on variety and never sees the same woman more than once.

One thing that these cases collectively bring out is that it is not obvious that treating people as fungible is always wrong.

In the case of Georgia, many of us will feel that there is something wrong with her attitude to Katie: that she has cast her aside and 'replaced' her rather casually in a way that is both morally problematic and makes us doubt whether their supposedly 'close, intimate, and loving' relationship was really as 'loving' as people thought. Of course, cases like this are complicated in reality and it is difficult to screen out other worries, such as ones to do with (for example) Katie's welfare and the breaking of commitments and promises (features that we can only speculate about given the limited case description). Nonetheless, even if these other worries are set to one side, it still seems that there is something to be concerned about and that that something is fungibilization. Georgia seems to be viewing Katie as merely an instantiation of a particular *kind of* person (call this the Type-K person) and it seems that provided that she has the company of a Type-K person then she's content —just as someone who desires a Cobra beer will be happy with a bottle of Cobra, regardless of which particular bottle it is.

Turning now to Scott and Evan, treating people as fungible in this case seems unproblematic and I would suggest that there is (other things being equal) no significant moral difference between Scott's and Evan's hairdressing preferences. It is permissible to have a preferred stylist and equally permissible not to care who cuts one's hair. Sandra Marshall puts it as follows:

> it is not difficult to see how fungibility can be an aspect of a market relation. One well-trained waiter is just as good as another, one paying customer is just as good as another. There may be nothing wrong with this: to treat people as interchangeable within the market activity need not be in any way damaging. Indeed, it is perfectly possible to imagine that with developments in robotics we could do without waiters altogether without loss.[18]

Marshall's remarks remind us that, in many contexts, regarding people as fungible is morally unproblematic. I am not obliged to care which particular hairdresser, or taxi driver, or 'checkout operative' happens to service me—and while personal engagement with people in these roles may well be pleasing and desirable, it is surely not morally required.

---

[18] Sandra Marshall, 'Bodyshopping: The Case of Prostitution', *Journal of Applied Philosophy*, 16 (1999), 139–50: 145.

It is harder to say with any certainty what we should think about Hayden and Gabriel not least because commercialized sex is itself such a complicated and controversial moral issue. Perhaps in the case of Gabriel (the one who likes variety) it is clearer that he is treating these women as fungible, whereas there would be more chance for Hayden to develop a personal relationship with his preferred sex worker. However, that is only speculation and it is by no means certain that any sort of mitigating personal relationship would develop. Anyway, the sex case seems to occupy a rather borderline or contested position. One view of sex is that it is an intrinsically morally neutral activity that can in principle be commercialized in morally unproblematic ways. People who think this may think that the Hayden and Gabriel Case is essentially the same as the Scott and Evan Case—because (as far as intrinsic moral status is concerned) paid hairdressing and paid sex are basically the same. An opposite view is that sex is morally (and perhaps also emotionally and psychologically) special and that this specialness entails inter alia a duty not to regard the other in sexual encounters as fungible.[19] If this latter view of sex is correct then this will tell against many forms of commercialized sex, although not all forms because there are possible versions in which neither party is regarded as fungible (specifically those which rely, in one way or another, on personal engagement with the other). Similarly, this view of sex would count against some sorts of non-commercial 'casual' sex and perhaps also against Georgia's actions. Anyhow, it looks as if treating people as fungible is morally problematic some but not all of the time and I shall return shortly to the question of what differentiates cases in which fungibility is morally problematic from those in which it is not. But first I want to take a look at another closely related notion: uniqueness.

Uniqueness

Radin tells us that 'the idea of fungibility . . . undermines the notion of individual uniqueness'.[20] Perhaps she is right about this but, as we have just seen, the problem with applying this idea to persons is that, in many respects, people do not appear to be terribly unique. At least as occupational role occupants, one customer, or hairdresser, or waiter is much like another. Or, even if we do not want to go that far, it is clear that before applying the idea of uniqueness to persons we need to know much more about the kind of uniqueness that is at stake. That is, the uniqueness thesis stands in need of clarification, so that we can say what it is that we are supposed to be wrongfully disregarding when we treat people as fungible. All of which takes us to

[19] For discussion see e.g., Piers Benn, 'Is Sex Morally Special?' *Journal of Applied Philosophy*, 16 (1999), 235–45.

[20] Margaret Jane Radin, *Contested Commodities* (Cambridge, MA: Harvard University Press, 1996), 120.

the question that I want to pose in this subsection. How exactly is the claim that each individual human being or person is unique to be understood? And ought we to believe it?[21]

There are three main interpretations of this uniqueness thesis. Under the first, it is an empirical claim about diversity. People (in this view) *need not* be, but as a matter of fact *are*, unique—meaning just that they, as a matter of fact, differ from one another considerably (for example, supporters of this view sometimes claim that genetics is on their side, because each human being has its own 'unique' set of genes). There are at least two problems with this version of the uniqueness thesis. First, it is very hard non-arbitrarily to specify what should count as difference or diversity and what should count as sameness or similarity. For this reason, unqualified statements such as 'everyone's basically the same' and 'everyone's a unique individual—we're all different' are hopelessly vague and lacking in content. The second problem, bearing in mind that uniqueness is supposed to be an ethically significant notion, is that this version of the thesis makes people's moral status dependent on accidental and seemingly irrelevant differences between them and others. This seems (at best) odd. To see why, consider hypothetical identical twins who are exactly similar in all respects. These twins are not (*ex hypothesi*) unique: that is, they do not differ from one another significantly. Yet it would be bizarre to claim that they lack the same moral status as other people, or that it is okay to treat them (but not other people) as fungible, or that their moral status would be higher if the other twin died, or if the other twin had never been born. For these reasons, we must reject the first interpretation of the uniqueness thesis.

Under the second interpretation, the uniqueness thesis is supposed to be a necessary truth about persons, something along the following lines: *no two persons share all the same properties*. The problem with this interpretation is that it appears to be either false or *trivially true* (i.e. true, but lacking in content or importance). There is clearly a sense in which two people could have all the same (non-relational) properties. For example, I could (in theory) be replicated, or split into two persons. And surely it would then be at least possible for me and the replicant to have all the same properties, both mentally and physically. At this point, defenders of this version of the uniqueness thesis will have to resort to such things as *spatio-temporal properties*. For example, they might say that the replicant is 41 miles closer to Seattle than I am and therefore different from me in this respect. Furthermore, they might say that we are *necessarily* different, because our spatio-temporal properties must *always* differ (since two different objects cannot occupy the same space at the same time). Hence, it can be argued, even the replicant and I are unique because we are never in exactly the same place at the same time; we never share all the same spatial properties. However, this renders the uniqueness thesis *trivially*

---

[21] Wilkinson, *Bodies for Sale* 49—52.

true. Or at least it is far from clear why this is a morally significant kind of uniqueness, because ants and pebbles on the beach are as unique in this sense as persons.

The third interpretation of the uniqueness thesis says that what is unique about persons is consciousness or 'the self'. It is extraordinarily hard to know what to make of such claims—not least because, as I suggested earlier, it is very hard non-arbitrarily to specify what counts as being different or unique. Is my consciousness or 'self' unique? Well, I can think of no reason to believe that my lived experiences are radically qualitatively different from anyone else's. This is not to deny that people have different experienced lives. As far as I can tell, they do. But this is not going to be enough to ground a non-trivial uniqueness claim, because just as some people have very different experienced lives to mine, others may well have rather similar ones.

Perhaps though this misunderstands the point. Maybe the claim is not so much that my 'self' is *qualitatively different* from other 'selves' but rather that I am unique and irreplaceable in the sense that *there will only ever be one Stephen Wilkinson* (though there are, of course, other people *called* Stephen Wilkinson). There is certainly a sense in which this is true. Unfortunately for the uniqueness thesis though, this has more to do with the way proper names work than with the existence of some more profound philosophical truth about uniqueness. In other words, the reason why 'there will only ever be one Stephen Wilkinson' is true is just that 'Stephen Wilkinson' is being used as a proper name. Proper names are what Saul Kripke famously calls *rigid designators*.[22] This means that they pick out the very same individual in all possible worlds and are to be contrasted with *definite descriptions* such as 'Stoke-on-Trent's wittiest bioethicist' which though it may (or may not) designate Stephen Wilkinson in the actual world, can designate other individuals in other possible worlds. So uniqueness of this sort seems to be just a function of naming which makes the uniqueness thesis look ethically insignificant. For I may as well call my toaster 'Lucy' and claim that 'there will only ever be one Lucy' and that Lucy is irreplaceable and unique. This will be true so long as Lucy is understood as a proper name and in spite of the fact that, in practical terms, Lucy is highly replaceable.

What can we conclude from all this? There appear to be two fundamental problems with using uniqueness in ethical arguments. The first is that it is hard to make sense of the claim that persons are unique. Depending on how it is interpreted it seems to be false, or trivially true, or morally insignificant. And (of course) if persons are not really unique in any interesting sense then it is not clear why we are obliged to regard them as unique. Indeed, doing so seems irrational. The second problem is that there are clearly lots of contexts in which treating people as fungible is ethically unproblematic. The most clear-cut cases are perhaps ones where someone is filling a particular social or economic role: e.g. driver, teacher, waiter. Here, at least in uncomplicated cases, it

---

[22] Saul Kripke, *Naming and Necessity* (Oxford: Blackwell, 1980).

is hard to see why we should not regard individual role occupants as replaceable and non-unique, at least qua role occupant. These considerations suggest that we should regard appeals to uniqueness with a fair degree of scepticism.

Special Relationships

So appeals to the (alleged) uniqueness of persons cannot justify moral claims about fungibilization. There may, however, be special contexts in which the claim that we ought to treat people as non-fungible makes some sense and should be accorded some weight. The Georgia Case discussed earlier was, I suggested, an example of this. Similarly, not-treating-as-fungible seems to be an important part of personal friendship. Part of B's being A's friend is that A cares that the particular person with whom she is talking, or going out to dinner with, or going on holiday with is B, and not merely *someone like* B. In other words, viewing B as replaceable or substitutable is incompatible with true friendship. Perhaps this is because, in the case of friendships, something approaching a meaningful uniqueness claim is plausible, for instance, because of friends' shared histories. Or perhaps the demand for non-fungibility can be explained in terms of other things such as the idea of loyalty, or the fact that (given certain expectations) to treat a friend as fungible (for example, to 'swap' her for another on trivial grounds) would be immensely harmful. Whatever the explanation, it does seem that the idea of treating persons as non-fungible has more applicability in personal relationships than in other contexts. If this is right (and I have only suggested rather than argued for it here) then perhaps the idea of fungibilization will have more relevance to some areas of bioethics than to others. Thus, in the sale of body parts debate, where close personal relationships between vendors and recipients are unlikely, perhaps it has little relevance; while, in family and reproductive ethics, when considering the relationships between parents and children, concerns about fungibility may have more force. For it seems plausible that parents should regard and treat their offspring as non-fungible; they should, rather obviously, be unwilling to 'swap' their child for another with similar characteristics and should grieve over the death of a child even if another similar one comes along later.

A more subtle application of this idea arose in a widely publicized sex selection case, that of Alan and Louise Masterton (described at the start of Chapter 1). They had four sons and one daughter, Nicole, who died in a bonfire incident.[23] The Mastertons wanted to use PGD to sex select another daughter. Their request was turned down by the HFEA whose rules only permitted sex selection in order to avoid sex-linked genetic disorders (such as haemophilia, muscular dystrophy, and cystic fibrosis). As

[23] BBC News, *Couple Fight for Baby Girl*, 4 Oct. 2000, <http://news.bbc.co.uk/1/hi/scotland/955251.stm> (last accessed: Sunday, 12 Apr. 2009).

well as the usual concerns about sex selection, the Masterton Case provoked another kind of criticism: that they might be trying to *replace* Nicole with another similar child and that this would be wrong because it would involve treating both Nicole and the new daughter as interchangeable or replicable. For example, in a BBC News Online Scotland webcast, the Mastertons were asked:

If you don't want a daughter to replace your lost daughter, why do you want one?[24]

The accusation of wanting to replace Nicole is one that was denied by the Mastertons and, as far as I know, they were right to do so. Nonetheless, it is worth noting that claims and counterclaims about one child replacing another were prominent in the media debate about this case. This suggests that concerns about fungibilization are in wide circulation, although they are rarely of course *called* this.

Parents, Prospective Parents, and Fungibility

I would grant then that reasonable concerns about treating-as-fungible arise in the context of parenting (although, as ever, giving an account of which particular behaviours count as treating-as-fungible and why will be tricky). However, as has already been noted on several occasions, the obligations of actual and prospective parents may differ: the latter do not necessarily have all the duties that the former have. So it does not follow from the fact that parents should not treat their children as fungible that *prospective* parents have an obligation to treat their *possible* children as non-fungible (if indeed we can make sense of this).

In this subsection then I shall attempt to say, first, what an obligation to treat one's possible children as non-fungible would amount to and, second, whether such an obligation exists.

The idea that people ought not to view their possible future children as fungible is quite hard to make sense of because it is not as if prospective parents (at least in standard embryo selection cases) are in a position to be well acquainted with merely possible future individuals. Perhaps the best interpretation is as follows: to treat one's possible future children as fungible is not to care which particular possible individual comes into existence, provided that it has a certain range of desired characteristics. So imagine a case in which prospective parents are choosing between five different embryos and in which all of the embryos meet the parents' criteria (for example, none has a serious genetics disorder). In this case, to treat as fungible would mean not caring which one was implanted, to believe that they are, for all practical purposes, interchangeable.

---

[24] BBC News, *The Mastertons Webcast: Transcript*, 23 Oct. 2000, <http://news.bbc.co.uk/1/hi/scotland/981703.stm> (last accessed: Sunday, 12 Apr. 2009).

The fundamental question here is: how can concerns about fungibilization be taken from the parenting context and applied to prospective parents, especially those facing pre-existential selection decisions, such as the decision about which embryo to implant? There seem to be two plausible answers to this and, whichever one we choose, it looks as if concerns about fungibilization will not tell against selective reproduction. The first answer is that it is not possible to apply the idea of fungibilization to merely possible future children because it is an idea that only makes sense in cases where one person is acquainted with a determinate other. The moral wrong of fungibilization comprises viewing as replaceable someone who you ought to treat as irreplaceable. But it is hard to see how or why one can view as irreplaceable an other about which one knows almost nothing. And this applies a fortiori when the other is a merely possible person, someone who does not presently exist.

The second answer is that fungibilization does apply to pre-existential selection decisions in the following way. To view a set of possible future persons as fungible is not to care which one is created provided that it has a sufficient number of your desired characteristics (with the set of desired characteristics varying, perhaps markedly, from prospective parent to prospective parent). This though is not something that tells against selective reproduction. For the fungibilization problem, if there is one, arises not in *selective* reproduction but in cases where the prospective parents *do not care* which embryo is implanted and regard the embryos as interchangeable. So to have an attitude of non-fungibility would be to be *ultra-selective*, to desire the creation not just of a child with certain characteristics, but the creation of a particular determinate (possible, future) person.

Now it seems that viewing unimplanted embryos as fungible is probably sensible, at least insofar as they all meet the prospective parents' selection criteria (which may be quite basic, such as not having serious genetic disorders, or may be more demanding). Indeed, the idea of prospective parents preferring one of a set of relevantly similar embryos is rather bizarre and it is hard to think of any reason why a rational person could have such a preference. If that is right, then something like the first answer is correct: moral concerns about fungibilization are inapplicable to merely possible future persons, such as unimplanted embryos (depending on what one thinks of their moral status). If, however, I am wrong, then something like the second answer holds and fungibilization *does* apply to pre-existential selection decisions. But, as we have just seen, if it does apply, then it fails to count against selective reproduction: for treating (for example) unimplanted embryos as fungible means *not caring which one is implanted*, which is the opposite of selective reproduction. So either way, concerns about fungibilization (although perhaps valid in some contexts, such as parenting and personal friendship) are incapable of supporting an ethical objection to selective reproduction.

5.4 Summary and Conclusions

The prospect of using selective reproduction not in order to give higher levels of health and welfare to the child created, but rather to benefit other existing people raises several ethical questions; these have been the subject of this and the preceding chapter.

In this chapter, I examined the idea that saviour siblings, and indeed all children created via selective reproduction, might be treated as commodities. This examination meant, among other things, analysing the concept of commodification and two of its components, instrumentalization and fungibilization, and asking how these concepts apply to embryo selection cases. My conclusion is that these claims about children being treated as commodities are generally misleading and unjustified. On the best available understandings of 'commodity' and 'commodification', embryo selection does not necessarily involve treating children as commodities, nor is there much reason to believe that there is a contingent connection between embryo selection and the commodification of children. Embryo selection may well involve the instrumentalization of the embryos themselves, but this should not be troubling for people who do not think that embryos are persons or 'ends-in-themselves'.

6

Eugenics and the
Expressivist Argument

in activist literature, genetics becomes a coherent and consistent plot to eliminate
disabled people.[1]

At present, selection technologies, such as preimplantation genetic diagnosis (and
similarly prenatal screening and testing accompanied by selective termination), are
used primarily to avoid the birth of children with genetic disorders or, to put it
more positively, to help parents have healthy children. Furthermore, this view that
the proper purpose of PGD (and selective reproduction generally) is to avoid genetic
disorders is not merely part of established ethics and practice but (in the UK at least)
enforced by the regulator. For example, the HFEA's *Code of Practice* says that:

The use of PGD should be considered only where there is a significant risk of a serious genetic
condition being present in the embryo.[2]

In addition, the Human Fertilisation and Embryology Act 2008 now lays down a
restrictive list of reasons for which embryo testing may be carried out under licence,
the main one for our purposes being:

in a case where there is a particular risk that the embryo may have any gene, chromosome
or mitochondrion abnormality, establishing whether it has that abnormality or any other
gene, chromosome or mitochondrion abnormality[3]

Other permissible grounds under this legislation include saviour sibling selection
(discussed in Chapter 4) and testing to check biological parenthood (in cases where
uncertainty has arisen).[4]

---

[1] Tom Shakespeare, *Disability Rights and Wrongs* (London: Routledge, 2006), 85–6.
[2] Human Fertilisation and Embryology Authority (HFEA), *Code of Practice* (7th edn., 2007), G.12.3.2.
[3] Human Fertilisation and Embryology Act 2008, Section 14(4).
[4] Human Fertilisation and Embryology Act 2008, Schedule 2 (Activities that may be Licensed under
the 1990 Act), Section 3.

Presumably, the main rationale for this position is child welfare, the thought being that children with serious genetic disorders generally have worse lives than those without. There is also, I imagine, a 'cost of care' rationale relating both to the parents' emotional, financial, and practical costs and to the material costs to the National Health Service. In previous chapters, I discussed and cast some doubt upon these rationales and so I will say little more about them here. Instead, in this and the next chapter, I shall address two further issues. One is whether using PGD to avoid serious genetic conditions is morally preferable to using it for other purposes, such as the selection of (possible, future) children with 'enhanced' features. This is the main concern of Chapter 7. A second is: are there any moral arguments that count specifically *against* using PGD to reduce the prevalence of disease and disability? As we shall see, there are several such arguments and evaluating them is the main aim of this chapter. In general terms, the arguments divide into two categories. First, there is the Eugenics Argument. In its direct form, the Eugenics Argument says that using PGD to select out disability and/or disease is an instance of eugenics and that since (it is assumed) eugenics is wrong then so is this use of PGD. There are also several *indirect* versions of the Eugenics Argument. One of these is the claim that, although using PGD may not itself be eugenic, it is likely to lead down the proverbial slippery slope to other attitudes and practices that are. Second, there is the Expressivist Argument. This says that striving to avoid the births of children with disabilities or diseases (using PGD and the like) expresses an erroneous and morally unacceptable attitude towards such people.

6.1 What Is Eugenics?

The basic structure of the Direct Eugenics Argument is as follows.

1. Using PGD (and other selection techniques) to select out disability and/or disease is a case of eugenics.
2. Eugenics is morally wrong.
3. *Therefore*: using PGD (and similar techniques) to select out disability and/or disease is morally wrong.

This argument is logically valid: that is, (1) and (2) do jointly entail (3). However, questions can be raised about both of the premises: specifically, is PGD an instance of eugenics and is eugenics (always) morally wrong? Not surprisingly, both of these questions depend on what we mean by the word 'eugenics' and, as we shall come to see, this is a contested issue with different sides in the debate using the term rather differently. In this and the following few sections, I shall attempt to clarify the meaning, or meanings, of 'eugenics'. In this section, I shall look at what *descriptive* accounts of eugenics are available before, in 6.2, moving on to address the question of whether eugenics is necessarily wrong and the more complicated question of how different views of the term's *moral* force relate to the different descriptive accounts of eugenics.

Although these questions are abstract and philosophical they do nonetheless have considerable practical importance. The following quotation from Diane Paul shows why:

> As a historian of modern genetics, I am often asked whether human genetics represents disguised, or incipient, or possibly a new kind of eugenics. Those who pose the questions may not be certain how to define eugenics, but they are almost always convinced that it is a bad thing, one which should be prevented. Indeed, fear of a eugenics revival appears to be a principal anxiety aroused by the Human Genome Project (HGP), in Europe as well as the United States ... While almost everyone agrees that eugenics is objectionable, there is no consensus on what it actually is. Indeed, one can be opposed to eugenics, and for almost anything. As Sir Isaiah Berlin remarked about the protean uses of 'freedom', its meaning 'is so porous that there is little interpretation that it seems able to resist'. To denounce eugenics is to signal that one is socially concerned, morally sensitive (and if a geneticist, perhaps worthy of public trust). But it does not predict one's stance on any particular reproductive issue.[5]

So we are in a situation where eugenics is commonly cited as a major concern about, and objection to, contemporary genetic and reproductive science, but in which there is also considerable confusion and disagreement about what exactly 'eugenics' means. This is a regrettable state of affairs, and the stakes are high, since contemporary genetic and reproductive science is capable of delivering substantial benefits to humankind. So if we allow its development to be held back by unsound objections, based around vague worries about 'eugenics', unnecessary and unjustified harm may be inflicted on those who stand to benefit from these new technologies. On the other hand, if there really are sound eugenics arguments in play then we need these to be clearly and unambiguously articulated. Only then will we know which technologies to ban or restrictively regulate, and understand properly the reasons for doing so. This is vital if we are to avoid erroneously permitting or encouraging dangerous or unethical eugenic practices. So, either way, we need a good grasp of the concept of eugenics.

A Working Definition of 'Eugenics'

The term 'eugenics' dates back to 1883, when it was coined by Francis Galton.[6] Galton defines 'eugenics' as the study of 'the conditions under which men of a high type

---

[5] Diane Paul, 'Is Human Genetics Disguised Eugenics?' in Michael Ruse and David Hull (eds.), *Biology and Philosophy* (Oxford: Oxford University Press, 1998), 536–49: 536–7.

[6] Mary Coutts and Pat McCarrick, 'Eugenics', *Kennedy Institute of Ethics Journal*, 5 (1995), 163–78: 163; *Oxford English Dictionary* (<www.oed.com>).

are produced' and as 'the science which deals with all influences that improve the inborn qualities of a race'.[7] Eugenics though is not merely a field of study and, as Paul notes, 'it is less often identified as a science than as a social movement or policy, as in Bertrand Russell's definition: "the attempt to improve the biological character of a breed by deliberate methods adopted to that end" '.[8] Other similar definitions include those found in the *Oxford English Dictionary*, which defines 'eugenic' as 'pertaining or adapted to the production of fine offspring, *esp.* in the human race', and in the *Routledge Encyclopaedia of Philosophy* which defines 'eugenics' as 'the attempt to improve the human gene pool'.[9] This last definition is particularly relevant for our present purposes, since my primary concern is with genetics and reproductive technologies, and it will therefore be adopted as my initial definition. However, this is only a *working* definition and much more will need to be said about what eugenics is and about the different possible kinds of eugenics that there are.

Ends, Means, and the Diversity of Eugenic Practices

Eugenics can take many forms and a wide variety of different means can be, and have been, deployed in order to achieve the eugenic end of 'improving the gene pool'. Thus, at one extreme (the most brutal end of the scale) eugenic ends can be pursued via compulsory sterilization programmes and the killing of those deemed 'unfit'; while, at the other, relatively innocuous attempts to persuade the middle classes to have more children have been used to achieve similar ends. Likewise, eugenic ideologies have enjoyed support from those across the political spectrum with Nazis but also many liberals and progressives supporting versions of eugenics.[10] So when assessing the moral standing of eugenics it is vitally important to separate out questions about the morality of pursing eugenic ends from those about whether this or that *means* of achieving them is acceptable. Since my main concern here is whether eugenics is intrinsically wrong, rather than with the moral standing of particular ways of implementing eugenics, I shall for the rest of the chapter focus solely on the putative wrongness of pursuing eugenic *ends* and will leave to one side questions about means. A very wide range of actions and policies could be used to further eugenic ends and it would be hopelessly overambitious to try to say something informative about each of these. After all, any of the following could be

[7] *Oxford English Dictionary* (<www.oed.com>); Francis Galton, *Essays in Eugenics* (Honolulu: University Press of the Pacific, 1909), 35.

[8] Paul, 'Is Human Genetics Disguised Eugenics?', 537.

[9] Ruth Chadwick, 'Genetics and Ethics', in Edward Craig (ed.), The *Routledge Encyclopaedia of Philosophy* (London: Routledge, 1998).

[10] Ann Kerr and Tom Shakespeare, *Genetic Politics: From Eugenics to Genome* (Cheltenham: New Clarion Press, 2002).

used eugenically and it goes without saying that each raises very different ethical concerns and issues:

- Gamete Selection
- Embryo Selection
- Selective Abortion
- Encouraged, Voluntary Sterilization of Selected Adults
- Compulsory, Coerced Sterilization of Selected Adults
- Selective Infanticide
- Selective Killing of Adults.

I do, however, want to say something about two distinctions that are often drawn within eugenics: the distinction between authoritarian and liberal or laissez-faire eugenics, and the distinction between positive and negative eugenics.

Authoritarian Eugenics

The distinction between what have been termed 'authoritarian' and 'laissez-faire' eugenics is really a continuum, with some eugenic policies and practices being more or less permissive (and more or less authoritarian) than others. At the authoritarian end of the range sit Nazi eugenics, compulsory sterilization programmes, and the like. These are to be contrasted with what Kitcher calls laissez-faire eugenics:

The brutal compulsion of the Nazi eugenics program prompted an important change in postwar efforts to apply genetic knowledge. Everyone is now to be her (or his) own eugenicist, taking advantage of the available genetic tests to make the reproductive decisions she (he) thinks correct. If genetic counselling ... is a form of eugenics, then it is surely *laissez-faire* eugenics.[11]

Similarly, at the permissive extreme, sits what Nozick terms the 'genetic supermarket', in which children are produced according to 'the individual specifications (within certain moral limits) of prospective parents': a social set-up which, for Nozick, 'has the great virtue that it involves no centralized decision fixing the future of human type(s)'.[12]

Laissez-faire eugenics then occurs when private individuals practice eugenics with no, or minimal, State involvement. Authoritarian eugenics is a little harder to

---

[11] Philip Kitcher, *The Lives to Come: The Genetic Revolution and Human Possibilities* (London: Penguin, 1996), 196.

[12] Robert Nozick, *Anarchy, State, and Utopia* (Oxford: Blackwell, 1974), 315.

characterize. Its main defining feature is that prospective parents are *compelled* to behave eugenically and are *forced* to reproduce, or to refrain from reproducing, or to reproduce in a particular way. However, more needs to be said, first, about who or what is doing the forcing and, second, about what counts as forcing.

Regarding the first of these, the main question is: does the compulsion have to come from the State in order for it to constitute authoritarian eugenics? Normally, what people have in mind when they talk about authoritarian eugenics is State compulsion. However, there seems to be no reason in principle to exclude other sources of authoritarianism, such as organized religion, families, or indeed any group of eugenics enthusiasts that wants to force others to act in accordance with its beliefs. Thus we might distinguish, within authoritarian eugenics, between State eugenics, Church eugenics, transhumanist eugenics, etc.

The second question (what counts as forcing?) is more difficult because it depends on a philosophically troublesome distinction between those actions which are (fully, truly) voluntary and those which are not, and on the similarly tricky concept of coercion. This is not the place to give a full account of these concepts; nonetheless, a rough outline is called for.

A practice is authoritarian eugenics only if *either* (a) prospective reproducers are physically forced to reproduce, or prevented from reproducing, in certain ways (for example, a woman might be kidnapped and forcibly inseminated or sterilized, or a pregnant woman might be subjected to prenatal testing and selective termination without her consent) *or* (b) prospective reproducers are allowed to decide for themselves whether or not to reproduce in particular ways, but their decisions are somehow *coerced*. In what follows, my main concern is with (b). This is partly because (a) is relatively straightforward (and obviously wrong, at least in the contexts that concern me here) and partly because, more often than not, it is concerns about relatively subtle forms of involuntariness and pressure that figure in contemporary debates about genetic and reproductive technologies, not worries about outright physical force. Thus, Turnbull, for example, speaks of 'eugenic pressure' which 'starts very humbly, with genetic labelling', 'occurs through language and context', and 'appears in the guise of medical beneficence'.[13]

As Greene rightly points out, 'unfortunately, confusion over what the term "coercion" stands for has not stopped people from using it'.[14] Coercion is a hugely

---

[13] D. Turnbull, 'Genetic Counselling: Ethical Mediation of Eugenic Futures', *Futures*, 32 (2000), 853–65: 856.
[14] J. Greene, 'Coercion: Description or Evaluation', *International Journal of Applied Philosophy*, 10 (1996), 7–16: 7.

complicated and interesting moral concept and what I say here does not do justice to that complexity. A fuller, but by no means comprehensive, account can be found in my *Bodies for Sale*, and a *much* fuller account is Alan Wertheimer's *Coercion*.[15] For now, though, I am going to offer a comparatively simple account of at least the more straightforward cases of coercion, which is that A coerces B into X (some action or omission) if A threatens to make B worse off if B does not do X. Thus, coercive *threats* are contrasted with incentivizing *offers*, cases in which A offers to make B better off if B does do X. One of the main complicating factors when applying the idea of coercion is that it is sometimes hard to tell whether a proposal is an offer or a threat. Nozick famously discusses a case in which someone in a boat could easily save a drowning man but asks him to pay for being rescued.[16] Is this threat or an offer? In one sense, the sailor is offering to make the drowning man better off: he would be better off paying and not drowning, than not paying and drowning. But then given that there is an (predictive or moral) expectation that rescue should be freely provided in such circumstances, there is also a sense in which the sailor is *threatening not to* save him, proposing to make him worse off—worse off, that is, than he ought to be or than he could reasonably expect to be. If the threat-interpretation of this case is correct then the drowning man is being coerced into paying. If not, then he is merely being offered a welcome additional option (being saved for a fee). Anyway, as I have said, I would not be going into any more detail about the idea of coercion here, and I mention this case merely to flag up the fact that applying the idea, and in particular distinguishing between threats and offers, can be difficult.

Going back to eugenics and selective reproduction, one interesting application of the idea of coercion (specifically 'subtle' or 'structural' coercion) relates to the levels of service offered to people with disabilities and their carers. During research interviews in 2005, one participant said to me:

> I've sometimes referred to eugenics as an emergent property. It's not one element that's eugenic, but it's the conglomeration of unfree choices in a prejudiced environment in a world that doesn't support disability, it could be said to be emergent eugenics.[17]

This argument can be reconstructed along the following lines. Prospective parents (through prenatal testing and, to a lesser extent, PGD) are offered the choice of whether to have a disabled child or not. This decision could *in principle* be voluntary. However, prospective parents are, more often than not, on the receiving end of a

---

[15] Alan Wertheimer, *Coercion* (Princeton: Princeton University Press, 1987); Stephen Wilkinson, *Bodies for Sale: Ethics and Exploitation in the Human Body Trade* (London: Routledge, 2003).

[16] Robert Nozick, 'Coercion', in Sidney Morgenbesser, Patrick Suppes, and Morton White (eds.), *Philosophy, Science and Method: Essays in Honour of Ernest Nagel* (New York: St Martin's Press, 1969), 440–72: 449, emphasis added.

[17] Anon., *Expert Interview* (2005).

systemic form of coercion. It works like this. The State (or society generally) ought to provide a certain level of support to people with disabilities and their carers. However, it in fact provides much less support than this and furthermore this position is unlikely to change in the foreseeable future. The State is then in effect coercing people into refraining from having children with disabilities by threatening them with poverty and social disadvantage—poverty and disadvantage that it has a moral responsibility to ameliorate, and for which it is therefore at least partly responsible. I have a great deal of sympathy with this form of argument, although whether it in fact applies to our present society is an open question that depends on two questions that I am unable to answer here. First, there is the thorny *political* question of what exactly (for example, in terms of welfare benefits and services) the State owes to its disabled citizens and their carers. Second, there is the equally tricky *empirical* question of whether this posited standard of care (whatever it is) is in fact met by the State's services.

So much for the *definition* of coercion and of authoritarian eugenics. I want now to say something about its *significance* to debates about selective reproduction. There are two main reasons for engaging with the distinction between authoritarian and laissez-faire (or liberal) eugenics. The first is simply that the distinction is commonly used in the literature and therefore a properly contextualized account of eugenics requires an exposition of it. The second is that arguably many concerns about eugenics are really about *authoritarian* eugenics and so it is important to emphasize that eugenics is not *necessarily* authoritarian or otherwise coercive. As Caplan et al. tell us, while it is admittedly:

morally objectionable for governments or institutions or any third party to compel or coerce anyone's reproductive behaviour . . . the goals of obtaining perfection, avoiding disease, or pursuing health with respect to individuals *need not involve coercion or force*.[18]

In other words, it is possible for people to pursue 'individual eugenic goals' without being on the receiving end of coercion; individuals can do such things voluntarily. Thus, in this respect at least, eugenics may be morally unproblematic.

So when it comes to an assessment of eugenics' moral status we must be careful not to assume that it will be authoritarian. For, as Caplan et al. note, it is perfectly possible to support broadly eugenic aims while eschewing coercion and authoritarianism—just as one might support the goal of improved public health without thinking (for example) that the State has a right to control people's eating or exercise habits.

Positive and Negative Eugenics

Academic work on eugenics often utilizes a distinction between positive and negative eugenics. Much of this work assumes that the distinction is morally significant and

[18] A. Caplan, G. McGee, and D. Magnus, 'What Is Immoral about Eugenics?' *BMJ* 319 (1999), 1284, my italics.

that positive eugenics is worse than negative eugenics (at least, other things being equal). Despite its pervasiveness and supposed importance, however, the nature of the positive–negative distinction remains unclear and the terms 'negative' and 'positive' are used in several different ways. The following characterizations of the positive–negative distinction are fairly typical of those found in the ethics literature:[19]

'positive eugenics' . . . aims to increase desirable traits rather than reduce undesirable ones[20]

positive eugenics attempts to increase the number of favorable or desirable genes in the human gene pool, while negative eugenics attempts to reduce the number of undesirable or harmful genes, e.g., genes that cause genetic diseases.[21]

'Negative eugenics' refers to the elimination of diseases or defects, whereas 'positive eugenics' refers to the enhancement of traits.[22]

Negative eugenics is a systematic effort to minimize the transmission of genes that are considered deleterious, in contrast to positive eugenics, which aims to maximize the transmission of desirable genes.[23]

The aim of negative eugenics is disease prevention and health promotion, not enhancement of normal capacities.[24]

On these definitions, most selective reproduction presently practised in the UK at the moment is *negative* eugenics (if it is eugenics at all) since its aim is to 'screen out' conditions such as beta thalassaemia, cystic fibrosis, Duchenne muscular dystrophy, and Huntington's disease.[25] If, however, embryo selection could be used instead to create children with dispositions to be exceptionally athletic, or attractive, or intelligent, then this would be *positive* eugenics (on the assumption that these features are desirable).

Characterizing the positive–negative distinction may, however, be less straightforward than it at first appears. For in most, maybe even all, cases the same eugenic practice can be described as both 'negative' and 'positive'. This arises most obviously in cases where the characteristic in question is a matter of degree, such as athleticism,

[19] R. Barnett, 'Keywords in the History of Medicine: Eugenics,' *The Lancet*, 363 (2004), 1742; Ruth Chadwick, *Genetics and Ethics*; Ruth Chadwick et al., 'Genetic Screening and Ethics: European Perspectives', *Journal of Medicine and Philosophy*, 23 (1998), 255–73: 268; Rachel Iredale, 'Eugenics and its Relevance to Contemporary Health Care', *Nursing Ethics*, 7 (2000), 205–41: 207; Tom Shakespeare, 'Choices and Rights: Eugenics, Genetics, and Disability Equality', *Disability and Society*, 13 (1998), 665–81: 668.

[20] Diane Paul, 'Eugenic Anxieties, Social Realities, and Political Choices', *Social Research*, 59 (1992), 663.

[21] David Resnik, 'The Moral Significance of the Therapy–Enhancement Distinction in Human Genetics', *Cambridge Quarterly of Healthcare Ethics*, 9 (2000), 365–77: 373.

[22] Jean Chambers, 'Women's Right to Choose Rationally', *Cambridge Quarterly of Healthcare Ethics*, 12 (2003), 418–28: 418.

[23] B. Elger and T. Harding, 'Huntingdon's Disease: Do Future Physicians and Lawyers Think Eugenically?' *Clinical Genetics*, 64 (2003), 327–38: 335.

[24] Walter Glannon, 'Genes, Embryos, and Future People', *Bioethics*, 12 (1998), 187–211: 197.

[25] HFEA, *HFEA Licenses PGD for Inherited Colon Cancer (Press Release)* (1 Nov. 2004), <www.hfea.gov.uk> (last accessed: Monday, 13 Apr. 2009).

attractiveness, or intelligence. For, in such cases, the negative feature is just the absence of the positive feature (and vice versa). So, for example, selecting *out* low(er) intelligence ('negative eugenics') might be the same practice as selecting *in* high(er) intelligence ('positive eugenics'). Moreover, this does not apply only to cases in which the desirable trait is a matter of degree. Take, for example, a single gene disorder, such as cystic fibrosis, which is caused by a malfunctioning gene on chromosome 7.[26] Although the symptoms of cystic fibrosis can vary in their severity, whether someone has the condition or not is not itself a matter of degree. Nonetheless, the same problem applies. For while we would normally say that we were selecting *against* cystic fibrosis, and *against* this malfunctioning gene (both negative features), there appear to be no reasons for not also saying that we are selecting *in favour of* copies of chromosome 7 with fully functioning genes and *in favour of* future persons with fully functioning respiratory systems (both positive features). So if we tried to make sense of the positive–negative distinction solely in terms of 'selecting out the bad' vs 'selecting in the good', it would turn out to have little or no determinate meaning, for just about anything could count as positive or as negative if suitably described.

I shall return to this in the next chapter, as part of my discussion of the distinction between enhancement and disease-avoidance. For it seems to me, for reasons that will emerge later, that that distinction has a lot in common with the positive–negative eugenics distinction.

6.2   The Moral Standing of Eugenics

These days, it is rare to hear people say positive things about eugenics and general anti-eugenics statements are often treated as obvious and uncontroversial truths that we should all sign up to. For instance, the *Charter of Fundamental Rights of the European Union* advocates:

the prohibition of eugenic practices, in particular those aiming at the selection of persons.[27]

But ought we to *define* 'eugenics' such that being eugenic is always a wrong-making, or morally bad, property of actions or policies? Is 'eugenics' what Bernard Williams terms a *thick moral concept*—one 'such as treachery and promise and brutality and courage, which seem to express a union of fact and value'.[28]

---

[26] Richard Twyman, 'Cystic Fibrosis', Wellcome Trust website, 30 July 2003, <www.wellcome. ac.uk> (last accessed: Monday, 13 Apr. 2009).

[27] *Charter of Fundamental Rights of the European Union* (2000/C 364/01), Article 3 ('Right to the Integrity of the Person').

[28] Bernard Williams, *Ethics and the Limits of Philosophy* (London: Fontana, 1985), 129.

The main reason for thinking of 'eugenics' as a negative moral term is that most people who use it in contemporary debates do so to express condemnation, and it is rare for people who support embryo selection to describe it as 'eugenic'. During 2005, I conducted some expert interviews with (among others) UK-based academics, campaigners, and health professionals. One of my aims was to discover what key participants in debates about reproductive ethics thought about the term 'eugenics'. Not surprisingly, the most enthusiastic users of 'eugenics' were those campaigners who are generally critical of reproductive and selection technologies:

We use it ['eugenics'] whenever we can and we won't be distracted or diverted into using any other word, not least because it's not a popular word. It's not a word that people like to hear; it's got a lot of nasty connotations. So we're not going to cop out and try to find a more palatable word.[29]

While, on the other side, those with 'pro-choice' views generally avoid the word:

I almost think we should ban the term ['eugenics']. If you just say 'eugenic' nobody knows what you mean. We should say what it is about the statement or the policies that we object to, and examine that. It's like saying 'you're a fascist!' It's an unexamined assertion that's used for rhetorical effect, so it just seems lazy to me. It's not a coherent or well-specified critique. And it's very insulting to doctors[30]

I think on any occasion when the issue might be raised there would probably be a desire to avoid using it because of its pejorative connotations. It suggests Nazis before we even start to consider the issues.[31]

So nearly everyone agrees that 'eugenics' is hugely emotive and negative. As Raanon Gillon puts it, 'Eugenics is widely regarded as a dirty word'.[32] But while, for some, this is a reason to avoid it, for others, this makes the term 'eugenics' a good way of getting their message across. A useful comparator here is the expression 'unborn child'. Many people with 'pro-life' views use this to draw attention to (putative) similarities between foetuses and children (or indeed to express the view that foetuses *are* children); while those with 'pro-choice' views generally avoid this expression since they have the opposite aims and views. The same goes for 'eugenics'. Those hostile to embryo selection often use 'eugenics' to draw attention to (putative) similarities between practices, such as PGD, and historical atrocities associated with eugenics movements of the past; while those who support PGD generally avoid the word 'eugenics' in order to avoid drawing attention to these (putative) similarities, or because they do not think that there are any such similarities.

---

[29] Anonymous expert interview with the author (2005).
[30] Anonymous expert interview with the author (2005).
[31] Anonymous expert interview with the author (2005).
[32] Raanon Gillon, 'Eugenics, Contraception, Abortion and Ethics', *Journal of Medical Ethics*, 24 (1998), 219.

One implication of all this is that defining 'eugenics' is itself complex and controversial. In particular, the working definition suggested at the outset was largely descriptive, 'the attempt to improve the human gene pool', and so how can this be squared with the view that 'eugenics' is a negative moral term?

One option is to treat 'eugenics' as a moral term by defining it as '*wrongfully* attempting to improve the human gene pool'; on this view, permissible attempts to 'improve the gene pool' do not count as eugenic. Alternatively, we could insist that 'eugenics' be descriptively defined and therefore that there is at least a theoretical distinction, within eugenics, between permissible and wrongful eugenics. On this latter view, we could still take account of the point made earlier about linguistic politics, about 'eugenics' being a 'dirty word', and there still being good reasons not to *use* it except in cases of wrongful eugenics, but at least in principle permissible eugenics would be a possibility.

I cannot hope to resolve fully the definitional issue at this point. Indeed, it probably cannot be resolved prior to an assessment of the substantive moral arguments against eugenics (descriptively defined).[33] This then is my next task: to look at some attempts to show that 'improving the human gene pool' is wrong, or at least morally problematic. If these attempts are successful then we will have reason to view all eugenics with suspicion (even if 'eugenics' is descriptively defined) and there may also be reason to build wrongness into the meaning of the word 'eugenics'.

6.3 Is the Very Idea of 'Genetic Improvement' a Mistake?

The next few sections move beyond the analytical and terminological issues and address the substantive ethical question of whether there is anything wrong with trying to improve the 'gene pool'. As we have seen, obviously *some* programmes that aim to improve the 'gene pool' are morally wrong because they use unacceptable means. This, however, will be disregarded for the present and I shall focus here on the question of whether aiming for genetic improvement is itself morally flawed, regardless of the means deployed (that is, even if the means used are, in and of themselves, morally innocent).

There seem to be two main objections to improving the gene pool. First, it may be claimed that the whole idea of genetic improvement is misguided and that the supposed 'improvements' aimed for are not really improvements. This section is devoted to a critical assessment of that idea. Second, some people have suggested

---

[33] Stephen Wilkinson, ' "Eugenics Talk" and the Language of Bioethics', *Journal of Medical Ethics*, 34 (2008), 467–71.

that using genetic selection to reduce the prevalence of impairment is likely to harm existing (and future) people who continue to live with impairment (those who are not 'screened out' or whose impairments are acquired after birth). This argument is the subject of 6.4.

So, is the very idea of 'genetic improvement' misguided? Obviously, some things that are touted as genetic improvements are not really improvements. If someone suggested using selective reproduction to reduce the incidence of homosexuality or to increase the incidence of blonde women with large breasts, we should be sceptical about whether these really are improvements. Similarly, the history of eugenics is full of cases in which (for example) cultural and racial differences are wrongly seen as defects that should be eliminated.[34] So we should approach 'improvement' claims with a high degree of caution. However, it does not follow from the fact that many people have misused the idea of genetic improvement that the notion is irredeemable. We must though be clear in each case what kind of improvement we are talking about and also demand *reasons why* the thing in question is not merely a change but an improvement, a change *for the better*.

The most obvious type of genetic improvement that we can make sense of and endorse is health improvement: specifically, using selective reproduction to reduce the prevalence of genetic disease and impairment in future populations. On the face of it, this seems to be a kind of genetic improvement since almost all would agree that, other things being equal, a less diseased and disabled future population is preferable to a more diseased and disabled one. This of course is underpinned by a welfare justification. For if (a) on average, disease and impairment cause lower welfare and (b) higher welfare is preferable to lower welfare, it follows that we should (other things being equal) select (possible, future) populations with less rather than more disease and impairment. (In Chapter 3, I explored in some detail various problems with this way of thinking about the welfare of possible future populations but will leave these to one side for the purposes of the present discussion.)

So is reducing the prevalence of genetic disease and impairment through selective reproduction (something that many would label 'eugenic' and which does appear to meet my descriptive working definition of 'eugenics') a genuine instance of improving the 'gene pool'?[35] It seems that it is on account of the welfare reasons just mentioned.

---

[34] Bernadette Baker, 'The Hunt for Disability: The New Eugenics and the Normalization of School Children', *Teachers College Record*, 104 (2002), 663–703; Barnett, 'Keywords'; Daniel Kevles, 'Eugenics and Human Rights', *BMJ* 319 (1999), 435–8.

[35] John Gillott, 'Screening for Disability: A Eugenic Pursuit?' *Journal of Medical Ethics*, 27 (suppl. ii), (2001), ii21–ii23; Suzanne Holland, 'Selecting Against Difference: Assisted Reproduction, Disability, and Regulation', *Florida State University Law Review*, 30 (2003), 401–10; Human Genetics Alert *Newsletter*, issue 1 (Dec. 2001); Julian Savulescu, 'Procreative Beneficence: Why We Should Select the Best Children', *Bioethics*, 15 (2001), 413–26.

However, this view is challenged by what I have elsewhere termed the Equal Value Principle and so I shall now outline this principle and explain what is wrong with it.[36]

Shortly after its creation in 2000, the Disability Rights Commission (DRC) was asked by LIFE for its view on Section 1(1)(d) of the Abortion Act 1967 (as amended by the Human Fertilisation and Embryology Act 1990) which permits (without any time limit) termination on the ground that 'there is a substantial risk that if the child were born it would suffer from such physical or mental abnormalities as to be seriously handicapped'.[37] In response, the DRC said that while 'Section 1(1)(d) is not inconsistent with the Disability Discrimination Act' it is, nonetheless:

offensive to many people; it reinforces negative stereotypes of disability; and there is substantial support for the view that to permit terminations at any point during a pregnancy on the ground of risk of disability, while time limits apply to other grounds set out in the Abortion Act, *is incompatible with valuing disability and non-disability equally.*[38]

In the same statement, the DRC informs us that:

Throughout its programme of work on ethical issues, the DRC will be guided by two principles: *valuing disability and non-disability equally*, and the right of individuals to make informed, autonomous choices.[39]

It is the first of these principles, the Equal Value Principle, that I shall focus on here. For it seems as if this principle could underpin an ethical argument against any reproductive practice which selects against disability. After all, if disability and non-disability were valued equally then why would anyone have reason to select the latter and deselect the former? Furthermore, if disability and non-disability were valued equally then we could not regard reducing the prevalence of genetically based disability and impairment as an improvement, since improvement means moving from something less valuable to something more valuable, from something worse to something better. It may be argued then that using PGD (and similar techniques) to select out disability is wrong because it violates the Equal Value Principle.

Two questions are raised by the Equal Value Principle. First, does 'screening out' disability necessarily involve failing to value disability and non-disability equally? And second, how plausible is the Equal Value Principle itself?

Taking the first question first, one view is that clinicians who offer embryo testing and selective implantation to prospective parents are not themselves making value

[36] Stephen Wilkinson, 'Eugenics, Embryo Selection, and the Equal Value Principle', *Clinical Ethics*, 1 (2006), 26–51.

[37] Disability Rights Commission, *DRC Statement on Section 1(1)(d) of the Abortion Act 1967*, <www.drc-gb.org> (last accessed, 26 Oct. 2005), my emphasis. The Disability Rights Commission was subsequently replaced by the Equality and Human Rights Commission in Oct. 2007.

[38] Disability Rights Commission, *DRC Statement.*

[39] Disability Rights Commission, *DRC Statement.*

judgements about disability. Rather, they are offering *choice* to the parents. So, on this view, the doctors have not acted badly because they are merely facilitating choice.

This could be true in some possible cases. However, there are reasons to doubt whether this degree of neutrality exists in many actual cases, and whether the general policy context within which clinical practice takes place can support such a neutral stance. One such reason is that clinicians offering specific preimplantation genetic tests usually know what the prospective parents' preferences and values are and, more often than not, are only carrying out the tests because they know that the parents wish to select against a particular genetic disorder. This does not of course *entail* that the clinicians involved do not value disability and non-disability equally. Nonetheless, it does at least raise the question of whether a clinician who subscribes to the Equal Value Principle should really support and collaborate with parents' attempts to avoid disability or disease.

Another more policy-oriented reason is that (as explained at the start of this chapter) the HFEA may only license embryo testing for certain purposes, with the main one of these being to 'select out' embryos with genetic disorders ('abnormalities'). And, as we saw in Chapter 3, the Human Fertilisation and Embryology Act 2008 now specifically rules out 'preferring' embryos with abnormalities that would generate disease or disability to 'healthy embryos'.[40] It cannot therefore be argued convincingly that the aim of the overall system of PGD is *merely choice*, because the system is so clearly oriented towards disease-avoidance and disability-avoidance (which presumably stem from valuing non-disability more highly than disability, and health more highly than disease). So, rightly or wrongly, the general policy context in which selective reproduction occurs at present is very much shaped by the medical goals of disease-avoidance and disability-avoidance and it is hard to see why someone would have such goals unless she positively valued non-disability and the absence of disease.

Turning now to the second question, how plausible is the Equal Value Principle? It seems that the principle is not as compelling as the DRC has suggested, mainly because its proponents apparently neglect an important distinction between valuing disability and non-disability equally, and valuing disabled and non-disabled *people* equally. Clearly, we should value disabled and non-disabled *people* equally and give them equal respect and rights as human beings, but it does not follow from this that we must value disability and non-disability equally.

This is clearest when the disability in question involves a straightforward physical injury. Take, for example, people with injured and permanently non-functional legs. Obviously, we should value people with and people without functioning legs equally and grant them equal respect; indeed, we should go further and grant people without functioning legs additional resources to compensate for their reduced mobility,

---

[40] Human Fertilisation and Embryology Act 2008 (Chapter 22), Section 14(4).

and (where practicable) modify built environments to facilitate access. None of this, however, requires us to value functioning and non-functioning legs equally. On the contrary, most of us have a strong and rational preference for functioning legs. Furedi makes the point as follows:

I find it difficult to believe that the actor Christopher Reeve . . . values his condition as a paraplegic as much as he values his former ability to ride horses and act in Superman films. This is not to say that he values himself as a person less, or that he values his life less. It simply means that most people in these circumstances would surely choose to return to health if they could. Which of us could honestly say that, when we are planning a child, we are indifferent as to whether . . . it is healthy? We value health above ill-health. This does not mean that we accord less value to blind, deaf, paraplegic or ill people.[41]

So while people with and people without disabilities should be treated as equals in terms of their moral status, given a choice, non-disability is usually preferable to disability.

This point is bolstered by another argument against the Equal Value Principle, which claims that the principle has absurd, or at least unpalatable, consequences. For commitment to this principle entails that we should not seek to cure people when they acquire disabilities, and certainly should not use public resources to do so, because this would suggest that disability is less valuable than non-disability. Indeed, if we do not value non-disability more highly than disability then (with the exception of non-curative interventions, such as pain relief) it is hard to see what rationale there could be for having a medical profession and for making people pay taxes to fund the National Health Service.[42] So the Equal Value Principle appears to have unacceptable implications and should be rejected.

One possible defence of the principle is to claim that it applies only to disabilities, not to diseases (or to disorders, which I take to be equivalent to diseases for the present purposes). On this view, valuing health over disease is acceptable but valuing disability over non-disability is not.

Defining disease and defining disability are both vast topics and I cannot hope to do justice to them here.[43] As I argued in Chapter 3, perhaps the key, though not the

[41] Ann Furedi, ' "Disability Cleansing"—or a Reasonable Choice?', *Spiked Online*, <www.spiked-online.com>, 29 Aug. 2001.

[42] Steven Edwards, 'Disability, Identity, and the "Expressivist Objection" ', *Journal of Medical Ethics*, 30 (2004), 418–20.

[43] Steven Edwards, 'Dismantling the Disability/Handicap Distinction', *Journal of Medicine and Philosophy*, 22 (1997), 589–606; John Harris, 'Is There a Coherent Social Conception of Disability?' *Journal of Medical Ethics*, 26 (2000), 95–100; Richard Hull, 'Defining Disability: A Philosophical Approach', *Res Publica*, 4 (1998), 199–210; Lennart Nordenfelt, 'On Disability and Illness, A Reply to Edwards', *Theoretical Medicine and Bioethics*, 20 (1999), 181–9; Lorella Tersi, 'The Social Model of Disability: A Philosophical Critique', *Journal of Applied Philosophy*, 21 (2004), 141–57.

only, defining feature of physical disorders is that they involve the malfunctioning, or the subnormal functioning, of a bodily part or process. It is this feature (along with pain) that makes most of us want to avoid disorders, and makes us prefer health to disease (all other things being equal). For, generally speaking, more functionality is better than less. However, functionality and health are not *intrinsically* valuable; rather, they are merely *means* to other valued ends, helping people to achieve their goals and to have a higher quality of life. Hence, there are many possible (and, I suspect, some actual) cases in which it would be sensible not to care about functionality, or indeed to prefer less to more. To illustrate this: whether colour blindness or infertility (both functional impairments) negatively impact on someone's quality of life depends to a very great extent on the person's preferences and priorities. In the first case, wanting to pursue certain occupations would make colour blindness have much more serious effects.[44] In the second case, disliking children may make infertility positively advantageous. Conversely, having 'perfect pitch' (a functionally better-than-normal ability) is unlikely to be advantageous to a person with no interest in music. A more extreme example of this would be people with Body Integrity Identity Disorder who actively pursue elective amputation. In some of these cases it is claimed that physically unnecessary amputation vastly increases quality of life owing to a strong desire to be without the limb in question, despite a loss of mobility and functionality.[45] So, in the case of physical disorders, while *usually* normal is preferable to subnormal functionality it is not *necessarily* preferable.

Given this understanding of disease or disorder, how are we to understand disability? One initial difficulty in trying to distinguish the two is that, in ordinary usage, many disabilities are or contain disorders, often termed *impairments* in this context. For example, the UK's Disability Discrimination Act 1995 defines 'a person as having a disability for the purposes of the DDA where he has a physical or mental impairment which has a substantial and long-term adverse effect on his ability to carry out normal day-to-day activities'.[46] Similarly, the Disability Rights Commission, on its Definition of Disability web page, suggested that all of the following have disabilities:

people with cancer, diabetes, multiple sclerosis and heart conditions; people who have a hearing or sight impairment or a significant mobility difficulty, caused for example by arthritis . . . people who have mental health conditions or learning difficulties.[47]

Thus it is tempting to see disability as a *kind of* disorder, with disabilities (on the DDA definition) being those disorders that prevent people from carrying out normal

---

[44] Jonathan Glover, *Choosing Children: Genes, Disability, and Design* (Oxford: Clarendon Press, 2006), 9.

[45] Tim Bayne and Neil Levy, 'Amputees by Choice: Body Integrity Identity Disorder and the Ethics of Amputation', *Journal of Applied Philosophy*, 22 (2005), 75–86; Carl Elliot, 'Costing an Arm and a Leg', *Slate*, <www.slate.com>, 10 July 2003.

[46] Disability Discrimination Act 1995, s1(1).

[47] DRC, *Definition of Disability*, <www.drc-gb.org> (last accessed: 12 Dec. 2006).

day-to-day activities (and do so over the long term). So, even if one takes seriously (as we certainly should) the idea that many of the disadvantages that people with disabilities face are caused by social factors (discriminatory attitudes, bad planning, lack of resources, etc.), it still seems as if all, or nearly all, disabilities have an important impairment or functional limitation aspect to them and that, if it were not for this lack of functionality, these disabilities would not exist. Indeed, it looks very much as if the existence of malfunction or subnormal function is what marks out *disability* as a specific category—as opposed to purely social discrimination, such as racism, or bias against redheads or against those who are (non-pathologically) fat. As Tom Shakespeare puts it:

Impairments may not be a sufficient cause of the difficulties which disabled people face, but they are a necessary one. If there is no link between impairment and disability, then disability becomes a much broader, vaguer term which describes any form of socially imposed restriction.[48]

This brings us to a crucial issue—*is being disabled (more) like being ill, or is it (more) like being the victim of social discrimination?* As I suggested in Chapter 3, the most plausible answer is that it has something in common with both, and that it depends which particular disability we are talking about.[49] Facial disfigurement is an interesting case to start with. In cases where the face is functionally unimpaired (in terms of the capacity to eat and talk, etc.) most of the disadvantage suffered will be caused by other people's negative attitudes, by the fact that they do not like, or feel uncomfortable about, the appearance of the disfigured person. So being disadvantaged by disfigurement closely resembles (or is a case of) being a victim of social discrimination; put crudely, it means being badly treated because people do not like the way you look. At the other end of the spectrum, there are cancers and heart conditions. It is certainly possible for people with these to suffer from social discrimination. However, unlike disfigurement, cancer and heart disease are independently harmful for reasons that have nothing to do with social discrimination. For cancer and heart disease usually cause significant dysfunction and disadvantage, up to and including premature death, *regardless of whether of not sufferers are discriminated against.* In-between are more complicated and contentious cases, such as the example of deafness discussed in Chapter 3.

The purpose of this short detour into the disease–disability distinction was to see whether it might be used to defend a version of the Equal Value Principle according to which, while valuing health over disease is acceptable, valuing disability over non-disability is not. As we have seen, this view is problematic because many disabilities (those with large functional impairment elements, such as having

---

[48] Tom Shakespeare, *Disability Rights and Wrongs* (London: Routledge, 2006), 85–6.

[49] Richard Hull, 'Cheap Listening? Reflections on the Concept of Wrongful Disability', *Bioethics*, 20 (2006), 55–63: 56.

permanently non-functional legs) consist at least partly of disease or injury. In such cases, it is impossible to distinguish clearly between disease and disability.

Perhaps then the most plausible view is this. There is nothing wrong with assigning a negative instrumental value to functional impairment (and a positive value to its absence) and hence nothing wrong with assigning a negative value to the functional impairment aspects of disability. As we have seen, though, this negative valuation of impairment does not entail and ought not to be accompanied by a negative valuation of the *person* with the impairment. Furthermore, we must recognize that different forms of social and environmental organization render the adverse effects of functional impairment more or less severe and, in some cases, can eliminate these effects altogether.

Conclusion

This section has aimed to answer the following question.

Is the very idea of improving the 'gene pool' fundamentally flawed?

With some qualifications, the answer is *no*. There have of course been many versions of 'eugenics' that have incorporated dangerously flawed ideological and pseudo-scientific beliefs, such as Nazi racial 'science'. However, there is no need to assume that all attempts to improve the 'gene pool' will be similarly flawed, and we can imagine versions of 'gene pool' improvement, such as the attempt to create healthier future populations, that would and should attract very widespread support. So perhaps (for example) improving the 'gene pool' in ways that improve future public health would be morally acceptable (and even desirable). Against this, some people (notably proponents of the Equal Value Principle) have argued that even the attempt to improve population health is unethical because it is premised on valuing non-disability more highly than disability. However, it seems that this argument (along with the Equal Value Principle itself) is unsound and should be rejected. There is nothing wrong with assigning a negative value to the functional impairment aspects of disability and this negative valuation of impairment does not entail and need not be accompanied by any negative valuation of the *person* with the impairment.

6.4 Social Problems Caused by Reducing the Prevalence of Disease and Disability

Other arguments against using selective reproduction to reduce the prevalence of disability and disease appeal to the (alleged) harm that this would cause for people who continue to live with disability and disease. One source of this harm, it is claimed, is the sending out of a 'negative message' about disability; this is the Expressivist Argument discussed in the next section. Another (the subject of this section) is the fact that (so it is claimed) if disability were to become rarer as a result of PGD and PND, this would both increase societal intolerance of disability and weaken the economic and political case for making social institutions and the built environment 'disability-friendly'.

Let us look at the environmental-organizational point first. Assume that there are presently 750,000 wheelchair users in the country. Then also assume that this number could be gradually cut to 250,000 by using PGD and PND to screen out the birth of (possible, future) people who would have been susceptible to mobility impairment. (This is of course rather unlikely because most people who use wheelchairs do so because of accidents or the effects of ageing, rather than anything genetic, so this is just an illustration.) If this population decrease were to occur then one possible effect would be on the economics of access. The government might, for example, have decided that it is willing to spend public funds on making buildings wheelchair-accessible only when those buildings are visited by wheelchair users three times per working day on average (say, 750 visits per year). This particular policy may or may not be justifiable, but one can imagine a cost-effectiveness rationale for it and there certainly must be *some* cost-per-wheelchair-visit threshold above which expenditure on access would be irrational, with the money better used elsewhere. Given this policy, the wheelchair user community may well see a very substantial reduction in the number of buildings made accessible if preimplantation and prenatal screening reduced their numbers by two-thirds, because the number of buildings meeting the government's criterion would be drastically reduced. So while we may welcome the fact that 500,000 fewer people have mobility disabilities, the remaining 250,000 wheelchair users could end up being *worse off* than they would have been because fewer buildings will be accessible. This model of the detrimental effects of reducing prevalence seems reasonably plausible, or at least it does so for certain kinds of impairment. Other characteristics for which it seems plausible include visual impairment (for example, it will only be worth providing 'talking books' if there is more than a certain level of demand); deafness (similarly, it may only be worth providing signing and written materials if more than a certain number of people want to make use of them); and obesity (for, in a 'slimmer' world, clothes for the larger person may be unavailable, and chairs may become smaller).

I am less convinced by the other suggested form of harm: the idea that society would become less tolerant of disability if there was less of it about. That is not to say that it is false; it is just that it could go either way, depending on many other variables. Anyway, for now, this is an empirical unknown and so I shall focus on the first form of harm: the claim that prevalence-reduction would take away some of our economic and political reasons for making social institutions and the built environment more 'disability-friendly'. If this were true (and, as I have said, it is highly believable) what would follow from it?

Well, it would have been established that we have *some* reason not to use selective reproduction to reduce the prevalence of disability: that reason being that (in the case discussed earlier) our 250,000 remaining wheelchair users will *suffer harm* if a selecting out policy is enacted. However, this reason will of course have to be weighed against other countervailing reasons. Foremost among these is that fact that (if we're looking at 'same number' selection) 500,000 future non-disabled people will be created instead of 500,000 future wheelchair users: something that many of us would regard as positive, on the assumption that *not* having a mobility disability is good for people's welfare (other things being equal). Deciding how to perform this 'balancing act' will not be easy and this issue is a microcosm of population ethics as a whole, raising difficult questions about the morally best distribution of welfare across different (possible, future) populations.

If we were to be crudely utilitarian about it we might reason as follows. In one scenario (the one where selective reproduction is *not* practised) we will end up with something like the following:

Scenario 1
750,000 wheelchair users with average WELFARE LEVEL 10
(*aggregate welfare 7.5 million*)

If, however, we practise (*same number*) selective reproduction, we will end up with:

Scenario 2
250,000 wheelchair users with average WELFARE LEVEL 8
500,000 non-disabled people with average WELFARE LEVEL 12
(*aggregate welfare 8 million*)

The 250,000 wheelchair users are worse off in the second scenario because of the worsening of access and facilities, but the 500,000 'substitutes' are better off than the wheelchair users because of the (supposed) advantages of not having a mobility disability. So given the above welfare values, the utilitarian calculus favours selective reproduction, because aggregate welfare is increased by half a million units.

However, this by no means gives us a decisive argument in favour of allowing selective reproduction to take place. There are several reasons for this. First, and most obviously, the numbers I have just used were made up and there is no reason to believe that things would work out this way: for example, it may be that population depletion would have a more detrimental effect on the remaining wheelchair users than I stipulated, or that the 500,000 non-disabled 'substitutes' would not have such good lives as I suggested. Second, it might be argued (plausibly) that utility maximization is not the only relevant consideration. There are also issues of distributive justice and so *even if* allowing harm to the remaining wheelchair users is the option with most overall utility it may still be unfair and wrong. Third (at least in some circumstances, depending on the selection mechanisms used), it may be argued that the reduction in the welfare of the remaining wheelchair users is more morally important than the overall population utility gain, because the former constitutes a harm to identifiable individuals whereas the latter (the utility gain) is only an *impersonal* improvement (one which does not *benefit* any individual) because it is achieved by 'swapping' one (possible, future) population for another (a disabled population for a non-disabled one).

So the argumentative state of play thus far is as follows: the fact that reducing the size of the disabled population would make remaining people with disabilities worse off *is* a reason not to do it, although not necessarily a decisive one. This, however, must be weighed (perhaps in some pretty complicated ways) against other kinds of consideration: most notably, against any overall welfare gain caused by reducing the prevalence of the disability. It seems then as if it is nigh-on impossible to provide a *general* answer to the question—*does this argument work?*—because the answer will depend both on the details of the particular situation under consideration and on some intractable questions in moral theory about, inter alia, how to weigh utility against equality and impersonal welfare gains against harm to determinate individuals.

Before moving on though I would like to consider one further objection to this argument. It has been claimed that *if* reducing the size of the disabled population through selective reproduction makes the remaining people with disabilities worse off *then* this is a reason not to reduce the size of the disabled population. This suggestion, however, may be vulnerable to a number of counterexamples, such as:

> **The Cure Case.** *It becomes possible to remove impairment from 50 per cent of the existing population: for example, possible to make wheelchair users walk and run normally. Doing this would be immensely beneficial to those who lose their impairments, but it would also (for population depletion reasons) be harmful to those who remain unable to walk.*

What we are meant to think about the *Cure Case* is this: the fact that those who must continue to be wheelchair users would be harmed is *not* a reason to stop the other 50 per cent from getting rid of their impairments. And if this is true of the *Cure Case* then surely it is also true of attempts to achieve similar results (a reduction in the prevalence of disability) by selective reproduction.

I think, however, that this is mistaken. The fact that those who must continue to be wheelchair users would be harmed *is* a reason to prevent the other 50 per cent from becoming unimpaired. However, it will (depending on the circumstances of the case) generally be an *insufficient* reason and will be outweighed by both the benefits to those who lose their impairments and by our duty to respect the autonomy of those who wish to be cured. So the *Cure Case* does not, it seems, cast doubt on the general form of the argument we are considering. Furthermore, the *Cure Case* differs from the selective reproduction case in two important respects. One is that the welfare gain in the *Cure Case* benefits determinate individuals; whereas in the selective reproduction case, we are simply 'replacing' a disabled (possible, future) population with a non-disabled (possible, future) population. Another (as I have already suggested) is that, in the *Cure Case*, we are dealing with the interests of existing and (I presume) autonomous adults, which means that their wishes and rights must be taken into account; whereas, in the selective reproduction case, we are choosing between different (as yet non-existent) future populations. These differences explain why our intuitions about the *Cure Case* may be different from those about the selective reproduction case. And so the *Cure Case* need not make us change our view. The fact that wheelchair users (those who must *remain* wheelchair users, that is) would be harmed by a decrease in their numbers *is* a reason, albeit a defeasible one, not to reduce the size of the wheelchair user population, be that by cure or by selective reproduction.

6.5 The Expressivist Argument

The Expressivist Argument (also known as the Expressivist Objection) is supposed to give us a reason not to use preimplantation and prenatal genetic tests to screen out disability. According to this argument, what is wrong with these practices is that they send out a negative message to and about certain existing people: either people with disabilities generally, or specifically those with the characteristic being 'selected against'. Steve Edwards and Tom Shakespeare (respectively) outline the argument as follows:

A particular kind of objection is sometimes raised against the practice of prenatal screening for genetic anomalies associated with disabilities. According to the objection, such practices cannot be morally justified ... [because] such practices cause offence and hurt to people currently living with the kinds of conditions screened for.[50]

it may be claimed that prenatal diagnosis discriminates against disabled children and adults, because it sends the message that it would have been better if they, too, had not been born. The argument is often called 'the expressivist objection', because it suggests that genetic diagnosis and selective abortion 'expresses' discriminatory or negative views towards disabled people.[51]

Edwards goes on to give the following example:

---

[50] Steven Edwards, 'Disability, Identity, and the "Expressivist Objection" ', *Journal of Medical Ethics*, 30 (2004), 418–20. 418; See also Mary Mahowald, 'Aren't We All Eugenicists? Commentary on Paul Lombardo's "Taking Eugenics Seriously" ', *Florida State University Law Review*, 30 (2003), 219–35: 234.

[51] Shakespeare, *Disability Rights*, 35.

consider a person currently living with cystic fibrosis. Such a person might hold the view that prenatal screening for cystic fibrosis, with a view to termination on grounds of the presence of cystic fibrosis in the fetus, sends a negative message to the person to the effect that it would have been better had he not been born. Also, such a person might feel hurt or otherwise harmed as a consequence of that practice.[52]

Senders and Recipients

The first challenge when trying to make sense of the Expressivist Argument is that the key idea of 'sending out a message' is vague and requires clarification.

We should start with a general distinction between the message that the sender *intends to send out* and what the recipient *hears or receives* (or rather *thinks she* hears or receives). Because of the inevitable imperfection of human communication and because different actions and symbols mean different things to different people, the 'sender message' and the 'recipient message' often diverge. Thus, as we all know from personal experience, it is easy to cause offence without meaning to, for people to hear or perceive a message that we did not (or did not deliberately) send out. If this is a danger in personal interactions, it is an even bigger one when large issues of public policy are at stake and where the actors are not individuals but whole communities or corporate agents. So one possibility is that people who select out *do not mean to* send out a negative message about people with disabilities, but that those people feel, nonetheless, that such a message is being sent. Glover describes this possibility as follows:

there need be nothing wrong with the intention to have children with a better chance of flourishing as a result of not having a disability. But, even if the preference for normality is utterly untainted by . . . ugly attitudes, this may not prevent it from causing dismay to some people with disability.[53]

If this were the position, an adequate response to the Expressivist Argument would be not to refrain from selecting against disability (since there would be nothing wrong with this per se) but instead to take steps to ensure that people with disabilities did not *take it to be* expressing a negative view of them. Once more, Glover makes the point well:

we need to send a clear signal that we do not have the ugly attitudes to disability. It is important to show that what we care about is our children's flourishing: that this, and not . . . some horrible project of cleansing the world of [people with disabilities] is what motivates us.[54]

Glover suggests two main ways in which we can send this 'clear signal'. One is to point out that selecting out embryos with genetic impairments is fundamentally the same sort of activity as that carried out by the health services:

[52] Edwards, 'Disability', 418.   [53] Glover, *Choosing Children*, 34.
[54] Glover, *Choosing Children*.

We want to defeat cancer, not because we lack respect for people with cancer and want to rid the world of them, but because of what cancer does to people.[55]

Second, we must be consistent and not single out the avoidance of impairment for unmerited special treatment. If our fundamental concern is the flourishing of children, then we must act on this consistently and, insofar as we can, act against other impediments to flourishing including poverty, poor quality (or non-existent) schooling, child abuse, and environmental causes of disability (such as road accidents). Furthermore (again, in order to be consistent) selective reproduction would have to be expanded (where technically possible) to encompass *all* interventions that promote flourishing, not just those that reduce the prevalence of disability. Thus, if some forms of enhancement selection become possible then (other things being equal) these too should be permitted if they are likely to advance human flourishing. David Wasserman, advocating a position rather like this in relation to prenatal testing, argues persuasively:

for the comparative virtues of an unrestricted regime of prenatal testing over a régime restricted by a criterion of 'severity'—the severity of either the medical condition of the fetus, or the impact on the family. My primary argument [is] a moral, not an empirical one—that an unrestricted regime will avoid or mute the expressive significance of prenatal selection for impairment: the 'message' that the prospect of severe impairment provides a categorically better reason for refusing to bring a child into the world than the indefinite number of other potentially burdensome traits and conditions that a child may have.[56]

I would also add two other ways in which we can make it clear that, when we 'select against' disability, we are not doing it for (what Glover terms) 'ugly reasons'. One is to provide existing people with disabilities with good levels of support and with a comprehensive set of civil rights and anti-discrimination measures. Another is that people involved in prenatal and/or preimplantation genetic diagnosis (be they health care professionals, service users, or indeed bioethicists) should pay careful attention to the language that they use when discussing these sensitive matters. For, as Tom Shakespeare points out:

One of the strengths of the expressivist objection is that it forces us to attend to the language of prenatal diagnosis, and the wider messages which it conveys. There are many examples of highly prejudicial language being used about disabled people in the literature on genetics and screening[57]

The conclusion of this subsection then is that we must distinguish between the intended message and the message that is received (or perceived) by people with

---

[55] Glover, *Choosing Children*, 35.

[56] David Wasserman, 'A Choice of Evils in Prenatal Testing', *Florida State University Law Review*, 30 (2003), 295–313: 313.

[57] Tom Shakespeare, *Disability Rights*, 89.

disabilities. If this discrepancy is minimized, then some of the concerns raised by the Expressivist Argument will have been dealt with without our practices having been substantially altered. However, proponents of the Expressivist Argument may argue that the problem cannot be dealt with just by looking at communications and consistency issues because there is something *fundamentally* objectionable about the motives and attitudes underlying selection against disability. This is the subject of the next subsection.

The Underlying Message: 'it would be better if you did not exist'

> the reality is that people do think the world would be a better place without people with disabilities[58]

> every other day, newspapers report yet another 'exciting breakthrough' in prenatal screening . . . common reaction among people with severe disabilities is the cold inner grip of a feeling never far from the surface—that we are tolerated only on sufferance, and that society would really prefer us to be quietly eliminated.[59]

The main worry here is that selecting out disability must be based on the view that the world would be a better place if people with disabilities (or people with the particular disabilities being selected against) did not exist. For this seems to follow from, or to be the best rationale for, the aim of the practice, which is to stop (possible, future) people with disabilities from coming into existence.

In order to evaluate this view we need first to distinguish between the different possible meanings of '*the world would be, or would have been, a better place if you did not exist*'. In particular, we can distinguish between the following claims (where the 'you' in question is an existing person with a disability):

(A) The world would be a better place if you were killed now.

(B) The world would be a better place if you had not been born and if the world population was therefore one less than it is today.

(C) The world would be a better place if your parents had used selection technology to create/select a different child instead of you: if they had had the same number of children but, rather than creating you, created a happier and healthier alternative person instead.

[58] Anonymous expert interview with the author (2005).
[59] Alison Davies, *A Disabled Person's Perspective on Pre-Natal Screening* (1999), <http://www.leeds.ac.uk/disability-studies/archiveuk/Davis/davis.htm> (last accessed: Sunday, 12 Apr. 2009).

(A), the most extreme claim, is relatively easy to deal with. For most of us, the permissibility of deselecting an embryo with a genetic impairment does not entail that murdering an existing person with the same impairment is similarly permissible. I say 'for most of us' because there are some people who believe that embryos are persons and have the same moral status as children or adults and, if they were right, then there would be no fundamental difference between destroying an embryo and murdering an adult. However, for reasons outlined in Chapter 1, I am leaving to one side these views. So I shall assume, at least for the time being, that not implanting an embryo with Condition X and murdering an adult with Condition X are fundamentally different.

The question of whether we are committed to (B) and/or (C) when we screen out genetic impairments is more complicated and depends on whether the choice made is a 'same number' or 'different number' one. Let us start with 'same number' choices as these seem, as far as the Expressivist Argument is concerned, less problematic.

As was noted in Chapter 1, many embryo selection decisions are 'same number'. In the standard 'same number' case, the prospective parents are committed to having one and only one (extra) child. So the question that faces them is not *whether* to have a child, or *how many* children to have, but *which* (possible, future) child to (try to) bring into existence. In many of these cases, health is a major factor in deciding and the prospective parents will want to make use of the embryo that provides the best chance of a child being born without a serious genetic disorder. So what message does this kind of choice, in favour of health or against impairment, send out?

With some qualifications (that I shall explore later) there do seem to be reasons for thinking that selection decisions of this kind rest on the principle expressed in (C) (above) and therefore that they send out a Type-(C) message. This is because the prospective parents, in our embryo selection scenario, appear to be acting on the principle that health is better than disease or disability (presumably on child welfare grounds, and perhaps also on 'cost of care' grounds) and so, if they think this of their own case, then they must (if they are consistent and rational) think the same of other relevantly similar cases. So what if our embryo-selecting parents meet Jack, an existing person with an incapacitating and painful genetic disorder? What attitude do they have to his existence? Well, they do seem committed to the view that the world would have been a better place if Jack's parents (assuming this to be possible) had used PGD instead to create Jacqueline, a different possible child without a genetic disorder. The rationale for this is that Jacqueline would have had a higher quality (for example, less painful) life than the one that Jack is having. None of this of course is a reason for thinking that Jack should be killed or would be better off dead. Rather, they are looking back at how the world *would have been better* if Jack's parents had created Jacqueline instead.

So embryo-selecting parents will often send out a Type-(C) message because the content of the message (that *ceteris paribus* the world would be a better place if people were born without genetic disorders) is the rationale for their selection decision. But is there anything wrong with sending out this message, or with acting on the principle it expresses? Here are some reasons that people sometimes offer for answering *yes* (sticking with the example of Jack).

1. Jack has made and continues to make a positive contribution to the world.
2. People love Jack and are glad that he is alive.
3. Jack has a life worth living and is glad that he is alive.

The first thing to say about these claims is that they are all true, or rather they will be true in many Jack-type cases. Also, it goes without saying that they are all good reasons (if any more are needed) for *not killing* Jack. However, as regards the embryo selection question, they all miss the point and for the same fundamental reason. Since we are (at the moment) dealing with 'same number' selection cases we are not simply comparing Jack with the absence of Jack. Rather, we are comparing the world with Jack in it with the world *as it would have been if Jacqueline had existed instead*. Thus, the reply to (1) is that, although admittedly Jack makes a positive contribution to the world, Jacqueline (for all we know) would have made an equally positive contribution *and* would have had a happier life owing to her good health. The response to (2) is that, had Jacqueline been born instead, we would (for all we know) have loved her as much as we do Jack and would have been glad that she was alive. And, as regards (3), no one is denying that Jack has a life that is worth living, but that is not the issue: the question rather is whether Jacqueline would have had an *even better* life than Jack. Now all of these comparisons will of course be dogged by uncertainty and maybe Jacqueline, her good health notwithstanding, would have had an utterly miserable life, one much worse that Jack's. But, at the point of preimplantation genetic diagnosis we can only go on what we know, and one thing that we do know is that incapacitating and painful genetic disorders reduce people's chances of flourishing and (at least on average) reduce people's levels of welfare (keeping in mind some of the caveats outlined in Chapter 3). So 'same number' embryo selection to avoid genetic disorders *does* normally send out message (C), because message (C) encapsulates the best rationale for this form of selection. But message (C) is not one that we should be embarrassed to send out because it is defensible. It is defensible because selecting higher over lower probable future welfare is permissible and rational (other things being equal).

It is important, however, to stress that this way of thinking need not and should not be confined to disease and disability. Glover (writing in the 1970s and so using the language of those times) tells us:

If someone with a handicap is conceived instead of a normal person, things turn out less well than they might have done. It would have been better if the normal person had been conceived. But things of this sort can be said about almost any of us. If my own conception was an alternative to the conception of someone just like me except more intelligent, or more athletic, or more musical, it would have been better if that person had been conceived.[60]

So what if *my* mother were to tell *me* that, around the time of *my* conception, she was offered, but refused, a reproductive technology that would have resulted in the creation of a different child: Stephanie rather than Stephen? Sex aside, Stephanie would have been like I am except more athletic and beautiful and less likely to suffer from obesity and heart disease. What attitude ought I to have to my mother's revelation and do I think that she made the right decision? Well I am glad to be alive, but I, nonetheless, believe that she made the wrong decision. Given the available evidence at the time, it would have been better to create Stephanie instead of me because, even though I cannot complain about my level of flourishing thus far, the chances are that Stephanie would have flourished *even more* over a whole lifetime. So the message in (C), as I have said, need not and should not single out people with disabilities for negative treatment. Rather, we should *all* take the view that, while we are glad to be alive (those of us that are), it would have been sensible to create other happier and healthier people instead of us if the opportunity arose.

'Same number' embryo selection to avoid genetic disorders does not, however, send out message (B), because message (B) is really about 'different number' selection, about cases in which we are choosing not to create a child at all rather than have a child with a disease or disability. It is to these choices and to message (B) that I now turn.

'Different Number' Selection: choosing not to have a child at all

Let us start by considering some examples of 'different number' selection.

> **Sean and Skye** are keen to have children but discover by chance that they are carriers of a serious genetic disorder, ABC Syndrome, for which there is presently no cure. It is highly likely that their offspring would suffer from ABC Syndrome, which is disabling and painful. After lengthy discussion, Sean and Skye decide not to have children and Sean arranges to have a vasectomy.

> **Lola** is twenty-weeks' pregnant. Prenatal testing reveals that the foetus has ABC Syndrome. After much soul-searching, Lola decides to have an abortion. This is in spite of the fact that, as a 41-year-old who found it very hard to become pregnant, she knows that her chances of having another child are remote.

---

[60] Jonathan Glover, *Causing Death and Saving Lives* (Harmondsworth: Penguin, 1977), 148.

These are both instances of 'different number' disease-avoidance because the prospective parents decide that not having a child at all is better than having a child with *ABC Syndrome*. The questions that we must answer are:

1. Does the behaviour of Lola and of Sean and Skye send out Message (B) to (in this instance) people with *ABC Syndrome*: that the world would be a better place if people with *ABC Syndrome* had not been born and if the world population was correspondingly smaller?
2. If this message is sent out, is it morally defensible?

With some qualifications (to which I shall return shortly) the answer to (1) seems to be 'yes'. Take Sean and Skye for instance. They are deciding between two (possible, future) worlds. In the first, they have a child with *ABC Syndrome*. In the second, they have no children. They decide that the second world is better than the first. Now Sean and Skye doubtless have no desire to *force* other parents to make the same decision as them. Furthermore, they would probably accept both that this is an issue about which reasonable people can disagree and that there are important subjective differences between people: for example, some people are better able to cope with caring for sick children than others. Nonetheless, Sean and Skye must presumably be committed to something like the view that the benefits of creating a child with *ABC Syndrome* are outweighed by the burdens, including both the burdens to the child itself (incapacity and pain) and those to the family and other third parties (the 'cost of care'). And if they think this then consistency demands that they must also think that the world would have been a better place if the parents of *existing* people with *ABC Syndrome* had, like them, decided to refrain from reproducing. So Sean and Skye are, it seems, sending out a version of Message (B) to people with *ABC Syndrome*, although (as I have said) this message may well be tempered by the recognition that there are important differences between families.

These differences mean that we must make one important qualification: that what consistency demands of Sean and Skye depends on the extent to which they see themselves as relevantly similar to the parents of existing *ABC* children. Imagine, for example, that Sean and Skye's reason for not having an *ABC* child was that they saw themselves as *exceptionally unsuitable* parents for such a child. If that was their thinking then all that consistency would require of them is a belief that the world would be a better place if all those parents *who are as exceptionally unsuitable as Sean and Skye* had refrained from reproduction. And so Sean and Skye's 'message', in this case, would be applicable only to those very few inappropriate people, not to parents of *ABC* children generally. But if, on the other hand, Sean and Skye do not see themselves as exceptional and view the creation of an *ABC* child as a bad thing, even for averagely suitable prospective parents, then their rationale, or 'message', will be much more generally applicable. What this suggests is that the extent to which Message (B) is conveyed depends in part on the reasoning of the prospective parents. Where their reasons for avoiding the birth of a child are largely to do with their own exceptionality then either the 'world would be a better place' message would not be sent out at all or its scope will be very limited. Cases of this type then will not fall foul of the Expressivist Argument. But where the prospective parents do not regard themselves as exceptionally unsuitable then their thinking will be more universalizable and widely applicable.

Let us turn now to consider the question of whether Message (B) is morally defensible. There is no generally applicable answer to this and whether the message is defensible will depend on the nature of the particular condition being 'selected against'. Thus, for any given condition, if it is true that the 'positives' of bringing into being a child with x are outweighed by the burdens, then sending out the message that the world would have been a better place if the existing people with x had not been created is permissible; while conversely sending out this message in cases where the burdens do not outweigh the benefits would be wrong. Indeed, this reveals an important structural feature (and structural limitation) of arguments like the Expressivist Argument: that is, of arguments which object to practices on the grounds that they send out a negative message. The limitation is that this will only normally count as an objection if the message sent is false, for (provided that the message is not communicated in an insensitive or disrespectful manner) there cannot, one would think, be much wrong with sending out a true message, even if it is negative. So Expressivist-type arguments, as well as establishing that a negative message is sent out, must show that the message is *unduly* negative.

In response to this, someone could claim that even true negative messages about people with disabilities ought not to be sent out because of their harmful effects. Thus, what is proposed would be a sort of beneficent deception, or at least a beneficent withholding of information. This view should be treated with a good deal of scepticism. One problem with it is that what is proposed is the withholding of information on a massive scale, something which is both intrinsically morally problematic (because of the degree of dishonesty involved) and unlikely to work. Another is that there is surely a moral difference between being asked *not to say* certain (true) things in order avoid harming and offending others, on the one hand, and being asked to create an (otherwise unwanted) child with a disability for similar reasons (and in spite of the fact that the reasons for not having that child are sound). The latter will generally be much more onerous than merely refraining from saying certain things and would surely be too much to ask.

Having said all that, I would concede that there are nonetheless some worrisome aspects of sending out Message (B) and that selecting against disease and disability by making a 'different number' choice (specifically, the choice not to have any child at all) is generally more troubling than the 'same number' embryo selection decisions discussed earlier.

One of these worries arises from the fact that, unless we confine ourselves to 'wrongful life' cases (which, as I suggested in Chapter 3, will be very rare indeed) the justification of decisions like Sean and Skye's must appeal not only to the welfare of the child created but also to others' interests: most obviously, those of the prospective parents. Thus, in reaching a judgement about whether or not to create the child, the prospective parents must appeal, among other things, to the impact on their own welfare and that of any other existing children. Therefore, the message sent out here may well be that the world would be a better place without people with *ABC Syndrome*, partly because people with this syndrome suffer, *but also partly because they are a burden on others*. And this is a troubling implication and an unpalatable message. (In fact, this also applies to *some* 'same number' selection decisions—we might, for example, choose between embryos on 'cost of care' grounds—but at least in 'same number' cases there will often be an adequate justification for selection that appeals solely to the welfare of the child created.)

So the Expressivist Argument does draw our attention to an important point: that, in cases (especially 'different number' cases) where the justification for 'deselecting' a (possible, future) person with a disability is (mainly) the 'burden of care' then there is at least a danger of sending out the message that it would be better if people with the disability in question did not exist *because of the extent to which they are a burden on others*.

One response to this is to point out that this message is not as bad as it sounds because there is a distinction between (a) the 'hindsight' view that it *would have been* better if certain people had not been created, and (b) the view that such people should be 'killed off' now. It might be argued that (a) does not entail (b) because at birth (or perhaps sooner) people acquire various rights, including the right to life and so, even if it is true that the world would be better without them, it would nonetheless be wrong to kill or otherwise mistreat them. This response does perhaps lessen the impact of the message. However, even once it is taken into account, the residual message is pretty unpalatable, for it says of (and to) a certain class of persons that it would have been better if they did not exist because they are 'a burden'.

Another response is to claim that Lola, Sean, and Skye (and many people like them) are not acting on moral reasons when they choose not to have a child. They are not (according to this response) acting on a belief that *the world* would be a better place without another child with *ABC Syndrome*. Rather, the motivating belief is that *their own lives* would be better if they did not have to care for a child with *ABC Syndrome*. This could be either because they feel that they could not cope with the demands that this would place upon them, or simply because they *do not want to* have these demands placed upon them—for example, they might prefer to spend time on their careers, hobbies, holidays, or pets, than to spend it caring for a child with *ABC Syndrome*.

I do not know how many prospective parents in the position of Lola, Sean, and Skye actually have this attitude. However, we can still usefully ask whether this more 'selfish' attitude is better or worse than evading parenthood for more impersonal reasons (ones to do with making the world, as opposed to one's own life, better). Ironically perhaps, there is at least one respect in which the more 'selfish' attitudes are less troubling. Imagine, for instance, that Lola wishes to pursue a successful career in law and believes this to be incompatible with being the parent of a child with *ABC Syndrome*. Now this judgement may or may not be correct (perhaps she is wrong and combining a career in law with the care role *is* achievable). Furthermore, there are important background issues about why it is that Lola has this belief (most obviously, are society and/or the State failing to provide adequate support for parents of children with *ABC Syndrome*?). But I would, nonetheless, suggest that the message sent out by Lola's decision to prioritize career over parenthood should be less troubling to people with disabilities than an otherwise similar decision based on the belief that the world would be better without an extra child with *ABC Syndrome*. For the latter is a universalizable moral judgement that (as we saw earlier) entails—or at least strongly suggests—that the world would have been better if the existing people with *ABC Syndrome* had not been born. Whereas Lola's 'selfish' decision does not suggest this so much as her own personal unwillingness to take on the extra demands of coping with a child with *ABC Syndrome*.

A useful comparison here is with people who decide not to have children for reasons unconnected to disability. Some of these will make the decision not to reproduce on 'selfish' grounds: weighing up the anticipated rewards of parenting against the advantages of non-parenting and deciding that the latter will probably deliver a higher overall quality of life. Others, however, will be misanthropes who believe that the world would be a better place if no one reproduced and if humanity gradually become extinct. The latter (misanthropic) position, it seems, is more morally suspect and troubling for the rest of us than the former ('selfish') one because of what it says about the existence of us all: that it would be better if we and our children did not exist. Holding the belief that the eradication of humankind is desirable is, it seems, a more worrying character trait than (for example) just being too lazy or career-focused to have a child. This distinction is analogous to that between people who want to avoid having a child with a disability because they think that not having one will make their (the prospective parents') lives go better, and those who want to avoid having a child with a disability because they think that the world would be a better place without such children. The latter looks like a more worrying attitude.

Does this mean that there is a version of the Expressivist Argument that succeeds, one that provides a sound moral objection to (at least some forms of) selecting out disability? With a couple of important qualifications, the answer is 'yes', although the version of the Expressivist Argument that survives will be much more limited in scope than what we started out with, and than many of the argument's proponents would like. For this reason, it is not clear that even the successful version of the argument has many, if any, implications for law and policy.

So what are these important qualifications? The first is that, as I explained earlier, the Expressivist Argument does not generally work well against 'same number' selection. This is because the pro-flourishing and pro-welfare rationale for 'same number' selection is defensible and there is nothing intrinsically wrong with sending out the message that we (other things being equal) prefer to create future populations with more rather than less health and welfare (although, as noted in Chapter 3, there are some *theoretical* problems with this, notably the danger that we will end up being committed to the Repugnant Conclusion). Hence, insofar as impairment reduces people's chances of flourishing, selecting against it is justifiable in 'same number' cases. The scope of the Expressivist Argument then must be narrowed so that it applies primarily to 'different number' cases: specially those in which people choose to avoid parenthood altogether rather than having a child with a disability or disorder. That is the first qualification.

The second qualification is based on a further distinction that can be drawn (for our purposes, within the remaining set of 'different number' cases) between (a) people who avoid having a child with a disability for self-interested reasons (for example, because they do not wish to take on the resultant caring responsibilities), and (b) those whose motives are more impersonal, specifically the belief that *the world considered overall would be a better place* if they did not have the (possible, future) child under consideration.

The first group of parenthood-avoiders (the 'self-interested' ones) are much less susceptible to the Expressivist Argument. These people are not sending out the message that the world would be a better place without disability, since this is not what motivates them. Rather, the worst that they are saying is that (as a matter of personal preference and self-interest) they would rather spend their lives doing something other than caring for a child with a disability or disease. One might of course also ask whether *this* message is acceptable. However, there is a powerful argument for thinking that it is (at least if we focus, for the time being, on the message's intrinsic properties, rather than additional complications such as the possibility of its being misinterpreted). This argument starts with the premiss that (at least in all but the weirdest thought experiments) parenthood is morally optional: there is no general moral obligation to have a child. It then proceeds by asking us to think about cases like the following.

> **Thomas and Tia** *have genetic tests which show that their chances of having a child with a genetic disorder are lower than the norm (i.e. it is very unlikely). They eventually decide, nonetheless, not to have a child because the burden of caring for it would be incompatible with their hobbies (including scuba-diving and skiing) and their desire to be high earners.*

> **Morgan and Millie** *have genetic tests which show that their chances of having a child with a serious genetic disorder are extremely high. They decide not to have a child because the burden of caring for a child with a serious genetic disorder would be incompatible with their careers and their desire to travel around the world on motorcycles.*

If we believe that parenthood is morally optional then it follows that Thomas and Tia have made an acceptable decision: it is morally permissible to prefer scuba-diving and affluence to child-rearing, and to avoid parenthood on those grounds. It also follows that there is nothing wrong with the message that Thomas and Tia are sending out because the message (if indeed there is a message) is just that for them, based on their own personal preferences, affluence and scuba-diving are more likely than parenthood to deliver (their own) flourishing and happiness.

The moral optionality of parenthood also, of course, entails that Morgan and Millie have made an acceptable decision. What is more, their reasons for steering clear of parenthood seem to be *even better* than Thomas and Tia's. For whereas Thomas and Tia would only have to contend with the normal demands of parenting, Morgan and Millie would be at high risk of having to contend with the special challenge of caring for a child with a serious genetic disorder—a task which, even with generous community and familial support (that may or may not be forthcoming), could be substantial and will almost certainly be more burdensome than the parenting challenges that Thomas and Tia would face.

So this pair of cases illustrates a general point: that if we believe in the moral optionality of parenting in cases, like Thomas and Tia, where disability and disease are not at issue, then we should surely believe that the moral optionality of parenting applies a fortiori to cases, like Morgan and Millie, where the decision is whether or not to have a child with a serious genetic disorder. This is because the self-interested reasons for avoiding parenthood will (on average) be even stronger for people like Morgan and Millie than for people like Thomas and Tia. The same goes for the messages that they send out (if any). In the case of Thomas and Tia, the message was just that for them, based on their own personal preferences, scuba-diving and affluence are more likely to deliver flourishing and happiness than parenthood. This, I suggested, is an acceptable message to send out. If that is correct, and if Morgan and Millie have better and stronger reasons for avoiding parenthood than Thomas and Tia's reasons, then Morgan and Millie's 'message' (that, given their particular circumstances and preferences, career advancement and world touring are preferable to caring for a child with a serious genetic disorder) must surely be at least as acceptable (quite possibly more acceptable) than Thomas and Tia's.

So that is the second qualification: the Expressivist Argument does not work against cases in which people avoid parenthood for essentially self-interested reasons, but only against those who do so for impersonal reasons (reasons to do with making *the world* better).

This takes us straight to the third qualification, which is (as we saw earlier, while discussing the Sean and Skye case) that not all people whose reasons for avoiding parenthood are impersonal are vulnerable to the Expressivist Argument. For some such people want to avoid having a disabled child because they see themselves as *exceptionally unsuitable* parents. And, as I argued earlier, these people are largely immune from the Expressivist Argument. The reason for this is the extremely narrow scope of their 'message': that the world would be a better place if the handful of parents who are *as bad at parenting as they would be* had not had children. And, by its very nature, this message does not speak to (or about) people with disabilities generally.

These qualifications leave us with a very particular kind of case against which the Expressivist Argument *does* work, one with the following features:

(1) It is a 'different number' case, typically one in which prospective reproducers decide to avoid parenthood altogether rather than have a child with a disability.

(2) Their reasons for deciding not to create the child are 'impersonal' rather than 'selfish': they think that *the world would be a better place* without their (possible, future) child in it.

(3) They do not see themselves as *exceptionally* bad or unsuitable parents (or, if they do, that is not why they refrain from creating the child).

(4) Their belief that the world would be a better place without their (possible, future) child in it *is false or unjustified*. If it were true (or justified)—for instance, if it were a potential 'wrongful life' case in which the child would have a sub-zero quality of life—then the message sent out would be defensible, and so there would be nothing wrong with sending it out (provided that it was not done insensitively). So some kind of defect in the content of the message (falsity, irrationality, etc.) is essential to the Expressivist Argument's working.

Cases of this kind do fall foul of the Expressivist Argument because a negative, damaging, and morally unjustified message is being sent out.

Conclusion

The Expressivist Argument says that what is wrong with selecting out disease and disability is that it sends out a negative message to or about people with disabilities: in its most extreme form, that the world would be a better place if they did not exist. What conclusions follow from my assessment of this argument?

First, when (as is often the case) what underlies our selecting-out practices is a desire to create a future population with less pain and more flourishing, we should make this clear. In particular, we should make it clear to existing people with disabilities that it is this and not any hatred of them, or desire to eliminate them, that lies behind our actions. Getting this message across may involve, among other things, ensuring that we act consistently to promote human flourishing across the board (for example, by providing health and social services and using enhancement technologies where these are known to be safe and effective). It will also involve explaining that there is a crucial ethical and legal distinction between (a) deselecting a (possible, future) person on the grounds that she would have characteristic x, and (b) killing or otherwise mistreating an existing person for having x, and making it clear that accepting (a) in no way entails accepting (b).

Even once the steps just outlined have been taken, residual concerns about the message sent may remain. Some of these are more well founded than others. In particular, as we have just seen, existing people with disabilities have more reason to be troubled by prospective parents who decide that *not having a child at all* is preferable to having a child with a disability (a 'different number' choice) than by those who use embryo selection to *choose between* (possible, future) children with and without disabilities (a 'same number' choice).

As far as the Expressivist Argument is concerned, 'same number' selection against disability should be seen as relatively innocuous because the rationale of this practice, and hence the fundamental message that it sends out, is morally defensible. Furthermore, this message does not (or should not) single out people with disabilities for especially negative treatment. For, as I have argued, if flourishing and welfare are what matter, then we should *all* (disabled or otherwise) take the view that it would have been better to have created alternative people instead of us if the opportunity arose, in cases where those (possible, future) people had a better chance of a high quality of life than we did. This general principle will often count against the selection of (possible, future) people with disabilities, because of disability's negative effects on flourishing and quality of life. Nevertheless, disability is by no means unique in this respect and *any* characteristic that reduces a person's chances of flourishing and happiness should be similarly selected against (other things being equal).

Finally, as I suggested earlier, one important structural feature of the Expressivist Argument is that it can only really work *either* against insensitive and misleading communication, *or* against messages that are false. Thus, very generally, whenever selective reproduction is performed on the basis of a moral or empirical error (for example, based on unduly negative attitudes to disability, or indeed to other characteristics such as sex—or on unduly *positive* views about certain traits, such as appearance or height) it will be vulnerable to a version of the Expressivist Argument. But when the underlying reasons for selecting are sound, then the Expressivist Argument cannot apply, except where communications issues mean that the underlying reasons are misunderstood.

6.6 Summary and Conclusions

The main business of this chapter was an examination of two arguments (or argument-*types*) that have been used against selective reproduction generally, but especially against the widespread practice of screening out disability and disease: the Eugenics Argument and the Expressivist Argument.

One of the main problems with the Eugenics Argument is the term 'eugenics' itself, which used to mean various different things. If a broad descriptive definition of 'eugenics' were adopted (such as 'improving the gene pool') then I would concede that (on this definition) many instances of screening out genetic disease are indeed eugenic. But then (given the descriptive definition) it would not follow from that that there was anything wrong with these practices, since there may well be acceptable forms of eugenics (again, on this descriptive definition). Alternatively, a more evaluative definition of 'eugenics' could be adopted, but then it is not obvious that selecting out genetic disorders is really eugenics, especially if the screening is voluntary (non-authoritarian) and based on genuine health and welfare criteria rather than malevolent 'racial science'.

Turning now to the Expressivist Argument, I started my analysis by making a distinction between (a) communication problems, difficulties caused by the way in which selecting out is presented and discussed, and (b) more fundamental concerns, specifically that the underlying rationale for selecting out contains a negative message about people with disabilities. The communications issues are, in theory if not in practice, relatively easy to deal with, and earlier I suggested some ways in which this might be done. A more interesting question for our purposes then concerns what the different rationales for selecting out might be and whether any of them do indeed contain an unacceptable message. My conclusion is that many of these rationales are defensible and hence do not send out a morally problematic message. However, some (specifically that which underpins a certain kind of 'different number' choice) are less defensible and, against these, the Expressivist Argument does enjoy some limited success.

So my overall conclusion is that the Eugenics Argument against selecting out disease and disability is entirely unsuccessful. While the Expressivist Argument is largely unsuccessful, but does work in a qualified way in the limited range of cases outlined at the end of 6.5.

7

Enhancement

This chapter aims to do four things. First, I will analyse and clarify some different accounts of enhancement. Second, I will identify and explain some ethical views about enhancement: notably, the view that it is especially morally problematic (compared to, say, therapy). Third, I will ask whether these ethical views are defensible. Finally, I will ask what implications (if any) the most defensible of these positions have for the ethics of selective reproduction and also for questions of law and regulation in this area.

7.1 What Is Enhancement?

Modification vs Selection

We need to start by restating the distinction between modification and selection. *Modification* involves altering the nature of a determinate individual who does or will exist and includes things like genetically altering ('engineering') an embryo or a foetus, and surgery on adults. *Selection*, on the other hand, specifically *selective reproduction*, involves deciding which out of a number of possible future persons will exist (using, for example, preimplantation genetic diagnosis, gamete selection, or selective abortion). As I explained in Chapter 1, the main concern of this book is the latter: selective reproduction. Nonetheless, I need to reintroduce the distinction at this point in order to head off a possible source of confusion. This is that it might be thought that the term 'enhancement' necessarily refers to modification, not to selection, because to enhance something (in the ordinary sense of the word) is to *improve* it, and the idea of improvement suggests altering something, changing a determinate object for the better. Certainly, in everyday parlance, that is the most common use of the term. However, at least in bioethics discourse, 'enhancement' can also be used to cover selection. For example, the Human Genetics Commission tell us that

In theory, embryo enhancement might involve either the selection of an embryo with genetic characteristics indicative of desirable traits such as beauty or intelligence, or a process of genetic modification to enhance such traits.[1]

Jean Chambers, while writing in the *Cambridge Quarterly of Healthcare Ethics*, tells us:

The very possibility of preimplantation embryo *selection* raises the issue of negative versus positive eugenics. 'Negative eugenics' refers to the elimination of diseases or defects, whereas 'positive eugenics' *refers to the enhancement of traits.*[2]

So it seems that we can enhance either by improving a determinate individual, or by selecting a better rather than a worse (possible, future) person. I should, however, add that (rather confusingly) there is some variation in practice here and some bioethics scholars do sometimes use 'enhancement' in a narrower sense, to mean *modifications* which improve, and then contrast this with selection. A recent example of this is a paper called 'Behavioural Genetics: why eugenic selection is *preferable to* enhancement'.[3] Anyhow, for my present purposes, I shall be using the term 'enhancement' in the wider sense to refer to both modification and selection and, as will be clear by now, my main interest here is the latter: selection. That said, many of the ethical arguments considered later apply equally to modification and selection and so will, I hope, speak to those whose foremost interest is (for example) in the use of genetic engineering, or even surgery, to achieve enhancement.

The Non-Disease-Avoidance Account of Enhancement

Having established that 'enhancement' can apply to both modification and selection, the next question is—with what are enhancement interventions to be contrasted? One answer, the dominant one in the bioethics literature, is that enhancement is to be distinguished from the avoidance, cure, or prevention of *disease*. The following passages from Cooke, Gardner, and Kamm (respectively) illustrate this:

one may be inclined to redistribute as much as possible and be as 'charitable' as possible, *going well beyond disease prevention, and into enhancement,* where height, good looks, physical strength,

---

[1] Human Genetics Commission, *Choosing the Future: Genetics and Reproductive Decision Making* (July 2004), 19.
[2] Jean Chambers, 'Women's Right to Choose Rationally: Genetic Information, Embryos Selection, and Genetic Manipulation', *Cambridge Quarterly of Healthcare Ethics*, 12 (2003), 418–28: 418. Emphasis added.
[3] Julian Savulescu, Melanie Hemsley, Ainsley Newson, and Bennett Foddy, 'Behavioural Genetics: Why Eugenic Selection is Preferable to Enhancement', *Journal of Applied Philosophy*, 23 (2006), 157–71. Emphasis added.

and intelligence, would be considered generous endowments of resources for one's future descendants.[4]

Enhancement . . . is the use of genetic engineering to supply a characteristic that a parent might want in a child that *does not involve the treatment or prevention of disease.*[5]

enhancement itself may take two forms: (a) improving humans so that they fare better than any current human with respect to some characteristic, and (b) bringing people to have *good characteristics, whose absence in them would not be a disease,* that are now already common to many but not all humans (e.g., high intelligence)[6]

This view of enhancement is what I term the *Non-Disease-Avoidance Account.* It says that human enhancement is any improvement (through modification or selection) that goes beyond, or is something other than, the avoidance of disease. (Improvement, in the case of selection, means a 'better' person rather than some 'worse' alternative.)

The Non-Disease-Avoidance Account rather obviously leads to the enormously complicated question, 'what is disease?' not something that I am going to attempt to answer here. Indeed, it is not a question that *needs* answering here because the Non-Disease-Avoidance Account of enhancement is neutral with respect to this issue and almost any theory of disease could be allied with it. One implication of this is that the Non-Disease-Avoidance Account, on its own, will not have much to say about particular cases or issues. That is because, unless it is allied with a particular theory of disease, it will not entail that x or y are enhancements (because we will not know if x or y are diseases). Another implication is that proponents of the Non-Disease-Avoidance Account of enhancement may well disagree among themselves about whether x or y are enhancements, if they also disagree with one another about the correct theory of disease.

Similarly, the Non-Disease-Avoidance Account of enhancement raises the question of what counts as an improvement, given that enhancements are *improvements* other than disease-avoidance. As with the nature of disease, the Non-Disease-Avoidance Account itself remains silent on this and so, in order to deliver substantive results about particular cases, it will need always to be allied with some supplementary theory of what counts as improving a person, and so what counts as a good person (though not necessarily in the moral sense of 'good'). Welfare, or the capacity to flourish and be happy, are among the more obvious candidates. Thus, when we ask why making people more muscular and giving them better memories are *improvements* (rather than

    [4] E. Cooke, 'Germ-Line Engineering, Freedom, and Future Generations', *Bioethics*, 17 (2003), 32–58: 37. Emphasis added.
    [5] W. Gardner, 'Can Human Genetic Enhancement be Prohibited?' *Journal of Medicine and Philosophy*, 20 (1995), 65–84: 65. Emphasis added.
    [6] France Kamm, 'Genes, Justice, and Obligations to Future People', *Social Philosophy and Policy*, 19 (2002), 360–88.

mere changes) the usual answer is that these characteristics are supposed (on average) to make people happier. However, there is nothing in the Non-Disease-Avoidance Account per se that commits its proponents to a welfare-oriented view and the account could in principle be allied with almost any view of the good human or person.

The Super-Normality Account of Enhancement

The Non-Disease-Avoidance Account is the most prevalent account in the bioethics literature. However, we need also to look at the other main account: the *Super-Normality Account*. Someone who seems to hold this view is Glannon, who says that enhancement:

aims to raise cognitive and physical capacities *above the normal range of functioning* for persons.[7]

According to the Super-Normality Account, enhancement consists of improving a person *beyond the normal range* for persons (regardless of whether or not this is an instance of disease-avoidance). The two accounts of enhancement will agree about many, perhaps even most, cases (which is, I suspect, why the distinction between the two is rarely alluded to). Take, for instance, the rather hackneyed example of making a person extraordinarily intelligent (or indeed making an extraordinarily intelligent person). The chances are that proponents of the two different accounts can agree that this is enhancement. For proponents of the Non-Disease-Avoidance Account, it is enhancement because it is (a) an improvement, but (b) nothing much to do with disease-avoidance, while for supporters of the Super-Normality Account, it is an enhancement because it is (a) an improvement, and (b) one which takes the person's capacities above the normal range. However, the two accounts will sometimes disagree about cases. To see how they differ, consider the following embryo selection case.

> **Embryo A** *is known to have a serious genetic disorder.*
>
> **Embryo B** *will probably develop with significantly below average intelligence, but not low enough to constitute a learning disability or mental disorder.*
>
> **Embryo C** *is likely to develop with an exceptionally effective immune system.*
>
> **Embryo D** *is likely to have significantly higher than average intelligence.*
>
> **Embryo E** *is average/normal in all known respects.*

Given fairly standard assumptions about what counts as disease and what counts as improvement, what will the two different accounts of enhancement say about these cases?

[7] Walter Glannon, 'Genes, Embryos, and Future People', *Bioethics*, 12 (1998), 187–211.

First, *if we were to deselect (select against) Embryo A and choose E instead would this be an instance of enhancement?* According to the Non-Disease-Avoidance Account, *no*, because the aim of the deselection is to avoid disease. And, according to the Super-Normality Account, *no*, because *Embryo E* is merely normal, not super-normal.

Second, *if we were to deselect (select against) Embryo B and choose E instead would this be an instance of enhancement?* On the Non-Disease-Avoidance Account, this *would* be an instance of enhancement because selecting normal intelligence over subnormal intelligence is (arguably) an improvement, but not a case of disease-avoidance. According to the Super-Normality Account, though, deselecting *Embryo B* is *not* a case of enhancement because in choosing *E* over *B* we are avoiding subnormality rather than selecting for super-normality.

Third, *would selecting Embryo C be a case of enhancement?* According to the Non-Disease-Avoidance Account this would *not* be enhancement because the aim of the selection is disease-avoidance (albeit future disease-avoidance). On the Super-Normality Account, however, it *would* be enhancement, for *Embryo C* is being selected on account of its *super-normal* immune system.

Finally, *would selecting ('selecting in') Embryo D be a case of enhancement?* Both accounts agree that this is enhancement selection. For it is not a case of disease-avoidance and it is a case of selecting in favour of a super-normal characteristic.

Table 7.1 illustrates some of the differences between the Non-Disease-Avoidance Account and the Super-Normality Account of enhancement. The shaded cells are the ones where the two accounts disagree.

Table 7.1.

Type of Selection	What does the Non-Disease-Avoidance Account say?	What does the Super-Normality Account say?
Selecting against embryos with genetic disorders	*Not* enhancement (because disease-avoidance)	*Not* enhancement (because *not* selecting super-normal characteristics)
Selecting against (non-pathologically) low intelligence	Enhancement (because not disease-avoidance)	*Not* enhancement (because *not* selecting in super-normal characteristics)
Selecting in favour of exceptionally effective immune systems	*Not* enhancement (because disease-avoidance)	Enhancement (because selecting super-normal characteristics)
Selecting in favour of extremely high intelligence	Enhancement (because not disease-avoidance)	Enhancement (because selecting super-normal characteristics)

So What is Enhancement?

It seems to me that there are not any completely decisive arguments in favour of one or other of the two accounts of enhancement. Essentially, what we are dealing with here are two different (but quite closely related) concepts. On the one hand, there is improvement that is not disease-avoidance and, on the other, there is the bestowing of super-normal characteristics. Both concepts are legitimate and useful and both have a place in the various ethical and policy debates. Which account of enhancement one chooses (and which is most useful) will very often depend on one's own ethical concerns and views. Someone who thinks, for example, that disease-avoidance is a morally special kind of activity may well find it useful to contrast this with 'enhancement' (meaning *non-disease-avoidance*); whereas someone whose concerns are more to do with the distribution of welfare, or with 'the natural', may want to claim that 'enhancement' (meaning *giving people significantly super-normal powers*) is especially problematic. So we can ask whether either of these 'camps' has a right to claim the word 'enhancement' for its own exclusive use. But at present I can see no compelling argument for this on either side. So provided that everyone is clear about what they mean by 'enhancement', and says what they mean by it and, in particular, which of the two senses outlined above is being used, then it is acceptable to use the term in either way. What we must, however, avoid is equivocation: sliding between the two senses (without noticing or saying so) during the course of an argument or discussion. For this reason, it may well be better if talk of enhancement, or at least *unqualified* talk of enhancement, were replaced by other less ambiguous terminology: for instance, one might talk about 'selecting for super-normality' rather than 'enhancement selection'.

Finally, I mentioned in the previous chapter that the idea of enhancement has a lot in common with the idea of positive eugenics and I am now in a position to say specifically what they have in common. It is that, just as there is a Non-Disease-Avoidance Account and a Super-Normality Account of enhancement, so too are there Disease-Avoidance and Super-Normality Accounts of the positive/negative eugenics distinction. Thus, one workable definition of 'positive eugenics' is: *improving the 'gene pool' in ways that are not (intentionally, primarily) to do with disease-avoidance*. Another is: *improving the 'gene pool' in ways that lead to the creation of (people with) super-normal characteristics (health-related or otherwise)*. Conversely, 'negative eugenics' can mean either *improving the 'gene pool' so as to avoid disease* or *improving the 'gene pool' by reducing the prevalence of (people with) subnormal traits (health-related or otherwise)*.[8]

[8] Stephen Wilkinson, 'On the Distinction between Positive and Negative Eugenics', in Matti Hayry, Tuija Takala, and Peter Herissone-Kelly (eds.), *Arguments and Analysis in Bioethics* (Amsterdam: Rodopi, in press).

7.2 The Moral Status of Enhancement

> The therapy-enhancement distinction occupies a central place in contemporary discussions of human genetics and has been the subject of much debate . . . In thinking about the morality of genetic interventions, many writers have defended somatic gene therapy, and some have defended germline gene therapy, but only a handful of others defend genetic enhancement, or even give it a fair hearing. The mere mention of genetic enhancement makes many people cringe and brings to mind the Nazi eugenics programs, Aldous Huxley's *Brave New World*, 'The X-Files,' or the recent movie 'Gattaca.'[9]

As the above quotation from Resnik suggests, many people believe that the idea of enhancement is ethically significant. Specifically, there is a widespread belief that, in controversial areas like genetics and reproduction, enhancement is more morally problematic and less defensible than (for example) promoting health and avoiding disease. The therapy-enhancement distinction also often figures in debates about priority setting or health care resource allocation, with one commonly held view being that enhancement is a relatively low priority compared to treatment. This is actually one area in which the distinction between the two accounts of enhancement offered in the previous section is relevant because it is sometimes said, in defence of enhancement, that immunization is an enhancement. However, whether this is so depends on which account of enhancement is adopted. For while it may well be enhancement on the Super-Normality Account, it clearly is not on the Non-Disease-Avoidance Account.

However, not *everyone* thinks that using genetics and/or selective reproduction to achieve enhancement is a bad thing and some people positively embrace the idea of enhancement, which is hardly surprising really given that enhancement necessarily involves some kind of *improvement* and so must presumably be good in some respects at least. An example of support for enhancement is the Transhumanist Movement. The World Transhumanist Association, for example, tells us that it:

> support[s] the development of and access to new technologies that enable everyone to enjoy better minds, better bodies and better lives. In other words, we want people to be *better than well*.[10]

---

[9] David Resnik, 'The Moral Significance of the Therapy-Enhancement Distinction in Human Genetics', *Cambridge Quarterly of Healthcare Ethics*, 9 (2000), 365–77: 365.

[10] World Transhumanist Association, *What is the TWA?*, <http://transhumanism.org/index.php/WTA/about> (last accessed: 23 Mar. 2009).

There is even a Transhumanist Declaration which begins as follows:

1. Humanity will be radically changed by technology in the future. We foresee the feasibility of redesigning the human condition, including such parameters as the inevitability of aging, limitations on human and artificial intellects, unchosen psychology, suffering, and our confinement to the planet earth.
2. Systematic research should be put into understanding these coming developments and their long-term consequences.
3. Transhumanists think that by being generally open and embracing of new technology we have a better chance of turning it to our advantage than if we try to ban or prohibit it.
4. Transhumanists advocate the moral right for those who so wish to use technology to extend their mental and physical (including reproductive) capacities and to improve their control over their own lives. We seek personal growth beyond our current biological limitations.[11]

Transhumanists put forward some interesting arguments and it is an intriguing social movement. Nonetheless, I will not say anything else about transhumanism here. This is because, in keeping with the general approach of the book, my main aim is to critically assess the arguments and positions of those who condemn, or advocate the restrictive regulation of, selective reproduction (or of particular forms, such as enhancement selection). This is a project that will, I imagine, be of interest to transhumanists, since I am to some extent critiquing the transhumanists' critics. But assessing *positive* arguments *for* enhancement and selective reproduction is outside the scope of my project, except insofar as attending to these is a necessary part of the critique.

So I shall spend the rest of this chapter assessing various arguments for the view that enhancement (especially enhancement selection) is morally problematic and/or ought to be prohibited. Before proceeding to consider these arguments, however, I need to say something more about the nature of this anti-enhancement view, or rather of *these* anti-enhancement views, for several different possibilities are available. For our purposes, there are three main anti-enhancement theses to look at. First, there is the *absolutist* anti-enhancement position: that *all* human enhancement is wrong (or that using genetic engineering and/or selective reproduction to bring about enhancement is always wrong). Second, there is the *defeasibilist* anti-enhancement view. This says that 'being an enhancement' is a morally negative or wrong-making feature of actions, but that some enhancements may, nonetheless, be justified, all things considered. For example, people with this view may think that a particular enhancement is justified (all things considered) because it massively increases welfare. But they will also think

[11] World Transhumanist Association, *The Transhumanist Declaration* (2002), <http://transhumanism.org/index.php/WTA/declaration> (last accessed: Monday, 13 Apr. 2009).

that its being an enhancement is nonetheless a (defeated or outweighed) reason not to do it, and furthermore that it would have been better if we had been able to find a different means of achieving this massive welfare gain, one that did not involve having to resort to enhancement. So this *defeasibilist* anti-enhancement view essentially says that enhancement is generally a bad thing and best avoided, but that avoiding enhancement is not the only moral consideration there is, and so sometimes we will, all things considered, have good reason to resort to enhancement. Third, and finally, there is the *pragmatic* anti-enhancement view. According to this, there is nothing intrinsically wrong with enhancement. However, enhancement is still usually best avoided for pragmatic and/or consequence-based reasons. For instance, these pragmatists may believe that enhancement tends to lead to reductions in welfare, or to unfairness, or that enhancement technologies are dangerous and liable to lead to abuse. Subtle variants of each of these views are available but for the time being I will group them into these three broad categories.

Finally, before moving on to consider the arguments, I should reiterate something about the scope of the present discussion. My sole concern at the moment is with people who think that achieving *enhancement through selective reproduction* is morally problematic, although (for stylistic reasons) I will not necessary say this each time. Thus, when I talk about arguments against enhancement, I mean *enhancement through selective reproduction* (enhancement selection). Indeed, I suspect that almost no one is opposed to enhancement *across the board*, for the view that improving people *whatever the means* would be a very odd one to hold and it is hard to think of any rationale for it. That said, although the present discussion is focused on selective reproduction, many of the arguments and counterarguments will apply in the other controversial areas mentioned earlier, such as genetic modification and contested surgeries.

7.3 The Goals of Medicine

When new technologies are employed in conventional medicine, the answers about ends are quite clear. We want to heal the sick. We want to relieve the suffering. And our new abilities might let us do so more effectively. But when the same technologies enable us to reach beyond the traditional goals of medicine to alter our bodies and minds for ends other than restoring health, we are in uncharted waters.[12]

---

[12] Leon Kass, 'Reflections on Public Bioethics: A View from the Trenches', *Kennedy Institute of Ethics Journal*, 15 (2005), 221–50: 235.

The Goals of Medicine Argument claims that disease-avoidance is preferable to other kinds of improvement (what would be enhancements on the Non-Disease-Avoidance Account) because whereas disease-avoidance is clearly a core goal (perhaps *the* core goal) of medicine, enhancement is not. Similar, but broader, versions of this argument could invoke the goals of the health care professions generally, or of the National Health Service. Resnik describes a version of this view as follows:

A slightly different approach to these issues asserts that genetic therapy is on solid moral ground because it promotes the goals of medicine, while genetic enhancement promotes other, morally questionable goals.[13]

The Goals of Medicine Argument is, however, flawed. One difficulty it faces is that saying what the goals of medicine are is not easy. Indeed, stating what exactly the goals of medicine are has become a bit of an academic sub-specialty in its own right with Bengt Brülde, for example, suggesting that there are as many as seven widely accepted and 'irreducible goals of medicine', namely:

- To promote functional ability, especially health-related functioning.
- To maintain or restore normal clinical status (structure and function), especially by preventing disease or injury, or by curing disease.
- To promote quality of life, especially by relieving pain and suffering.
- To save and prolong life, especially to prevent premature death.
- In certain cases, to help the patient to cope well with his or her condition.
- In certain cases, to improve the external conditions under which people live, either in order to promote freedom and independence (as in the case of handicap) or in order to prevent disease or injury.
- To promote the growth and development of children.[14]

So it is far from obvious that disease-avoidance is medicine's only goal. Other possibilities include promoting happiness and enabling people to exercise their autonomy, neither of which necessarily involve disease-avoidance, and both of which may require doctors to go beyond disease-avoidance. Furthermore, enhancement is already part of medical practice and many doctors (notably cosmetic surgeons and sports physicians) provide enhancement services.

A second criticism of the Goals of Medicine Argument is that it wrongly views as intrinsically valuable, something that is only instrumentally valuable (the avoidance of disease). What really matters (so the objection goes) is patient welfare, perhaps in conjunction with some other fundamental goods. Thus, doctors should not refrain

---

[13] Resnik, 'Moral Significance', 368. Resnik goes on to critique and reject this view.
[14] Bengt Brülde, 'The Goals of Medicine: Towards a Unified Theory', *Healthcare Analysis*, 9 (2001), 1–13: 5. See also Lennart Nordenfelt, 'On the Goals of Medicine, Health Enhancement, and Social Welfare', *Healthcare Analysis*, 9 (2001), 15–23.

from benefiting patients (or, in the case of reproductive medicine, from creating better off future patients) simply because what they require (or want) goes beyond the treatment of disease; conversely, they should not treat (or strive to avoid) disease unless doing so benefits the patient.

The third, and it seems to me the most telling, objection to the Goals of Medicine Argument is that, even if its claims are true, they only apply to members of the medical profession. So the argument can simply be bypassed by getting people other than doctors to deal with enhancement: for there is no reason why people other than doctors should feel constrained by the fact (if it is a fact) that what they are doing does not promote the goals of medicine.

Consider this analogy. The Plumbers' Union argues against the installation of garden sprinklers and decorative water features on the grounds that the 'goal of plumbing' is to provide householders with water for drinking and washing, not pointless ornamental items. Well, it may or may not be true that these things are a proper part of plumbing. But, even if they are not, this would hardly be an argument against sprinklers and water features per se. Rather, it would be an argument for getting people other than plumbers to install and maintain them. This is structurally exactly like the position of doctors who object to enhancement on 'goals of medicine' grounds. Indeed, it is analogous in other ways as well. For instance, we are naturally inclined to get plumbers to install water features because they have the right technical skills, just as we are naturally inclined to get doctors to do cosmetic surgery and reproductive enhancement because they have the right technical skills. But, in both cases, if there is a professional ethos that stands in the way of practitioners' carrying out the desired task, there is (in principle) nothing to stop us from just creating a new alternative group of professionals (enhancement practitioners, sprinkler installers, or whatever) part of whose remit is to carry out whatever it is the doctors and plumbers reject. These new professionals may well have exactly the same *technical* skills as the old ones but would have a different ethos and different conceptions of their professional goals (for example, the goal of the 'enhancement practitioners' would be enhancement rather than cure). So the Goals of Medicine Argument is doomed to failure on this ground. For the most it can show is that *doctors* ought not to enhance, and doctors are not the only possible enhancers. Furthermore, *all* similar arguments are bound to fail. For example, people sometimes claim that abortion, euthanasia, and providing recreational drugs should not be done because they are incompatible with the goals of medicine—but, again, the most that this shows is that these things should not be *done by doctors*. It is not an objection to their being done *by someone* (which is not to say that there are not other objections to these things).

It seems then that there are plenty of reasons to reject the Goals of Medicine Argument.

7.4 Positional Goods

This section considers the Positional Goods Argument against enhancement selection (or against certain kinds of enhancement selection).

What are Positional Goods?

We can answer this by drawing a distinction between two different ways in which traits can be advantageous. Some characteristics are *non-relationally* advantageous. These are properties that it is beneficial to possess (or to have more rather than less of) regardless of whether or not other people possess them, and regardless of whether other people have more or less of them than you do. So one way of deciding whether a property is non-relationally advantageous is to think about whether having it (or more of it) would be valuable on a desert island, or in a world with no other people. If it would be advantageous, the non-existence of other people notwithstanding, then it is a non-relational good. Perhaps health and physical strength fall into this category.

Non-relationally advantageous features are contrasted with relationally advantageous ones, or positional goods. Purely positional goods are properties that it is good to possess (or to have more of) *only* because this gives you a competitive advantage *over other people*. Thus, a purely positional good would be of no value to you in the desert island scenario. Being fashionable (by which I mean up-to-date rather than tasteful) is a good example. People who always wear 'the latest design' and are 'ahead of the game' may derive esteem and status by having clothes that are more fashionable than other people's. There are two reasons for thinking that fashionableness is a purely positional good. First, it would not be advantageous in the desert island scenario, if indeed we can make sense of what fashion would mean in such an environment. Second, fashion looks like a *zero-sum game*: by which I mean, if everyone started to wear clothes that were (say) two months more up-to-date than they used to, then no one (apart from clothes shops perhaps) would gain. The fashionable people would continue to be fashionable and those who lagged behind would continue to lag behind. Indeed, this is a general feature of purely positional goods. Social situations in which people chase them are zero-sum games; gain to one person is matched by loss to another.

Tallness is another standard example of a positional good. It is often said that being tall per se is not advantageous, but that being taller than other people is. Thus, tallness would not be advantageous in the desert island scenario, and environmental or genetic enhancements that made the whole population taller would be (at best) a waste of time because adding height is a zero-sum game. As Buchanan et al. put it:

pursuit of 'positional advantage' through enhancement of some traits, such as height, risks being either self-defeating or unfair. If all can do it, it may be self-defeating: no one gains a height advantage if everyone increases in height. If only the wealthiest can pursue enhancement, it seems unfair that advantages so ramify.[15]

When the goods secured by markets in genes are positional, as would arguably be the case with increased height for children, advantages won by some are by dint of logic disadvantages imposed on others.[16]

Now in fact is it not completely obvious that tallness is a purely positional good, or at least it may not be in some environments. For example, we can imagine desert island scenarios in which having a giraffe-like reach is good for you, even if there are no other people around for you to be taller than. This leads to my next point, which is that many properties are both non-relationally advantageous and positionally advantageous:

many traits that confer competitive advantage also have some instrumental and intrinsic value to people independently of these advantages. For traits valued in these more complex ways, their pursuit by everyone need not produce self-defeating coordination problems. For example, suppose everyone's intellectual performance could be enhanced in certain areas; no competitive advantage would result, but (arguably) society might be better off because of the enhanced abilities of all.[17]

Indeed, most of the examples that one can think of fall into this 'mixed' category. For example, having enhanced eyesight, hearing, and health are non-relationally good, but would probably also confer some competitive advantage. For these features, the best case situation for an individual would be one in which she was the only enhanced person. That way, she would get to enjoy both the intrinsic benefits of the enhancement *and* the positional advantage of being better than other people. However, for these 'mixed' features (unlike for *purely* positional goods) people could still all be better off in a world of universal enhancement, for the gains do not depend entirely on positional advantage; it is not a zero-sum game.

The Positional Goods Argument

Having outlined what positional goods are, we are now able to look at the structure of the argument, which is as follows.

[15] Allen Buchanan, Dan Brock, Norman Daniels, and Daniel Wikler, *From Choice to Chance: Genetics and Justice* (Cambridge: Cambridge University Press, 2000), 155.
[16] Buchanan et al., *From Choice to Choice*, 340.   [17] Buchanan et al., *From Choice to Choice*, 186.

1. If permitted, enhancement selection would be used (among other things) to confer positional advantage. Parents would seek to use selection technologies to 'chase' positional goods for their children.

2. *Either*: access to positional goods enhancement would be nearly universal, e.g. because of public funding, or because the techniques became very cheap and easy. *Or*: only a particular sector of society would be able to access enhancement, perhaps because a market in selection developed that only the rich could afford to access.

3. The first scenario (nearly universal enhancement) is objectionable because of the waste of resources involved. Because chasing (purely) positional goods is a zero-sum gain, there will be no overall benefit but the costs may be considerable.

4. The second scenario (in which only the rich can access enhancement) is, however, also objectionable because: (a) it would lead to additional distributive injustice; and (b) those people who were unable to afford enhancement would be harmed.

5. *Therefore*: enhancement selection of positionally advantageous traits should not be permitted because allowing it would (via one of the two scenarios mentioned above) lead to a morally objectionable outcome.

The first question to ask about this argument is—what is its scope? It is, in some way, supposed to be an anti-enhancement argument but its target is the selection of traits that are positional goods, which may not be the same as enhancement. Indeed, positional goods and enhancement are clearly distinct categories, regardless of which account of enhancement we choose. For some super-normal characteristics are non-relationally good (for example, having an exceptionally strong heart and lungs), and some characteristics unrelated to disease-avoidance are non-relationally good (such as having a fantastic memory). So, on either account, only some enhancements are positional goods. Hence, the Positional Goods Argument could only work directly against *some* enhancements, those that aim at selecting children with positionally advantageous traits.

That said, the Positional Goods Argument may still work *indirectly* against enhancement generally, particularly in a legal or regulatory context. For, it may be argued (for example) that, given the difficulty of distinguishing between non-relationally advantageous enhancements and positional enhancements, the only way of preventing a positional goods 'arms race' (and the associated unfairness and/or waste) is to draw the line at disease-avoidance: to allow disease-avoidance selection (which is primarily to do with non-relational goods, even if some positional advantage accrues as a side effect) and nothing else. For once we start allowing enhancement selection, then it will be very hard to draw a further line that prevents medical practice from moving into positional goods enhancement.

So while, from a 'pure ethics' point of view, the Positional Goods Argument counts only against positional enhancement, it may in policy discussions give us some reason to restrictively regulate *all* enhancements. Indeed, it may be that in general the Positional Goods Argument works better at a policy level than at the level of personal morality. Another instance of this is Premiss 3: the view that social situations in which a positional good is universally sought are morally objectionable and best avoided because of the waste involved. Again, this seems to speak primarily to policymakers who might have an opportunity to avoid these 'arms race' situations by putting in place disincentives or prohibitions that prevent people from chasing the positional good in question. Given the costs involved and the lack of benefit, it seems clear that any rational policymaker will seek to do this provided that there are no countervailing reasons (such as the costs of enforcement or people's unbending reluctance to give up the positional good). However, it is less obvious that private individuals, in these 'arms race' situations, are obliged to refrain from chasing the positional good. Say, for example, that nearly all schoolchildren take a safe and effective dietary supplement that will, in due course, make them 15 cm taller than they would otherwise have been. The Positional Goods Argument, it seems, offers us good reasons for banning or discouraging this practice, at least for children who are in the normal height range. But it is much less clear that individual parents have a personal moral duty to deprive their children of the dietary supplement, especially in a situation where 99 per cent of the other children are taking it. For doing this would seem to disadvantage their children without doing any good, unless (and this is perhaps an important exception) not giving their child the supplement was a means of bringing about a ban, or a change of social attitudes, perhaps as part of a political campaign.

Before moving on to consider some objections to the Positional Goods Argument, it is worth pausing for a moment to emphasize one feature of Premiss 4, which concerns the scenario in which only the rich can access positional enhancement. The feature I have in mind is this: the claim concerns not only distributive justice (the fact that the gap between rich and poor will widen) but also *harm*, in particular the idea that acquiring a positional good, in situations where only a few people can do so, harms those people who cannot acquire it.

A possible example of this is vehicle size. It has been claimed that the safest cars are the heaviest cars, but that this is (largely) a positional phenomenon. In other words, while having one of the heaviest cars is safer than having a lighter car, this is mainly a function of *relative* weight: what matters is that your car is *bigger than* the other driver's in a collision. So vehicle size (as far as safety is concerned) looks like a zero-sum game. If we all had bigger cars then no one would be any safer and we would all have wasted a lot of resources. So now imagine a (not terribly unlikely) scenario in which not everyone can afford one of the biggest cars, in which some people have to put up with smaller models. As well as any injustice involved, the (unwilling) drivers of small cars might reasonably claim that the drivers of heavy cars (who have 'upgraded' for safety reasons) have *harmed* them (when they suffer additional injuries in a collision with a heavy car) or that they have been *subjected to additional risk* (if they are lucky enough not to have been in a collision yet).

The fact that this is not only a claim about injustice, but also one about harm, strengthens, and widens the argument's appeal. For this means that it may persuade even those who are sceptical about the injustice claim and Millian liberals who believe that harm is the only valid reason to prohibit a practice.

Objections

In this subsection, I shall consider three possible objections to the Positional Goods Argument.

1. Positional Goods and Enhancement

The first objection is that, as was conceded in the previous subsection, positional goods and enhancement are distinct categories. Therefore, the Positional Goods Argument's conclusion applies not to enhancement generally, but only to those enhancements that are positional goods.

There are two ways of dealing with this. The first, which I also outlined in the previous subsection, is to claim that (at least for law and policy purposes) there is a contingent connection between positional goods and enhancement such that, if enhancement was allowed, this would lead to (or include) the chasing of positional goods. It is hard to say much in the abstract about this response since it depends largely on practical considerations that will vary from case to case. So perhaps all we can say is that there will be some situations in which there is a close connection between positional goods and enhancement, and some in which there is not. And so, for any given possible enhancement situation, we will need evidence about the extent to which positional goods are involved before making a decision.

The second response is simply to give ground and concede that the Positional Goods Argument only applies to *some* enhancements. One could still do this, however, and defend a qualified version of the view that the concept of enhancement has some relevance to ethics, particularly if the Non-Disease-Avoidance Account of enhancement is deployed. The justification for this would be as follows. It looks as if disease-avoidance will always (when it is a good) be a non-relational good. For the absence of disease characteristics, such as malfunction and pain, is intrinsically advantageous, regardless of other people's health status (although we should not rule out the possibility of good health being positionally advantageous *as well*). So disease-avoidance will never be vulnerable to the charge that it involves the chasing of (purely) positional goods because disease-avoidance always has some intrinsic value. Whereas enhancement selection will sometimes be vulnerable to this charge. Or to put it another way, it looks as if (as regards the characteristics of persons) being an enhancement is a necessary (but not sufficient) condition for being a positional good. So we do have more reason to be suspicious of enhancements than we do of disease-avoidance—because there is a risk that they are positional goods.

2. Are Many Enhancements Purely Positional?

A second objection simply questions whether many of the genetic enhancements that parents would wish to seek for their future children really are positional goods. This is an empirical objection (leaving aside a few conceptual issues about what counts as 'positional') and involves speculating about the kinds of traits that prospective parents might be interested in acquiring. Nonetheless, advocates of this objection might reasonably claim that (if available) things like the following would be near the top of the enhancement shopping list for many prospective parents:

- Good health
- A personality type (or, more plausibly, a tendency to acquire a personality type) that increases the child's chances of happiness
- Intelligence and other traits that increase the probability of success.

All of these are, I would suggest, non-relational goods—or, at worst, they are mixed goods with relatively small positional elements. Of course, other parents may well go for positional enhancements (appearance, height, etc.) but it does seem unduly pessimistic to assume that most prospective parents will be predominantly concerned with these, rather than the kind of non-relationally advantageous quality of life-oriented features listed above.

3. Consistency — Why Single Out Enhancement?

The final objection points out that chasing positional goods is all-pervading. Several existing and accepted practices involve attempts to acquire purely or predominantly positional goods (e.g. fashion, vehicle size, some aspects of land and property ownership); and, perhaps more tellingly, a very high proportion of our socio-economic practices (perhaps even most such practices) involve a mixture of non-relational and positional gain. So, given the ubiquity of positional goods chasing, it does not look as if enhancement is any worse than many other widely accepted social phenomena. This, so the objection goes, means that proponents of the Positional Goods Argument are faced with an unpalatable choice. Either they must concede that their argument has global and revolutionary implications: specifically, the condemnation and/or prohibition of positional goods chasing across the board. Or they must accept that, because positional goods chasing is acceptable in many areas other than enhancement (or, at least, allowed and tolerated in these areas), then the same should go for enhancement; it too should be accepted, or at least permitted.

Faced with this dilemma, can the Positional Goods Argument be defended? With some qualifications, it can. The first part of the defence is to concede that there is no fundamental moral difference between chasing positional goods through enhancing one's future children and doing so through other accepted means, such as buying a large SUV ('Sport Utility Vehicle') for safety reasons. Other things being equal, all of these practices are objectionable, and for the reasons offered by the Positional Goods Argument. So proponents of this argument should just admit that their argument applies not just to enhancement, but to a much wider range of practices. Against this, someone might claim that its conclusion then has counter-intuitive and revolutionary implications, in terms of the condemnation and prohibition of widely accepted social practices. But proponents of the Positional Goods Argument should, it seems to me, embrace these implications (insofar as they are revolutionary) and deny that they are counter-intuitive (since not all intuitions are conservative). For the Positional Goods Argument does reveal a serious problem with chasing positional goods, and it is a problem that applies to fashion and SUVs as much as to enhancement.

But, given this, is the Positional Goods Argument still an argument against enhancement? Well, it can only really claim to be: (a) an argument against *some* enhancements; and (b) not *only* an argument against enhancement. As regards the practical question of whether enhancement selection and fashion or SUVs (etc.) should be treated the same way in law and policy terms, this will depend largely on externalities: i.e. on factors outside the scope of the Positional Goods Argument itself. One of these is the practicalities of enforcement. For example, it is relatively easy to ban genetic enhancement because it must (at least at the moment) take place within a heavily regulated medical sector, but it is hard to know how we would set about banning fashion. Large vehicles are an interesting 'middle' case and it may well be possible to discourage these through regulation and taxation (as has indeed been done recently in the UK, although for different reasons). Another externality is the degree of harm involved in the chasing of the positional good, and it might plausibly be argued that genetic enhancement is more likely to harm the non-enhanced, than merely being unfashionably dressed. Hence, the case against enhancement might, for this reason, be stronger than that against fashion. Yet another externality, which applies to mixed goods (those with both non-relational and positional elements) is the question of how much real overall benefit is delivered by the non-relational aspect. Thus, if we were to prohibit intelligence enhancement (which probably has some non-relational and some positional aspects) we might lose out on an opportunity to increase average intelligence, something that may produce an overall utility gain. Anyway, as I have said, these questions are outside the scope of the Positional Goods Argument itself, but rather are interesting questions raised by it. Nonetheless, the Positional Goods

Argument does give us a reason (albeit a defeasible one) to be opposed to at least some forms of enhancement, those which are about giving solely or predominantly positional advantages to one's future children.

Conclusion

So how successful is the Positional Goods Argument? It does seem to give us a (defeasible) reason to discourage or prohibit the chasing of positional goods. Hence, we should (other things being equal) be supportive of attempts to prevent selective reproduction being used in ways that might lead to a positional goods 'arms race'.

Whether the Positional Goods Argument provides a reason to oppose enhancement selection *generally*, however, is another matter. As we have seen, the main problem with using the Positional Goods Argument against enhancement is that many enhancements are non-relationally, rather than positionally, advantageous. Thus, the Positional Goods Argument does not count against these. Or, if it does, it must do so through an indirect route, such as the fact (when it is a fact) that the only way of stopping *positional* enhancement selection is to ban *all* enhancement selection. There may, I would concede, be situations in which this indirect argument works. Whether we are in such a situation now, however, is questionable. I suggested earlier that many parents would, if it became possible, seek to use enhancement selection to acquire intrinsically (rather than merely positionally) advantageous features for their children, such as health, happiness, and intelligence. If this is right, then the extent to which the introduction of enhancement selection will lead to a positional goods 'arms race' is limited, although that is not to say that there will not be wider issues of access and social justice that need attending to. It is to some of these that I now turn.

7.5 Equality

In this section, I consider the argument that enhancement is wrong and/or ought not to be permitted because it is linked to inequality. Unlike the Positional Goods Argument, this objection to enhancement selection is meant to work directly against both intrinsically and positionally advantageous traits. It immediately raises two questions. First, must enhancement selection inevitably lead to increased inequality, and (if not inevitably) how strong are our reasons for thinking that it would, as a matter of fact, do so? Second, is inequality per se a bad thing?

Two main reasons are offered for thinking that enhancement would lead to further inequality. The first is empirical: that, if offered as a private service, then only the rich would be able to access enhancement. Hence, inequality would be worsened because wealthy children would not only be monetarily better off, but would also have advantageous genetic make-ups. The second reason involves a putative conceptual link between enhancement (using the Super-Normality Account) and inequality. The link is based on the fact that (on the Super-Normality Account) enhancement is all about the addition of super-normal characteristics, whereas non-enhancement selection[18] (that is, the selection of traits that are not enhancements) involves the elimination or reduction of subnormal ones. Assuming that most existing people have normal characteristics, reducing the number of future people with subnormal characteristics will have an equalizing effect: a higher proportion of the population will be close to the average quantity for that population. But enhancement will have the opposite effect, by 'replacing' (possible, future) people who would have been near the norm with ones who are super-normal and thus further away from the average. Table 7.2 illustrates this, using the example of height (although nothing depends on its being height, it could be any readily quantifiable feature, and need not be a positional good).

Table 7.2.

People's Heights (cm)	Natural State (%)	Enhancement Only (%)	Non-Enhancement Selection Only (%)	Both Forms of Selection (%)
120	10	10	Nil	Nil
140	20	20	10	10
160	40	20	60	40
180	20	20	20	20
200	10	30	10	30

The second column shows the 'natural state', the distribution of height without any selection having taken place. (Remember that this argument deploys the Super-Normality Account of enhancement.) The middle column shows how the distribution might go if there was height enhancement (taking values from normal to super-normal levels) but no other kind of height selection (which means leaving the 'bottom end' as it is); while, conversely, the fourth column shows how the distribution might go if there was only non-enhancement selection in favour of height (of a kind that takes values from subnormal to normal levels). Finally, the right-hand column shows a combination of both forms of selection. Obviously, there are some complications concerning what counts as equality or as inequality but, intuitively at least, we can see

---

[18] Strictly speaking, this is limited to non-enhancement selection aimed at improvement. Other forms of selection that are not enhancement, such as sex selection and saviour sibling selection do not need to involve the elimination or reduction of subnormal traits.

from the table that: (a) 'enhancement only' leads to the most unequal distribution of height; and (b) 'non-enhancement-selection only' leads to the most equal distribution. So that gives us a reason to view enhancement as worse (other things being equal) than other forms of selective improvement. The reason is that enhancement is an anti-egalitarian practice, one that by its very nature leads to additional inequality.

Objections

Turning now to possible objections, the first argument (the empirical one) is relatively easy to refute. It is claimed that, if enhancement was carried out in the private sector, this would disadvantage those who were unable to afford it. This is indisputable. However, this is not a special problem for enhancement, but an entirely general issue. Thus, we could likewise say that if preimplantation genetic diagnosis to avoid genetic disorders were privatized then this would adversely affect the poor, or that the privatization of education, or of health care, or of transport, would disproportionately affect the poor and exacerbate inequality.

In the case of enhancement selection, then, the best solution would be not to discourage or prohibit it, but rather to have public funding and universal access: at least for those enhancements that deliver genuine (and not merely positional) benefit at a reasonable cost. Indeed, if (as many of us think) there is a case for publicly funding education, then a similar case could be made for publicly funding selection for enhanced intelligence, if this became possible (although clearly there would be reasonable concerns about the extent to which this might increase State power and the danger of totalitarianism).

This leaves open the question of how to deal with enhancements that are either positional or not cost-effective enough to justify public funding. I have already suggested, in the previous section, that there is a case for prohibiting, or at least officially discouraging and restricting, positional goods enhancement. So that just leaves open the question of what to do with enhancements that are non-relationally advantageous, but which are not cost-effective enough to merit State funding. To some extent, this question will have to remain open because the best way of dealing with these situations will generally be determined by the details of the case. What we can say though is that these problems have much more to do with existing socio-economic inequality than with the nature of enhancement. For the question of whether to allow the rich to buy themselves expensive advantages that cannot feasibly be provided for everyone is a completely general issue in politics. So privatized enhancement selection would, as it were, be just one more thing for the rich to spend their money on. Of course, if enhancement selection was extremely effective then we might be concerned about its very dramatic effects on equality but then, by the same token, its effectiveness would strengthen the case for public funding.

The second argument, it seems, is mistaken about, or at least overstates, the extent to which enhancement and inequality are linked. Most obviously, if we imagine a scenario in which enhancement is universal, then that could easily contain more rather than less equality, provided that everyone was enhanced to the same extent. For instance, we could make it so that *everyone* grew to be 2.5 m tall (on the, rather dubious, assumption that that would be good for people). As regards the claims related to Table 7.2, it is of course true that *if* we 'replaced' normal (possible, future) people with tall people, while not doing anything to change the height distribution at the 'bottom end' of the scale, then increased inequality would ensue. But this is just one way in which we can choose to use enhancement and not necessarily one that I would recommend. It is not in the nature of enhancement that it must be used in this way. So the second argument appears to be fatally flawed on these grounds.

Finally (and this is a huge topic that I will not go into in much detail here) there are potential problems with the background theory on which all of these equality arguments rest. These arguments all depend on some version of egalitarianism, which I am taking here to be the view that there is something intrinsically bad about unequal states of affairs, and that there is something good about a situation in which inequality is removed. But there is more than one way of removing inequality, and the egalitarian seems committed to the view that there is something good about removing inequality however we do it, including by levelling down. And this is a standard problem for egalitarian theory. If welfare in a population is very unevenly distributed, and if (as egalitarianism claims) there is something bad about this state of affairs, then there will be *something* good about removing the differentials by bringing everyone down to the level of the lowest, even if it would not, perhaps for broadly utilitarian reasons, be overall the right thing to do. As Parfit suggests, for the egalitarian:

it would be in one way better if we removed the eyes of the sighted, not to give them to the blind, but simply to make the sighted blind.[19]

This conclusion—that there would be something good about a change which improves welfare for no one and reduces it for some—is so counter-intuitive that it erodes the attraction of the original egalitarian claim.[20]

As I have said, egalitarian theory is a huge topic in political philosophy and I cannot hope to do justice to it here. Nonetheless, it is worth noting that the underlying egalitarian commitments of these equality arguments may themselves be problematic.

---

[19] Derek Parfit, 'Equality or Priority?' in John Harris (ed.), *Bioethics* (Oxford: Oxford University Press, 2001), 347–86: 364.

[20] Deontic egalitarianism (in Parfit's taxonomy) is immune to this levelling-down objection, but has its own problems.

7.6 Summary and Conclusions

All enhancements are improvements, but not all improvements are enhancements: not as the term 'enhancement' is used in bioethics, at any rate. So, within 'improvement', we have a distinction *either* between enhancement and disease-avoidance (according to the Non-Disease-Avoidance Account of enhancement) *or* between enhancement and subnormality-avoidance (according to the Super-Normality Account of enhancement). Many people think that enhancement is morally problematic and the main aim of this chapter was to explain the case for thinking this, and then to subject that case to critical scrutiny. Three arguments were discussed.

First, there was the claim that enhancement is inconsistent with the goals of medicine. This argument was rejected: (a) because there is reason to think that enhancement may well be compatible with the goals of medicine; and (b) because, even if it were not, this would only be an argument for *doctors* not enhancing, and would not give other people (specialist enhancement practitioners perhaps) a reason not to enhance.

Second, there was the Positional Goods Argument. This does successfully provide reasons to discourage or prohibit (where practicable) positional goods 'arms races'. However, since many enhancements are not positional goods, the Positional Goods Argument does not establish a case against all enhancements. However, there may be some social situations in which acting against enhancement generally is justified, because that is the only way to prevent a destructive chase for positional goods.

Finally, there was the claim that enhancement is more likely than other forms of improvement to generate inequality. This argument was rejected on the grounds that there is nothing in the nature of enhancement that makes it more liable to cause inequality. Clearly enhancement *can* be used in ways that worsen inequality, but then the same goes for almost anything, including notably disease-avoidance.

The chapter's overall conclusion then is that the arguments against enhancement selection are unsuccessful, with the specific exception of enhancing in order to acquire positional goods.

8

Sex Selection

> it may be argued that permitting selection of embryos on the basis of their sex
> would lead to demographic disaster or the reinforcement of sexist attitudes, both
> of which would be harmful to the wider society.[1]

As well as its intrinsic interest, sex selection serves as an illuminating example from a
much wider set of questions about the legitimacy of certain reproductive choices, and
about the extent to which law should constrain procreative liberty. For a number of
reasons, sex selection is a particularly interesting case. First, unlike some of the more
fanciful bioethical examples of parental choice (selecting for intelligence and the like)
sex selection is (or can be) technically uncomplicated and is already easy to deliver
reliably. Thus, it is a pressing practical issue that has already received considerable
attention not just from academics, but from the policy community.[2] Second, sex
selection (with the exception of selection to avoid sex-linked genetic disorders) is
a reasonably clear case in which parental desire or preference is the immediate
motivation, rather than considerations relating to the health or welfare of the
future child. Thus, it is perhaps a clearer or purer case of the exercise of reproductive
autonomy than (for example) using preimplantation genetic diagnosis to avoid disease.
Third, sex selection raises in very direct ways issues of sex or gender discrimination;
that is not to say that other forms of selection do not raise such issues, but sex selection
is undoubtedly the clearest case. Finally, sex selection is a topic where bioethics, public
policy, and law are particularly closely related and where philosophical analyses of
ethical arguments (such as those in this chapter) are particularly relevant to the
formation and understanding of law and policy. This is because, more often than

---

[1] House of Commons Select Committee on Science and Technology, *Inquiry into Human Reproductive Technologies and the Law, Eighth Special Report of Session 2004–2005* (2005), 20.

[2] See e.g. Human Fertilisation and Embryology Authority (HFEA), *Sex Selection: Choice and Responsibility in Human Reproduction* (consultation document) (2002), 5 and *Sex Selection: Options for Regulation (A Report on the Human Fertilisation and Embryology Authority's (HFEA's) 2002-3 Review of Sex Selection Including a Discussion of Legislative and Regulatory Options)* (2003), 25; House of Commons Select Committee on Science and Technology, *Inquiry, Eighth Special Report*, 179; Human Genetics Commission, *Making Babies* (2006), 19.

not, the reasoning offered by policymakers and lawmakers for allowing or prohibiting particular forms of sex selection is essentially ethical argument. Hence, ethical analysis can both *explain* (substantially though not completely) why we have the policies that we do and *critique* these policies by discovering whether or not the moral reasoning behind them is sound.

There is a range of possible views about prenatal and embryonic sex selection. At one extreme, some think that *all* sex selection is wrong and should be banned, although those who take this line are often driven by quite general concerns about (for example) the destruction of embryos or the wrongness of 'playing God', rather than objections that apply uniquely to *sex* selection. At the opposite end of the scale are libertarians who may favour either a 'free market' in sex selection, or perhaps a lightly regulated market: one controlled just enough to ensure technical competence and safety. In-between are various intermediate positions. One of these is the regulatory position in the UK (described below). According to this, embryonic sex selection is permissible only for one purpose: ensuring that the child created does not have a sex-linked genetic disorder.[3] A second, slightly more permissive, intermediate position is that sex selection is acceptable (and should be allowed) *both* for the purposes of disease-avoidance *and* in order to deliver family balancing (defined below).

This chapter proceeds as follows. Sections 8.1 and 8.2 are mainly introductory, placing the sex selection debate in its context within bioethics, and describing the legal position in the UK. Sections 8.3 and 8.4 are both concerned with the view that sex selection for family balancing purposes is morally better than other forms of social sex selection, and with the related view that family balancing should be legally privileged (for example, allowed even though other forms of sex selection are not). Two main arguments for this view are considered: that family balancing is (allegedly) less likely to cause population sex imbalance than other forms of sex selection, and that family balancing is (allegedly) less likely to be sexist. It is concluded that both arguments are weak, as is (therefore) the case for privileging family balancing. Having dealt specifically with family balancing, subsequent sections move on to look at more fundamental and/or general arguments for and against sex selection and ask whether *any* form of social sex selection should be permitted, and whether *any* form is ethically defensible. Sections 8.5 and 8.6 revisit the population sex imbalance and sexism arguments to see whether these count decisively against all forms of sex selection. It is concluded that they do not, although they may work in particular social circumstances. Sections 8.7

---

[3] HFEA, *Code of Practice* (7th edn., 2007). This is also the position taken in the 1997 *European Convention on Human Rights and Biomedicine* (the *Oviedo Convention*), Article 14 of which states that 'the use of techniques of medically assisted procreation shall not be allowed for the purpose of choosing a future child's sex, except where serious hereditary sex-related disease is to be avoided', <http://conventions.coe.int/Treaty/EN/Treaties/Html/164.htm> (last accessed: Monday, 13 Apr. 2009).

and 8.8 deal with two further objections to sex selection. The first is that prospective parents' (especially prospective mothers') consents to sex selection are likely to be rendered invalid by social pressure to conform to sexist values. The second is that sex selection in Western countries, while perhaps permissible considered in isolation, is (all things considered) wrong because of the message that it would send out to other countries (those where, because of different social circumstances, sex selection would be wrong). Section 8.7 concludes that, while there are *possible* social circumstances that would vitiate prospective parents' consents, there is little reason to believe that these obtain generally in the UK at present—or, at least, if they do obtain, then flawed consents are ubiquitous and there is no *particular* problem for sex selection. Section 8.8 concedes that we must of course *take into account* the international ramifications of our domestic policies (along with all the other consequences of our actions). However, it is argued that these considerations are not sufficient to justify prohibiting sex selection in the UK. One of the main reasons for this is that, if sex selection were (considered in isolation) morally permissible in the UK, but not in some other country, then it should be possible to explain to the people in that other country why the moral status of sex selection is not the same 'here' as 'there': to explain what the social differences are that underpin this ethical difference. Finally, Section 8.9 considers a particular argument in defence of clinical sex selection: the claim that, since hardly anyone objects to 'folk' methods of sex selection (such as diet, or using certain sexual positions) it would be inconsistent for us to object to (a fortiori to ban) clinical methods of sex selection (like sperm sorting and embryo selection) since these differ from 'folk' sex selection only in their efficacy.

The overall position defended in this chapter is that sex selection is morally problematic insofar as it is sexist or harmful, and that often it is both (and hence problematic). However, I also argue (with some caveats) against the legal prohibition of social sex selection in the UK and in other relevantly similar Western countries. Two of the main reasons offered for this are, first, that it would be possible to regulate sex selection in ways that make it fairly harmless and, second, that any sexism enshrined in a British system of regulated sex selection would be no worse than that contained in many other permitted practices; and, while all sexism is morally to be condemned, making all of it *illegal* is neither practicable nor desirable.

8.1 Bioethical Context

In this section I narrow the focus of the chapter by introducing two distinctions. The first is between generic arguments that apply to all (or most) forms of selection (that is, selection between different possible future children—via, for example, embryo selection) and arguments that apply uniquely to *sex* selection. The second is between objections to sex selection per se and objections to *particular means* of sex selecting.

Most of the generic anti-selection arguments considered in earlier chapters apply to sex selection. Leading examples include the following claims:

1. Prospective parents should accept their (possible, future) children (unconditionally perhaps) and this attitude is not consistent with selective reproduction (see Chapter 2).
2. Selection somehow violates the child's right to an open future (see Chapter 2).
3. Selection would have an adverse effect on child welfare (see Chapter 3).
4. Selection constitutes, or may encourage, the wrongful 'commodification' of children and/or reproduction and/or women (see Chapter 5).
5. Selection constitutes, or may encourage, eugenics (see Chapter 6).

The important feature of all these for our present purposes is that each attacks selection *generally* and therefore such arguments will not differentiate between *sex* selection and other forms. Hence, since the justifiability specifically of sex selection is what concerns me here, I shall leave them to one side for the present. Moreover, these arguments have already been discussed in detail in previous chapters and, in most cases, found wanting.

My concern in this chapter then is with arguments that purport to show that *sex* selection is *especially* morally problematic. I start by looking for arguments that count against (non-medical) sex selection but which (some people claim) do so less strongly in family-balancing cases than in other cases. This is because I want initially to critique the view that sex selection should be permitted only for family balancing (or to avoid a sex-linked disorder). The second part of the chapter then addresses the more fundamental issue of whether sex selection in general is morally wrong and a proper object of legal prohibition.

Turning now to the second distinction, moral concerns about sex selection can usefully be divided into those about the *means* used to sex select and those about the *end* of sex selection itself—about the whole project of attempting to determine sex. The extent to which objections of the first kind (the means used) are applicable will depend on what sex selection techniques we are debating. All of the following are possible 'techniques':

- killing female (or male) babies;
- aborting female (or male) foetuses;
- sexing IVF embryos, implanting male (or female) ones, and discarding those of the undesired sex;
- prior to insemination, using sperm sorting to increase greatly the probability of having a boy (or girl);

- having sexual intercourse only at certain points in the menstrual cycle in order to increase slightly the probably of having a boy (or girl).

I imagine that most of us would regard the practices near the top of the list as much more morally problematic than those at the bottom: believing that while (to understate it somewhat) there is something troubling about killing infants, choosing to deselect and discard a certain class of sperm is relatively innocuous. In the case of sex selection then, the now real possibility of using sperm sorting greatly reduces ethical concerns about methods and means, since (unlike embryos or babies) hardly anyone wishes to ascribe moral significance to sperm.

In what follows, for the sake of argumentative clarity and simplicity, I am going to focus on sex selection via either sperm sorting or embryo selection, so as to be able to leave to one side any extra ethical or legal complications relating to selective abortion (or a fortiori to infanticide, which I take not to be an acceptable option). This leaves me to focus on the *end* of sex selection itself—on the question of whether attempting to determine sex is wrong, irrespective of the methods used.

8.2 Legal–Regulatory Context in the UK

The case which has perhaps done more than any other in recent times to put sex selection, and in particular family balancing, on to the policy agenda was that of Alan and Louise Masterton. In May 1999, their 3-year-old daughter, Nicole, suffered severe burns after a gas balloon fell on to a bonfire in their garden. Nicole was admitted to the Royal Hospital for Sick Children in Edinburgh, but sadly died two months later.[4] Prior to her death, the Mastertons had had five children of which Nicole was the only daughter. They were left with four surviving sons then aged between 8 and 14.

By March 2000, it emerged that the Mastertons were keen to have another daughter using embryonic sex selection and were lobbying the HFEA to allow them to do this. According to a *Times* report, they wrote to the HFEA enclosing a photograph of Nicole and a note which said:

This is our precious daughter Nicole. The joy and happiness she brought into our lives, her spirit and her place in our family and our hearts are the driving force behind this appeal.[5]

At that time (as now) embryonic sex selection for social reasons (that is, for reasons other than disease-avoidance) was not allowed in the UK. The basis for

---

[4] M. Mega, 'Couple Fight to Pick Sex of Baby', *The Sunday Times*, 12 Mar. 2001, 32.
[5] G. Harris, 'Grieving Couple Fight to Choose Sex of Next Baby', *The Times*, 13 Mar. 2000, 11.

this was as follows. The Human Fertilisation and Embryology Act 1990, s. 3, states that:

(1) No person shall —
    (a) bring about the creation of an embryo, or
    (b) keep or use an embryo, except in pursuance of a licence

Thus, because embryonic sex selection requires the creation and use of embryos, it fell under the ambit of the HFEA and its codes of practice and standard licence conditions. The *Code of Practice* in force at that time (the 4th edition, revised in July 1998) stated that:

7.20 Centres should not select the sex of embryos for social reasons

and that

7.21 Centres should not use sperm sorting techniques in sex selection.[6]

Sex selection 'for social reasons' (which is banned) is contrasted with *medical sex selection* (which is permitted)—i.e. sex selection where the aim is to avoid creating a child with a sex-linked disorder. The HFEA informs us that:

There are approximately two hundred known sex-linked diseases, most of which only affect males. These diseases vary in severity from colour blindness to haemophilia and Duchenne's muscular dystrophy.[7]

Subsequently, the Human Fertilisation and Embryology Act 2008 has put the regulatory prohibition of (non-medical) embryonic and gametic sex selection on to a statutory footing. Embryo selection and sperm sorting can only be done under HFEA licence and the 2008 Act states that such licences 'cannot authorise any practice designed to secure that any resulting child will be of one sex rather than the other'.[8] The 2008 Act does, however, lay out some specific types of selection that *may* be licensed (the above mentioned, general prohibition notwithstanding) including medical sex selection:

in a case where there is a particular risk that any resulting child will have or develop—

    (i) a gender-related serious physical or mental disability,
    (ii) a gender-related serious illness, or
    (iii) any other gender-related serious medical condition[9]

So the 2008 Act essentially enshrines in legislation what had been the HFEA policy position previously: that all forms of sex selection, except embryonic sex selection to

---

[6] HFEA, *Code of Practice* (4th edn., July 1998), 45.

[7] HFEA, *Sex Selection* (consultation document) (2002), 7.

[8] Human Fertilisation and Embryology Act 2008, Schedule 2 (Activities that may be Licensed under the 1990 Act), Sections 3 and 4.

[9] Human Fertilisation and Embryology Act 2008.

avoid sex-linked disease or disability, are prohibited. The latest HFEA *Code of Practice* (in draft form only at the time of writing) summarizes the post-2008 position as follows:

The law requires that the centre should not, for social reasons:

- select embryos of a particular sex
- separate sperm samples, or use sperm samples that have been separated, for the purpose of sex selection, or
- participate in any other practices designed to ensure that a resulting child will be of a particular sex.[10]

It is perhaps also worth noting that family balancing is not mentioned in this document (nor was it in the 4th edition) and is not officially distinguished from other social reasons to sex select.

Returning to the Mastertons, one obstacle that they faced was that the HFEA would not hear a direct appeal from prospective patients but required a clinic to apply for a licence to treat them. However, none of the available clinics were willing to do this (presumably being aware of the ban on social sex selection in the *Code of Practice*).[11] Thus, the Mastertons in effect had to ask the HFEA not to consider *their case* but rather to reassess the existing *policy* on sex selection. At the time, press reports claimed that the Mastertons planned to use the Human Rights Act 1998 to challenge HFEA's refusal to hear their case without the intercession of a clinic (specifically in relation to Articles 6 and 8—the Right to a Fair Trial and the Right to Respect for Private and Family Life) although it does not appear that they ultimately pursued this.[12]

In October 2000, Ruth Deech (then HFEA chair) said publicly that there would be no change of policy on social sex selection, citing HFEA's 1993 consultation,[13] after which 'the policy of only permitting sex selection using licensed treatments for the avoidance of serious sex-linked genetic conditions was confirmed'.[14] At this point, the Mastertons (both already in their forties) reportedly travelled to Rome to receive treatment, although ultimately this was unsuccessful resulting only in a male embryo (which they decided to donate to an infertile couple).[15]

---

[10] HFEA, *Code of Practice* (8th edn. in draft, 2008).

[11] R. Young, 'Couple Seek Right to a Daughter', *The Times*, 4 Oct. 2000, 4.

[12] S. English, 'Parents Battle to Choose a Girl', *The Times*, 5 Oct. 2000, 3.

[13] HFEA, *Sex Selection: Public Consultation Document* (1993); K. Scott, 'IVF Selection Still Off Limits', *The Guardian*, 19 Oct. 2000, 15.

[14] HFEA, *Sex Selection* (consultation document) (2002), 3.

[15] L. Duckworth, 'IVF Couple Give Away "Wrong Sex" Embryo', *The Independent*, 5 Mar. 2001, <http://www.independent.co.uk/life-style/health-and-wellbeing/health-news/ivf-couple-give-away-wrong-sex-embryo-694608.html> (last accessed: Monday, 13 Apr. 2009). See also House of Commons Select Committee on Science and Technology, *Human Reproductive Technologies and the Law (Fifth Report of Session 2004–2005), Volume II (Oral and Written Evidence)*, Mar. 2005, Ev 336.

Later, in 2001, some procedural aspects of the HFEA's handling of the Mastertons were criticized by the Parliamentary Ombudsman and an apology was issued. In particular, when they initially provided the HFEA with a detailed (thirty-page) presentation of their case, the Mastertons were wrongly told (or at least it was implied) that this would be given full consideration by the HFEA membership at its meeting on 27 January 2000. Alan Masterton is reported to have said:

Right up until the day before the meeting at which our case was to be discussed we were told that a copy would be given to each member. It was not until the day after that we got information that the members of the authority had not actually seen the document.[16]

In fact, consideration could (or would) only have taken place following an application to sex select by a licensed clinic.

While the Masterton case did not directly affect policy it was arguably one factor that led (in September 2001) to the Minister for Public Health asking the HFEA to carry out a review of its sex selection policy.[17] As part of this review, the HFEA launched a public consultation in October 2002. Unlike the 1993 HFEA consultation document, the 2002 version (which was generally longer and much more detailed) mentioned and highlighted the idea that family balancing might be a special ground for sex selection. Indeed, a noteworthy feature of the 2002 consultation document is the assumption (albeit qualified in places) that family balancing sex selection is less morally problematic than other forms of (non-medical) sex selection. For example, the *Executive Summary* says:

The arguments put forward against the permissive view may be tested against what is supposedly the least objectionable non-medical reason for sex selection, family balancing, to assess whether any form of sex selection, by any means, that is not carried out for serious medical reasons is morally acceptable.[18]

Underpinning this appear to be two thoughts, both of which are scrutinized later in this chapter. The first is that (unlike unfettered social sex selection):

if sex selection were restricted to family balancing it would not significantly alter the overall sex ratio.[19]

The second is that family-balancing sex selection is (or is less likely to be) objectionably sexist than other forms of (non-medical) sex selection:

For many people [sex discrimination] is an important consideration, especially for those proponents of the permissive argument whose liberal position includes a commitment

---

[16] S. Templeton, 'Couple in Battle to Choose the Sex of their Baby Win an Apology', *Sunday Herald*, 20 May 2001, 1. See also House of Commons Select Committee on Science and Technology, *Human Reproductive Technologies*, Ev 336.

[17] HFEA, *A Summary of the 111th Meeting of the Human Fertilisation and Embryology Authority* (28 Sept. 2001).

[18] HFEA, *Sex Selection* (consultation document) (2002) at 3.   [19] HFEA, *Sex Selection*, 26.

to opposing discrimination on grounds of sex. They might respond that there are some non-medical reasons for sex selection which are not based on objectionable forms of sex discrimination. The standard case here is that in which prospective parents who have one or more children of one sex seek to ensure that a future child is of the other sex. This is sometimes known as family balancing[20]

an implication of these arguments against sex selection [is] that the best case for sex selection for non-medical reasons is where it rests on the wishes of prospective parents who already have one or two children of one sex, to have a child of the other sex. For where this is the rationale behind it, objectionable forms of sex discrimination are not involved.[21]

The main outcomes of the HFEA consultation process were, however, fairly conservative at least inasmuch as no liberalization of sex selection (not even for family balancing) was proposed.[22] According to the HFEA, the status quo position of embryonic sex selection being available only for the purposes of disease-avoidance should (and would) be maintained. This position is instantiated in the HFEA *Code of Practice* in force at the time of writing, which states that:

G.8.7.1 The centre should not, for social reasons:

(a) select embryos of a particular sex, or
(b) separate sperm samples, or use sperm samples which have been separated, for the purpose of sex selection.[23]

In addition, HFEA's standard licence conditions state:

A.13.7(d) . . . that Centres should not use any information derived from tests on an embryo, or any material removed from it or from the gametes that produced it, to select embryos of a particular sex for social reasons[24]

8.3 Family Balancing and Population Sex Imbalance

We can now turn to the arguments for permitting family balancing while not allowing other sorts of sex selection. But first what exactly is family balancing? The broadest definition says that an instance of (non-medical) sex selection is family balancing if the family in question (and I note in passing that there would be further definitional work to do on 'family') has more children of one sex than the other (say, four girls

---

[20] HFEA, *Sex Selection*, 25. [21] HFEA, *Sex Selection*, 29.

[22] HFEA, *Sex Selection: Options for Regulation* (2003), 26.

[23] HFEA, *Code of Practice* (7th edn., 2007). As noted above, the 8th edn. is, at the time of writing, in draft form.

[24] HFEA, *Code of Practice* (7th edn., 2007).

and three boys) and sex selects (in this case, a boy) with the aim of evening things up, of reducing or eliminating the sex differential. As the HFEA (Human Fertilisation and Embryology Authority) put it in its 2002 consultation document, 'family balancers':

already have children predominantly of one sex and would like a child of the other sex to complement their existing family[25]

Later in the document however, HFEA does imply two possible ways of narrowing the definition of family balancing. One is to make having *no existing children of the desired sex* a necessary condition; so selecting a girl would be family balancing if the family started off with *no* girls and three boys, but not if it started off with *one* girl and three boys. The other possible narrowing is to require a sex differential of two or more in the existing family; thus, selecting a girl where boys outnumber girls four-to-*two* would be family balancing, but it would not be family balancing if boys outnumbered girls by only four-to-*three*. These additional criteria were combined for HFEA's 2002 questionnaire, which asked whether:

sex selection . . . should be permitted for non-medical reasons when a family has at least two children of one sex and none of the other sex.[26]

Based on reasoning contained elsewhere in the consultation document, it looks as if the thought was that this is the least contentious and most clear-cut version of family balancing. Hence, if any form of non-medical sex selection is acceptable, this is.[27]

I should also mention at this stage a concern about the expression 'family balancing'. The worry is that such language is pejorative and implies that families not containing boys and girls in roughly equal numbers are somehow defective.[28] And while many parents (and prospective parents) do desire sex 'balance',[29] it is difficult to see how one could justify any suggestion that families with all girls or all boys are objectively inferior.

Let us turn now to the arguments in favour of privileging family-balancing sex selection. The first of these says that this form of sex selection is less likely to cause a population sex differential (an 'imbalance') than other kinds.[30] As Savulescu suggests:

if you were concerned . . . about the sex ratio, you would simply allow sex selection only for family balancing and there would be no effect on the sex ratio[31]

---

[25] HFEA, *Sex Selection* (consultation document) (2002), 5.

[26] HFEA, *Sex Selection: Options for Regulation* (2003), 25.

[27] HFEA, *Sex Selection* (consultation document) (2002), 3.

[28] Soren Holm, 'Like a Frog in Boiling Water: The public, the HFEA, and Sex Selection', *Healthcare Analysis*, 12 (2004), 27–39: 31.

[29] T. Jain, 'Significant Proportion of Infertile Couples Requests Preimplantation Sex Selection', *Fertility Weekly* (Mar. 2005), 9–10.

[30] HFEA, *Sex Selection* (consultation document) (2002), at 26.

[31] Professor Julian Savulescu, Oral Evidence, in House of Commons Select Committee on Science and Technology, *Human Reproductive Technologies*, Ev103 (Q796).

In order for this argument to work, three things would need to be established.

1. Population sex differentials (or differentials above a certain level) are a bad thing.
2. Unfettered social sex selection would cause population sex differentials to rise significantly beyond desirable levels.
3. Family balancing alone would *not* cause population sex differentials to rise—or, at least, its effects on population sex differential would be much less marked than those of unfettered social sex selection.

The sorts of reason typically offered for believing (1) are well summarized by Rogers, Ballantyne, and Draper, who tell us:

Further harm from SSA [sex selective abortion] lies in the resultant severe imbalance in the sex ratio, leading to millions of men being unable to find a partner and found a family ... The long-term consequences are currently unfolding, with estimates of 23 million men in China being unable to partner (the so-called bare branches). The likely social effects are thought to include increased criminal behavior and social disruption with banditry, violence and revolutions historically more common in areas with large numbers of excess males.[32]

It should, however, be noted that these reasons only apply in certain types of society: those where, for example, the preference is for males, heterosexual monogamy (or polygyny) is the norm, and there are insufficient opportunities for single men to live contented and fulfilled lives. And, while I would be happy to concede that population sex imbalance is a problem in such societies, it is (as McCarthy, among others, has argued) far from obvious that is a necessary or general problem with sex selection. For instance, perhaps a predominantly female human world would be preferable to the present one given that men are responsible for more than their fair share of crime and violence. Or perhaps women would be better off if there were fewer of them because 'they would be rarer and therefore more valued'.[33]

Turning to (2) and (3), would unfettered social sex selection, especially in the UK, cause population sex differentials to rise? Views vary on this but the HFEA, in its post-consultation document, told us that it had commissioned (from Catherine Waldby) a systematic literature review of material relating to the social and ethical issues raised by sex selection and this cites (among other things):

recent studies in the UK [that] showed no significant overall preference for one sex over the other although a disproportionately high percentage of those actively seeking sex selection

---

[32] Wendy Rogers, Angela Ballantyne, and Heather Draper, 'Is Sex Selective Abortion Morally Justified and Should It Be Prohibited?', *Bioethics*, 21 (2007), 520–4: 522; See also Neil Levy, 'Against Sex Selection', *Southern Medical Journal*, 100 (2007), 107–9.

[33] Levy, 'Against Sex Selection', 107.

were from ethnic populations originating from outside Europe. Amongst these there was a marked preference for male children although this was from families who already had more than one female child and were nearing the end of their reproductive lives.[34]

HFEA concluded:

These findings did *not* demonstrate that permitting controlled sex selection for non-medical reasons would lead to a skewing of the sex ratio in the UK.[35]

As an ethicist, it is not for me to say whether or not social sex selection would in fact cause population sex differentials to rise significantly. What is clear though is that this premiss is at best contentious and that this is therefore a weak point in the argument. It should, however, be conceded that what HFEA terms 'ethnic populations originating from outside Europe' may raise special issues if their sex selection preferences differ substantially from those of the population overall. I shall return to this issue in 8.6.

Let us turn now to (3), the claim that the effects of allowing only family-balancing sex selection (on population sex ratios) would be less severe than allowing sex selection more widely. As we have already seen, one possible objection to this is that the effects of allowing unfettered sex selection might not themselves be all that noticeable (at least in many Western countries). Another is that, if there is a potential problem with population sex ratios, then either restricting sex selection to family balancing would be ineffective, or this policy would be less effective than some conceivable alternatives. Dahl suggests several different ways of preserving population sex balance, including:

setting up waiting lists for couples who wanted a child of the more frequently chosen sex, always pairing couples who wanted a boy with a couple who wanted a girl, and, as a last resort, even taxing parents of the preponderant sex more heavily.[36]

Alternatively, sex selectors could be encouraged or made to donate their viable spare embryos thus almost completely eliminating any unbalancing effects (and doing some good besides).[37]

Some of these alternatives have apparent advantages over a system in which the only permitted form of (non-medical) sex selection was family balancing. For instance,

[34] HFEA, *Sex Selection: Options for Regulation* (2003) at 10–11.

[35] HFEA, *Sex Selection*. See also Professor Martin Richards's written evidence in House of Commons Select Committee on Science and Technology, *Human Reproductive Technologies*, Ev 364; Levy, 'Against Sex Selection', 107.

[36] Edgar Dahl, 'Sex Selection: Laissez-Faire or Family Balancing?' *Healthcare Analysis*, 13 (2005), 87–90: 88.

[37] This suggestion can be found in written evidence to the HC Select Committee on Science and Technology from Mr Paul Rainsbury, Professor Gedis Grudzinskas and Professor Alan Handyside. House of Commons Select Committee on Science and Technology, *Human Reproductive Technologies*, Ev 330.

the pairing system, under which clinics must select roughly equal numbers of boys and girls looks like a more robust way of ensuring that there are no detrimental effects on population sex ratios than simply privileging family balancing. The pairing system would guarantee almost no effect. Whereas if there was (for example) a widespread preference for boys, then family-balancing sex selection would be used mainly by 'unbalanced' all-girl families seeking boys. The effects of this would be less dramatic than unfettered sex selection, but it could, nonetheless, lead to a preponderance of boys, and restricting sex selection in other ways may be more effective.

So if population sex imbalance is really the worry, restricting sex selection to family balancing probably is not the best answer, and it may not be an answer at all. Even in countries with sex imbalance problems, restricting sex selection to family balancing will probably be a less good option than either preventing sex selection from taking place altogether or using one of the alternatives mentioned above.

8.4 Family Balancing and Sexism

sex selection represents sexism in its purest most blatant form[38]

It might be said that the sex of one's child would matter only to someone who has objectionable sexist attitudes—who thinks that little girls should be sweet and quiet, for example, or boys tough and brave—and will try to impose these views on the child.[39]

The second argument in favour a 'family balancing only' policy is that this is less likely to be sexist than other types of sex selection. Like many arguments of this kind, there is a causal or consequence-based version and a more straightforward direct version. The latter says that family-balancing sex selection is less likely to *be* sexist and to be motivated by sexist beliefs and attitudes. Whereas an example of the consequence-based version would claim that, if we permitted unfettered sex selection, this would change social attitudes and make sexism more widespread—while the same is not true of family balancing.[40] For the present, I shall focus just on the direct version of the argument. This is partly because the consequence-based version relies on an empirical claim whose truth is very hard to assess. It is also partly because if

[38] Jonathan Berkowitz and Jack Snyder, 'Racism and Sexism in Medically Assisted Conception', *Bioethics*, 12 (1998), 25–44.
[39] Bonnie Steinbock, 'Sex Selection: Not Obviously Wrong', *Hastings Center Report*, 32 (2002), 23–8: 25.
[40] HFEA, *Sex Selection* (consultation document) (2002), 29; the European Society of Human Reproduction and Embryology (ESHRE) Ethics Task Force, 'Preimplantation Genetic Diagnosis', *Human Reproduction*, 18/3 (2003), 649–651: 651.

the direct version fails then the causal/indirect version will most likely fail too. For if family balancing *is not itself* less sexist (than other types of sex selection) it is hard to see why we should think it less likely to *cause* sexism. Of course, because this is a causal rather than a logical matter, this scenario is not *impossible* (that is, there are *possible* situations in which, although family balancing is in itself no less sexist than other forms of sex selection, it is, nonetheless, less likely to cause additional sexism than the other forms). However, we are entitled at least to make a *presumption* that if family balancing is as sexist as other forms then the risks of its *causing* further sexism are the same as for the other forms (a presumption that could only be overturned if there was empirical evidence specifically showing that the negative effects of allowing family-balancing sex selection would be less severe). Thus, even though ultimately this is an empirical matter, the causal argument indirectly depends on the extent to which family balancing is *intrinsically* more or less sexist than the other sex selection practices.

So what is the sexism argument for privileging family-balancing sex selection? The main claim is that the motives of would-be sex selectors are suspect, except in cases of family balancing, because in 'non-family-balancing' cases, would-be sex selectors' preferences are driven by sexist views. The most obvious of these is sex supremacism, the belief that one sex is better than the other; another is sex stereotyping, which involves an exaggerated view of the difference that sex makes to people's personal characteristics and behaviour. Both supremacism and stereotyping are often allied with other discriminatory views about the moral status and rights of women (and possibly men).

Family-balancing sex selection, so the argument goes, is not (as) vulnerable to the charge of sexism because what family-balancing sex selectors aim at is balance, rather than a particular sex. Other forms of sex selection however *do* aim at a particular sex and may therefore be based on supremacism, stereotyping, or other sexist attitudes. In the next few pages, I shall look first (and quite briefly) at the claim that other types of sex selection are liable to be driven by supremacism, and then (in a little more detail) at the claim that they are likely to involve stereotyping.

An initial (and indeed fundamental) problem with the claim about supremacism is that regular ('non-family-balancing') sex selection does not have to be underpinned by sex-supremacist beliefs. For there is an important distinction between *preferring to have* a child of a particular sex and *believing that sex to be superior*. As Steinbock suggests:

The desire for a son . . . might be based on the recognition that the experience of parenting a boy is different from that of parenting a girl.[41]

---

[41] Steinbock, 'Sex Selection', 25.

Indeed, someone could prefer a child of a particular sex because he viewed that sex as weak and wanted to be surrounded by (perceived) weaklings. So desiring a given sex and believing it to be superior are clearly different things and, similarly, it is possible to prefer the company of one or other sex without believing that sex to be superior. Conversely, while regular sex selection is not *necessarily* supremacist, family balancing *can* be supremacist. For example, a father who believes females to be second-rate might suffer (what he sees as) the misfortunate of numerous daughters and want to even things up, not because he desires balance, but because he believes that boys are better. So it looks, first, as if sex selection in general need not be supremacist and, second, as if the distinction between supremacist and non-supremacist sex selection has little or nothing to do with that between regular and family balancing sex selection.

Turning now to stereotyping, perhaps these concerns have more solid foundations than those about supremacism. Berkowitz and Snyder argue along these lines (although in the context of a more general attack on sex selection, not a defence of family balancing).[42] They tell us:

Sexism in . . . sex selection occurs when parents choose the sex of a child in anticipation of the social roles that child will perform in the future. For example, a man may desire a son with whom he may pursue such 'masculine' activities as fishing or baseball. This preference implies that boys, when compared to girls, are more desirable or capable companions for these activities. Conversely, a woman may desire a daughter because she would like a shopping companion. Such assumptions are sexist in that they presume one sex is superior to, or more appropriately suited for certain social tasks: presumptions which perpetuate and foster stereotypical social roles.[43]

Thinking along similar lines, Levy tells us that:

there are sexist beliefs other than the belief that one gender is inherently superior to the other. There is also, and far more commonly today in the developed world, the sexist belief that though the genders are of equal value, they are specially suited to different roles and occupations. It is true that there are differences between the cognitive styles of men and women, but these differences are subtle, showing up at the level of groups. Though women are (for instance) better at certain kinds of linguistic reasoning than men, it is sexist to channel women in the direction of certain activities and certain roles because of this group-level profile. It is also sexist to have expectations of children because of their gender alone.[44]

There are two worries here. One is about how the child will be treated once it comes into existence—will it be forced into an unduly narrow or restrictive 'gender

---

[42] Berkowitz and Snyder, 'Racism and Sexism',
[43] Berkowitz and Snyder, 'Racism and Sexism', 32.
[44] Levy, 'Against Sex Selection', 108.

role' (boys made to fish and girls to shop, to use Berkowitz and Snyder's examples)? Concerns of this kind have, in general terms at least, already been dealt with during earlier chapters (for example, in the discussions of the child's right to an open future and the welfare of the child). So I shall focus here on the second worry, which is that the sex selection is driven by sexist attitudes and beliefs.

In what way are they sexist? Well, for Berkowitz and Snyder it appears largely to be a matter of 'essentializing' (to biological sex) characteristics that are not in fact essential—or at least a matter of *exaggerating* biological differences and their effects on personal and social traits. So what would be wrong with selecting a girl because you want your child to enjoy flower arranging, housework, and shopping is this: that these traits are not (or at least not directly) determined by or essential to biological femaleness. Hence, sex selectors of this kind are acting on a false view of biological sex difference *and* (both simply by making this choice and by the ways in which they plan to treat their children) doing something that will promulgate and perpetuate such false views of sex. As Berkowitz and Snyder put it:

Unlike the inability of men to become pregnant, there are no genetic barriers to girls fishing or boys shopping.[45]

So, as far as stereotyping is concerned, it may be permissible (if a little weird) for a woman to select a girl so that she can share with her experiences of childbirth and menstruation; and it may be similarly permissible for a man to select a boy so that they can share experiences of beard growing, erectile function (or dysfunction), and prostate enlargement. For these characteristics uncontroversially *are* determined by sex (or, at the very least, are heavily dependent on sex) regardless of social determinants. Of course, such cases of sex selection may still be morally problematic on other grounds. For example, one might question whether it is entirely appropriate or healthy to want to talk to one's (as yet non-existent) future children about such bodily matters, and might question why the prospective parents could not just talk to other existing relatives and friends about such things. But, since our present concern is specifically with sex stereotyping, I shall leave such worries to one side.

If Berkowitz and Snyder are right about what it takes for a case of sex selection to involve sexist stereotyping then many cases of sex selection will turn out to be sexist:

when carefully examined, many of the motivations for preferring a certain sex are probably rooted in sexist preconceptions.[46]

This is because relatively few prospective parents would want to sex select for the kinds of purely biological reason just mentioned. Rather, what interests them are behavioural and personality factors.

---

[45] Berkowitz and Snyder, 'Racism and Sexism', 32.
[46] Berkowitz and Snyder, 'Racism and Sexism'.

Before turning to see how this argument applies to family balancing, a further complication (or perhaps objection) should be mentioned. The difficulty is that the question of which personal characteristics are (wholly or partly) determined by *biology* (including sex) and which are (wholly or predominantly) *socially* determined—part of the 'nature–nurture' debate—is immensely complicated and controversial. Hence, in advance of settling the 'nature–nurture' question, it may be very difficult indeed to work out which views about sex difference are sexist stereotyping and which are simply reasonable views about the difference that biology does make to character. As Steinbock argues, it seems plausible that biology (including sex) has *some* role in shaping people's characters even if this is mediated by social determinants and even if its influence is only defeasible and probabilistic: that is, sex might make it *more likely* that one will have personality trait x, but having x is not an *inevitable* consequence of one's sex.[47] Anyway, for our purposes, the point is that insofar as it is hard to tell which aspects of a person's character are biologically determined, it is similarly hard to tell which claims about sex difference are true and which are exaggeration or stereotyping.

A further complication is that prospective sex selectors must make their decisions in the real social world, an environment that may well be sexist and which will almost certainly impact on future children's characters whether the parents like it or not. Thus (to stick with the hackneyed examples for simplicity's sake) even if there is nothing in a girl's *biological* make-up that makes her more inclined to shop than to fish, in a sexist society, it may still be true that (albeit for social reasons) parents who choose a boy are more likely to end up with an angler than a recreational shopper (and vice versa). So what are we to say of parents who choose to have a boy because they want an angler rather than a shopper, and do this knowing that the mechanism linking maleness to fishing is social rather than biological? Are they stereotyping? Not necessarily, provided that their assessment of the situation is factually correct. It may, however, be that their behaviour should be criticized either because it is an instance of *collusion* with a sexist society, or because of the social consequences of 'going along with' and possibly reinforcing gender role stereotyping.

While not perhaps decisive objections, all of these complications do serve to weaken the stereotyping argument against sex selection because it is difficult to condemn (a fortiori ban) a practice when there is so much uncertainty about the fundamentals which supposedly underlie this condemnation.

We can now return to family balancing and ask whether this fares any better than regular sex selection when it comes to the stereotyping question. As with regular sex selection, whether family balancing involves stereotyping depends on

---

[47] Steinbock, 'Sex Selection', 25.

what the parents are aiming at. If what they want is a 'balance' of plainly biological features (if they want half their children to be capable of strong beard growth and other half to develop breasts, for example) then (as explained previously) while we may think that this is weird or objectionable in other ways, it does not seem to involve stereotyping, for the desired sex-linked characteristics really are largely biologically determined (although not of course without exception). If, on the other hand, the sort of 'balance' that they are after is less clearly related to biology and more to do with character traits that may or may not be determined by physical sex, then there is a significant risk that the parents are guilty of stereotyping.

It seems then that such stereotyping is as likely in the case of family-balancing sex selection as it is in regular sex selection. Consider these two cases. Family A want all of their children to have aggression and sporting prowess and so select all boys; Family B want half their children to have aggression and sporting prowess, and the other half to be caring and musical, and so use (family-balancing) selection to have half boys and half girls. Whatever the general merits of these choices, it seems clear that, as far as sex stereotyping is concerned, the families are in the same position; both are guilty of sex stereotyping. A similar point can be found in a Human Genetics Alert campaign briefing from 2002:

Even in the case of family balancing ... which the HFEA views as relatively acceptable, rigid gender expectations are clearly operating. In how many cases where parents are 'desperate for a girl' will they be hoping for a loud tomboy that grows up to be an engineer? Society must continue to fight sexist gender stereotypes, not allow them to dictate who is born.[48]

Thus, it seems that sex stereotyping is as likely to underpin family-balancing sex selection as it is any other type.

Given the above objections, only a very weak empirical version of the sexism argument could survive—the (as far as I know, unproven) empirical claim that regular sex selectors are *more likely* to be motivated by sexism than family-balancing sex selectors. Even if there was some evidence to support this, it seems a fairly flimsy basis on which to base a regulatory distinction. And, as regards the *ethical* question, what we should pay attention to is the distinction between sexist and non-sexist sex selection distinction, rather than that between family balancing and non-family balancing. Sexists can use either family-balancing or non-family-balancing sex selection and are to be equally condemned in both cases for their sexism.

---

[48] Human Genetics Alert, *The Case Against Sex Selection (Campaign Briefing)* (Dec. 2002).

8.5 Sexism as a Fundamental Objection to Sex Selection

My main aim, up to this point, has been to assess whether family balancing is *ceteris paribus* morally better than other forms of (non-medical) sex selection, and whether it should receive preferential treatment in law. As we have seen, the two main arguments for privileging family balancing are both weak, and I have concluded that we do not have good reason to make an ethical or regulatory distinction between family balancing and other types of sex selection. This, however, leaves open the bigger question of whether social sex selection in general should be permitted and it is to this that I now turn. I shall start to answer this by revisiting the arguments reviewed in the previous sections (those concerning sexism and population sex imbalance) and asking what implications they have for the more fundamental and general questions of whether sex selection is morally permissible, and of whether it should be allowed.

I start by revisiting sexism. We have seen that family-balancing sex selection is unlikely to be any less sexist than 'regular' sex selection. But is 'regular' sex selection itself sexist enough: (a) for it to be morally wrong; and (b) (in the UK context) for prohibition to be justified?

Levy (one of many proponents of sexism arguments against sex selection) argues as follows:

If people choose to have a child of a particular gender, for reasons of family balancing or because of a preference for one gender, it is because they attribute certain psychological qualities to the members of that gender. This belief is the product of sexism: it expects certain gendered characteristics of an individual based on their group membership. The effects of sex on psychological dispositions and abilities is far too subtle, and too uneven, to justify any [such] expectation.[49]

As was argued in the preceding sections, what Levy says here has considerable plausibility. The way I framed this earlier was that sex stereotyping is a form of sexism, and that sex stereotyping amounts to having an exaggerated view of the difference that sex makes to (such things as) the future person's character and mental (or indeed physical) aptitudes. Sex selection (as both Levy and I have argued) does not *necessarily* involve sex stereotyping. But not many people who sex select will do so on plainly biological grounds (which, although rather weird, at least would not involve stereotyping). Rather, people tend to sex select because of their aspirations regarding the type of *personality* their future child should have. So we are agreed that there is

---

[49] Levy, 'Against Sex Selection', 108.

a good chance that sex selection, even in a UK context, would be driven by sexist attitudes. And, given that sexist attitudes are morally flawed, sex selection would be similarly tarnished by the sexism lying behind it. (One extra caveat, also discussed earlier, is that *if* a strong biological essentialist view of the difference that sex makes to character were true, then sex selecting in order to get a child with a certain personality type may not involve stereotyping.)

Whether this is sufficient to justify prohibiting sex selection though remains an open question. Levy makes the point as follows:

Though sexist attitudes are objectionable, people ought to be free to hold and—within limits—to express them.[50]

My own view of this is that, as with many aspects of the sex selection debate, a lot depends on consequences, context, and details. For one can readily imagine both scenarios in which banning social sex selection is justified and ones in which it is not. On balance, though, it does seem that the present real world situation the UK is *not* one in which concerns about sexism are sufficient to justify prohibition and, in the remainder of this section, I shall outline some reasons for this.

First, by way of a starting point, it is worth restating some basic principles outlined at the start of the book. One is that we should presumptively favour liberty: that, where practicable and where there are no compelling reasons for doing otherwise (such as harm to other people) we should allow individuals to make their own choices. Another is the particular importance of reproductive liberty. Robertson puts this as follows:

Because of the importance of reproduction in an individual's life, the freedom to make reproductive decisions has long been recognized as a fundamental moral and legal right that should not be denied to a person unless exercise of that right would cause significant harm to others.[51]

So (while, unlike Robertson, I would allow *some* arguments not based on third-party harms to enter the fray) we start with a strong presumption in favour of permitting sex selection.

Second, it is worth distinguishing between different kinds of sexist act: specifically, between those that unjustly cause substantial harm to one or other sex (usually, in debates about sex selection, to women) and those which are harmless, or almost harmless. (I am using 'harm' here to mean something like 'set back the interests of'; thus, not all wrongful acts are harmful on this definition—see Chapter 3 for more on the definition of 'harm'.) For brevity, let us call these two kinds of sexist act *harmful*

[50] Levy, 'Against Sex Selection.'
[51] John Robertson, 'Preconception Gender Selection', *American Journal of Bioethics*, 1 (2001), 2–9: 3.

(meaning *substantially harmful*) and *harmless* (meaning *not substantially harmful*). While (as I have said) I would not wish to rule out a priori the existence of cases in which prohibiting harmless acts is justified, the justification in such cases would have to be exceptional, and the distinction between justified and unjustified prohibitions does often track that between harmful and harmless acts. This, I would argue, applies in the case of sexism and sex selection. Thus, while there are plenty of clear cases in which sexist acts are and should be banned, these are generally ones which harm individual women, or women as a group. So outlawing sex discrimination in education and the workplace is justified since it is both sexist and harmful to women, whereas it is far from clear (in the particular social context we are looking at here) that permitting social sex selection *via* sperm sorting will be harmful to women. And indeed many women (those who wish to make use of sex selection services but are prevented from doing so) may be harmed by the ban on sex selection. Hence, even though sex selection is (often) sexist, the case for prohibiting it is weak because it is probably also fairly harmless.

Some of the reasons why (if permitted in the UK) it would be harmless in terms of its social effects have already been discussed in relation to family balancing. Others (including potential harms related to ethnic subgroups, to consent, and to effects on other countries) are discussed in subsequent sections. In addition, it is worth reiterating that (because gametic and embryonic sex selection are identity-affecting) the chances of existential harm befalling the selected child are minimal (see Chapter 3).

The sexism argument is also sometimes allied with the claim that sex selected children are more likely to be on the receiving end of excessively controlling parenting. As Levy puts it:

[parents] are not entitled to impose them [their sexist attitudes] on their children because so doing violates the child's right to an open future, the requirement that a range of significant life plans be available to the child, and that she be able to choose among them without undue pressure from parents or from society. By taking steps to raise the probability (or, as they might see it, to ensure) that their children have certain psychological dispositions, parents signal that they will channel their children in certain directions.[52]

However, such arguments have already been dealt with and dismissed, in general terms, in earlier chapters. In particular, I have argued both that we should treat the so-called 'child's right to an open future' with considerable scepticism (see Chapter 2), and that we should be careful to keep separate existential issues (*should this child be prevented from coming into existence?*) from questions about what happens to the child once it exists (see Chapter 3). Thus, if we were to come to the view that a particular set

---

[52] Levy, 'Against Sex Selection', 108. Note that in this paper, Levy remains agnostic about whether sex selection should be banned.

of parents was going to inflict such a degree of sexist parenting on a child that State interference was justified, then it would surely make more sense for this to be a social services intervention aimed at rescuing the child, than an intervention that stopped the child from coming to exist at all (by banning sex selection).

This use of the distinction between harmful and harmless acts of sexism fits well into (and is supported by its apparent role in) other controversial debates. For example, one plausible view of pornography and sexual services is that while both probably involve sexism (in the main, there could be non-sexist forms too) there is only a case for prohibition for those parts of these practices that are not merely sexist, but also substantially harmful to women (either directly or indirectly through damaging societal attitudes). These aspects can justifiably be banned but others, those that are merely distastefully sexist without harming, are to be condemned *morally* but are not suitable objects of prohibition.

Finally, additional support is lent to the view that only harmful forms of sexism should be banned by asking what the legal system would look like if it strived to ban all forms of sexism, harmful or otherwise. Obviously, as ever, there are some difficult empirical issues here but it does seem to me that sexism (especially sex stereotyping) is pretty widespread and may be involved in practices ranging from jokes, to social expectations around dress and appearance, to marriage and relationships, and beyond. Thus, the scale of State intervention required to prohibit sexism in all its forms would be immense and such a policy is neither feasible nor desirable.

I conclude then that, while much (though not all) sex selection would in practice be based on sexist beliefs and attitudes (and that this is morally bad), this is not a sufficient reason to ban it: both because of the importance attached to reproductive liberty and because most sex selection in a UK context would be fairly harmless. This latter point, however, is of course contentious and does rely on some of the complex arguments engaged with in earlier chapters and in subsequent sections of this chapter.

8.6 Population Sex Imbalance, Subgroups, and Social Context

Not surprisingly, the extent to which the population sex imbalance argument against sex selection succeeds varies according to where and when it is deployed. For it is a consequence-based argument and as such works in some contexts and not others, depending on what the consequences are. In the UK context, the argument can be given fairly short shrift. This is first because, as we have seen, even with unfettered sex selection, a population sex imbalance would be unlikely to ensue. And second because there are a variety of regulatory options (like those suggested by

Dahl above) that could easily prevent sex selection from becoming unduly biased in favour of one sex or the other.[53] For example, we could insist that sex selection only took place in licensed clinics and that clinics were only allowed to produce a maximum of 60 per cent boys or 60 per cent girls. So, in most Western countries, the correct response to the population sex imbalance argument is to point out: (a) that imbalance is unlikely to be a problem; and (b) that (as a 'belt and braces' measure) we could use our already well-developed regulatory framework to prevent it from ever becoming one.

There are, however, two complications. The first (mentioned earlier) is that some ethnic subgroups within the UK population have a strong preference for boys. Thus, while (if regulated sex selection were permitted) the total population would probably remain in balance, some sub-populations may well become unbalanced. A second is that permitting social sex selection in the UK could 'send out the message', to distant countries and cultures with a strong preference for boys, that sex selection is acceptable.

Taking the first of these complications first, it is worth bearing in mind that the ethnic or religious dimension of this is only a contingent and incidental feature (albeit one of great practical significance) and that the very same issue could in principle arise for subgroups of any kind. There could, for example, be societies in which the working class, or aristocrats, or poets, or opera lovers, had extraordinarily strong son preferences. *If they did, would this be a problem?*

There are at least two circumstances in which it may be. One is if the subgroup in question does not mix much with the rest of society, especially when it comes to marriage, procreation, and the like. Thus, if the strongly son preferring opera lovers only want to have sex and have children with other opera lovers (and leaving in place, for simplicity's sake, the usual assumptions about heterosexual monogamy), and if they practice pro-male sex selection, then they will end up with a sex imbalance problem: one that is *to some extent* like that which arises when whole countries do this. However, there is one important difference. In the scenario we are considering, where the country as a whole does have (something like) a 50:50 sex ratio, then there *are* potential 'local' partners available for the 'surplus' opera loving men: namely, women who do not (presently) love opera. So the plight of the wifeless opera lovers is almost certainly less serious than that of wifeless men in countries where there is a shortage of women *overall*. How much less serious depends on a number of complex and subtle questions about the subgroup. If marrying another opera lover is a mere preference about what the couple like to get up to in their spare time, or if persuading presently uninterested women ('outsiders') to love opera is quite easy, then 'marrying out' may be no big deal for the opera lovers. But if opera loving is a deeply rooted cultural

[53] Edgar Dahl, 'Sex Selection', 88.

practice, one that is somehow constitutive of one's social identity, and if it is practically impossible for women 'from outside' to come to properly understand it, then the 'surplus' opera loving men may have their quality of life adversely affected by having to chose between a life alone and life with an 'outsider'. And obviously it may be that membership of some of the ethnic and religious groups invoked in the sex selection debate is more like the latter: that there are sociocultural goods that are accessible only in relationships between members of the subgroup.

What conclusions should we draw from this? One is that prospective parents from a given subgroup, considering son selection,[54] do have a prima facie moral reason not to select a son if they know, or ought to know, the following:

(a) he would be born into a relatively isolated social group in which there is (or will be) a shortage of female partners, *and*
(b) heterosexual monogamy (or, even worse, polygyny) is the norm, *and*
(c) the subgroup is such that relationships with women 'from outside' are likely to be impossible or unsatisfactory, *and*
(d) the absence of a relationship, or having to 'make do' with a woman from 'outside' will have an adverse effect on his quality of life, *and*
(e) all things considered (because of (a)–(d)) the overall expected quality of life of a (possible, future) girl would be higher than that of a (possible, future) boy.

Indeed, if they know (or ought to know) (a)–(e) then they have reason, not merely to avoid selecting a boy, but actively to select girls. And this applies not only to subgroups but to prospective parents living in countries with overall population sex imbalance. So I am happy to allow that there is something wrong (*ceteris paribus*) with selecting a boy under these circumstances, although it is worth reiterating that this is not because there is anything wrong with selecting per se but just because (possible, future) boys will be worse off than (possible, future) girls in the scenario outlined above. It is also worth pointing out that the reason in play here is an impersonal welfare one, not one based on any determinate individual's being harmed. As mentioned in Chapter 3, there are various complications with such moral reasons and limits on the extent to which they are capable of justifying restrictive regulation. Specifically, it is not obvious that we should generally enforce prospective parents' prima facie obligations to select the 'happiest available' (possible, future) child. Thus, selecting a boy in the aforementioned case is perhaps rather like selecting *for* a (relatively minor, but quality of life affecting) disability. In both cases, there are impersonal welfare reasons for not doing it, but these are not anti-selection reasons so much as reasons to select in 'the other direction' (against disability, against maleness).

---

[54] Obviously, the same goes for either sex. I am sticking with male selection for stylistic simplicity and because, in reality, this is usually the worry.

So what implications does this have for policy? How should we respond to the fact (if it is a fact) that some subgroups will be heavily biased in favour of boys and that this may have an effect on (future) men's quality of life. Indeed, this scenario may also have a negative impact on women's quality of life for, as Levy notes:

when females become rare in high sex ratio societies that are also deeply sexist, they become valuable but only as *commodities*.[55]

One option is to apply special restrictions to the affected subgroups. We could, for example, insist that clinics, *within the opera loving population*, produce a maximum of 60 per cent boys. However, I suspect that this would not work in practice because people could easily deny that they were opera lovers in order to access services. More realistically, it is easy to imagine a scenario in which people felt driven to lie about their religious or cultural affiliations. And attempts to assess, independently of people's testimonies, what their real religious or cultural backgrounds are would run the risk of both excessive intrusion into their private lives and of discrimination and racism.

So, in the UK context, it looks as if we do have to choose between: (a) allowing sex selection and accepting the fact that some subgroups (although not the population as a whole) will encounter population sex imbalance; or (b) banning sex selection on the grounds that population sex imbalance, even if confined to subgroups, should not be tolerated. It seems to me that, with some qualifications, (a) is preferable (provided that no other independent reasons to prohibit sex selection can be found). The main qualification is that, as I have suggested, much depends here on the effects of any decision, and one can certainly imagine *possible* situations in which these effects are so dire that they do justify prohibition (for instance, if something like a bloody war between subgroups might result from sex selection).

What then are the reasons for preferring (a)? First, we need to keep in mind that, for the usual 'non-identity' reasons, the 'surplus' men (those who cannot find female partners from their own subgroup) are not harmed by being created or by being selected (although they are probably harmed during their lifetimes by the experience of not finding a suitable partner). Thus, the reasons for avoiding their births altogether and for creating girls instead are merely impersonal ones. As I have said, such impersonal reasons do give prospective parents a prima facie moral obligation not to select a boy in these circumstances, but (for reasons discussed in Chapter 3) it is not clear that such reasons are (except in the most extreme cases) sufficient to justify legal prohibition or compulsion. Second, there are several complications relating to the isolation and separateness of subgroups. One of these is uncertainty about the future. Perhaps the children we are creating now will not need a life partner, if indeed they need one at all, until the year 2040 and inter-ethnic relations could change a great deal between

[55] Levy, 'Against Sex Selection', 107.

now and then. (Compare, for example, attitudes to 'mixed race' marriage in the 1970s and today.) Another is that the isolation and separateness of subgroups may not itself be morally neutral. Perhaps the world would be a better place if groups interacted more with each other, and perhaps allowing a sex imbalance to build up in some subgroups will encourage, in a positive way, more 'mixed marriage'. Furthermore, if extreme subgroup separateness is a bad thing (which arguably it is) then by basing our sex selection policies on continued separation, and by applying sex selection policies that may allow or encourage separation to persist, we are colluding with a morally undesirable form of isolationism. Third and finally, there are proportionality issues. According to 2001 Census data, for example, 'non-white ethnic groups' in England and Wales comprise only 7.9 per cent of the population and the proportion for which unbalanced sex selection would be a problem would be even smaller than this, perhaps less than 5 per cent.[56] So, if we were to prevent *everyone* from accessing sex selection, on the grounds that a subgroup (or, more likely, set of subgroups) comprising less 1-in-20 of the population would, as it were, misuse sex selection by choosing nearly all boys, the 19-in-20 may understandably feel rather hard done by. And any harm done to the majority (such as the disappointment that prospective sex selectors might experience when unable to have the child of their choice) must be weighed against the interests of minority groups. Which way this balancing goes will depend on detail of the situation. If the harm to frustrated sex selectors were relatively minor, while the social damage to minority groups were catastrophic, then prohibiting sex selection for the sake of minority groups may be justified (*ceteris paribus* and, in particular, leaving aside the other reservations mentioned above). But we cannot just assume that things will be like this and there will be other situations in which any social damage to the minority groups will not be sufficiently serious to justify frustrating prospective sex selectors' aspirations.

The main conclusions of this section then are as follows. I am happy to allow, as a matter of personal moral responsibility, that prospective parents deciding whether or not to sex select, and indeed which sex to select, should (insofar as they are able) take account of population sex imbalance issues, including those within relevant subgroups. Specifically, if their (possible, future) sons would have worse lives than their (possible, future) daughters (because the sons would run the risk of failing to find a wife, owing to shortage of women) then the parents have a prima facie moral reason to select girls (or, at the very least, not to select boys). But although this holds for personal morality, I have also considered and rejected the claim that sex selection in the UK should be banned on account of its likely impact on population sex ratios within some ethnic subgroups.

---

[56] Office for National Statistics, <http://www.statistics.gov.uk/glance> (last accessed: Monday, 13 Apr. 2009).

8.7 Pressure and Consent

I said earlier that there are two reasons to be concerned about allowing sex selection when there are subgroups with strong son preferences. The first, as we have seen, is that sex imbalance may result within the subgroups. The second is that subgroups with strong son preferences may exert pressure on prospective parents (especially women), and that this pressure will (at least in some cases) vitiate their consent to the sex selection process. The prospective parents will, so the argument goes, be (in some sense) forced to select a son. Hence, their consents will lack one of the essential features of valid consent: voluntariness. Rogers, Ballantyne, and Draper (although discussing sex selective abortion in *countries* with strong son preferences) make the point as follows:

The birth of a son may ensure better treatment for [the mother] and the child, increase her status within the family and society, and increase the chance that her child will receive enough resources to survive. For these reasons, it may be a rational choice for a woman to elect to abort a pregnancy that would otherwise result in the birth of a female child. It is not clear however, that a rational choice necessarily amounts to an autonomous choice. Autonomous choices are usually characterized as occurring intentionally, with understanding and without controlling influences. In the case of a woman electing to have a SSA, in a situation in which she will suffer significant harms including vilification and physical and mental abuse if she bears a daughter, we need to question whether a decision to abort is voluntary on any plausible account of autonomous choices.[57]

There are two main versions of this worry. The first concerns direct pressure: instances in which individual women are subjected to specific acts of coercion, manipulation, or violence. This would include the 'vilification and physical and mental abuse' cited by Rogers et al. The second is about indirect pressure stemming from entrenched and quite possibly internalized social expectations and values.[58]

As regards pressure of the first kind, certainly this is to be condemned if and when it occurs, and we should support the principles of respect for autonomy and valid consent underlying this concern. Whether that is a sufficient reason to prohibit sex selection in general, however, is another matter. It is another matter first because, as just discussed, there are questions of proportionality, with the extent of the vitiated

---

[57] Rogers, Ballantyne, and Draper, 'Sex Selection Abortion', 521.

[58] Sheldon and Wilkinson discuss a very similar issue in relation to female genital mutilation or modification. See: Sally Sheldon and Stephen Wilkinson, 'Female Genital Mutilation and Cosmetic Surgery: Regulating Non-Therapeutic Body Modification', *Bioethics*, 12 (1998), 263–85.

consent problem needing to be weighed against the restriction of other women's reproductive choice that banning sex selection would entail. Second, and more importantly (at least when we are thinking about subgroups within the UK) there are ways of dealing with the consent problem using regulation and good clinical practice. An example of such a system would be the UK regulations governing unrelated organ transplantation, which impose specific safeguards to ensure that consent is valid and uncoerced.[59] No such system can be perfect and there will always be some cases where the quality of the consent is insufficiently high. Nonetheless, we can minimize the number of such cases by using vigilant consent procedures. Furthermore, problems of this kind are ubiquitous and there are surely many cases, in both clinical practice and research, where consents are not as voluntary as they should be. I say this not in any way to condone it, but just to make the point that (with robust consent regulations in place) sex selection would be no more problematic than many other aspects of health care practice and research. I should add, however, that things may well be rather different in the *whole country* situations that are the primary concern of Rogers, Ballantyne, and Draper: those where systemic pressure is placed upon *all* women. The chances of consent procedures succeeding in these situations may be *much* less.

Turning now to *indirect* pressure, this is more complicated, particularly when we are thinking of cases in which the women themselves have internalized the sexist values that most likely underpin strong son preference. Imagine, for example, the following case.

> **Victoria**, *a 30-year-old graduate, is a member of a subgroup that attaches immense value to the production of sons, especially to one's firstborn child being a boy. Victoria endorses her community's values and wishes to use sex selection to produce a son as her first child. According to her religious beliefs, having a son is a great honour and a blessing from God.*

What should we say about people like Victoria? Perhaps the first thing to strike us is that her beliefs are themselves unethical insofar as they are sexist. This may well be true, but is not relevant to the particular issue under discussion, which is her ability to give autonomous and voluntary consent, not the morality of her beliefs or character. Indeed, in general, the fact that people are bad does not remove their capacity to give valid consent. What matters most for our purposes then is—are her beliefs and preferences autonomously held, or has she been brainwashed or indoctrinated into holding them (for instance, by being exposed to religious training as a child)? If the latter, then we may reasonably complain that her choice of, or consent to, sex selection is defective because it is driven by beliefs or desires that are

---

[59] Human Tissue Authority, *Code of Practice: Donation of Organs, Tissue and Cells for Transplantation (Code 2)*, July 2006.

not autonomously held, but which have been somehow foisted upon her. I will say more about what it takes for a belief or desire to be autonomously held in a moment, but first want to ask how this idea might underpin a general argument against (social) sex selection.

The argument must take something like the following form:

1. As a matter of fact, the preference for sons held by many members of UK subgroups (people like Victoria) is based on non-autonomous beliefs and/or desires.

2. When a consent is based on non-autonomous beliefs and/or desires, it is invalid. Medical procedures should not take place based on such consents.

3. The occurrence of clinical sex selection procedures without valid consent is something that health law and policy should strive to avoid.

4. The best, or only, means of avoiding the widespread occurrence of sex selection procedures without valid consent is the general prohibition of (social) sex selection.

5. *Therefore* (from 3 and 4): (social) sex selection should be prohibited.

While I endorse some elements of this argument (in particular, the importance attached to valid consent) it does seem flawed. Perhaps the best way into this is to ask what is meant by *non-autonomously held beliefs and desires*. This could, not surprisingly, mean several different things and this is not the place to get into a prolonged discussion of the nature of autonomy. In brief, though, one (or both) of two thoughts could lie behind the claim that these beliefs and/or desires are not autonomous. One is about the way in which the person's mental states were *acquired*. Thus, we might contrast beliefs gained through independent study and investigation with those caused by brainwashing, indoctrination, or mind-altering drugs. The former are (arguably) autonomously acquired while the latter are not, and this is the idea underlying the distinction between education and indoctrination. The other thought concerns not so much how the mental states were originally acquired, but rather the extent to which the holder of the beliefs and desires is presently capable of subjecting them to rational critique and reflection, and of changing or losing the beliefs and desires in the light of such reflection. Although these two ideas are analytically distinct they may be linked in practice insofar as autonomously *acquired* beliefs and desires are more likely to be autonomously *held*, whereas those acquired through (say) brainwashing might be harder for the person to rationally critique or to rid themselves of through reflection.

This sketch of the nature of autonomous belief and desire reveals immediately some problems with the argument above. One is that distinguishing between beliefs and desires that are autonomously acquired and/or held and those that are not may be terribly difficult and require huge amounts of information about the person. So the claim that many members of UK subgroups have non-autonomously acquired and/or held beliefs would take a lot of establishing, if indeed it can be established at all. Another is that, given the account just sketched, the possession of non-autonomously acquired and/or held beliefs is likely to be very widespread and not just confined to subgroups that are strongly religious or sexist. For even many feminist atheists will have beliefs that do not meet these autonomy criteria, having perhaps themselves been non-rationally influenced by advertising, parents, peer group pressure, or teachers. So we cannot just help ourselves to the view that strongly religious and sexist subgroups have a particular problem with non-autonomous beliefs and desires. Yet another difficulty is that, when dealing with valid consent in a medical ethics context, we normally require simply that the consenter is mentally competent (which includes a certain level of autonomy, but at the level of the whole agent rather than each particular belief and desire), that she is adequately informed, and that she is not coerced or manipulated (in other words, the consent must be voluntary). So, while the standard medical ethics model of consent would disallow consents based on extreme and ongoing forms of 'mind control' (because of the voluntariness requirement), and would similarly disallow consent from someone who, considered as a whole agent, had very low levels of rationality and autonomy (because of the competence requirement, which in turn requires adequate reasoning and understanding), it does not require the complete absence of non-autonomous mental states in the consenter's motivational set. And, if it did, then there would not be much valid consent around.

This point is bolstered by the fact that many of what we might term our *basic* desires are not autonomously held (on the accounts suggested above). Basic desires are things like wanting food, sex, warmth, and water, wanting to avoid physical pain, or perhaps wanting to stay alive. Such desires are often non-autonomous in that they are neither acquired through conscious rational processes, nor can be readily eliminated or modified by critical reflection. That is not to say that modification in the light of rational reflection is completely impossible for these desires. But they are at least generally *resistant to elimination* by reflection such that, for example, people find it very difficult to think their way out of wanting food or wanting not to die (except in special circumstances, such as when the person is in intractable pain). The relevance of this to our present concerns is that many central cases of choice or consent in a biomedical setting are reliant on these basic non-autonomous desires. For example, consenting to a pain-relieving intervention would be based on the patient's non-autonomous desire to avoid pain. We do not, however, regard this as problematic provided that the patient, *considered as an agent overall*, is autonomous and competent, and provided that the consent meets the other standard conditions for validity. So again we see that valid consent cannot require the complete absence of non-autonomous mental states in the consenter's motivational set; for, if it did, there would be almost no cases of valid consent, especially in a biomedical setting. The same goes for consent to sex selection: prospective parents can validly consent to this, provided that they are sufficiently autonomous *agents*, even if some of the particular beliefs on which their consents are based are non-autonomously held.

This section has considered the claim that some subgroups with strong son preferences would exert pressure on prospective parents (especially women), and that this pressure would (at least in some cases) vitiate their consent to the sex selection process. It is concluded that, while this is a danger that we should remain wary of, cases in which sex selection was not validly consensual could be kept to a minimum, provided that careful consent procedures were used. With adequate safeguards in place, consent in sex selection clinics need be no more problematic than in many other areas of health care practice and research.

8.8 Sending Out the Wrong Message

Earlier, I suggested that the permissibility of sex selection depends on social context and that while worries about population sex imbalance may justify prohibition in some countries (specifically those with very strong son preferences), such arguments do not apply to most Western democracies. I also mentioned one possible problem with this view: that permitting social sex selection in the UK could 'send out the message' that sex selection is acceptable to distant countries and cultures with a strong son preference. The House of Commons Select Committee on Science and Technology summarized the argument as follows:

It could be argued that by permitting people to choose the sex of their child in this country we are legitimising the choices among cultures where boys are preferred . . . What is allowed here will . . . be cited as a precedent by other countries. It may also make it harder for the UK to criticise sex selection in other countries, however abominably it is presently carried out, for instance by the murder of baby girls in some countries or by abortion.[60]

The worry then is that while these other countries and cultures are importantly different from ours (such that sex selection is acceptable 'here' and not 'there') these differences may be overlooked by those wanting to practice sex selection in contexts where it would be wrong. Such people may use our allowing of sex selection as a way of justifying their behaviour and (at least in political, as opposed to academic, debates) permitting it in our country would make it harder for us unequivocally to

[60] House of Commons Select Committee on Science and Technology, *Inquiry into Human Reproductive Technologies and the Law, Eighth Special Report of Session 2004–2005* (2005), 63.

condemn wrongful sex selection practices (possibly even including infanticide and forcing women to sex select).

Like many other arguments about sex selection, this one is about the potential *bad consequences* of permitting sex selection in the UK (although with the consequences being elsewhere). As such, we must concede that it is a type of argument that could in principle serve to justify prohibiting sex selection provided that the consequences of allowing it really were sufficiently calamitous. And of course whether, in the real world, they would be is an empirical matter.

That said, there are, nonetheless, reasons to be sceptical about this argument against sex selection in the UK. The first, a practical point (and one that opponents of sex selection are usually rather keen to remind us of) is that sex selection in places like China and India is already happening on a grand scale anyway, notwithstanding the fact that the UK does not allow social sex selection.[61] So our 'setting a good example' by prohibiting sex selection does not seem to be doing much good. And if it is not doing much good, if China and India are not taking much notice of what we do, then we may as well not pay much attention to their behaviour when formulating our own policies. Now of course it is open to opponents of sex selection in the UK to say that things would have been *even worse* in China and India were it not for the British ban. And again this is an empirical matter. Nonetheless, in the absence of solid evidence for this, it seems no better than idle speculation. Indeed, it is not even a form of speculation with much intuitive plausibility. This is first because it seems to take far too seriously the influence of UK assisted reproduction policy on the behaviour of Chinese and Indian sex selectors (many of whom are, in any case, acting outside their own laws). For how many Chinese and Indians even know what HFEA rules and British legislation say about sex selection? (I would be rather surprised if even 1 per cent of the Chinese population are familiar with our new Human Fertilisation and Embryology Act, for example.)[62] Indeed, how many British people know the details of this? Second, it is worth bearing in mind that relationships between countries and cultures are rarely straightforward and we cannot just assume that some form of imitation will be the way that other countries respond to what we do. It may go the other way and other countries may want to distance themselves from what they want to see as Western depravity. If this were the case (which it clearly is in some parts of the world) then interestingly the best way to put other countries off the idea of sex selection would be for us to encourage a rather unfettered and distasteful version of it here. This then takes us back to the general limitations of such consequence-based arguments: one of which is that they can serve (putatively) to justify pretty much anything, depending on how the predicted consequences turn out.

[61] Shirish Sheth, 'Missing Female Births in India', *The Lancet*, 367 (21 Jan. 2006), 185–6: 185.
[62] Human Fertilisation and Embryology Act 2008.

A second reason to be sceptical about the argument is that it overlooks an important and fundamental point: that the UK cannot surely set a bad example unless it is doing something wrong. There is a kind of dilemma here for those who wish to base their argument against UK sex selection on other countries' reactions. For *either there are* independent reasons (i.e. reasons that have nothing to do with the reactions of other countries) why sex selection as it would be practised here would be wrong, in which case citing the reactions of other countries is unnecessary (since we would already have reasons for not doing it here). *Or there are not* any independent reasons why sex selection (as it would be practised) is wrong, in which case how can we be setting a bad example? How can permissible behaviour be an example of something bad?

In response, opponents of sex selection might point out (rightly) that if the first 'horn' of the above dilemma were true (if there *were* independent reasons to avoid sex selection) then the appeal to other countries would not be completely redundant, as it might still *amplify* the case against sex selection: sex selection would then be both wrong (for some independent reason) and made even worse because of the example it sets. This is true, although the argument based on other countries would still be wholly *parasitic* on some other argument against sex selection and could only work if that other argument worked too.

Those opposed to sex selection may also point out that it is possible to encourage bad behaviour by doing things that are not wrong but which *seem* to be wrong to others. That is certainly true. Permissible acts can appear wrong and sometimes it is important to be *seen* to be right, as well as to be right. Having said that, we should not just give in too easily to this argument and there are various ways in which it might be dealt with or undermined.

One solution would be to make it very clear (to outside observers) what exactly it is that we are doing in this country when we sex select, why it is permissible, and why the policy and/or the circumstances here are relevantly different from those in other countries (the ones for which we are allegedly setting a bad example). These relevant differences have already been discussed: such as that we would not have a problem with population sex imbalance and that our motives are less likely to be underpinned by extreme sexism than those of sex selectors in some other countries (which is not to deny that there would be some sexism involved in some British cases). In addition, and more importantly, there are moral differences between the sex selection practices that we would allow in the UK and those that are most frequently condemned in China and India. There is, for example, an enormous moral difference between situations in which women are forced to sex select and those in which they freely choose to do so. And there are similarly differences between sex selection via infanticide and sex selection via embryo or gamete selection. Practising the latter need in no way imply support for the former.

Now of course it is *possible* for someone to fail to notice the above mentioned distinctions and to think that consensual and carefully regulated sex selection via sperm sorting is no different from forcing mothers to kill their female babies. But then it is also *possible* for someone to fail to notice the difference between consensual extramarital sex and rape, or the difference between employment and slavery. In all these cases, our first response should be to explain what the differences are, and why our doing the first does not lend support to the second. Such distinctions are crucial and, by advocating sex selection in the specific circumstances outlined above, we would not be endorsing either infanticide, or coerced sex selection, or actions that cause major population sex imbalance.

That leaves the question of whether other countries (or more generally other people) are capable of understanding these distinctions. Again this is ultimately an empirical matter. I have already said that I doubt whether many people in China and India in fact take much notice of UK reproductive policy, or even know what it is. But insofar as they do, is there any reason to think them incapable of understanding that there are (for example) differences between infanticide and sperm sorting, and between coerced and voluntary sex selection? The ethical issues surrounding these distinctions can be complex but nonetheless, it is condescending and implausible to claim that people overseas could not understand the distinctions that we are drawing (and even those with rather 'pro-life' views are likely to concede that not making use of a particular spermatozoon is a different practice from killing a female infant). So the claim that other nations will not understand the fact that our sex selection policy (were it to be liberalized) would be very limited in scope and carefully regulated, does not seem at all plausible. And no nation capable of understanding these distinctions could, without disingenuity, cite the UK's limited endorsement of pre-conception or preimplantation sex selection as a justification for infanticide and other immoral practices. Of course, some states, and some individuals, will behave dishonestly, but there is very little that we can do to prevent this and it is certainly not a sound basis for constraining UK law.[63]

Indeed, there is something rather troubling in general with the idea that we should, as it were, 'dumb down' our policies so that they do not make use of subtle distinctions, on the grounds that observers (be they here or elsewhere) will allegedly be incapable of understanding that permitting x does not mean condoning y (when there are morally relevant differences between x and y). Giving in to such arguments makes it less likely that our laws and policies will be capable of tracking or reflecting the ethical complexity that exists in many areas of life.

---

[63] Centre LGS, *Response to the Public Consultation on the Human Fertilisation and Embryology Act*, Nov. 2005, <http://www.kent.ac.uk/clgs/centre-files/consultation_responses.html> (last accessed: Monday, 13 Apr. 2009).

8.9 Innocuous Means of Sex Selection

> Paradoxically, it is legal to attempt periconceptual sex selection by 'natural means', even if these employ technology developed specifically for that purpose.[64]

Next, I want briefly to consider the Innocuous Means Argument for the permissibility of sex selection. The form of the argument is as follows:

1. There are several 'folk' means of practising sex selection, such as modifying one's diet, or having intercourse using certain positions or at certain times.
2. There is nothing wrong with using these 'folk' methods of sex selection and they certainly should not be banned.
3. There are no fundamental moral differences between 'folk' and 'scientific' forms of sex selection (such as sperm sorting and embryo selection): especially given that they aim at the same thing.
4. *Therefore (from 3)*: in order to be rational and consistent—
   (a) people who regard 'technological' sex selection as wrong ought also to regard 'folk' sex selection as wrong (and vice versa);
   (b) people who regard 'folk' sex selection as permissible ought also to regard 'technological' sex selection as permissible (and vice versa);
   (c) people who think that 'technological' sex selection ought to be banned ought also to think that 'folk' sex selection should be banned (and vice versa); and,
   (d) people who think that 'folk' sex selection should be allowed ought also to think that 'technological' sex selection should be allowed (and vice versa).
5. *Therefore (from (2), (4b), and (4d))*: 'technological' sex selection is morally permissible and ought not to be prohibited.

Does this argument work? We can start to assess it by asking whether there really are any innocuous 'folk' means of sex selection. There do seem to be on the face of it. Savulescu, for example, tells us that:

Periconceptual choice of sex is based on the observation that conception close to ovulation is more likely to result in a boy. Attempts to predict the time of ovulation have been made by measuring hormonal levels, polarity of the egg membrane, and cervical mucous thickness. Other 'folk' methods include positioning during intercourse, vaginal douching, and so on.[65]

---

[64] Julian Savulescu, 'Sex Selection: The Case For', in Helga Kuhse and Peter Singer (eds.), *Bioethics: An Anthology* (Oxford: Blackwell, 2nd edn., 2006), 145–9: 145.

[65] Savulescu, 'Sex Selection', 146.

And, in April 2008, research was reported (not for the first time) suggesting that women's diets can influence the sex of their future children. Specifically, women are more likely to have boys if they have a high-calorie diet in the run-up to pregnancy:

Scientists at Oxford and Exeter universities asked 740 women, who had become pregnant for the first time, about their eating patterns in the year before they conceived. They then divided the women into high, medium and low calorie groups. They found that 56% of women in the high calorie group gave birth to boys compared with 45% in the lower calorie group.[66]

Fiona Matthews, a researcher from the University of Exeter, adds:

We were able to confirm the old wives' tale that eating bananas and so having a high potassium intake was associated with having a boy, as was a high sodium intake. But the old tale about drinking a lot of milk to have a girl doesn't seem to hold up. In fact, it meant they were again more likely to have a boy.[67]

The study also showed that 59 per cent of women who ate breakfast cereal every day had boys, compared with only 43 per cent of women who rarely or never ate cereal:

If you're looking for a boy, then eating breakfast cereal every day and within safe limits, having a reasonable intake of sodium, potassium and calcium, plus a good intake of protein looks like a sensible option. It's the converse of that if you're hoping for a girl[68]

Other (as far as I am aware) less well-evidenced folk methods include:

douches (alkaline for a boy; acidic for a girl), positions for intercourse (from the rear for a boy; missionary for a girl); female orgasm (before male orgasm for a boy; not at all for a girl); frequency of coitus (more for boys)[69]

Armed with this knowledge, it seems that women can increase or decrease their chances of having a son by adjusting their breakfast cereal and banana intakes. So let us assume for the sake of argument at least that the means are available. But are these innocuous means? What, for instance, should we think of the following case?

> **Zara**, who already has two boys, is keen to have a girl as her third, and probably final, child. This is not for any sexist reasons (she is keen to stress that she values men and women as equals) but because she wants to have the experience of a mother–daughter relationship and this will almost certainly be her only chance to do that. Having read various books and press reports about

[66] Ian Sample, 'Bananas and Cereal—Scientists Reveal What Little Boys Are Made Of: Pregnancy Diet Influences Baby's Gender, Study Says Fewer Calories Mean Greater Chance of a Girl', *The Guardian*, 23 Apr. 2008, 2.

[67] Sample, 'Bananas and Cereal'.   [68] Sample, 'Bananas and Cereal'.

[69] Helen Bequaert Holmes, 'Choosing Children's Sex: Challenges to Feminist Ethics', in Joan Callahan (ed.), *Reproduction, Ethics, and the Law* (Bloomington: Indiana University Press, 1995), 148–77: 156.

influencing the sex of one's future children, Zara stops eating breakfast cereal and bananas and has
sex only in the 'missionary position' while trying to become pregnant.

Is there anything wrong with what Zara is doing and should it be allowed? The second part of the question is the easiest for surely no one is going to say that she should be *compelled* to eat bananas and cereals, or to employ a more imaginative range of sexual positions. To most of us, I imagine that similar thoughts will apply to the moral dimension of the question: that is, refraining from banana eating and the like seems not to be something that should attract any sort of moral condemnation. So there is (I imagine) a widespread *intuition* that some forms of attempted sex selection are morally unproblematic.

Quite what this shows and what underlies the intuition, though, is more contentious. One issue is whether we can, in the context of an argument purporting to demonstrate the permissibility of sex selection, help ourselves to the thought that Zara's acts (omissions, in fact) are morally neutral. For what an ardent opponent of sex selection could say is that Zara *is* acting badly because there *is* something wrong with doing things calculated to influence the sex of one's future children. So perhaps we cannot (without begging the question) just assume that Zara is morally in the clear.

This is probably right, but serves to reveal another problem for opponents of sex selection (the one alluded to in the Savulescu quotation at the start of this section). The problem is that their view seems to have two unpalatable implications: (a) that Zara is acting immorally by giving up bananas and alternative sexual positions; and (b) (worse still) that there is a prima facie case for forcing Zara to eat bananas and to employ alternative sexual positions. Perhaps (a) is something that the opponents of sex selection can live with and one can imagine coherent versions of this view, although it is certainly not one that will win them many allies. Being committed to (b) though does seem more fundamentally problematic and, in response, critics of sex selection would need to argue that there is a pragmatic distinction to be drawn between, on the one hand, regulating sex selection clinics and, on the other, regulating the everyday sex lives and eating habits of individuals. Their position then would be that while, in principle, the same prima facie case for State intrusion applies to both, there are reasons for treating sex selection clinics and private individuals' lifestyle choices differently. One of these is simply pragmatic: we cannot realistically police people's kitchens and bedrooms, as we do clinics. The other is more principled: that stronger rights to privacy exist in relation to people's kitchen and bedroom behaviour, than in relation to their dealings with medical establishments.

These are, up to a point, decent responses, but they do leave the opponents of sex selection with residual problems. The first of these (concerning the 'pragmatic' response) is that the fact that there is no practical way to force Zara to eat bananas or to use more imaginative sexual positions is a woefully inadequate, and extremely fragile, basis for our not so forcing her. For essentially what we would be saying (if we thought this) is that if we could find a practical and cost-effective way of forcing her then we should, but it just so happens that we cannot. I doubt that many people, even those instinctively opposed to sex selection, will regard this as an acceptable view. The second residual problem is that it is by no means obvious that people's eating habits and sexual actions are any more supported by privacy rights than their relations with the health care staff who might perform sex selection procedures. Indeed, privacy in relation to medical treatment (especially when it concerns such intimate matters as reproduction and sex) is generally regarded as a very important moral principle and arguably underpins some of the centrepieces of medical ethics, notably confidentiality and informed consent. This is not the place to get into a lengthy discussion of the nature and scope of privacy. Nonetheless, it is worth pointing out (as I have) that the difference between what happens to a person in a sex selection clinic and what happens in her own home may not be as obvious, or as great, as opponents of sex selection would need them to be in order to draw a principled distinction between making Zara eat bananas, etc. and stopping someone from accessing clinical sex selection services.

Finally, as regards our intuitions about Zara's attempt to sex select, it may be argued that the reason why we think of her actions as innocuous is either because we do not think that they will work at all, or that we think they will (at best) only slightly increase the probability of her having a girl (which, indeed, does seem to be what the evidence suggests). Whereas the success rates for sperm sorting or embryo selection would be much higher and so the degree of control exerted by someone using these scientific methods would be correspondingly much greater. This then, opponents of clinical sex selection may argue, is the moral difference between Zara's acts and medicalized sex selection: the latter is much more effective.

It is easy to see how this difference might underpin some consequence-based arguments. Most obviously, the more ineffective a method of sex selection is, the less likely it is to cause a population sex imbalance (with completely ineffective methods being best of all). But such arguments have already been dealt with and, to a large extent dismissed, at least in the UK context that is my primary concern. So what concerns us here is whether 'folk' sex selection is *intrinsically* any better than 'scientific' sex selection (by virtue of its being less effective), and it is by no means clear that it is. (I am also sidelining here concerns about the selection and destruction of sperm or embryos, to which I shall turn next.) For surely if there is something in the nature of sex selection that makes it wrong, then attempting it *through whatever means* is wrong. For instance, if it were the case that sex selection were necessarily grounded in sexist attitudes, or constituted an act of sexism, then this would apply regardless of the effectiveness of the methods used. For what would matter would be the fact that the selector *intended* what she was doing to result in a boy, or in a girl.

What conclusions then can we draw from the Zara case? The fundamental challenge for opponents of sex selection is this: can they consistently oppose sex selection via embryo or gamete selection while also denying that Zara is acting immorally, or even worse that she should be forced to eat bananas and to utilize a wider range of sexual positions? Leaving aside consequence-based arguments, which were dealt with and (at least partially) dismissed earlier, it looks as if it will be difficult for the opponents of sex selection to maintain a distinction between these two forms of sex selection. And probably the best that they can do is either maintain that there are pragmatic differences between 'folk' and 'scientific' sex selection (a position which, for reasons just given, is rather unsatisfactory) or claim that what differentiates Zara's behaviour from medical sex selection is that the latter involves the selection and destruction of sperm and embryos. It is to this latter claim that I now briefly turn.

This book has little to say about the moral status of the embryo and about the wrongness or otherwise of creating and destroying human embryos. I explained the reasons for this in 1.6. The most relevant one for our present purposes is that concerns about the destruction of embryos are really too general to underpin arguments that count specifically against selective reproduction, or a fortiori specifically against sex selection. For such concerns do not count *specifically* against selection, but instead against a very wide range of practices including IVF, abortion, and some birth control techniques. Having said that, one could take the view that embryos are morally significant inasmuch as we should only destroy them (and create them with a view to destroying some of them) when there is a weighty positive moral justification for doing so. Such positive justifications might include enabling an otherwise childless person to have a child (which is potentially positive both for the parent and for the resultant child) or enabling us to 'select out' life shortening and/or painful medical conditions. But, it may be argued, no such positive justification exists in the case of (non-medical) sex selection which delivers no real benefit other than the satisfaction of the parents' desires. Thus, we have an argument that is specifically against sex selection: whereas many other forms of IVF and selection are sufficiently valuable to outweigh the *dis*value of embryo destruction, sex selection is not.

This is a valid form of argument, but there are some available responses that serve to defend sex selection from at least its strongest conclusions. The first, a practical point, is that the possibility of sex selection via sperm sorting enables us to bypass concerns about embryos, since it is not sensible to assign the sort of positive value to sperm that some people do to an embryo: not least because almost all sperm are destined for death (without fertilization) whatever one does. Second (returning to sex selection via embryo selection) one might argue that the positive justification in the case of sex selection is not *fundamentally* different from that in the case of IVF for the purposes of alleviating childlessness. For in both cases parental welfare is increased (when things go well). I would concede there is usually a difference of degree here, with unwanted childlessness generally having a bigger impact on welfare than having a child of the 'wrong' sex. But what this suggests is not so much that there is an ethical difference between 'regular' IVF and embryonic sex selection, but rather that the 'all things considered' ethical judgement about each individual case should vary depending on the extent of the benefits (or harms) to prospective parents. Thus, there will be some people who, while desiring IVF to alleviate unwanted childlessness, would nonetheless have equally good future lives with or without children. For these people (according to the line of argument we are considering) the positive prima facie case for permitting 'regular' IVF would be quite weak, because the benefits to the prospective parents would be negligible or non-existent. Conversely, there will be some prospective sex selectors who are (right or wrongly) so invested in having (say) a girl that their lives would be ruined by having to settle for a boy. Here (leaving aside, for now, worries about the quality of such people's parenting) the positive prima facie for permitting sex selection (grounded in parental welfare considerations) would be very strong.

What then does the existence of apparently innocuous means of sex selection, like banana eating, tell us about the sex selection debate? While not providing a decisive argument one way or the other, it does put some additional pressure on those who oppose sex selection, and especially on those who advocate a ban. This pressure comes from the requirement to be consistent. Thus, those who are opposed to sex selection in clinics need to say why they are not also opposed to banana eating for the purposes of sex selection. Perhaps such reasons can be found, although I have attempted in this section to problematize some of the leading candidates. It looks as if the best reasons for treating clinical and 'folk' sex selection methods differently are practical ones: for example, it is a lot easier to regulate assisted reproduction than it is banana consumption. But this position is unattractive on two counts. First, it seems rather unfair to restrict users of one sex selection method rather than another just because one set of sex selectors (those going down the clinical route) are, as it were, soft targets—just because it is easier to control their behaviour. Second, opponents of clinical sex selection would still be committed to the rather unpalatable view that we should prohibit or restrict 'folk' sex selection methods as well if we could.

8.10 Summary and Conclusions

The central concern of this chapter has been non-medical (also known as *social*) sex selection (that is, sex selection for reasons other than the avoidance of sex-linked disability or disease), especially when this is delivered using either embryo selection or gamete selection. The first substantive ethical questions considered were:

Is family balancing morally preferable to other forms of non-medical sex selection?

and:

Should family balancing be given a privileged legal and/or regulatory status compared to other forms of non-medical sex selection (for example, such that family balancing is the only permitted form)?

The answer to both of these is *no*.

Two main arguments for preferring family balancing to other types were considered. There is, first, the claim that family balancing is less likely to cause population sex imbalance and, second, that family balancing is less sexist (or less likely to be sexist). Both of these were rejected. In the case of population sex imbalance, I argued both that this is unlikely to be a problem in most Western countries (my concern here) and that, even if it were a potential problem, there are ways of regulating sex selection (ways other than allowing only family balancing) that could deal with it (for example, limiting the proportion of boys/girls that licensed clinics could select). As regards sexism, I argued that, insofar as sex selection in general is vulnerable to accusations of sexism, then family balancing is not immune from such criticisms. All forms of sex selection *can* be driven by morally problematic sexist attitudes; conversely it is possible for all (or most) forms to be underpinned by more innocent motives.

Having dealt with family balancing, I turned to the more fundamental questions of whether any form of social sex selection is morally acceptable, and of whether any form of sex selection should be allowed. Similar arguments were again in play, especially concerns about sexism. In response to these, although I was happy to concede that a good deal of social sex selection would be driven by sexist beliefs and attitudes (and that such views are, at best, mistaken and, at worst, morally reprehensible), this fact is not enough to justify the prohibition of social sex selection in the UK. This is both because of the importance attached to reproductive liberty but also crucially because the kind of sexism involved would often be fairly harmless. This does not mean that morally it is to be condoned, just that it is not sufficiently harmful or serious to justify prohibitive State intervention. Several further objections to permitting sex selection were considered and rejected. These included specific concerns about ethnic minority populations and about the international consequences of UK domestic policy.

So the overall view defended here is as follows. Social sex selection is not *necessarily* sexist although *often* it is and, where it is, this is a reason morally to condemn it. However, neither the sexism argument nor the various other consequence-based arguments are sufficient to justify prohibition. It is important, however, to note that this conclusion is context-sensitive and that there may be countries in the world (notably ones with a very strong son preference) where prohibition is the best policy—perhaps because no other form of regulation will work, because cultural factors serve to vitiate the consent of prospective parents (especially women), or generally because the prevalence and severity of sexism is much greater in those countries than in the UK.

BIBLIOGRAPHY

Abuja, Anjana, 'The Ethics of Sex Selection Should Not Be Down to the Public', *The Times*, 12 Nov. 2003, 22.

Albrecht, G., and Devlieger, P., 'The Disability Paradox: High Quality of Life Against All Odds', *Social Science & Medicine*, 48 (1999), 977–88.

Alexandra, Andrew, and Walsh, Adrian, 'Exclusion, Commodification, and Plant Variety Rights Legislation', *Agriculture and Human Values*, 14 (1997), 313–23.

Anderson, Elizabeth, 'Is Women's Labor a Commodity?' *Philosophy and Public Affairs*, 19 (1990), 71–92.

—— 'Why Commercial Surrogate Motherhood Unethically Commodifies Women and Children: Reply to McLachlan and Swales', *Health Care Analysis*, 8 (2000), 19–26.

Archard, David, 'What's Blood Got To Do With It? The Significance of Natural Parenthood', *Res Publica*, 1 (1995), 91–106.

—— Wrongful Life, *Philosophy*, 79/3 (2004), 403–20.

Asch, Adrienne, 'Distracted by Disability', *Cambridge Quarterly of Health Care Ethics*, 7 (1998), 77–87: 78.

ASH (website), *Tax and Smuggling: Frequently Asked Questions*, <http://old.ash.org.uk/html/smuggling/html/taxfaq.html> (last accessed: Wednesday, 25 Oct. 2006).

Ashcroft, Richard E., Dawson, Angus, Draper, Heather, and MacMillan, John (eds.), '*Principles of Health Care Ethics*' (2nd edn., Chichester: John Wiley & Sons Ltd, 2007).

Ayres, Chris, 'When IVF Turns into an IQ Test', *The Times*, 11 Dec. 2007, 14.

Baker, Bernadette, 'The Hunt for Disability: The New Eugenics and the Normalization of School Children', *Teachers College Record*, 104 (2002), 663–703.

Barendregt, Jan J., Bonneux, Luc, and van der Maas, Paul J., 'The Healthcare Costs of Smoking', *New England Journal of Medicine*, 337 (1997), 1052–7.

Barnett, R., 'Keywords in the History of Medicine: Eugenics', *The Lancet*, 363 (2004), 1742.

Bayne, Tim, and Kolers, Avery, 'Parenthood and Procreation', in Edward Zolta (ed.), *The Stanford Encyclopedia of Philosophy* (Stanford: Centre for the Study of Language and Information), <http://plato.stanford.edu>.

—— and Levy, Neil, 'Amputees by Choice: Body Integrity Identity Disorder and the Ethics of Amputation', *Journal of Applied Philosophy*, 22 (2005), 75–86.

BBC News, *Couple Fight for Baby Girl*, 4 Oct. 2000, <http://news.bbc.co.uk/1/hi/scotland/955251.stm> (last accessed: Sunday, 12 Apr. 2009).

—— *Genetics Storm Girl 'Responding Well'*, 19 Oct. 2000, <http://news.bbc.co.uk/1/hi/health/979884.stm> (last accessed: Sunday, 12 Apr. 2009).

BBC News, *The Mastertons Webcast: Transcript*, 23 Oct. 2000, <http://news.bbc.co.uk/1/hi/scotland/981703.stm> (last accessed: Sunday, 12 Apr. 2009).

—— *Hashmi Decision Sparks Ethics Row*, 22 Feb. 2002, <http://news.bbc.co.uk/1/hi/health/1836827.stm> (last accessed: Sunday, 12 Apr. 2009).

—— *Couple 'Choose' to Have Deaf Baby*, 8 Apr. 2002, <http://news.bbc.co.uk/1/hi/health/1916462.stm> (last accessed: Sunday, 12 Apr. 2009).

Benatar, David, 'Why It Is Better Never to Come into Existence', *American Philosophical Quarterly*, 34 (1997), 345—55.

—— 'The Wrong of Wrongful Life', *American Philosophical Quarterly*, 37 (2000), 175—83.

—— 'To Be or Not to Have Been?: Defective Counterfactual Reasoning about One's Own Existence', *International Journal of Applied Philosophy*, 15 (2001), 255—66.

—— *Better Never to Have Been: The Harm of Coming into Existence* (Oxford: Oxford University Press, 2006).

Benn, Piers, 'Is Sex Morally Special?' *Journal of Applied Philosophy*, 16 (1999), 235—45.

Berkowitz, Jonathan, and Snyder, Jack, 'Racism and Sexism in Medically Assisted Conception', *Bioethics*, 12 (1998), 25—44.

Boyle, Robert, and Savulescu, Julian, 'Ethics of Using Preimplantation Genetic Diagnosis to Select a Stem Cell Donor for an Existing Person', *BMJ* 32 (2001), 1240—3: 1241.

Brecher, Bob, 'The Kidney Trade: or, The Customer is Always Wrong', *Journal of Medical Ethics*, 16 (1990), 120—3.

Britten, Nick, 'Couple to Create "Saviour Sibling" ', *Daily Telegraph*, 6 May 2006, 6.

Brock, Dan, 'The Non-Identity Problem and Genetic Harms—The Case of Wrongful Handicaps', *Bioethics*, 9 (1995), 269—75.

Brook, S., 'How Our Designer Baby Saved His Brother's Life', *The Sun*, 3 Feb. 2005, 36.

Brulde, Bengt, 'The Goals of Medicine: Towards a Unified Theory', *Healthcare Analysis*, 9 (2001), 1—13.

Buchanan, Allen, Brock, Dan, Daniels, Norman, and Wikler, Daniel, *From Choice to Chance: Genetics and Justice* (Cambridge: Cambridge University Press, 2000).

Burnie, Joan, 'A Poor States To Be In; Let's Just Ban the USA', *Daily Record* (Glasgow), 12 Apr. 2003, 25.

Burwood, Les, 'How Can We Assess Whether It Is Rational to Fall in Love?' *Journal of Social Philosophy*, 30 (1999), 223—35.

Campbell, Alistair, 'Surrogacy, Rights and Duties: A Partial Commentary', *Health Care Analysis*, 8 (2000), 35—40.

Caplan, A., McGee, G., and Magnus, D., 'What Is Immoral about Eugenics?' *BMJ* 319 (1999), 1284.

Card, R., 'Infanticide and the Liberal View of Abortion', *Bioethics*, 14 (2000), 340—51.

Centre LGS [Law, Gender, and Sexuality], *Response to the Public Consultation on the Human Fertilisation and Embryology Act*, Nov. 2005, <http://www.kent.ac.uk/clgs/centre-files/consultation_responses.html> (last accessed: Monday, 13 Apr. 2009).

Chadwick, Ruth, 'Genetics and Ethics', in Edward Craig (ed.), The *Routledge Encyclopedia of Philosophy* (London: Routledge, 1998).

—— Have, Henk ten, Husted Jørgen, Levitt, Mairi, McGeenan, Tony, Shickle, Darren, and Wiesing, Urban, 'Genetic Screening and Ethics: European Perspectives', *Journal of Medicine and Philosophy*, 23 (1998), 255–73.

Chambers, Jean, 'Women's Right to Choose Rationally: Genetic Information, Embryos Selection, and Genetic Manipulation', *Cambridge Quarterly of Healthcare Ethics*, 12 (2003), 418–28.

Cooke, E., 'Germ-Line Engineering, Freedom, and Future Generations', *Bioethics*, 17 (2003), 32–58.

Coutts, Mary, and McCarrick, Pat, 'Eugenics', *Kennedy Institute of Ethics Journal*, 5 (1995), 163–78.

Dahl, Edgar, 'Sex Selection: Laissez-Faire or Family Balancing?' *Healthcare Analysis*, 13 (2005), 87–90.

Davies, Alison, *A Disabled Person's Perspective on Pre-Natal Screening* (1999), <http://www.leeds.ac.uk/disability-studies/archiveuk/Davis/davis.htm> (last accessed: Sunday, 12 Apr. 2009).

Davies, Dena, *Genetic Dilemmas: Reproductive Technology, Parental Choices, and Children's Futures* (London: Routledge, 2001).

Davies, Julie-Anne, ' "Designer" Baby Goes Ahead', *The Age*, 12 Mar. 2003 <www.theage.com.au/articles/2003/03/11/1047144972401.html> (last accessed: Sunday, 12 Apr. 2009).

Dawson, Angus, *Vaccination Ethics: Law, Public Goods & Public Health* (Cambridge: Cambridge University Press, in press).

Dejevsky, Mary, 'Parents Have Baby to Produce Life-Saving Stem Cells for Sister', *The Independent*, 3 Oct. 2000, 13.

Department of Health, *Review of the Human Fertilisation and Embryology Act 1990—A Public Consultation* (2005).

—— *Review of the Human Fertilisation and Embryology Act: Proposals for Revised Legislation (including Establishment of the Regulatory Authority for Tissue and Embryos)* (Dec. 2006).

Derbyshire, David, and Petre, Jonathan, 'Parents Win Right to Have Donor Babies', *Daily Telegraph*, 22 July 2004.

Devolder, Katrien, 'Preimplantation HLA Typing: Having Children to Save Our Loved Ones', *Journal of Medical Ethics*, 31 (2005), 582–6.

Disability Rights Commission, *DRC Statement on Section 1(1)(d) of the Abortion Act 1967*, <www.drc-gb.org> (last accessed: 26 Oct. 2005).

—— *Definition of Disability*, <www.drc-gb.org> (last accessed: 12 Dec. 2006).

Draper, Heather, and Chadwick, Ruth, 'Beware! Preimplantation Genetic Diagnosis May Solve Some Old Problems But It Also Raises New Ones', *Journal of Medical Ethics*, 25 (1999), 114–20.

Duckworth, L., 'IVF Couple Give Away "Wrong Sex" Embryo', *The Independent*, 5 Mar. 2001, <http://www.independent.co.uk/life-style/health-and-wellbeing/health-news/ivf-couple-give-away-wrong-sex-embryo-694608.html> (last accessed: Monday, 13 Apr. 2009).

Dworkin, Gerald, *The Theory and Practice of Autonomy* (Cambridge: Cambridge University Press, 1998).

Edwards, Steven, 'Dismantling the Disability/Handicap Distinction', *Journal of Medicine and Philosophy*, 22 (1997), 589–606.

Edwards, Steven, 'Disability, Identity, and the "Expressivist Objection" ', *Journal of Medical Ethics*, 30 (2004), 418–20.

Elger, B., and Harding, T., 'Huntingdon's Disease: Do Future Physicians and Lawyers Think Eugenically?' *Clinical Genetics*, 64 (2003), 327–38.

Elliot, Carl, 'Costing an Arm and a Leg', *Slate*, <www.slate.com> 10 July 2003.

English, S., 'Parents Battle to Choose a Girl', *The Times*, 5 Oct. 2000, 3.

Ethics Committee of the Human Fertilisation and Embryology Authority, *Opinion: Ethical Issues in the Creation and Selection of Preimplantation Embryos to Produce Tissue Donors*, 22 Nov. 2001, ELC (12/03) 04.

European Society of Human Reproduction and Embryology (ESHRE) Ethics Task Force, 'Preimplantation Genetic Diagnosis', *Human Reproduction*, 18/3 (2003), 649–51.

Feinberg, Joel, 'The Child's Right to an Open Future', in Joel Feinberg (ed.), *Freedom and Fulfilment: Philosophical Essays* (Princeton: Princeton University Press, 1980), 76–97.

—— *Harm to Others: The Moral Limits of the Criminal Law*, i (New York: Oxford University Press, 1984).

—— *Freedom and Fulfillment* (Princeton: Princeton University Press, 1992).

Finnis, John, 'The Rights and Wrongs of Abortion', *Philosophy and Public Affairs*, 2 (1973), 117–45.

Flinter, Frances, 'Preimplantation Genetic Diagnosis Needs to be Tightly Regulated', *BMJ* 322 (28 Apr. 2001), 1008–9.

Frankfurt, Harry, 'Freedom of the Will and the Concept of a Person', *Journal of Philosophy*, 102 (1971), 129–39.

Furedi, Ann, ' "Disability Cleansing"—or a Reasonable Choice?' *Spiked Online*, <www.spiked-online.com>, 29 Aug. 2001.

Fuscaldo, Giuliana, 'Genetic Ties: Are They Morally Binding?' *Bioethics*, 20 (2006), 64–76.

Galton, Francis, *Essays in Eugenics* (Honolulu: University Press of the Pacific, 1909), 35.

Garavelli, Dani, 'Live and Let Live', *Scotland on Sunday*, 22 June 2003, 15.

Gardner, W., 'Can Human Genetic Enhancement Be Prohibited?' *Journal of Medicine and Philosophy*, 20 (1995), 65–84.

Garrard, Eve, and Wilkinson, Stephen, 'Does Bioethics Need Moral Theory?' in Matti Hayry and Tuija Takala (eds.), *Scratching the Surface of Bioethics* (Amsterdam: Rodopi, 2003), 35–45.

—————— 'Mind the Gap: The Use of Empirical Evidence in Bioethics', in M. Hayry, T. Takala, and P. Herissone-Kelly (eds.), *Bioethics and Social Reality* (Amderstam: Rodopi, 2005), 73–87.

—————— 'Selecting Disability and Welfare of the Child', *The Monist*, 89 (2006), 482–504.

Gibson, Susanne, 'The Problem of Abortion: Essentially Contested Concepts and Moral Autonomy', *Bioethics*, 18 (2004), 221–33.

Gillon, Raanon, 'Eugenics, Contraception, Abortion and Ethics', *Journal of Medical Ethics*, 24 (1998), 219.

Gillott, John, 'Screening for Disability: A Eugenic Pursuit?' *Journal of Medical Ethics*, 27 (suppl. ii) (2001), ii21–ii23.

Gitter, Donna M., 'Am I My Brother's Keeper? The Use of Preimplantation Genetic Diagnosis to Create a Donor or Transplantable Stem Cells for an Older Sibling Suffering from a Genetic Disorder', *George Mason Law Review*, 13 (2006), 975–1035.

Glannon, Walter, 'Genes, Embryos, and Future People', *Bioethics*, 12 (1998), 187–211: 197.

Glover, Jonathan, *Causing Death and Saving Lives* (Harmondsworth: Penguin Books, 1977).

—— *Fertility and the Family: The Glover Report on Reproductive Technologies to the European Commission* (London: Fourth Estate, 1989).

—— *Choosing Children: Genes, Disability, and Design* (Oxford: Clarendon Press, 2006).

Greene, J., 'Coercion: Description or Evaluation', *International Journal of Applied Philosophy*, 10 (1996), 7–16.

Haimes, Erica, 'What Can the Social Sciences Contribute to the Study of Ethics? Theoretical, Empirical and Substantive Considerations', *Bioethics*, 16 (2002), 89–113.

Hales, Steven, 'The Impossibility of Unconditional Love', *Philosophy and Public Affairs*, 9 (1995), 317–20.

Hanson, Mark, 'Biotechnology and Commodification within Health Care', *Journal of Medicine and Philosophy*, 24 (1999), 267–87.

Harris, G., 'Grieving Couple Fight to Choose Sex of Next Baby', *The Times*, 13 Mar. 2000, 11.

Harris, John, *The Value of Life* (London: Routledge, 1985).

—— 'The Welfare of the Child', *Health Care Analysis*, 8 (2000), 27–34.

—— 'Is There a Coherent Social Conception of Disability?' *Journal of Medical Ethics*, 26 (2000), 95–100.

—— *On Cloning* (London: Routledge, 2004).

Harvey, J., 'Paying Organ Donors', *Journal of Medical Ethics*, 16 (1990), 117–19.

Haworth, Lawrence, *Autonomy: An Essay in Philosophical Psychology and Ethics* (New Haven: Yale University Press, 1986).

Henderson, Mark, 'Older Mothers "Put Their Daughters at Risk of Infertility"', *The Times*, 25 Oct. 2006, <http://www.timesonline.co.uk/article/0,,11069–2419970,00.html> (last accessed: Sunday, 12 Apr. 2009).

Holland, Suzanne, 'Selecting Against Difference: Assisted Reproduction, Disability, and Regulation', *Florida State University Law Review*, 30 (2003), 401–10.

Holm, Soren, 'Like a Frog in Boiling Water: The Public, the HFEA, and Sex Selection', *Healthcare Analysis*, 12 (2004), 27–39.

Holmes, Helen Bequaert, 'Choosing Children's Sex: Challenges to Feminist Ethics', in Joan Callahan (ed.), *Reproduction, Ethics, and the Law* (Bloomington: Indiana University Press, 1995), 148–77.

Hooft, Stan van, 'Commitment and the Bond of Love', *Australasian Journal of Philosophy*, 74 (1996), 454–66.

House of Commons Select Committee on Science and Technology, *Inquiry into Human Reproductive Technologies and the Law, Eighth Special Report of Session 2004–2005* (2005).

—— *Human Reproductive Technologies and the Law (Fifth Report of Session 2004–2005), Volume II (Oral and Written Evidence)*, Mar. 2005, Ev 336.

Hull, Richard, 'Defining Disability: A Philosophical Approach', *Res Publica*, 4 (1998), 199–210.

—— 'Cheap Listening? Reflections on the Concept of Wrongful Disability', *Bioethics*, 20 (2006), 55–63.

Human Fertilisation and Embryology Authority (HFEA), *Sex Selection: Public Consultation Document* (1993).

Human Fertilisation and Embryology Authority (HFEA), Sex Selection: Public Consultation Document (1993).

—— Code of Practice (4th edn., July 1998), 45.

—— A Summary of the 111th Meeting of the Human Fertilisation and Embryology Authority (28 Sept. 2001).

—— Sex Selection: Choice and Responsibility in Human Reproduction (consultation document) (2002).

—— Code of Practice (6th edn., 2003).

—— Sex Selection: Options for Regulation (A Report on the Human Fertilisation and Embryology Authority's (HFEA's) 2002–3 Review of Sex Selection Including a Discussion of Legislative and Regulatory Options) (2003).

—— HFEA Licenses PGD for Inherited Colon Cancer (Press Release) (1 Nov. 2004), <www.hfea. gov.uk> (last accessed: Monday, 13 Apr. 2009).

—— Tomorrow's Children: A Consultation on Guidance to Licensed Fertility Clinics on taking in [sic] Account the Welfare of Children to Be Born of Assisted Conception Treatment (2005).

—— Code of Practice (7th edn., 2007).

—— Code of Practice (8th edn. in draft, 2008).

—— and Advisory Committee on Genetics Testing (ACGT), Consultation Document on Preimplantation Genetic Diagnosis (1999), <http://www.hfea.gov.uk/cps/rde/xbcr/hfea/ PGD_document.pdf> (last accessed: Sunday, 6 Sept. 2009).

—— and Human Genetics Commission (ACGT), Outcome of the Public Consultation on Preimplantation Genetic Diagnosis (2000), <http://www.hgc.gov.uk/uploadDocs/DocPub/Document/ pgdoutcome.pdf> (last accessed: 6 Sept. 2009).

Human Genetics Alert, Newsletter, issue 1 (Dec. 2001).

—— The Case Against Sex Selection (Campaign Briefing) (Dec. 2002).

Human Genetics Commission (HGC), Choosing the Future: Genetics and Reproductive Decision Making (July 2004), 19.

Human Genetics Commission (HGC), Making Babies: Reproductive Technologies and Genetic Decisions (Jan. 2006), 50.

Human Genetics Commission (HGC), Making Babies: Reproductive Decisions and Genetic Technologies (Jan. 2006), <www.hgc.gov.uk>, 63 (last accessed: Sunday, 12 Apr. 2009).

Human Genome Research Project (Dunedin, New Zealand), Choosing Genes for Future People (Dunedin: Otago University Print, 2006).

Human Tissue Authority, Code of Practice: Donation of Organs, Tissue and Cells for Transplantation (Code 2) (July 2006).

Hursthouse, Rosalind, 'Virtue Theory and Abortion', Philosophy and Public Affairs, 20 (1991), 223–46.

Iredale, Rachel, 'Eugenics and its Relevance to Contemporary Health Care', Nursing Ethics, 7 (2000), 205–41: 207.

Jackson, Emily, Regulating Reproduction: Law Technology, and Autonomy (Oxford: Hart Publishing, 2001), 7.

Jain, T., 'Significant Proportion of Infertile Couples Requests Preimplantation Sex Selection', Fertility Weekly (Mar. 2005), 9–10.

Johnson, Martin, 'The Medical Ethics of Paid Egg Sharing in the UK', Human Reproduction, 14 (1999), 1912–18.

Kamm, Frances, 'Genes, Justice, and Obligations to Future People', *Social Philosophy and Policy*, 19 (2002), 360–88.

Kass, Leon, 'Reflections on Public Bioethics: A View from the Trenches', *Kennedy Institute of Ethics Journal*, 15 (2005), 221–50.

Kaveny, M. Cathleen, 'Commodifying the Polyvalent Good of Healthcare', *Journal of Medicine and Philosophy*, 24 (1999), 207–23.

Kevles, Daniel, 'Eugenics and Human Rights', *BMJ* 319 (1999), 435–8.

Kerr, Ann, and Shakespeare, Tom, *Genetic Politics: From Eugenics to Genome* (Cheltenham: New Clarion Press, 2002).

Kilner, John, *The Ends Don't Justify the Genes*, Center for Bioethics and Human Dignity, <http://www.cbhd.org/resources/genetics/kilner_2002-07-19.htm>, 19 July 2002 (last accessed: Sunday, 12 Apr. 2009).

King, David, 'How Far Is Too Far?' *Sunday Herald* (Glasgow), 25 June 2006, 12.

Kitcher, Philip, *The Lives to Come: The Genetic Revolution and Human Possibilities* (London: Penguin, 1996).

Kolers, Avery, 'Cloning and Genetic Parenthood', *Cambridge Quarterly of Healthcare Ethics*, 12 (2003), 401–10.

Kornegay, R., 'Is Commercial Surrogacy Baby-Selling?' *Journal of Applied Philosophy*, 7 (1990), 45–50.

Kripke, Saul, *Naming and Necessity* (Oxford: Blackwell, 1980).

LaFollette, Hugh, *Personal Relationships: Love, Identity, and Morality* (Oxford: Blackwell, 1995).

Langton, James, 'Lesbians: We Made Our Baby Deaf on Purpose', *London Evening Standard*, 8 Apr. 2002, 9.

Laurence, Jeremy, 'Mother's Diet Linked to Baby's Sex', *The Independent*, 23 Apr. 2008, 16.

Levitt, Mairi, 'Better Together? Sociological and Philosophical Perspectives on Bioethics', in M. Hayry and T. Takala (eds.), *Scratching the Surface of Bioethics* (Amsterdam: Rodopi, 2003), 19–27.

Levy, Neil, 'Reconsidering Cochlear Implants: The Lessons of Martha's Vineyard', *Bioethics*, 16 (2002), 134–53.

—— 'Against Sex Selection', *Southern Medical Journal*, 100 (2007), 107–9.

Lewis, David, *On the Plurality of Worlds* (Oxford: Blackwell, 1986), Ch. 4.

Lillehammer, Hallvard, 'Benefit, Disability, and the Non-Identity Problem', in Nafsika Athanassoulis (ed.), *Philosophical Reflections on Medical Ethics* (London: Palgrave-Macmillan, 2005), 24–43.

Lindley, Richard, *Autonomy* (Basingstoke: Palgrave MacMillan, 1986).

Mackenzie, Catriona, and Stoljar, Natalie (eds.), *Relational Autonomy: Feminist Perspectives on Autonomy, Agency, & the Social Self* (New York: Oxford University Press, 2000).

Macrae, Fiona, 'Fathers Surplus to Requirements', *Daily Mail*, 17 Aug. 2005.

Mahowald, Mary, 'Aren't We All Eugenicists? Commentary on Paul Lombardo's "Taking Eugenics Seriously" ', *Florida State University Law Review*, 30 (2003), 219–35: 234.

Marquis, Donald, 'Abortion and Human Nature', *Journal of Medical Ethics*, 34 (2008), 422–6.

Marshall, Sandra, 'Bodyshopping: The Case of Prostitution', *Journal of Applied Philosophy*, 16 (1999), 139–50.

Mason, J. K., and McCall Smith, A., *Law and Medical Ethics* (Oxford: Oxford University Press, 5th edn., 1999).

McClean, Sheila, *Modern Dilemmas: Choosing Children* (Edinburgh: Capercaillie Books, 2006).

McDougall, Rosalind, 'Acting Parentally: An Argument Against Sex Selection', *Journal of Medical Ethics*, 31 (2005), 601–5.

McLachlan, Hugh, 'The Unpaid Donation of Blood and Altruism: A Comment on Keown', *Journal of Medical Ethics*, 24 (1998), 252–6.

McMahan, Jeff, 'Wrongful Life: Paradoxes in the Morality of Causing People to Exist', in J. Coleman and C. Morris (eds.), *Rational Commitment and Social Justice* (Cambridge: Cambridge University Press, 1998).

Mega, M., 'Couple Fight to Pick Sex of Baby', *The Sunday Times*, 12 Mar. 2001, 32.

Messant, Maureen, 'Mum's Too Old', *Birmingham Evening Mail*, 7 Jan. 2005, 24.

Mill, John Stuart, *On Liberty* (London: Watts & Co., 1929), 11.

—— and Gray, John, *On Liberty and Other Essays* (Oxford: Oxford University Press, 1998).

Mills, Claudia, 'The Child's Right to an Open Future?' *Journal of Social Philosophy*, 34 (2003), 499–509.

Morgan, J., 'Religious Upbringing, Religious Diversity, and the Child's Right to an Open Future', *Studies in Philosophy and Education*, 24 (2005), 367–87.

Narain, Jaya, 'My Sister, My Saviour: Cell Transplant from Baby Girl Gives Boy Hope', *Daily Mail*, 23 Mar. 2005, 37.

Narveson, Jan, 'Utilitarianism and New Generations', *Mind*, 76 (1967) 62–72.

National Institute of Neurological Disorders and Stokes (US), NINDS Anencephaly Information Page, <www.ninds.nih.gov/disorders/anencephaly/anencephaly.htm#What_is> (last accessed: Sunday, 12 Apr. 2009).

Nordenfelt, Lennart, 'On Disability and Illness, a Reply to Edwards', *Theoretical Medicine and Bioethics*, 20 (1999), 181–9.

—— 'On the Goals of Medicine, Health Enhancement, and Social Welfare', *Healthcare Analysis*, 9 (2001), 15–23.

Nozick, Robert, 'Coercion', in Sidney Morgenbesser, Patrick Suppes and Morton White (eds.), *Philosophy, Science and Method: Essays in Honour of Ernest Nagel* (New York: St Martin's Press, 1969), 440–72.

—— *Anarchy, State, and Utopia* (Oxford: Blackwell, 1974).

Odone, Christina, 'We All Lose in the Baby Business', *The Times*, 17 Jan. 2005.

Office for National Statistics. <http://www.statistics.gov.uk/glance> (last accessed Monday, 13 Apr. 2009).

Parfit, Derek, *Reasons and Persons* (Oxford: Oxford University Press, 1984), 356.

—— 'Equality or Priority?' in John Harris (ed.), *Bioethics* (Oxford: Oxford University Press, 2001), 347–86.

Paul, Diane, 'Eugenic Anxieties, Social Realities, and Political Choices', *Social Research*, 59 (1992), 663.

—— 'Is Human Genetics Disguised Eugenics?' in Michael Ruse and David Hull (eds.), *Biology and Philosophy* (Oxford: Oxford University Press, 1998), 536–49.

People, Science, & Policy Ltd. (for the Department of Health), *Report on Consultation on the Review of the Human Fertilisation Act 1990*, Mar. 2006.

Persaud, R., 'Smoker's Rights to Healthcare', *Journal of Medical Ethics*, 21 (1995), 281–7.

Priaulx, Nicolette, 'Rethinking Progenitive Conflict: Why Reproductive Autonomy Matters', *Medical Law Review*, 6 (2008), 169–200.

Putnam, Hilary, 'Cloning People', in Justine Burley (ed.), *The Genetic Revolution and Human Rights: The Oxford Amnesty Lectures* (Oxford: Oxford University Press, 1999), 1–13.

Quinn, Warren, 'Abortion: Identity and Loss', *Philosophy and Public Affairs*, 13 (1984), 24–54.

Radin, Margaret Jane, *Contested Commodities* (Cambridge, MA: Harvard University Press, 1996).

Resnik, David, 'The Commodification of Human Reproductive Materials', *Journal of Medical Ethics*, 24 (1998), 388–93.

—— 'The Moral Significance of the Therapy-Enhancement Distinction in Human Genetics', *Cambridge Quarterly of Healthcare Ethics*, 9 (2000), 365–77.

Roberts, Melinda, 'A New Way of Doing the Best That We Can: Person-based Consequentialism and the Equality Problem', *Ethics*, 112 (2002), 315–50.

—— 'Is the Person-Affecting Intuition Paradoxical?' *Theory and Decision: An International Journal for Methods and Models in the Social and Decision Sciences*, 55 (2003), 1–44.

Robertson, John, *Children of Choice: Freedom and the New Reproductive Technologies* (Princeton: Princeton University Press, 1996).

—— 'Preconception Gender Selection', *American Journal of Bioethics*, 1 (2001), 2–9.

—— 'Procreative Liberty in the Age of Genomics', *American Journal of Law and Medicine*, 29 (2003), 439–87.

Robertson, John A., Kahn, Jeffrey P., and Wagner, John E., 'Conception to Obtain Hematopoietic Stem Cells', *Hastings Center Report*, 32 (2002), 34–40.

Rogers, Wendy, Ballantyne, Angela, and Draper, Heather, 'Is Sex Selective Abortion Morally Justified and Should It Be Prohibited?' *Bioethics*, 21 (2007), 520–4.

Ryberg, Jesper, and Tännsjö, Torbjörn (eds.), The *Repugnant Conclusion: Essays on Population Ethics* (Dordrecht: Kluwer Academic Publishers, 2004).

Ryberg, Jesper, Tännsjö, Torbjörn, and Arrhenius, Gustaf, 'The Repugnant Conclusion', in Edward Zalta (ed.), *The Stanford Encyclopedia of Philosophy* (Spring 2006 edn.), <http://plato.stanford.edu/archives/spr2006/entries/repugnant-conclusion> (last accessed: Sunday, 12 Apr. 2009).

Salmon, Nathan, *Reference and Essence* (Oxford: Blackwell, 1982).

Sample, Ian, 'Older Mothers Risk Fertility of Daughters', *The Guardian*, 25 Oct. 2006, <http://www.guardian.co.uk/medicine/story/0,,1930727,00.html> (last accessed: Sunday, 12 Apr. 2009).

—— 'Bananas and Cereal—Scientists Reveal What Little Boys Are Made Of: Pregnancy Diet Influences Baby's Gender, Study Says Fewer Calories Mean Greater Chance of a Girl', *The Guardian*, 23 Apr. 2008, 2.

Savulescu, Julian, 'Procreative Beneficence: Why We Should Select the Best Children', *Bioethics*, 15 (2001), 413–26.

—— 'Deaf Lesbians, "Designer Disability" and the Future of Medicine', *BMJ* 325 (10 May 2002), 771.

—— 'Sex Selection: The Case For', in Helga Kuhse and Peter Singer (eds.), *Bioethics: An Anthology* (Oxford: Blackwell, 2nd edn., 2006), 145–9.

Savulescu, Julian, Hemsley, Melanie, Newson, Ainsley, and Foddy, Bennett, 'Behavioural Genetics: Why Eugenic Selection Is Preferable to Enhancement', *Journal of Applied Philosophy*, 23 (2006), 157–71.

Scott, K., 'IVF Selection Still Off Limits', *The Guardian*, 19 Oct. 2000.

Scott, Rosamund, 'Choosing Between Possible Lives: Legal and Ethical Issues in Preimplantation Genetic Diagnosis', *Oxford Journal of Legal Studies*, 26 (2006), 153–78.

Shakespeare, Tom, 'Choices and Rights: Eugenics, Genetics, and Disability Equality', *Disability and Society*, 13 (1998), 665–81: 668.

—— *Disability Rights and Wrongs* (London: Routledge, 2006).

Sheldon, Sally, 'Saviour Siblings and the Discretionary Power of the HFEA', *Medical Law Review*, 13 (2005), 403–11.

—— and Wilkinson, Stephen, 'Female Genital Mutilation and Cosmetic Surgery: Regulating Non-Therapeutic Body Modification', *Bioethics*, 12 (1998), 263–85.

—— —— 'Hashmi and Whitaker: An Unjustifiable and Misguided Distinction?' *Medical Law Review*, 12 (2004), 137–63.

—— —— 'Should Selecting Saviour Siblings Be Banned?' *Journal of Medical Ethics*, 30 (2004), 533–7.

—— —— 'Saviour Siblings, Other Siblings, and Whole Organ Donation', in Jeff Nisker, Francoise Baylis, Isabel Karpin, Carolyn McLeod, and Roxanne Mykituk (eds.), *The 'Healthy' Embryo* (Cambridge: Cambridge University Press, 2009).

Sheth, Shirish, 'Missing Female Births in India', *The Lancet*, 367 (21 Jan. 2006), 185–6.

Sikora, Karol, 'How Old Is Too Old to Be a Mother?' *The Observer*, 7 May 2006, 12.

Simoncelli, Tania, 'Preimplantation Genetic Diagnosis and Selection: From Disease Prevention to Customized Conception', *Different Takes*, 24 (2003).

Smith, Ed, 'Death, Not Disability, Is the End of the World', *CBC News Online*, 3rd Feb. 2005, <http://www.cbc.ca/news/viewpoint/vp_disabilitymatters/smith_20050203.html>, (last accessed: Sunday, 12 Apr. 2009).

Spanton, Tim, 'A Designer Baby Would End Our Heartache', *The Sun*, 11 Apr. 2002, 51.

Spital, Aaron, 'Donor Benefit is the Key to Justified Living Organ Donation', *Cambridge Quarterly of Healthcare Ethics*, 13 (2004), 105–9.

Spriggs, Merle, 'Lesbian Couple Create a Child Who is Deaf Like Them', *Journal of Medical Ethics*, 28 (2002), 283.

—— and Savulescu, Julian, 'Saviour Siblings', *Journal of Medical Ethics* (2002), 289.

Steinbock, Bonnie, *Life Before Birth: The Moral and Legal Status of Embryos and Foetuses* (New York: Oxford University Press, 1992).

—— 'Sex Selection: Not Obviously Wrong', *Hastings Center Report*, 32 (2002), 23–8.

Teather, David, 'Lesbian Couple Have Deaf Baby by Choice', *The Guardian*, 8 Apr. 2002, 2.

Templeton, S., 'Couple in Battle to Choose the Sex of Their Baby Win an Apology', *Sunday Herald*, 20th May 2001.

Tersi, Lorella, 'The Social Model of Disability: A Philosophical Critique', *Journal of Applied Philosophy*, 21 (2004), 141–57.

Thomson, Judith Jarvis, 'A Defense of Abortion', *Philosophy and Public Affairs*, 1 (1971), 47–66.

Thornton, Jacqui, 'Lesbian Bid to Have Girlfriend's IVF Baby', *The Sun*, 19 Apr. 2005, 22.

Tooley, Michael, 'Abortion and Infanticide', *Philosophy and Public Affairs*, 2 (1972), 37–65.

Truog, Robert, 'The Ethics of Organ Donation by Living Donors', *New England Journal of Medicine*, 353 (4 Aug. 2005), 444–6.

Turnbull, D., 'Genetic Counselling: Ethical Mediation of Eugenic Futures', *Futures*, 32 (2000), 853–65.

Twyman, Richard, 'Cystic Fibrosis', Wellcome Trust website, 30 July 2003, <www.wellcome. ac.uk> (last accessed: Monday, 13 April 2009).

Vehmas, Simo, 'Response to "Abortion and Assent" by Rosamund Rhodes and "Abortion, Disability, Assent, and Consent" by Matti Hayry', *Cambridge Quarterly of Healthcare Ethics*, 10 (2001), 433–40.

Wasserman, David, 'A Choice of Evils in Prenatal Testing', *Florida State University Law Review*, 30 (2003), 295–313: 313.

Wertheimer, Alan, *Coercion* (Princeton: Princeton University Press, 1987).

Wertheimer, Roger, 'Understanding the Abortion Argument', *Philosophy and Public Affairs*, 1 (1971), 67–95.

Wilkinson, Stephen, 'Smokers' Rights to Healthcare: Why the "Restoration Argument" is a Moralising Wolf in a Liberal Sheep's Clothing', *Journal of Applied Philosophy*, 16 (1999), 275–89.

—— 'Commodification Arguments for the Legal Prohibition of Organ Sale', *Health Care Analysis*, 8 (2000) 189–201.

—— *Bodies for Sale: Ethics and Exploitation in the Human Body Trade* (London: Routledge, 2003).

—— ' "Designer Babies", Instrumentalisation and the Child's Right to an Open Future', in Nafsika Athanassoulis (ed.), *Philosophical Reflections on Medical Ethics* (London: Palgrave-Macmillan, 2005), 44–69.

—— 'Eugenics, Embryo Selection, and the Equal Value Principle', *Clinical Ethics*, 1 (2006), 26–51.

—— 'Commodification', in Richard Ashcroft, Angus Dawson, Heather Draper, and John MacMillan (eds.), *Principles of Healthcare Ethics* (2nd edn., Chichester: John Wiley & Sons, 2007), 285–92.

—— 'Sex Selection, Sexism, and "Family Balancing" ', *Medical Law Review*, 16 (2008), 369–89.

—— ' "Eugenics Talk" and the Language of Bioethics', *Journal of Medical Ethics*, 34 (2008), 467–71.

—— 'On the Distinction between Positive and Negative Eugenics', in Matti Hayry, Tuija Takala, and Peter Herissone-Kelly (eds.), *Arguments and Analysis in Bioethics* (Amsterdam: Rodopi, in press).

Williams, Bernard, *Ethics and the Limits of Philosophy* (London: Fontana, 1985).

Winterson, Jeanette, 'How Would We Feel if Blind Women Claimed the Right to a Blind Baby?' *The Guardian*, 9 Apr. 2002, <www.guardian.co.uk/Archive/Article/0,4273,4390038,00.html> (last accessed: Sunday, 12 Apr. 2009).

Woodward, James, 'The Non-Identity Problem', *Ethics*, 96 (1986), 804–31.

World Transhumanist Association, *The Transhumanist Declaration* (2002), <http://transhu manism.org/index.php/WTA/declaration> (last accessed: Monday, 13 Apr. 2009).

—— *What is the TWA?* <http://transhumanism.org/index.php/WTA/about> (last accessed: 23 Mar. 2009).

Wrigley, Anthony, 'Genetic Selection and Modal Harms', *The Monist*, 89 (2006), 505–25.

Yablo, Stephen, 'Essentialism', in Edward Craig (ed.), *Routledge Encyclopaedia of Philosophy*, <www.rep.routledge.com>.

Young, R., 'Couple Seek Right to a Daughter', *The Times*, 4 Oct. 2000, 4.

Zussman, R., 'The Contributions of Sociology to Medical Ethics', *Hastings Center Report*, 30 (2000), 7–11.

Zyl, Liezl van, 'Intentional Parenthood and the Nuclear Family', *Journal of Medical Humanities*, 23 (2002), 107–18.

INDEX

DATE DUE

DATE DUE	
APR 0 8 2011	